# of Apacheria

BY DAN L. THRAPP

UNIVERSITY OF OKLAHOMA PRESS : NORMAN AND LONDON

By Dan L. Thrapp

Al Sieber, Chief of Scouts (Norman, 1964)
The Conuest of Apacheria (Norman, 1967)
General Crook and the Sierra Madre Adventure (Norman, 1972)
Juh: An Incredible Indian (El Paso, 1973)
Victorio and the Mimbres Apaches (Norman, 1974)
A Cavalryman in Indian Country (ed.) (Ashland, Oreg., 1974)
Dateline Fort Bowie: Charles Fletcher Lummis Reports on an Apache War
   (Norman, 1979)

Library of Congress Catalog Card Number: 67-15588

ISBN: 0-8061-1286-7

7   8   9   10   11   12   13   14   15   16   17   18   19   20

For Margie

Who made all things worth the doing

Introduction

From 1710 onward Apacheria shows on Spanish maps as a wide and deep area across much of Arizona and extending to the Rio Grande. It was not limited to the range of the Athapascan peoples but lapped into those of their neighbors, the plains tribes on the east, the Navaho on the north, the Yuman on the west and the Yaqui to the south. Dominant within this vast area were the bands who called themselves the *N'de* or *Dine* or some variant meaning, simply, "the people," but who were called by the whites "Apaches" from the Zuni word for "enemy." Perhaps relative newcomers to the Southwest,[1] the Apaches had become so locally famed that other peoples, unrelated to them, were called Apache-this or Apache-that; the Apache-Mohaves, for instance, who were really the Yavapai, a Yuman tribe, related to the Walapai and Havasupai, living between the high Mazatzals and Pinal Mountains and the country of the Chemehuevi, and from the Bill Williams-Santa Maria rivers to the Gila. The Walapai lived north of the mouth of the Bill Williams. The Havasupai had been pushed into canyons along the Colorado.

Then there were the Apache-Yuma, another Yuman people linguistically unrelated to the Apache, dwelling between the lower Colorado and the Yavapai. And the Tonto-Apache, a mixture of Apache, Yavapai, Yuma, and Maricopa.

The true Apaches were confusingly identified less through cultural or racial characteristics than by accident of geography, the regions where they usually were found.

Thus the Chiricahuas (called Cherrycows by many pioneers) resided in what is now southeastern Arizona. The Warm Springs, or

[1] This view is disputed by Jack D. Forbes, *Apache, Navaho, and Spaniard*, xiii–xxv.

Ojo Caliente band, preferred southern New Mexico, but they and the Chiricahuas considered themselves virtually the same people, although by whites they are often held to be distinct. Many parallel cases could be cited. The Apaches, never numbering more than about six thousand, approximately their population today, were not a cohesive tribe, but were gathered in certain rather large groupings.

The Gilenos, centered on the broken country about the upper Gila River, included the Chiricahuas, the Warm Springs, the Mogollon band, and the Mimbrenos. The San Carlos group included many bands formerly unassociated directly with that river. Among them were the Aravaipas, the Pinalenos, the Coyoteros, the White Mountain or Sierra Blanca Apaches, and many local bands. The Mescaleros, sometimes included with the Lipans among the Llaneros, or plains Apaches, were usually associated more closely with the Warm Springs Indians. And there were the Navahos, usually regarded as a separate tribe, although with a closely related language.

To his primordial weapons of rocks, bows with stone-tipped arrows, lances,[2] knives, and clubs (but no tomahawks), the Apache added by theft or trade the weapons of the white man. Apaches solved their perennial problem of obtaining ammunition in many ways. They traded for it with the Zuni villages, or with renegade whites. They stole much ammunition. Many of the murders and ambushes had as their reason the Apache need for ammunition. One young white man wrote that he had seen Indian bullets of lead, gold, and stone.[3] Some believed the Apaches used silver bullets, silver being easier to come by than lead. The traditional Apache weapon, however, was the bow, usually made of mulberry, the bowstring of the sinew of deer or, later, of cattle or horses, the arrows of cane, fletched with hawk or eagle feathers, the heads of flint or obsidian; the maximum effective range was about one hundred and fifty yards. An experienced warrior usually carried a spare bowstring and perhaps an extra bow stave as

[2] Daniel Ellis Conner, *Joseph Reddeford Walker and the Arizona Adventure*, denies that the Indians ever used lances or poisoned arrows, but the evidence is strongly against him.

[3] Thomas Edwin Farish, *History of Arizona*, III, 222.

Apacheria

well. Some Indians used an arrow poison, made of a plant substance, of snake or spider poison, or of rotted and impregnated deer gall, but it could not have been swift acting.

Apacheria itself was enormous in extent. It stretched from the willow thickets along the Colorado into the broken mountains beyond the Rio Grande, and from the great canyons of the north southward for a thousand miles into Mexico, excepting of course the agricultural empire of the peaceful Papagos and Maricopas along the Gila and other streams tributary to it. The tribes of Apacheria were a product of their habitat, harsh, cruel, and pitiless. Its topography seems at first a meaningless jumble of mountains and canyons, rioting rivers and forested uplands, barren deserts and near-Arctic peaks. Yet there is a pattern to it.

In the beginning the land was nearly flat and then, for reasons not clear even to the geologist, there came a gradual change. A huge upswelling began and extended over millions of years. This bowing of the earth's crust was slow enough to accommodate the erosive power of the rivers, so that the Colorado, for instance, could maintain its course, sluicing away the rising rock, eating deeper into the swollen upthrust until today's result is the mile-deep and still deepening Grand Canyon and tributary gorges. Bordering it to north and south are heavily wooded plateaus, the surface of the bulging arch. To the north the plateau gets lost in Utah. But to the south it becomes part of our story. The highlands here descend gradually until they terminate in the scenic escarpment called the Mogollon Rim, or, locally, the Tonto Rim. The plateau is pierced at intervals by tributaries to the Little Colorado.

The Mogollon Rim diminishes to the southeast, as it slashes diagonally across Arizona, punctuated now and again by such massive uplifts as the White Mountains; the San Franciscans, just across the line into New Mexico; the Mogollons, Stein's Peak Range, and so on. Farther to the east are separate systems, having no connection with the dwindling rim, but parallel to its tag-end mountains: the Black Range and, beyond the Rio Grande, the San Andres. Eastward, in western Texas, are other uplifts, the Sierra Blanca and the Sierra

Diablo. To the south, in Old Mexico, are far loftier mountains, the Sierra Madre and other ranges, rolling upheavals forming a major part of the huge tectonic revolution that had created the Colorado River bulge itself.

The great rivers of Apacheria were few—the Colorado and the Rio Grande and, in the south, the fishhook-shaped Bavispe, the Rio Yaqui, Santa Maria, and Rio de Casas Grandes, and the tributaries to some of these: the Gila system in Arizona, the Alamosa, Palomas, and Cuchillo Negro, of the Rio Grande, and the flowing children of the Bavispe.

In all of this immensity of desert, peaks, and mesas, of rivers, springs, and seeps, the most spectacular portion is what one sees from the Mogollon Rim gazing southward.

Within sight lies the beginning of the great basin which probably saw more Indian fighting than any other part of America, terrain in the process of formation even as the sheets of rock curved upward to create the great bulge. No sooner had the movement begun than the streams quickened under the incentive of enhanced gradient, leaching more rapidly back into the rising headlands, eating at the rock until, over a period too grand for comprehension, they will have destroyed the uprise itself. As the streams carve away the soil and rock, they leave hills, and buttes, and peaks and swales and valleys that bear names bestowed by hardy frontiersmen or by the Indians who preceded them: Hardscrabble Mesa, Turret Butte, the Mazatzals, Diamond Rim, Natanes Plateau, Bloody Basin, Big Prairie, and so forth. Other features, as well, are distinguishable: Hell Canyon, Jumpoff Gulch, Tonto, Fossil and Cibicue creek beds.

South of the Gila the scene changes. Here lies the desert, softer, if deadlier, mauve and charcoal and hazy blue, threaded by shallow, undependable streams or washes, its features labeled with gentle Spanish words: the Santa Cruz, Tres Alamos, Cienega, Dos Cabezas, Rincon, and Cerro Colorado; and with raspier names bestowed by prospectors who would brave any danger to pursue their star: Outlaw Mountain, Altar Wash, the Dragoons, the Mule and Winchester Mountains, Sawed-off Butte, Squaretop Hill, Biscuit Peak. And there are still others, reminiscent of those who once alone knew them: Geronimo, Cochise Head, Massai Point, Chiricahua, Huachuca, Aravaipa Canyon.

This, then, was Apacheria. A land of almost infinite extent and, in the nineteenth century, of equal peril.

So savagely contested was it, and so worthless did it appear, that General William Tecumseh Sherman, supreme Army commander, once growled, "We had one war with Mexico to take Arizona, and we should have another to make her take it back."[4] Again he wrote, "The best advice I can offer is to notify all settlers and miners to get out of Arizona and then withdraw the troops and leave the country to the tribes as a perpetual Indian territory where they can plunder and kill each other to their hearts' content."[5]

But he must have expressed himself tongue in cheek, for he knew that Arizona was thought to be rich in minerals, and where wealth lay, white men would go, even if they were forced to fight the most implacable savages on the American continent to get there. Fight them they and the soldiers did, and this book is the story of that long and varied war.

[4] *Ibid.*, III, 1.
[5] Sherman to W. W. Belknap, Secretary of War, January 7, 1870, quoted in Ralph Hedrick Ogle, *Federal Control of the Western Apaches: 1848–1886*, 73.

xii

Contents

	Introduction	*page* vii
I	The Saga of Bill Rood	3
II	The Conflict Begins	6
III	Civilians Take a Hand	24
IV	The Walapais War	39
V	The Hunting of Big Rump	53
VI	Death of Howard Cushing	63
VII	The Whitman Affair	79
VIII	Crook Takes Over	95
IX	Raids and Punishment	113
X	The Offensive Begins	119
XI	The Offensive Concludes	131
XII	Lieutenant Almy	144
XIII	The Renegades Destroyed	156
XIV	John Clum Takes Over	162
XV	Victorio!	182
XVI	Nana's Raid	211
XVII	Cibicu	217
XVIII	Loco	231
XIX	Dry Wash and Crook Again	251
XX	A New Raid	267
XXI	The Mexican Adventure	283
XXII	Who Captured Whom— or, Did Geronimo Take Crook?	295

XXIII Ka-ya-ten-nae   303
XXIV Geronimo—1   311
XXV Geronimo—2   328
XXVI Geronimo—3   350
        Bibliography   368
        Index   385

MAPS

Apacheria   *page* ix
The Walapais War   47
Cushing's Last Scout   71
Victorio's Fight   191
Tonto Basin Country   219
The Mexican Theater   317

Illustrations

Apache Pass
Fort Bowie
Ojo Caliente
Stein's Peak
Fort Whipple
Salt River Cave
Turret Mountain
Howard Bass Cushing and
    monument
Cochise
General Oliver Otis Howard
General George Crook
William J. Ross
Guy V. Henry

Albert E. Woodson
Victorio's editorial
Loco
Luis Terrazas
Victorio
Mike Burns
John P. Clum, Diablo,
    and Eskiminzin
Eskiminzin
Dead Shot
John P. Clum and his
    Indian police
Nachez
Peaches

following page 112

Mangus
Nana
James Cook
General Crook's Apache campaign
General George Crook
Sam Bowman and
    Lt. Charles B. Gatewood
Mickey Free and Chatto
Albert Payson Morrow
General Orlando B. Willcox
Wirt Davis

Colonel S. B. M. Young
Middleton Ranch
Geronimo and Nana
Geronimo
General George Crook, officers,
    and scouts
General Crook's conference
    with Geronimo
Lieutenant and
    Mrs. Charles B. Gatewood
General Nelson A. Miles and staff

Tenth Cavalry and
Indian prisoners

Apaches leaving Fort Bowie
for Florida

following page 240

The Conquest of Apacheria

The Saga of Bill Rood

Bill rood, or Rhodes,[1] was a frontiersman. Being an American and a borderer, he was an individualist, though in courage and resourcefulness he was perhaps no different from hundreds of other pioneers.

In company with a Mexican he set out one day in 1861 for his ranch, eighteen miles north of Tubac on the road to Tucson, to gather some loose horses. The pair stopped at Canoa, a stockaded inn about four miles from Rood's ranch, finding two men there cooking supper, and went on, gathered their stock, and drove it back to Canoa.

A scene of utter wreckage met their gaze. In the hour or more since they had left, the Apaches had visited the place, killed the two occupants, and withdrawn into the surrounding brush. Rood discovered them a few hundred yards off the path, and he and the Mexican, clapping spurs to their mounts, fled toward Tubac. They were hotly pursued by a hundred mounted Apaches and many more afoot. About a mile from Reventon, an inn along the way, Rood's horse seemed to be playing out, so he, with an arrow through his left arm, separated from his companion, veered toward the mountains, drawing after him the Indian riders, sure now of their triumph.

---

[1] Rood, whose name also was spelled Rhodes, Roods, Rude, Rode, Rhoade, and perhaps in other ways, was born four miles south of Knoxville, Tennessee, about 1819. He went west from Illinois in 1849 with the Jayhawker Party and in Death Valley carved his name and date on a rock. After various adventures he left California for Arizona in 1855 and became a prospector and cattleman south of Tucson. He moved to the Colorado River north of Yuma with the La Paz gold rush of Civil War times, and was drowned under mysterious circumstances April 29, 1870. Harold and Lucille Weight, *Wm. B. Rood, Death Valley 49er, Arizona Pioneer, Apache Fighter, River Ranchero*; Carl I. Wheat, "Trailing the Forty-Niners Through Death Valley," *Sierra Club Bulletin*, Vol. XXIV, No. 3 (June, 1939), 74–108, and Plate XXXIII, following page 62.

Scarcely two hundred yards ahead of pursuit, he threw himself from his horse and crawled into a thicket, lying close to the warm, soft earth in a small *charco*, or mudhole, near its center. The thicket was very dense. Rood spread his revolver loads and caps before him. He snapped off and drew out the arrow. Feeling the loss of blood, he buried his wounded elbow in the earth to clot the wound. All this was the work of a minute.

The Indians formed a cordon around his hiding-place. Rood brought down the first who charged toward him. Each succeeding brave met the same fate until six shots had been fired. The Apaches, believing his weapon empty, then charged with a loud yell, but the cool frontiersman had reloaded after every shot, and a seventh ball brought down the foremost of the attackers, and the eighth another one.

The Indians fired volley after volley into the thicket. Bullets and arrows coursed within inches of his head, snipping off twigs that showered down upon him, and sent up little puffs of dirt as they chunked into the ground. Miraculously all missed him.

Rood at length had but two bullets left. With one of these he killed another Indian; the rest whirled off and stood within shouting distance.

One of them, who knew him well by name, called out: "Don Guillermo! Don Guillermo! Come and join us; you're a brave man, and we'll make you a chief." The ranchman was not to be fooled. "You devils!" he called. "I know what you'll do with me if you get me!" He added, "I'll kill the last one of you before you shall take me!"

The Indians consulted, apparently concluded Rood was unbeatable that day, and galloped wildly off. The frontiersman waited until he was sure they were gone, then staggered into Reventon.

"Thus happened one of the most remarkable defences and escapes, and one that could have been carried out only by a cool courage, such as few men even with a long frontier experience can command," wrote a man who knew Rood well and greeted him next day.[2]

[2] Raphael Pumpelly, *Across America and Asia: Notes of a Five Years' Journey*

Yet this was but one incident in the long and sanguinary record of Indian-white affairs in Apacheria over a period that endured for three decades. No one knows, no one can even estimate accurately, how many brave men, women, and children fell in this bloody period of warfaie, but they were very many, and perhaps uncountable.

What led to these years of horror and disaster, of which the Rood affair was so typical? What set the red man and the white man at each other's throats? What began those years, and what perpetuated them, and how were they finally brought to a close?

They started in the mists of time before record; they were finished in a blaze of publicity and confusion that is only now clearing up. But the conquest of Apacheria, stained red with the blood of thousands, and washed in the heroism and valor of men of different races, is an American saga and one that needs to be told. Through it was seized the last great block of continent to be made a part of the American commonwealth. Through it was resolved for all time the question of supremacy between aborigine and settler, white man and red. Through it was perpetuated grief and terror and bloody-handed savagery and nobleness until the inevitable was brought about, until the land was lost to and made secure for the whites.

Whether this was for good or ill we cannot judge, for we are as partisan as our forefathers. But the deed was finished. The why, we cannot know, but here was how they did it . . .

Around the World and of Residence in Arizona, Japan and China, 45–47; Andrew Wallace, (ed.), *Pumpelly's Arizona*, 88–89, 97n., 98n.; J. Ross Browne, *A Tour Through Arizona*, 146.

II

The Conflict Begins

IT REQUIRED more than three hundred years for Apacheria to be settled by whites to the point of mortal conflict with its original inhabitants. There are those who would say that abrasion and fighting was inevitable, and there are those who would deny it. But friction between the races did come, and with it the sanguinary struggle.

In a book of this size and with this purpose it is not possible to trace in detail the development of exploration and settlement which brought the whites to Apacheria for profit and eventual residence. Perhaps the first European to come this way was Alvar Núñez Cabeza de Vaca, although his exact course westward across the American continent starting in 1528 is disputed. Somewhat less controversial are the entradas of later explorers, Fray Marcos de Niza in 1539, Francisco Vásquez de Coronado, the following year, Antonio de Espejo, who in 1582 or so probably reached central Arizona, and Juan de Oñate, who in 1604 reached the Colorado westerly from the Moquis villages. Settlements were made at Tubac, about 1752, at Tucson in 1769, and at other places at various times.

American trappers had penetrated Arizona on occasion. Among them were James Ohio Pattie and his father, who pursued beaver for four years in and about Apacheria. In the course of their adventures, young Pattie apparently was a member of the Michel Robideau party, most of whom were massacred by Pimas and Maricopas in 1826, one of the very rare occasions on which members of these tribes attacked white men.[1] Other trappers may have preceded the Patties, and many

[1] See *The Personal Narrative of James O. Pattie* (ed. by William H. Goetzmann), 74–79; Joseph J. Hill, "New Light on Pattie and the Southwestern Fur Trade," *Southwestern Historical Quarterly*, Vol. XXVI, No. 4 (April, 1923), 243–54.

followed them: Ewing Young, David Jackson, Kit Carson, Pauline Weaver, and Charles Kemp among them.[2]

The Mexican War left about as much impress upon Apacheria as a summer shower, but the Treaty of Guadalupe Hidalgo, which closed it, included this paragraph which concerns us:

> Considering that a great part of the territories, which, by the present treaty, are to be comprehended for the future within the limits of the United States, is now occupied by savage tribes, who will hereafter be under the exclusive control of the Government of the United States, and whose incursions with the territory of Mexico would be prejudicial in the extreme, it is solemnly agreed that all such incursions shall be forcibly restrained by the Government of the United States . . . and that when they cannot be prevented, they shall be punished by said government . . . with equal diligence and energy, as if the same incursions were meditated or committed within its own territory, against its own citizens.

The Gadsden Treaty, ratified in 1854, abrogated this provision, but the impression remained with the Mexicans, and with some justification, that America ought to prevent reservation Apaches from raiding at will into Sonora and Chihuahua. The Americans, for their part, resented the fact that a pool of hostiles remained more or less unmolested in the Sierra Madre. The result was an agreement put into force from time to time by which troops of either country in "hot pursuit" could penetrate as deeply as necessary into the other nation, and this, at long last, helped make possible the solution to the Apache problem.

Conflict between the western Apaches and the Spaniards commenced in the seventeenth century,[3] and was carried on with greater or less ferocity for more than two hundred years. Sometimes a truce would last for years, then war would break out again. Ignacio Zuñiga, commander for several years of the northern presidios of Sonora, wrote in 1835 that since 1820 no fewer than five thousand lives had

---

[2] Hubert Howe Bancroft, *History of Arizona and New Mexico*, 407.

[3] Bancroft, *Ibid.*, 170, says in 1672; other authorities put the start variously.

been lost to the Apaches, at least one hundred ranchos, haciendas, mining camps, and other settlements had been destroyed, between three and four thousand settlers had been forced to quit the northern frontier, and that "nothing was left but the demoralized garrisons of worthless soldiers," although, by the time he wrote, the Apache raids had slacked off, largely "for lack of anything worth plundering."[4]

Whether that report is entirely accurate, it seems evident that warfare between Apache and Mexican had by that time become general, and would continue that way. Not steadily, nor everywhere, however. It was a common Apache, and Mexican, practice to maintain close commercial relations on one side of the mountain and murder and pillage each other on the reverse. Thus an enterprising Apache might steal cattle or mules or women in Sonora and profitably dispose of them in Chihuahua or at Santa Fe, steal more on the way back and turn a fresh profit near the point of origin.[5] It would continue that way, to some degree, until the end of the wars.

Military measures against the Apaches proved largely ineffective. A series of well-planned presidios, or frontier garrisons, all too often failed to stem the menace because of their weakness through poor soldiery, or for other reasons.[6] The raising of effective civilian forces for punitive action likewise proved illusory,[7] and recourse from time to time was had to paying professional killers for scalps, which were presumed to be of hostile Apaches, although in fact this was not always so.[8]

[4] Farish, *History of Arizona*, I, 78–79.

[5] Many writers have commented on this and the custom continued until the very end of the Apache troubles. General Crook's spies reported it still was common practice as late as 1886. The reasons were many. They included the virtual isolation of Chihuahua from Sonora, and consequent lack of community interest, the profiteering motive, and so forth. Revolutionary activities of innumerable self-aspiring leaders did not create an over-riding national cohesiveness, either.

[6] Robert C. Stevens, "The Apache Menace in Sonora 1831–1849," *Arizona and the West*, Vol. VI, No. 3 (Autumn, 1964), 212–13, 218.

[7] *Ibid.*, 215–16.

[8] Stevens, *Ibid.*, 219, said the Sonoran government "returned to the old Spanish method" of offering scalp bounties, but does not cite any more ancient example. Other peoples, including the French and British, occasionally had offered scalp bounties earlier than this. Bancroft, *History of the North Mexican States and Texas*,

Typical of these *proyectos de guerra* was the scalp bounty law established in 1835 by Sonora, offering one hundred pesos (a peso was roughly equivalent to a dollar) for each warrior's scalp. Two years later Chihuahua formally offered one hundred pesos for a warrior's scalp, fifty for that of a woman, and twenty-five for a child's. The policy frankly sought extermination, evidence that genocide has widespread roots and was not a modern invention of a single nation. The policy was unwise quite aside from its moral failings, in that by the means chosen it could never prove decisive and served only to acerbate the situation.

Two questions naturally occur: how many Apaches fell before the scalp hunters, and how did the whites, in adopting this cruel policy, rationalize the murder of their antagonists? With respect to the former, no one can ever know.[9] No complete estimate has ever been made, but scores of scalp hunters busied themselves in the field for long periods, and their toll—of tame and of wild Indians, and others —must have been considerable. With respect to the second question, a complete answer must be left the psychologists. There was no sanction for this measure in history, in federal law, or, least of all, in church teachings, despite suggestions that it was then taught that Indians, being non-Christian and pagan, had no souls and hence were fair game. The Reverend Francis J. Connell, dean emeritus of the Catholic University of America's school of theology, assures that "the

II, 653–54. See also various articles by Ralph A. Smith, among them: "Apache Plunder Trails Southward, 1831–1840," *New Mexico Historical Review*, Vol. XXXVII, No. 1 (January, 1962), 20–42; "Apache 'Ranching' Below the Gila, 1841–1845," *Arizoniana*, Vol. III, No. 4 (Winter, 1962), 1–17; "The Scalp Hunter in the Borderlands 1835–1850," *Arizona and the West*, Vol. VI, No. 1 (Spring, 1964) 5–22; "The Scalp Hunt in Chihuahua—1849," *NMHR*, Vol. XL, No. 2 (April, 1965) 116–40; "John Joel Glanton, Lord of the Scalp Range," *The Smoke Signal*, No. 6, Tucson, Westerners, Fall, 1962, pp. 9–16 (this issue also includes Ray Brandes, "Don Santiago Kirker, King of the Scalp Hunters," 2–8); see also Mayne Reid, *The Scalp Hunters*, a novel based on Reid's experiences and observations in the Southwest from 1838.

[9] Kirker himself reported that he and his band killed 487 Apaches with the loss of only three men; "Benjamin David Wilson's Observations on Early Days in California and New Mexico," ed. by Arthur Woodward, *Historical Society of Southern California* (1934), 74–150, 130).

Church has never taught that pagans have no souls," or that their slaughter could be morally justified. "Christ commanded His apostles to preach the Gospel to *every* creature—indicating that every human being . . . must have an intellectual soul. . . . Any ideas to the contrary that the Mexicans may have had must be ascribed to their gross ignorance and their avarice."[10]

Apache-American hostilities in effect began with such laws and the monetary incentive they held out to erstwhile trappers, mountain men, Delawares, and other Indians. The bounty system had about it the smell of vengeance and was no more truly effective than a bounty system on any sort of wild game; it failed for the same general reasons. It served to cancel out any tendency on the part of the Apaches to become tame and drove the wilder spirits deeper into the mountains where, if anything, they became more implacably hostile.

The turning point in relations between Americans and Apaches, which had been fairly amicable, give or take a few killings now and then, mostly involving trappers, occurred in 1837 with the slaughter by a scalp hunter of Juan José Compá and some of his followers.

Juan José, a Mimbres Apache, had been educated for the priesthood in Catholic schools, it is said, and was described by an acquaintance as a good and able Indian. When his father was murdered by Mexicans, however, his attitude toward them underwent a fundamental change. Raids and depredations increased. Because of his education, Juan José was uncommonly successful. His men captured dispatch pouches so that Juan might learn enemy plans,[11] and the information sometimes was put to good use. Juan José and his Mimbres band were located in the vicinity of the Santa Rita copper mines, east of present-day Silver City, in southern New Mexico.

Enter James Johnson, a part-time scalp hunter, who touched off the assassination of Juan José and a long and bloody series of new depredations. It is discouraging to note that he lived out a fairly comfortable old age in California, for he was as black-hearted a

[10] Letter to author, April 5, 1966.
[11] Josiah Gregg, *Commerce of the Prairies*, 205. Wilson, "Observations," *Hist. Soc. So. Calif.*, 78.

murderer as ever disgraced the frontier. John C. Cremony says he was an Englishman,[12] and Benjamin D. Wilson, one more likely to know the facts, believed him to be an American.[13] He had married a Mexican woman and operated a trading post at Oposura, in Sonora. He was acquainted with Juan José.

Of the two major accounts of what transpired, the bloodiest, and least likely, is told by Cremony, who got it many years later by hearsay and, in substance, reported that Johnson and his men killed nearly four hundred Apaches. The version given by Wilson, who had camped not far distant and who obtained his facts from eyewitnesses, can be accepted more confidently. It is savage enough.

Wilson, who later became the first mayor of Los Angeles, made Juan José's acquaintance while trapping on the Gila, in 1835 or perhaps two years later; accounts differ.

He said that a party of Missourians, led by one Eames had gone into Sonora to purchase mules, but found the Apaches had stripped the countryside of them. En route home they stopped by Johnson's trading post and that worthy persuaded them to detour by way of Juan José's country. Innocently they agreed and Johnson, with an accomplice named Gleason, or Glisson, accompanied them. Concealed on a pack mule was a weapon described by Wilson as a "blunderbuss," by Cremony as a "six-pounder," by J. P. Dunn, Jr., as a "howitzer," and which was planned as the instrument of execution.[14] Juan's scouts had intercepted a dispatch reporting an offer made by Mexican officials to Johnson for the Indian's scalp, but, being a man of honor himself, he did not think his white friend would betray him.

"Don Santiago," Juan is reported to have said, "you have never deceived me, and, if you give me your word of honor that the report is false, come to my camp with your men and pass the night with us."

Arriving at Juan's camp, Johnson told the chief he had brought a sack of pinole, or cornmeal, for his people. It was placed at a selected

---

[12] John C. Cremony, *Life Among the Apaches*, 31.

[13] Wilson, "Observations," *Hist. Soc. So. Calif.*, 78.

[14] *Ibid.*, 80; Cremony, *Life Among the Apaches*, 31; J. P. Dunn, Jr., *Massacres of the Mountains*, 315.

spot and the Apaches gathered hungrily around. Gleason invited Juan out to inspect a mule, in order to make sure of him. Johnson personally fired the lethal weapon on the crowd around the pinole, killing and wounding many of them, while Gleason shot Juan, but did not kill him outright. Juan grappled with him, calling for Johnson to come to his rescue as he did so. As the pair toppled to the ground, Juan raised his knife, but said to Johnson, in Spanish, "For God's sake, save my life! I could kill your friend, but don't want to do it!" Even as he urged Johnson to pull Gleason away, Johnson coldly shot Compa to death.

"I knew him well," said Wilson of Juan José, "and can vouch for the fact that he was a perfect gentleman, as well as a kind-hearted one."

Recovering from their initial surprise, the Indians counterattacked and slew some of the more or less innocent Missourians, but the arch-leaders escaped, having killed, it is said, about a score of Apaches.[15] In bloody retaliation the Indians wiped out a twenty-two member trapping expedition under Charles Kemp, seventy miles down the Gila,[16] and other parties in New Mexico. The three-man group of Wilson's, only thirty miles distant, was captured, Wilson escaping by a hair's breadth, probably through intercession of Mangas Colo-radas. He made his way to Santa Fe.

Mangas was perhaps the greatest of all Apache war leaders during the last century. He was born between 1790 and 1795, probably somewhere in southern New Mexico, and, as in the case of most of his noted fellows there are legends, probably originating with those who refuse to believe in the intellectual capacity of any Indian, that he was at least half white, the son of an Apache warrior and a Mexican woman.[17] He was a huge man, some said six feet, six inches tall, with a proportionate brain and intelligence. He was a giant stalking the desert mountains, who made his own legends and whose fame and the terror of whose name reverberated from Durango in the

[15] Gregg, *Commerce*, 206.

[16] Gregg, *Ibid.*, 206, and Dunn, *Massacres*, 315, say fifteen men were in this group.

[17] James H. McClintock, *Arizona: Prehistoric, Aboriginal, Pioneer, Modern*, I, 176.

south to the Navaho country in the north, from the Davis Mountains of West Texas to the Santa Ritas below Tucson.

In 1845 his southern raids were said to be of such proportions that the Mexicans mobilized one thousand men for a grand campaign against him, but a revolution distracted them. The next year Mangas met General Stephen Watts Kearny, pledged friendship with the *norteamericanos* and his fighting men as allies should the new rulers of the southwest desire to plunge into Chihuahua, Durango, and Sonora. The offer was refused.[18]

Several Apache chiefs, including Mangas, concluded a treaty on July 1, 1852, negotiated by Major John Greiner and Colonel E. V. Sumner.[19] It had only a slight permanent effect, but the recorded discussion preceding it led to an interesting exchange between the great Indian and the whites. Greiner asked Mangas why he continued his war so savagely with the Mexicans, and the Apache replied:

"I will tell you. Some time ago my people were invited to a feast; aguardiente, or whiskey, was there; my people drank and became intoxicated, and were lying asleep, when a party of Mexicans came in and beat out their brains with clubs. At another time a trader was sent among us from Chihuahua. While innocently engaged in trading . . . a cannon concealed behind the goods was fired upon my people, and quite a number were killed. . . . How can we make peace with such people?"[20]

It is said that Mangas united his three daughters in marriage to Cochise, the powerful Chiricahua, to a Navaho chief, and to a neighboring band of Apaches,[21] thus extending his influence and binding

---

[18] Dwight L. Clarke, *Stephen Watts Kearny: Soldier of the West*, 183–84.

[19] Greiner was appointed Indian agent in New Mexico on March 12, 1851, and in the spring of 1852 took over the duties of Superintendent of Indian Affairs for James S. Calhoun, governor and ex-officio superintendent. Greiner's services appear to have ended about September 30, 1852. On July 1, 1852, he and Colonel E. V. Sumner, commander of the Ninth Military Department, concluded a treaty with several Apache chiefs, including Mangas.—Letter to author from Jane F. Smith, archivist in charge, Interior Branch, National Archives.

[20] Farish, *History of Arizona*, II, 151–52.

[21] Novelist Will Levington Comfort, in his well-researched story of Mangas, *Apache*, 195, says, however, the first daughter was given to Cochise, the second to

to his standard hundreds of the bravest and most resolute warriors in the Southwest. He kept in hand larger bands of fighters than had been known until his time among the Apaches, and they ravaged the countryside for great distances.

These marriages, if they were deliberately planned, hint at the statesmanlike qualities in this big Indian. They suggest he had the notion that the white peril was bigger than native rivalries and that one small band, no matter how ably led, could not solve it. If he was willing, as it seems, to subordinate inter-tribal, or inter-band independence to the good of the whole, he was virtually the first Indian since Tecumseh to have that idea.

Yet the only alliance of any real effect was with Cochise.

The story of Cochise, of the wrongs done him by the whites, and of his abundant vengeance, of his strange pact with a lone white man, and of his final pledge to cease warring against Americans, has often been told and will be only summarized here.[22] It is not the purpose of this book to trace in detail the development of Apache-American troubles, but to show how these were militarily solved.

A Chiricahua, Cochise was born about 1823 or 1824. He was described in August, 1870, in his maturity, by one who had an opportunity to study him, as "five feet nine and one-half inches high; . . . weight 164 pounds; broad shoulders; stout frame; eyes medium size and very black; hair straight and black . . . ; scarred all over the body with buck-shot; very high forehead; large nose, and for an Indian straight."[23]

By the tradition of his people, Cochise and his band were in perpetual feud with the Mexicans but, aside from minor depredations, largely the running off of stock and so on, Cochise gave no important

---

Kutu-hala of the White Mountain Apaches, and a third to Cosito, of the Coyotero Apaches.

[22] For a reliable and unemotional account see Frank C. Lockwood, *The Apache Indians*, 100–30.

[23] *Arizoniana*, Vol. I, No. 3 (Fall, 1960), 24, reprinted from the *Weekly Arizonian* of September 17, 1870.

trouble to North Americans until 1861.[24] The son of Nachi, he succeeded that chief as leader of his people, as his son, Taza, was to succeed him. Cochise was well known to travelers across the Southwest even before the Civil War. He appears to have been generally regarded as an affable, intelligent Indian, in whom one could have confidence.

In the winter of 1860–61 the chief had a contract to supply the Butterfield Stage Line with wood for its station at or near Puerto del Dado, the Apache Pass spring near which Fort Bowie would shortly be erected. On the languidly beautiful Sonoita River, meanwhile, about a dozen miles west of Fort Buchanan, established in 1856 between the present towns of Sonoita and Patagonia, there lived on a squalid ranch John Ward and his Mexican mistress, Jesusa Martinez, with their mixed family. Jesusa had thus far lived a life of adventure and misery. She may have been a servant in a party of Mexicans that left Santa Cruz, Sonora, on September 30, 1849, for Magdalena, seventy-five miles distant. The party, says one account, was ambushed by Pinal Apaches, and she was captured. She formed a liaison with a warrior, from whom she escaped in 1855, after birth of a son. The following year she reached Santa Cruz again, and in 1860 she met and agreed to share the life of John Ward. Or, as another account has it, she was born and raised at Santa Cruz, married a light-haired, blue-eyed man named Tellez, or something similar, possibly of Irish origin, and by whom she had two children, a boy, Felix, and a girl.[25] After Tellez died, she met Ward.

Ward had come to the presidio of Tubac afoot in 1857. He has been described as "a castoff from the Vigilance Committee in San Francisco, and . . . in all respects, a worthless character," which may

[24] James H. Tevis, *Arizona in the '50's*. See also Barbara Ann Tyler, "Cochise, Apache War Leader," *Journal of Arizona History*, Vol. VI, No. 1 (Spring, 1965), 1–10.

[25] This is the version I prefer. It is contained in statements given by Santiago Ward, a son of Jesusa and John, to Mrs. George F. Kitt of the Arizona Pioneers' Historical Society on March 12, 1934. A copy of the interview is on file at the APHS library at Tucson.

or may not have been a fair delineation.[26] By Jesusa he had another son, Santiago. By 1860 Felix Ward, who later came to be known as Mickey Free, was eleven or twelve, wiry and lively, and there must have been some affection between him and his foster father.

One day Apaches, probably Pinals, swept down on the Ward place, scooped up Felix along with some work oxen and perhaps other cattle, and made off. Ward reported the outrage to Fort Buchanan, whose commanding officer dispatched a scouting party which returned with the report that the raiders had split into three parties, and their trails lost. Neither Jesusa nor Ward ever saw their boy or, for that matter, the cattle again, and they died believing that Felix had been killed.[27]

Why no more was done immediately to recover the boy and stock is not known; perhaps it took time for suspicion to crystallize against the Puerto del Dado Chiricahuas. At any rate, in late January of the following year, Second Lieutenant George Nicholas Bascom[28] was sent with fifty-four men[29] to Apache Pass. Ward and an interpreter,

[26] Farish, *History of Arizona*, II, 30. The documentary evidence is sparse and contradictory on John Ward and Jesusa Martinez. Charles Poston, who should have known better, describes them and events concerning them in a most garbled and inaccurate fashion in the *Overland Monthly* for September, 1894, Vol. XXIV, No. 141, 293–94, "Building a State in Apache Land." Charles T. Connell, writing in the Tucson *Citizen* of April 10, 1921, is the source for the version citing Jesusa's capture by Apaches, but he says that her baby was fathered by an Indian, while most students appear to believe he was half Irish.

[27] John Ward died in 1867, leaving an estate worth $400 and bills of nearly that much. Jesusa died about this time. Santiago heard in 1881 that his half-brother was still alive and an interpreter at San Carlos. "So I went to see him," he told Mrs. Kitt. "I did not know him at first, but he looked very much like his sister, fair and grayish eyes. They called him Mickey Free. I do not know why. I tried to get him to come home, but he would never do it."

[28] A Kentuckian, Bascom was graduated from West Point in 1858 and reached Buchanan in 1860. He was promoted to first lieutenant, Sixteenth Infantry, in May, 1861, and to captain in October. Bascom was killed at twenty-six in the battle of Valverde, New Mexico.—George W. Cullum, *Biographical Register of the Officers and Graduates of the U.S. Military Academy at West Point, N.Y.* He appears to have been an able officer.

[29] Farish, *History of Arizona*, II, 31, says twelve men under Sergeant Reuben F. Bernard, but he is probably wrong. See also: B. J. D. Irwin, "The Apache Pass Fight," *The Infantry Journal*, Vol. XXXII, No. 4 (April, 1928); Robert M. Utley,

Antonio, accompanied him. They soon established contact with Cochise who, with several companions, joined Bascom in an army tent February 4 for a parley, the tent soon being surrounded by soldiers. Cochise denied knowledge of the boy, but Bascom, who did not believe him, told the Indian he would be held as hostage until Felix was returned.

According to the generally accepted story, Cochise whipped out a knife, slashed the rear wall of the tent, and burst through the cordon of surprised soldiers, gaining the safety of surrounding hills despite the fifty or more shots fired at him. Six Indians were seized as hostages. The next day Cochise and some of his warriors called a stage station keeper, a hostler, and a stage driver named Wallace from the stage station for a talk. They knew Cochise and did as he asked, when he sought to capture them. The hostler and station keeper broke away, and dashed toward the station amid a hail of bullets that killed the latter. The hostler had almost reached the station when he was shot from inside by soldiers who thought he was a charging Apache. Cochise also sacked a small wagon train two miles west of the mail station that evening, probably to get more hostages, which he reportedly did.

In shooting affairs February 5 and 7 or 8, two sergeants were officially reported wounded "slightly," yet this cannot be, because Bascom, sending for more men, also asked medical assistance, the latter not, as a matter of policy, being available to most scouting expeditions in the field for two more decades. On February 6 Cochise had appeared before the soldiers' position, reportedly bringing Wallace along as interpreter, and offered to exchange him and sixteen government mules for the Indian prisoners. Bascom refused to trade, it was said, unless the boy, Felix, was returned. That evening a note was received from Wallace reporting that Cochise held other prisoners, and would agree to the exchange.

"The Bascom Affair: A Reconstruction," *Arizona and the West*, Vol. III, No. 1 (Spring, 1961), 59–68; Benjamin H. Sacks, "New Evidence on the Bascom Affair," *Arizona and the West*, Vol. IV, No. 3 (Autumn, 1962), 261–78; Arthur Woodward, "Side Lights on Fifty Years of Apache Warfare 1836–1886," *Arizoniana*, Vol. II, No. 3 (Fall, 1961), 3–14.

Here arises a serious question: with both Cochise and Bascom agreed on a peaceful trade of prisoners, why did it fail to come off and why did bloodshed result? The answer can only lie, I think, in the arrival of Army Surgeon Bernard J. D. Irwin and an escort, from Fort Buchanan on February 10, and the later arrival of First Lieutenant Isaiah N. Moore from Fort Breckenridge with seventy men— all before Cochise could obtain the boy from the Apache band which had stolen him. With the massing of this considerable force in Apache Pass, the chief must have believed, was signalled a relentless military operation against him, and on February 17 or 18 the mutilated bodies of his prisoners, which numbered either three or six, were found.

On February 19 Bascom permitted his three adult male prisoners, and Irwin the three Coyoteros his men had captured en route to the Pass, to be hanged near the remains of the murdered whites. Bascom at first demurred, but Irwin, his superior in rank, insisted on hanging *his* three prisoners, anyway, so the lieutenant gave in, the deed was done, and a quarter century of tumultuous Apache hostilities were touched off.

Cochise's fury, it is said, was enhanced because three of those hanged were his close relatives. Within sixty days one hundred and fifty whites were killed, and it has been charged that the series of blunders which loosed Cochise upon the whites eventually cost "five thousand American lives and the destruction of hundreds of thousands of dollars worth of property."[30] No traveler, no settler, no miner, no small party of soldiers, no small community was safe from the avenging warriors. With the outbreak of the Civil War the troops were withdrawn from much of the country, and this added to the subsequent depopulation of a considerable part of the Southwest. Indians under Mangas joined in plundering, and many settlements were abandoned.

A brief description of two typical fights will illustrate the innumerable encounters between whites and Apaches during this period.

[30] Ogle, *Western Apaches*, 45n.; Farish, *History of Arizona*, II, 32–33, makes the latter estimate, which is probably too high.

About the end of March, 1861, William S. Oury of Tucson and others charged with moving Butterfield Stage Line livestock and equipment to a more northerly route, learned of a party that had left Mesilla by coach for Tucson. This group included Michael Neiss; John James Giddings, of San Antonio; a driver, Briggs; Anthony Elder, a conductor; and Sam Nealy, a company employee.

"Just at dawn of day, as they were approaching the station at Stein's Peak," wrote Oury, "the ever to be remembered Apache chief Cachise, with a large party of his savage people, fired upon the coach from a stone parapet prepared for the purpose along the margin of an arroyo. At the first volley they killed the driver, Briggs, and the brave conductor, Anthony Elder . . .

"The mules, being left without a guide and frightened by the near blaze of fire, started on a run, left the road, and ran for about a mile and a half to the foot of the mountain, where the coach was capsized and everything brought to a standstill."

Instead of fleeing to some place of greater security, the party apparently listened to Michael Neiss, "who had been for a long time road agent of the mail company on that section, that Cachise was a great friend of his." If so, Cochise had forgotten. "Poor kind hearted old man, how little he knew of the character of the relentless savage!" wrote Oury. "He was ruthlessly seized, as were also the other two, and dragged into the mountains to undergo God only knows what amount of excruciating torture."

Cochise boasted of his part in the affray to two Americans at Janos a couple of years later, Oury reported. He said "in derision of poor Neiss and Giddings that they had died like poor sick women, but that Sam Nealy (whom he described as having gold in his teeth) had fought bravely, only succumbing after having killed three of the savages."[31]

The Free Thompson party put up a better fight, one that was a legend on the border for many years. This group of six veteran frontiersmen, en route to California, were attacked by Mangas and Cochise in bloody Doubtful Pass in the spring of the same year, but

[31] Tucson *Star*, July 20, 1879.

the Indians found their work no sinecure. Each white was armed with an "improved" rifle, and together they had two thousand rounds of ammunition. They were assailed by perhaps several hundred warriors.

Whoever was driving the stage sized up the situation at the outset and, obviously an experienced Indian fighter, swung his teams off the road and whipped them cross-country to the only possible site for defense, a small mound where the party hastily threw up a small stone breastwork. The fight lasted three days, according to Indian accounts.

"The whites were unable to get water, and the little food they had was soon exhausted," it was reported. "The Indians finally killed them, but at the loss of something like . . . forty-five men."

The last man, heavily wounded and bleeding freely, dragged himself from one vantage point to another around the hill, to better fire at the enemy, according to signs found later by the Tucson men who buried the victims. Cochise expressed admiration for the Free Thompson group. He said "they were the bravest men he ever knew or heard of, that if all his band were equal in bravery and endurance . . . he would undertake to whip the whole United States."[32]

The story of the abortive Mangas- and Cochise-led ambush of General James H. Carleton's California Column in Apache Pass during the summer of 1862 has been told many times. The ambush was unsuccessful, but it did show the close alliance between the two great chieftains, as well as the greatest massing of Apache warriors for a fight in written history.

Mangas, now about seventy, had nearly exhausted his span of warfare, diplomacy, intrigue, and power. He and some of his band were encamped near the abandoned mining settlement of Pinos Altos in January, 1863, and military leaders had become convinced they could never thoroughly pacify the country while he lived.

There arrived in the vicinity about this time the forty or more adventurers known to history as the Walker Party, led by the vet-

[32] Ibid.; Farish, History of Arizona, II, 59–60; Comfort, Apache, 253–55, says the party traveled by pack train.

eran mountain man, Joseph Reddeford Walker. Leaving California the group, bolstered by additions from time to time, had crossed northern Arizona, visited Colorado, come south the length of New Mexico, and now was working west toward Arizona again. The primary purpose of its members was to seek gold, but they became interested in the capture of Mangas partly because brushes they had had with Indians had convinced them that the giant Apache might solve their difficulties. If they could capture him as hostage, "we would be able to proceed with far less difficulty," wrote one.[33] J. W. (Jack) Swilling,[34] a member of the party, headed the attempt to capture Mangas. This group was joined by Captain Edmond D. Shirland, First Cavalry, California Volunteers, and a military unit.

By a ruse Mangas was taken and the whites hurried him to Fort McLane[35] where they were met by more California Volunteers, commanded by General Joseph R. West[36] who, because of his rank, assumed command. He interviewed Mangas privately and then put him under a guard of soldiers.

Mangas "had prominent, bloodshot eyes and disdained to notice anyone and was a head and shoulders above any paleface present," Daniel E. Conner recalled. "He wore a cheap checked shirt and ordinary blue overalls cut off at the knees and a white straight-brim sombrero with a square crown like a quart cup and much too small for him. The hat was tied to his tremendous head by a string under his chin. He had a head of hair that reached his waist. His nose was

---

[33] Daniel Ellis Conner, *Joseph Reddeford Walker and the Arizona Adventure*, 34.

[34] Jack Swilling was one of the notable characters of early Arizona. Born in Georgia in 1831, he emigrated to Missouri, then to Texas and, about 1859, to Arizona. He made and lost fortunes, was prominent in irrigation development in the central valley of Arizona, but because of pain from early wounds became something of a drug addict and on August 12, 1878, died in prison while awaiting trial on a charge of holding up a stage.

[35] Fort McLane was occupied only in 1860 and 1861. It was fifteen miles south of the Santa Rita mines. Malcolm F. Farmer, "New Mexico Camps, Posts, Stations, and Forts," Santa Fe, Museum of New Mexico.

[36] Born in Louisiana, West enlisted as a private in 1847 and rose to brevet major general of volunteers, before being mustered out in 1866. He died in 1898.— Francis B. Heitman, *Historical Register and Dictionary of the United States Army, from its Organization, September 29, 1789, to March 2, 1903*, I, 1020.

aquiline and was his one delicate feature, both in size and form. His receding forehead was in keeping with his receding jaws and chin. His wide mouth resembled a slit cut in a melon, expressionless and cruel."

Night came on, and turned cold. The sentries built a hot fire, and his two guards brought Mangas to it; he rolled up in a single blanket on the ground. The two soldiers, one a noncommissioned officer, had been carefully warned not to let the prisoner escape. They accepted the implication.

"About 9 o'clock I noticed the soldiers were doing something to Mangas, but quit when I returned to the fire and stopped to get warm," Conner said. He was on routine guard.

"Watching them from my beat in the outer darkness, I discovered that they were heating their bayonets and burning Mangas's feet and legs. This they continued to do [until] Mangas rose upon his left elbow, angrily protesting that he was no child to be played with. Thereupon the two soldiers, without removing their bayonets from their Minie muskets each quickly fired into the chief, following with two shots each from their navy six-shooters. Mangas fell back into the same position . . . and never moved.

"An officer came, glanced at the dead body and returned to his blankets . . . In twenty minutes all was still again. The next morning I took some trinkets from the body . . . A little soldier giving his name as John T. Wright, came to the dead body and scalped it with an Arkansas toothpick [Bowie knife]." Five soldiers lifted the body, blanket and all, into a convenient ditch and covered it with a foot and one-half of earth. Later the surgeon, Captain D. B. Sturgeon, secured Mangas's tremendous skull and sent it to a phrenologist, Professor O. S. Fowler, who determined that it was of greater size than Daniel Webster's.[37]

Several years afterward charges of brutality were brought against General West concerning the Mangas affair, but the officer asserted he had placed "seven soldiers, including a noncommissioned officer, over Mangas, to be sure he could not escape; that Mangas was cap-

[37] Conner, *Joseph Reddeford Walker*, 34–42.

tured by his command red-handed in a fight with the soldiers, and was killed at midnight while he was rushing his guard to escape." None of his statements was true.[38]

Mangas's feats were not without significance. In a sense he inspired the spectacular careers both of Victorio and Geronimo, Mimbres like himself. Both were said to have been present at the Apache Pass fight. Neither was wounded there. But they took from it, no doubt, much that would have meaning in their own careers, not least being the dictum to avoid pitched battles with regular troops unless the soldiers were at a disadvantage, and then to make it short, sharp, and decisive.

[38] McClintock, *Arizona*, I, 177.

III

Civilians Take a Hand

THE JOE WALKER PARTY journeyed at night through perilous Doubtful Canyon, where perhaps more skirmishes took place than at the more noted Apache Pass to the southwest, visited Tucson and the Pima-Maricopa villages briefly, and arrived in May, 1863, at what became known as Walker's Diggings, or Walker's Camp, in central Arizona. Samuel C. Miller,[1] probably the youngest member of Walker's group, made the first gold strike, on a stream named Lynx Creek because he stamped to death a wildcat there, and a minor stampede of prospectors and settlers was generated which resulted in the founding of Prescott. It was gold that ultimately defeated the Apaches and wild Indians in much of the West, for it was gold that brought in population, and the Army to protect it, and the farmers and ranchers to feed the soldiers, and the communication lines the Army needed, and, at long last, the civilization with which the fetterless savages could not cope. Man for man they often were as good fighting specimens, or better, than the whites, but in numbers and in ingenuity they could never compete. It was gold that brought in the numbers, and the numbers that encouraged ingenuity.

Walker's men went to prospecting, killed off the game, and there was never food enough at first, though there was lots of freedom. "This was the freest country on earth at that time," Conner recalled, dryly. "No civilization, laws or books. No restriction nor anything

[1] Born November 4, 1840, at Peoria, Illinois, Miller hiked to California at fifteen and led a most adventurous life, dying near Prescott October 12, 1909. He once reportedly slew seven Indians at his ranch near Prescott. Miller was believed largely responsible for the Walapais War, caused when he wantonly shot an important chieftain.—Farish, *History of Arizona*, II, 257–62.

to eat. Democracy was in her prime."[2] Walker and Pauline Weaver,[3] representative mountain men, among the fiercest individualists America had yet produced, spelled the doom for the old, free life in the wilderness, by guiding the parties that struck gold and thus engendered the heavy inrush of prospectors and others. Weaver was unlike the typical mountain man, although he was of that breed. Wandering through the desert country, he had been engaged in working up peace treaties with various bands along the Colorado when Abraham H. Peeples discovered him and easily talked him into guiding an expedition that discovered the La Paz gold placers along the river. It was no trick at all to get Pauline later to guide a party that found the even richer deposits on Rich Hill and Antelope Peak and that indirectly led to other discoveries. But neither Weaver nor Walker ever profited extensively from the mines. Pauline idled around the boom camps named for him and, after a while, yawned and wandered up to the Verde country to scout for the Army. Joe Walker stuck it out for four years before boredom overcame him and he returned to California. He left behind him a burgeoning settlement, the establishment of a relatively stable government and the institutions of civilization, not all of which he created, by any means, but whose development his efforts vastly enhanced.

Prescott, founded in April, 1864, was named for the historian William Hickling Prescott, historian of Spanish conquests in the New World, because of the erroneous impression that pueblo and cliff-dwelling ruins nearby were of Aztec origin.[4] The city was protected

[2] Conner, *Joseph Reddeford Walker*, 249.

[3] Weaver has been neglected by biographers of mountain men. The best sketch of his life is Sharlot M. Hall's "First Citizen of Prescott: Pauline Weaver, Trapper and Mountain Man." This reproduces an address Miss Hall delivered October 27, 1929, when his remains were returned to Prescott from a national cemetery at San Francisco. The pamphlet, with an introduction by Alpheus H. Favour, appeared perhaps in April, 1930, under auspices of what is now known as the Sharlot Hall Historical Museum of Arizona at Prescott. His obituary appeared in the Prescott *Miner*, July 13, 1867.

[4] For a brief history of the founding of Prescott, see Pauline Henson. *Founding a Wilderness Capital: Prescott, A.T. 1864.*

by nearby Fort Whipple, at first surrounded by a log palisade until it was found unnecessary in Apache country. Prescott contained as colorful a galaxy of rogues and gentlemen, miners and Indian fighters, farmers and mule packers, honest men and thieves as could be found anywhere.

The first recorded shooting of a white by an Indian, and of Indians by whites in the Prescott area involved George Goodhue and Sugarfoot Jack.[5] Goodhue had gone with some companions toward Prescott when Jack heard firing in that direction and ran toward it. He saw about fifteen Indians coming toward him single file, waited behind a rock until they were within ten paces, then killed the first Indian and wounded the second, the rest fleeing. Sugarfoot fired after them, believing he had killed a third and wounded still another, when Goodhue and his surviving companions hastened up. They found Jack calmly awaiting them, smoking his pipe.[6]

Over at Weaver's Diggin's the killings already had commenced when two Indian boys, come to town to see the sights, were shot down by miners panicked by their own imaginations teased by fears of these representatives of a "warlike people, untamable, bloodthristy, unconquerable."[7] And from these days forward, Arizona's hills were washed in blood, with thousands of men, women, and children, white and red, giving up their lives or suffering grievous wounds, all as sacrifices to the gods of avarice, ignorance, and cruelty.

From these earliest days, large-scale civilian Indian-hunting expe-

---

[5] Farish, *History of Arizona*, III, 32; Conner, *Joseph Reddeford Walker*, 148–50, 265–68. Sugarfoot, whose real name no one knew, was said to be an escaped convict from Van Diemen's Land (Tasmania) who had enlisted in the California Volunteers, but was discharged either for thievery or for striking down his colonel. Albert Franklin Banta said he was as "brave as a lion, even if he was a notorious thief." He is probably not to be confused with Bill James, another escaped Van Diemen's Land convict, who was arrested from time to time at Prescott after indulging in thievery, and at length was chased out of town. Sugarfoot was said to have been stabbed fatally on the Rio Grande.

[6] Farish, *History of Arizona*, III, 32.

[7] The full story is in a clipping in the Los Angeles Public Library. There are two volumes of the clippings, all relating to Arizona Indian troubles. They were received as a gift in 1929, but the donor is unknown. Hereafter cited as L. A. Pub. Lib.

ditions were sent out. Often they were combined with prospecting and exploring projects, and thus were useful as well as "enjoyable" for active men, tired of hanging around the camps, bringing in crops, or pick-and-shovel labor at some dubious claim. The most noted leader of these early expeditions was King S. Woolsey, a man of intelligence, of undoubted courage, but something of an opportunist and, in one historian's words, "quite a rascal."[8] He was a "dignified, full-bearded man; farmer, miner, road-builder, guide, miller, merchant, Indian fighter, and legislator. He has been called 'the most notable, the most enterprising and the most courageous of all the great host of trail-blazers who first penetrated Arizona.' "[9]

Woolsey was born in Alabama in 1832, but was reared in Louisiana and reached California in 1850 and Arizona a decade later. Early suspected of Secessionist sympathies, he furnished supplies to Union forces after the California Column recaptured Arizona. He is said to have joined the Walker Party in 1863, but he was not so mentioned by Conner, and it is likely that he reached the Prescott area after Walker arrived.

Woolsey had an undying hatred for Indians, in common with many pioneers. On one occasion, while prospecting in the Bradshaw Mountains, he mixed pinole with strychnine and saw to it that some savages obtained the lethal concoction with disastrous results. This incident, which was by no means unique on the frontier, later became confused with his greatest Indian fight, when no poison was used.[10]

He had started one ranch at Agua Caliente, north of the Gila River, and later a second one on the Agua Fria, east of Prescott. Being about as far east as any ranch of its day, it was more subject to Indian raids than others, and Woolsey lost livestock accordingly. This led more or less directly to his first and most famous Indian hunt, although what triggered the expedition was stock thefts from another pioneer,

[8] Clara T. Woody to author, October 26, 1963.
[9] Bert Fireman. *Historical Markers of Arizona*, vol. II (no page numbers listed). Woolsey died at forty-seven on June 29, 1879, leaving an estate of $37,000 and debts of about two-thirds of that amount.—*Miner*, July 4, 1879.
[10] Clara T. Woody, "The Woolsey Expeditions of 1864," *Arizona and the West*, Vol. IV, No. 2 (Summer, 1962), 159.

Abe Peeples, co-discoverer of Rich Hill. Peeples had lost twenty-seven head of stock to one band of raiders, and he called for a retaliatory expedition, which Woolsey volunteered to lead.

The party crossed from the upper Hassayampa River to the Agua Fria, turned down it through Black Canyon and crossed below the mouth of that gorge, above what were called the Frog Tanks, on the east side of the Agua Fria about where Marinette is now. From here they passed to the plains of the lower Verde River, which they called the San Francisco, as did most of the early explorers. They had now fallen short of rations and sent a group under Peeples to the Pima villages for more. On the group's return, Woolsey was joined by fourteen Maricopas under Juan Chivaria, a noted war leader, a white man, Cyrus Lennan, and others, including some Pimas, who did not stay long. The combined party now toiled a day and a night through what they called Endless Canyon, which must have been the deep gorge of the Salt River, scaled the mesa on its south side, and, after some thirty-five miles, on January 24, 1864, slipped down into a wash.

It was a "pretty, sunny morning" when the whites, marching single file around a treeless mountain, of a sudden found a heavy force of Apaches winding around the same mountain above them. "They were all done up in paint and feathers and kept ominously silent," Conner recalled.[11] Some of the boys thought there were three hundred of them and others five hundred, but Conner guessed there were probably two hundred fifty, making the odds about six to one. The whites

[11] This account, unless otherwise specified, is based on Conner, a participant, *Joseph Reddeford Walker*, 171–76. Dunn, *Massacres*, 337, calls the Indians Pinals and Coyoteros. Most accounts say Peeples' losses were the prime reason for the expedition (see McClintock, *Arizona*, I, 185), but J. Ross Browne, in *A Tour Through Arizona*, indicates that the losses were more general. He reports (p. 120) that Woolsey had also lost thirty-three head of cattle, and settlers along Granite Creek, sixteen head. Authorities also differ on the number of Woolsey's party. McClintock, quoting Peeples, says there were eighteen white men and Maricopas and Pimas (pp. 185–86); Browne (pp. 170–71), says there were thirty whites plus Indians; Ogle, *Western Apaches*, 48, says the party included sixty whites and as many Indians; Conner, *Joseph Reddeford Walker*, 171, says there were "nearly forty men." The route is based on Browne (pp. 120–21), but with modifications to correct apparent errors of geography.

and their allies dismounted and arranged themselves for defense as best they could, someone joking as they did so: "Now we have found the stock and more of it than we want." The hostile parties faced each other at a distance of about one hundred paces, the whites expecting at any moment a crushing attack, although it seems unlikely the Apaches would have openly approached them if they meant war.

Woolsey shattered the unnatural stillness with a matter-of-fact greeting that seemed too loud. "*Buenos dias,*" he said. The Indians replied, in broken Spanish, and both sides relaxed. They agreed, through the efforts of Tonto Jack,[12] to talk. Six of their chiefs met five from the whites midway between the forces. Before stepping forward, Woolsey told his men that he would touch his hat or raise it with his left hand as a signal for them to start shooting. Whether or not he expected treachery, he intended it.

He, Joe Dye, Lennan, and the other whites stepped warily up for the parley, each wearing a brace of pistols under his coat. The Apaches, being less thoroughly clothed, had not the advantage of the whites and could conceal no arms save possibly knives, although one bore a lance. He trailed it at his heels to show his good intentions. One of the native leaders, a chief called Par-a-muck-a, said contemptuously that he could not sit on the bare ground. Woolsey called for a new, blood-colored blanket to be spread for him. Another was opened so that gifts of pinole and tobacco might be placed on it. Joe Dye reported that the Indians were insolent and taunting in their demeanor, and that a few secreted bows under their serapes, although this may be an attempt at justification for the succeeding events. The whites held one undoubted advantage. The Indians could not understand their language, and had no interpreter, so they could say what they liked while pretending to negotiate with their opponents. Woolsey seized upon this to assign "each of his companions [an] Indian to kill" and laughingly warned them in English "not to let one chief escape."[13] The Apache parleyers took their cue from Woolsey's ap-

[12] Jack apparently was a Yuma Indian, former prisoner of the Apaches, and now an employee of Woolsey's.—Farish, *History of Arizona*, II, 219.

[13] Conner, *Joseph Reddeford Walker*, 173.

parent good humor to shout back reports that brought howls of glee from their naked warriors, roosting on the stony hillsides above.

Everyone was in the best of humor, grinning amiably and chattering back and forth, when Woolsey with his left hand touched his hat.

In a crashing instant five of the six chiefs were slain, the blood of the most important pouring onto the scarlet blanket he had demanded. The sixth chief, shot twice through the body, raised a lance with a rusting Mexican saber for a blade, and rammed it through the heart of Cyrus Lennan,[14] who was to have killed him but botched the job. He slipped to the ground, muttering, "I am killed," as indeed he was. The hillside Indians, stunned by the shattering assault, fired an aimless volley and took to their heels.[15] The whites pressed them closely for half a mile up the wash, before straggling back to the scene of their treachery. The whole fight had lasted only seven or eight minutes, and the whites and their allies had lost but one man killed and several wounded, none seriously, although Tonto Jack took an arrow in the neck. They claimed officially that they had killed nineteen and wounded others. Unofficially the number of slain is often given as twenty-four, although Conner says, no doubt with truth, that "We never knew how many Indians were killed . . . and never waited to count them."[16] The whites hurriedly loaded their pack horses, lashed poor Lennan across an animal, and left that "unholy place," retiring to a lonely and wild site probably near the Salt, where Lennan was buried under a cottonwood on which was carved his name and date. A fire was built atop the grave to conceal it.[17]

[14] Lennan was a half-brother and partner of Ami White, prominent trader to the Pimas and Maricopas. Dye is said to have killed the Indian who slew him.— Conner, *Joseph Reddeford Walker*, 173n.; Browne, *A Tour Through Arizona*, 123.

[15] Conner, *Joseph Reddeford Walker*, 174–75, tells a story of the heroism and self-sacrifice of one of the Indians, who tried desperately to carry a wounded friend to safety, and finally died defending him from the whites.

[16] *Ibid.*, 175–76.

[17] Browne, *A Tour Through Arizona*, 123–24, says that the grave was at the junction of the Verde and the Salt. Conner, *Joseph Reddeford Walker*, probably mistakenly, places it on the Gila.

The question of where this fight took place has not been settled. It was long thought that it occurred at Bloody Tanks, at the head of Bloody Tanks Wash, the west branch of Pinal Creek, near Miami. Various artifacts and relics of some engagement have been found there. But an unpublished map of 1869 shows the fight to have been in Fish Creek Canyon, about twelve miles from the Salt River Canyon.[18] The Bloody Tanks relics are now thought to have originated with a fight Lieutenant Howard B. Cushing had with Pinal Apaches several years afterward.[19]

Conner, unpretentious and honest as salt pork, unlike many others who attempted to explain away the incident in later years, wrote: "Our apparent treachery . . . was justified because the men who composed [our] party were experienced in Indian fighting and they had learned this tricky lesson from the Apaches, who upon this occasion intended to do the same thing,"[20] which no doubt was what he believed. But it was supposition on his part. None of the whites knew the Apache language, and none could come close to divining the Indian intentions. This incident was really but an extension of the so-called extermination policy which, under General Carleton, was at this time receiving "as full and fair a trial as could possibly be given to it."[21] Carleton had solicited the aid of the governors of Sonora and Chihuahua, of Governor Richard C. McCormick in Arizona, and of the miners and Pimas and Maricopas in what was to be a massive assault on Apaches and Navahos alike. The results were most bloody—and inconclusive. Of Apaches alone, 216 were killed compared with 16 whites. The Woolsey incident was but a phase.

Nevertheless, it must be condemned, if not on moral grounds, then with the indisputable argument that it was shortsighted, if not stupid, and led inevitably into war, instead of averting it. Had it been possible to capture all the potentially hostile Indians, and then to anni-

[18] Bert Fireman, executive vice president of the Arizona Historical Foundation, to author, January 21, 1964. He believes the Woolsey expedition "didn't come anywhere close to Miami."

[19] Woody to author, July 8, 1964.

[20] Conner, *Joseph Reddeford Walker*, 176.

[21] Dunn, *Massacres*, 335.

31

hilate them, something could be said for the Woolsey method. But this, of course, was impossible. Since not all the Indians could be caught, the slaying of a mere nineteen or twenty-four was as nothing. Those who escaped bore only implacable hatred toward the whites. And under the fragmented nature of Indian society, any fear that might have been instilled into the hearts of those Apaches present, could not have extended nearly so far among the mountain bands as did the newly generated ripples of hatred and distrust and desire for revenge.

The three major Woolsey expeditions were not the only ones of their kind. Conner tells how miners often banded together, when they had little else to do, and went a-hunting Indians. When they could trap them, they killed them to the last man and, sometimes, to the last woman and child. The Indians, naturally, did the same to the whites and to other tribes. But, oddly enough, the whites seem to have begun the inter-racial strife and their cruel methods led to a brutalization of Indian warfare. "Both sides were becoming more and more exasperated, and vented their spleen in ways that only served to make matters worse. The Indians were adopting the practice of mutilating the dead, which was formerly contrary to their customs."[22]

The extermination impulse died hard and slow. It appears throughout the history of white-Indian strife and persists, in an altered form, to this day. On a small scale, the war between white and red soon became one of extermination as well. It is true that the Indians sometimes took prisoner children and women, and the whites on rare occasions spared them, but more often total massacre was the end sought, sometimes with horrifying and degenerate brutality. Conner tells how Sugarfoot Jack, after a rancheria was captured and put to the torch, discovered a live papoose and flung it into a flaming hut to watch it burn. He found another frightened child and dandled it upon his knee, playing with it until he had worked it into a fine humor, then drew his pistol and blew its brains out. This so disgusted even the hardened frontiersmen that they chased him into the brush and would have killed him had he not hidden until their tempers cooled. On

[22] *Ibid.*, 339.

another occasion someone was crude enough to rip off the scalp of a gray-haired woman, and brought down upon himself the wrath of what men of principle were with the party. The Apaches themselves did no scalping.

Despite the Woolsey expedition, and others like them, or perhaps because of them, the Indian menace grew steadily worse. Along the Hassayampa, Lynx Creek, the various tributaries to the Verde, the Salt, and the Gila—everywhere the story was the same: the whites lived on the reservations and the Indians occupied the country.[23] The military seemed incapable of controlling the natives, the settlers' attempts seemed inconclusive, but there was another alternative, and that was organization and maintenance of territorial rangers. The problem was payment for them.

Conner reports that a bill was introduced in the territorial legislature, and defeated by a single vote, that would have provided for one hundred rangers, the captains to receive five dollars a day and the privates three. This would have cost the territory $150,000 a year, and territorial tax collection was totaling about $1,400 annually and a debt "would have hung over the Territory like a dark cloud for generations."[24]

Nevertheless, the idea of such a force to combat the savage menace was all but irresistible, and in 1865–66 at least five companies were organized to replace the California Volunteers, heading home now that the Civil War was over.

Most of the Arizona Volunteers were Mexicans, recruited at Tucson and elsewhere below the Gila. For example, Company E was organized by Captain Hiram H. Washburn, who was assisted by Lieutenant Manuel Gallegos, a former captain in the Sonoran army of Governor Pesquiera and who had seen much Apache fighting. Company A was captained by Robert Postle, but most of the time was commanded by Lieutenant Primativo Cervantes of Wickenburg, a highly successful fighter. Company C was commanded by the half-

[23] Or so said Brigadier General William Starke Rosecrans, according to the San Francisco *Alta* of September 5, 1870.—L.A. Pub. Lib.
[24] Conner, *Joseph Reddeford Walker*, 334–35.

Indian Lieutenant John D. Walker, no relation to Joe Walker.[25] Company B was formed of Maricopas officered by First Lieutenant Thomas Ewing and Second Lieutenant Charles Reidt. Company F, also from the Tucson-Tubac area, was organized by Oscar Hutton, a well-known guide and Apache hunter, "a good and brave man," but inclined to be vain about such things as the fact that he had six toes on each foot. He died in the early 1870's after being kicked in the jaw by a mule, passing on, in the opinion of Captain John Gregory Bourke, "quite as much from chagrin at being outwitted as from the injury inflicted."[26]

This was the roster of Arizona Volunteers. Each of the companies saw combat, some repeatedly. Captain Washburn's Company E seems to have been as active as any, and the captain appears to have been a fertile idea-man. He wrote Governor John N. Goodwin suggesting that the intractable Cochise and perhaps four hundred warriors could be destroyed at Fronteras, just south of the border, where they were expected shortly for a spree. The Apaches would surely become drunk and then could easily be massacred, Washburn argued.[27] This was in the best traditions of the time, but was not acted upon.

Company E was sent to Camp Lincoln, later called Camp Verde, and a party from it, commanded by Gallegos, left camp on February 11, 1866, at 7:00 A.M., traveled two nights, resting by day until scouts found Apache sign and located a rancheria. The remainder of the wretchedly clad volunteers were drawn up in the night to within

[25] John Walker, born at Nauvoo, Illinois, about 1840, was a wagonmaster with the California Volunteers. Part Wyandotte, he settled among the Pimas and soon became virtually a member of that tribe. He compiled the first written grammar of their language and became a leader among them. He had studied medicine early in life, was of extraordinary intelligence and something of a scientist, was a surveyor and probate judge in Pinal County. When leading his Pimas into battle with Apaches he dressed in nothing but a breech-clout, whooped and yelled with them, and was merciless to the common enemy. He was adjudged insane late in life and died around the turn of the century. His estate was involved for years in bitter litigation, the U.S. Supreme Court finally holding that no part of it should go to his Indian daughter because a white man could not legally marry an Indian under laws of the territory.—Farish, *History of Arizona*, IV, 117–20; McClintock, *Arizona*, I, 194.

[26] John Gregory Bourke, *On the Border With Crook*, 14–15.

[27] McClintock, *Arizona*, I, 195.

striking distance of the enemy, located in some caves. About two in the morning Gallegos divided his force into three units and moved into position on a slope opposite the Apaches. So silently was the move made that not even the hostiles' dogs were aware of it. The slaughter was considerable. One war chief held a secure, elevated position and successfully defied the attackers, but his followers were not so fortunate. "All of the caves that were accessible were filled with dead and wounded," said a news report. "Some thirty are believed to have been killed outright. Thirteen scalps were brought to camp, and twelve prisoners, two squaws and ten children, one of the latter has since died." Seven of the volunteers were wounded, none seriously, in this savage little battle. A surgeon who accompanied the expedition offered each volunteer "a dollar's worth of tobacco for every Apache they kill in the future, that they may smoke the pipe of peace over the peaceable and harmless condition of those who fall under their guns."[28]

Company A made a good kill, of about twenty-two Apaches, a couple of months later in a daring expedition under Primativo Cervantes. John Walker and his Company C Pimas, plus forty men of Company B, the Maricopas, left the Pima villages March 27, and four days later had a fight, reporting the slaying of twenty-five of the enemy while losing one man killed and two wounded.[29] This may be the action in which Pimas shocked even some (but not all) of the rough miners by their exuberant smashing of Apache heads. The Apaches, perhaps learning it from the Pimas, followed the custom of flattening the faces of their victims, perhaps to escape identification in the next world. But the Pimas were most expert, sometimes carefully placing the head of the fallen on a flat stone so that when a huge rock came crushing down, it would suitably cave in the face. What disgusted Conner was that some of the whites observed approvingly while this was going on. Truly, he thought, "savage civilized men are the most monstrous of all monsters."[30]

[28] *Miner*, February 28, 1866.
[29] *Miner*, April 11, 1866.
[30] Conner, *Joseph Reddeford Walker*, 220–21.

Until their disbandment in the autumn of 1866, the Volunteers did good work, fighting Indians at every opportunity. On one occasion Sergeant Elias and six men of Company E fought twenty-seven Apaches while on wagon train escort near Prescott. Elias had a bullet through his hat during the two-hour fight, and one of his men was captured and recaptured three times, but the Indians quit just as the detail was running out of ammunition, and no one was killed on either side.[31] But the Volunteers could not solve the Indian problem.

The next expedient was organization of a ranger outfit with rugged Tom Hodges as captain.[32]

When depredations continued after the legislature adjourned without making provision for any form of defense organizations, the necessity for the rangers became apparent. For instance, Woolsey sent a team with four men from his Agua Fria ranch to the Bully Bueno Mill on upper Turkey Creek. Just short of Big Bug the outfit ran into an ambush, and three men were killed, the Indians making off with three of the four yoke of oxen. The fourth man, Harvey Twaddle, escaped the ambush, but not to live long.[33] His death was one of the freak affairs occasionally occurring on the frontier. One July day in 1867 Twaddle tracked some lost mules near Walnut Grove, and found them just as an Indian fired an arrow at him from ambush. Harvey shot at the redskin as a hasty second arrow was fired at him. He killed the Indian, and the arrow at the same time struck him in the chest. He pulled it out, killed a second Indian and wounded a third, and chased the mules back to camp. By the time he

[31] Farish, *History of Arizona*, IV, 110–11.

[32] Hodges was a saloon operator at Prescott and had many adventures in and about the settlement. According to McClintock, *Arizona*, I, 193, he was a "quarrelsome individual" and a "noted gunman" who later killed a man and fled to Mexico where he shortly died or was slain.

[33] *Miner*. November 10, 1866. The three killed were William Trahen, L. M. Linton, and Leroy Jay, an acquaintance of Conner, who went out with others to retrieve the bodies. They found them "literally cut to pieces. Their moustaches were picked with the lip and all, as if it had been trimmed from off the teeth. Their arms and fingers were cut off and they were really disjointed all over. Seventeen arrows were sticking into one of the trunks. They were otherwise mutilated in a manner too shocking to relate."—Conner, *Joseph Reddeford Walker*, 207.

reached there he was delirious, but recovered the next day sufficiently to describe his adventure in great detail. Harvey alternated between delirium and consciousness for nine days before he died. When his chest was opened, it was found that the arrow had penetrated his heart, "and it was wonderful that he had survived so long."[34]

These attacks, and others, prompted the Prescott *Miner* to exclaim: "Surely we need rangers, native volunteers, or more regulars to go in pursuit of the red rascals," and the populace apparently agreed. A public meeting was called November 23, 1866, at Prescott. Everybody came. They approved arrangements for their rangers there and then. "Thos. Hodges was requested to raise a company of 30 men to serve 90 days. A liberal sum was subscribed for the outfit, and also for Indian scalps."[35] As a further demonstration of popular support, the McGinley Theatrical Troupe, amateur thespians, gave a benefit performance for the Yavapai Rangers, raising "the handsome sum of $125. Every lady of that company should have an Apache scalp for a fashionable 'water fall.' "[36] A proposal to pay a $100 bounty for each Apache scalp failed to be approved by the legislature simply, in Conner's opinion, because there was no provision in it for a cut for "the speculators," who were as rife on the frontier as anywhere else.[37] So the business was turned over to Hodges, who was "an effective operator against the Apaches . . . and his men fought without money or price." They fought rather well.

On one expedition, Ranger scouts discovered Indian sign near the Willows, northwest of Prescott, and trailed the hostiles south. There was no indication that these Indians were marauders, but so what— they were Indians. At about midnight sixteen Rangers took the trail, leaving nine in camp and by midmorning the unsuspecting Indians were located in a rugged canyon, probably in the southern Aquarius Mountains.

[34] *Miner*, August 10, 1867; Conner, *Joseph Reddeford Walker*, 214–15.
[35] *Miner*, November 30, 1866.
[36] *Ibid.*, January 26, 1867.
[37] Conner, *Joseph Reddeford Walker*, 335. He was a member of the legislature at this session.

"The party divided and creeping cautiously down from the hills attacked the unsuspicious children of the forest, from two points in such a style that escape was almost impossible. A scene of carnage followed. One of the attacking party was killed and three wounded. The Indians fought bravely, but of all those who were surprised in their quiet home, only one, a dusky maiden of some twenty summers, is known to have escaped. Twenty-three Indians were killed, a renegade Mohave and his squaw being among the number. . . . Hurrah for the Yavapai County Rangers."[38] There must have been some local second thoughts about this indiscriminate slaughter of children, women, and the aged as well as fighting men, for the *Miner* shortly went out of its way to support the action:

> We are glad to know that our Yavapai Rangers do not think it worth the trouble to make prisoners of the murderous red skins. The custom heretofore adopted, even by our regular army, of making prisoners of women and children, and in many cases of the full grown bucks, seems to be dying out. . . . All in sight are made to bite the dust on the ground where they are discovered. . . . We have long believed there is but [one] sure and effectual mode of ridding our country of the treacherous wretches, and this seems to be fully comprehended by our Yavapai Rangers.[39]

The Rangers seem, however, not to have been a very long-lived organization. Being volunteer and working without pay, they could not have been. After all, Indian hunting was a laborious, tedious, and usually not very exciting occupation, with the moments of battle scarcely compensating for the weeks and months of following every lead and of fruitless searching of very rugged country. So, having tried many ways of combating the enemy, and finding him more of a nuisance than ever, the citizens came to depend once more upon the Army, though hastily organizing their own punitive expeditions as occasion arose. Sometimes they caught the Indians; more often they didn't even come close. A few times they ran into ambushes, and were lucky to escape.

[38] *Miner*, January 12, 1867.
[39] *Ibid.*, January 26, 1867.

IV

The Walapais War

WHITE IMPRUDENCE, one might almost say treachery, touched off the two-year war with the Walapais, a conflict the military was forced to muster a major effort to quell. There had been no major fighting in the northwest corner of Apacheria until that time, and virtually no incidents worthy of mention. One officer reported in 1859 that the Mohaves already were peaceably disposed, "having doubtless learned from experience that they have much to lose, and nothing to gain, from hostilities."[1] In 1863 a few Paiutes were reported harassing travelers along the San Bernardino Road,[2] and the following year there was a false report that Fort Mohave itself was to be attacked, but it wasn't.[3] Still later the Chemehuevis, across the river from the fort, committed a few depredations, but nothing a small scout could not handle.[4]

Among the Walapais in 1866 were three important men, all said to be chiefs: Wauba-Yuba, Scherum, and Walapais Charley, the latter two reportedly brothers. Most influential was Wauba-Yuba. Merchant William H. Hardy of Hardyville, nine miles up the Colorado from Fort Mohave and a man with a considerable interest in the dollar, had made a formal peace with the Indian in order to promote his freighting enterprises. He gave Wauba-Yuba a paper "treaty" he might show to other whites with whom he anticipated trouble. He

---

[1] Captain R. B. Gannett, commanding, Fort Mohave, to AAG, Department of California, October 31, 1859, Vol. 4, Letters Sent, Ft. Mohave, Records of U.S. Army Commands, Record Group 98. Hereafter cited by volume number, Ft. Mohave.

[2] Captain I. Ives Fitch, Fourth Infantry, to AAAG, Camp Drum, August 8 and 24, 1863, Vol. 5, Ft. Mohave.

[3] Captain Charles Atchisson, Fourth Infantry, to AAG, San Francisco, April 2, 1864, Vol. 5, Ft. Mohave.

[4] *Ibid.*, to AAAG, Drum Barracks, California, June 22, 1864; February 20 and March 5, 1865, Vol. 5, Ft. Mohave.

tried to show it to Sam Miller, late of the Walker Party, and therein made his final mistake. The Miller party was camped at Beale's Springs, near present-day Kingman, being uneasy over a report that a Walapais had recently killed a prospector named Edward Clower at the Willows, farther east, and Indian sign, which was all around. Miller's story was that Wauba-Yuba had ridden into camp, wanting to negotiate for flour, horses, and mules. After a brief argument, Miller picked up his Hawkins rifle "and sent a bullet crashing through the lungs of the Indian, tearing a hole in his body as big as his hand." A slightly different account said that Miller and other freighters consulted, decided the Indian meant mischief, "and he was at once shot." In either case it was murder, and a senseless one at that. The *Miner* rightly predicted that nothing but evil would result:

> While it is doubtless a fact that the actions of the Hualapais, or some of them, have of late been strange, and the fate of Clower is greatly to be deplored, and must be revenged, we think the conclusion that the tribe wished to wage war with the whites is premature, and that the killing of Wauba-Yuba will prove an unprofitable step. ... To have taken Wauba-Yuba ... was a harsh and, we fear, a most unfortunate measure.[5]

Miller was arrested at Fort Whipple, delivered to the United States marshal, examined by the United States commissioner, and held for the grand jury, which discharged him with "an unanimous vote of thanks." But the evil Miller loosed with his Hawkins was not so easily dismissed. Its legacy: "The road from Hardyville to Prescott is lined with graves ... and the early miners of Mojave County were waylaid while prospecting, and killed at their cabins, shafts and tunnels, until for a long time the mines were practically abandoned."[6]

Miners everywhere were subject to attack. Near Hardyville Ira Woodworth, first recorder of Mohave County, and Nathaniel Benjamin were fired upon while sinking a shaft. Both apparently were wounded. Woodworth ran forty yards and tumbled into an arroyo

---

[5] *Miner*, quoted by Farish, *History of Arizona*, II, 261; the grand jury approval is quoted by Edmund Wells, *Argonaut Tales*, 366–68.

[6] Richard G. Hinton, *The Handbook to Arizona*, 355.

where he was found with four bullets in him and his skull crushed to a jelly. Andrew Judson and Metcalf Baker tried to climb out of their mine and were smashed with rocks to the bottom of the shaft and killed. Sam Knodles and James L. Conover tried to fight off the Walapais, but found them too many. They escaped. A search party found Benjamin six miles away where, mortally wounded, he had staggered.[7] Few Mohave County residents failed to have brushes with the Walapais, and the Army, too, had its share of tiny battles, although for long it was too undermanned to mount major operations.

About two hundred fifty Walapais were reported to have attacked four soldiers and six civilians May 30, 1867, at Beale's Springs, one civilian being killed. An officer and twenty men pursued the hostiles toward Peacock Springs, to the southeast, but were driven back.[8] A month later the Indians killed the mail rider coming in from Prescott within sight of the Beale's Springs station, and then attacked eight men forted up in a man-high stone corral, sweeping off six mules while doing so. Still later, a citizen galloped up to Beale's Springs shouting "Indians!" and reporting he was followed by two soldiers, probably by then murdered. But one of the soldiers shortly rode in, asserting his companion had been hit and had told him to ride on as "he was mortally wounded & fell down from his horse."[9]

No one denied the Army was active. What was in dispute was its effectiveness. News stories suggested some officers and men were reluctant to press home their attack on the hostiles. For example, there was the case of Second Lieutenant Patrick Hasson, Fourteenth Infantry.[10] The lieutenant, new to the West, was ordered to take fifty

[7] *Miner,* October 13, 1866.

[8] Major William Redmond Price, Eighth Cavalry, to AAG, Department of California, San Francisco, June 16, 1867, Vol. 6, Ft. Mohave.

[9] Price to AAG, Department of California, June 28 and July 20, 1867, Vol. 6, Ft. Mohave.

[10] This account is based on articles appearing in the *Miner,* October 19, 1867, November 9 and 16, 1867, and on an account appearing in Wells's *Argonaut Tales,* 414–22. In the first of the *Miner* articles, the name is spelled Hartson, which is corrected November 9. Judge Wells calls the lieutenant a West Pointer, which he was not, and calls him Simpson. Hasson, born in Ireland, enlisted in the Army in 1856, was commissioned in 1861, and retired a captain in 1892.

men of Troop E, First Cavalry, with the veteran scout Dan O'Leary[11] and work from Fort Whipple northwesterly. His orders were simply to "Meet conditions." In other words, find the enemy, and fight him. On the third day out he went into camp near Mount Hope, above the Oaks and Willows, a noted oasis. Indian sign was plentiful; the hostiles apparently were camped nearby. Disgruntled soldiers described for the *Miner* what happened next:

> A halt was ordered. A corporal went forward about a hundred yards, saw a rancheria with Indians around it, who seemed to be totally unaware of the vicinity of the troops, and, returning, reported to his commander. The Lieutenant rebuked him sharply for going ahead without orders, ordered him under arrest, then called his bugler and ordered him to sound the assembly. The Indians, taking the alarm, commenced removing their goods and firing the rancheria. The Lieutenant inquired of the men if they had plenty of water; and receiving an affirmative reply, gave orders to dismount and camp for two hours.
>
> Before the two hours had expired, the Indians had reached a place of safety among the rocks above the Lieutenant's camp, and were shouting, so as to be heard distinctly: 'Come up here, you damned white sons of bitches!'

This taunt, continued the story, prompted the lieutenant to remark: "Thim rid divils is thryin' to decoy us intill an ambuscade; we'll go back to camp."

The *Miner* received a furious letter from the officer, who denied the published version was the true one and reporting that his "superiors have already judged" his conduct, and approved it. He gave no details, but Judge Edmund Wells, a contemporary who later wrote a book about pioneer incidents in that area, tells a slightly different version, which he may have obtained from O'Leary. This version has O'Leary sighting the rancheria at dusk and he and the officer planning the attack for dawn. The scout took a foot party out during the

---

[11] Dan O'Leary, born in Ireland about 1834, was the most famous of Arizona's guides of this period. He died at Needles, California, in 1900. See Dan L. Thrapp's, "Dan O'Leary, Arizona Scout," in *Arizona and the West*, Vol. VII, No. 4 (Winter, 1965), 287–98.

night to get on one side of the hostiles, and the officer was to take a mounted group to carry the brunt of the attack from another side. O'Leary got into position, but instead of hearing the rattling fire of the cavalry attack, he heard "a series of long, shrill and penetrating bugle blasts, the clarion notes of which pealed up the mountain slopes and striking the overhanging cliffs, caromed into the canyons below."

This, of course, flushed out the Indians. If this account is correct, what probably happened was that the lieutenant moved his mounted men into position, then halted them until O'Leary could get into position. While he was waiting, some thick-headed soldier went prowling ahead and stumbled onto the rancheria which Hasson would assume had alerted the enemy and sprung the trap. In his inexperience he ordered the bugles sounded, as was customarily done in those days, and thus the hostiles escaped. There is a suggestion that the *Miner* editor realized the injustice he had done the officer for he shortly took the opportunity to make amends in reporting, good-humoredly:

BRILLIANT SUCCESS OF LIEUT· HASSON

20 BUCK INDIANS KILLED

16 Squaws and Papooses Captured

It gives us unbounded pleasure to announce to our readers, and the balance of mankind, that Lieutenant Patrick Hasson, of the 14th U.S. Infantry, has lately made a brilliant and successful raid against the Hualapais. . . . This deed of the Lieutenant gives the lie to the slanderous charge against his courage, which was, no doubt, fabricated for base purposes by some enemy or enemies of his . . .

It reported that the lieutenant and seven of his men were wounded in the fight near Fort Rock, between Prescott and Hardyville.[12]

Everywhere in northwestern Arizona the fighting continued, sometimes with considerable heroism involved. Almost within earshot of Camp Willow Grove occurred a stubborn battle between a

[12] *Miner,* November 16, 1867. The *Chronological List of Actions, &c., with Indians, from January 1, 1866, to January, 1891* (hereafter cited as *Chronological List*) dates this fight November 5, reports thirty-two Indians killed and says nothing of white casualties.

lone white man and almost overwhelming numbers of Indians. It was on March 21, 1868, that mail rider Charley Spencer,[13] fought off the hostiles, as told in a letter to the *Miner* from Private James Deine, of Company E, Fourteenth Infantry:

> I am extremely sorry to inform you that Charles Spencer has been severely wounded by Indians, but, I am happy to state, not mortally. He is now in the hospital at this post, and is doing as well as could be expected. He, and the escort, started from this post with the mail for Hardyville and California, on the morning of the 21st inst., at the usual time, 9 o'clock. Before they got to the Cottonwoods, four miles from here, they were fired into by a party of Walapais Indians, and the escort, consisting of Corporal Troy and Private Flood, were killed at the first fire, as was, also, the mule which the mail carrier was riding. Spencer, as quick as possible, disengaged himself from the saddle, grabbed his seven-shooting rifle, and ran behind a greasewood bush, the only protection close at hand. Soon he saw a party of the savages go up to the dead body of the corporal, strip and mutilate it. While they were engaged in this brutal work, Spencer kept up a steady fire on them, and had the satisfaction of killing two of the red devils. The others then ran for shelter; Spencer did the same thing, and on reaching a safe retreat, and just as he was about to get securely covered, he was fired upon by about a dozen Indians, who were hid behind some rocks. One of their shots hit him in the thigh, passing through the fleshy part, causing him to fall. They then rushed towards him, thinking they had him sure. In this they were mistaken. For Charley had not yet commenced to fight. He soon gathered himself up, and made the savages hunt their holes. He then crawled into a cavity, between some rocks, and took a rest, which he needed. During all this time, a party of Indians were stripping the bodies of the murdered soldiers, and cutting up the carcasses of the horses and mules, which occupied them for about twenty minutes. They then surrounded Spencer, and tried to shoot him out, but he could shoot and

---

[13] Spencer, from Ohio, was a veteran Indian fighter whose hairbreadth escapes were legendary. He was shot and killed November 26, 1886, by a man with whom he had a dispute over one acre of ground.—Barnes, *Arizona Place Names*, 1st ed., 418; 2nd ed., Revised and Enlarged by Byrd H. Granger, 223–24. Where hereafter cited, the first edition is meant unless otherwise specified.

hit, too, and they found that that was no go. Then they tried to scare him out with yells, but he yelled back defiance at them, and, whenever opportunity offered, sent a bullet after them. Changing their tactics, they tried to blarney him by telling him to go home, that they did not want to kill him and would not shoot any more. But he would not be blarneyed, by them. At length, about 4 o'clock, they got up and dusted . . .

Once, during the afternoon, a single Indian approached Spencer's 'fortification,' telling him, in broken English, to come out and go home as they did not intend to kill any more soldier men; said he and the other Indians were going home, and then walked off over a hill. Spencer, soon after, placed his hat upon the rammer of his gun, raised it above the rocks, when, in an instant, it was riddled with bullets fired by Indians . . . who, no doubt, supposed his head was in the hat . . . [He planned] as soon as night was come . . . to crawl [for he could not walk] to the creek, wash and bathe his wound, and endeavor to reach the willows.

Attracted by the firing, a detachment of soldiers galloped up from the Willows, found the mutilated body of the corporal, and hurried back to their camp to report, supposing that all three men had been killed; Charley by this time was too weak to attract their attention. A lieutenant then brought up a wagon to collect the bodies, and Spencer, hearing the rumbling wheels but too lame to crawl out of his hole, yelled and fired his pistol, by which means he was located and brought to camp. He guessed there had been seventy-five Indians, "more than half of whom were armed with guns."[14]

If the Walapais War was to be liquidated, some comprehensive sort of campaign was necessary, and so the Grand Army of the Colorado was born. It was so named by a *Miner* correspondent, tongue in cheek, and it was the grandest military effort the territory had yet

[14] *Miner*, April 4, 1868. Spencer, in a letter of August 10, 1884, wrote: "I do not blame the Indians so much as some people think I ought. It was wartime for them, and their men, women and children had been killed by the whites; so why not retaliate . . . and besides, I have seen some of their children killed after having been taken captive . . . "—Herbert Welsh, "Report of a Visit to the Navajo, Pueblo, and Hualapais Indians of New Mexico and Arizona, 1885," 45.

seen. Supplies for a sixty-day campaign were gathered at various of the posts and in late September, when the edge had been honed from the summer heat, three columns moved out of Fort Mohave, guided by Dan O'Leary and Gus Spear, "better and more thorough mountaineers than whom, Kit Carson never was or will be."[15] The first "Grand Division," one hundred men and pack train, was under Major D. R. Clendenin. It left September 27, intending to follow up the river for fifty miles, then turn east into the Sacramento Valley. The "Second Division," also of one hundred men under a Lieutenant Traverse, crossed Union Pass the following day, and, also on September 28, the "Third Division," commanded by Lieutenant A. B. Wells, Eighth Cavalry and fifty men strong, left Fort Mohave to cross into the Sacramento Valley through Beale's Pass (Sitgreaves Pass), south of Fort Mohave. The whole Army, so-called, was under command of Colonel William Redwood Price, whose "rotund form" belied his energetic approach to the Indian problem.

Carefully combing the country, Clendenin's and Traverse's columns joined forces in the Sacramento Valley and by October 1 were in camp at Beale's Springs. Unfortunately a prolonged drought had blotted up most of the waterholes, creating hardships for the soldiers and lessening their chances of striking hostiles. Lieutenant Wells scouted for twelve days through the Hualapais Mountains, discovering several rancherias, whose water supply had dried up and which therefore were abandoned, and others from which the Indians fled on approach of the column. On October 6, however, the command attacked a party of Indians, killing seven, with no loss to themselves, and they drew into Beale's Springs later that day. In early October Major Clendenin with "a large force" was attacked by Indians at the base of the Hualapais Mountains and "was compelled to make a backward movement" for, he said, "the purpose of getting a better position." No casualties to either side were reported, although the Indians fired more than two hundred shots at him.[16] A subsequent three-day scout after Scherum and his band had better fortune. Thirty

---

[15] *Miner*, October 5, 1867.
[16] *Ibid.*, October 19, 1867. *Chronological List* does not report this action.

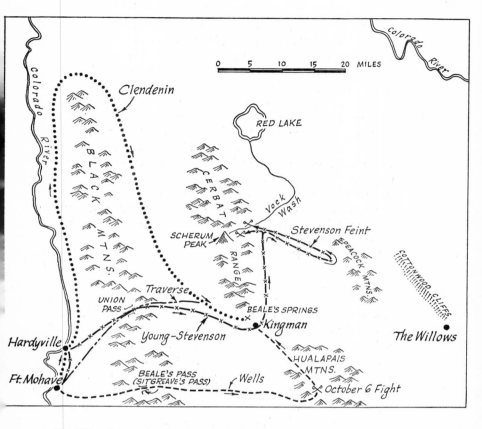

The Walapais War, showing the operations of the "Grand Army of the Colorado"
and of the Young-Stevenson expedition

miles northeast of Beale's Springs Major Clendenin drove the Indians from a ranch, finding there relics of a mining party which had been driven from a nearby district earlier with the loss of four men killed. On another scout in the same general direction, Wells routed the Indians at Bitter Springs, killing one.[17]

By early November headquarters had been shifted to the Willows. As active as it had been, the command had not accomplished much except to keep the hostiles stirred up. But, the *Miner* said, "it should be born in mind that the force is small, that the country in which they are operating is extremely rugged and mountainous, and that although they have guides, the Pah-Ute Indians who serve in that capacity are not well acquainted with the watering places."[18] The command was reported to have killed or captured more than one hundred Indians, and destroyed much of their matériel. The Army of the Colorado was dissolved by early February.

Perhaps the most vigorous battle of the campaign was undertaken by a column operating out of Fort Mohave in January, 1868. Its commander, Captain S. B. M. Young,[19] was convinced that military peregrinations through the Walapais country, attacking targets of opportunity, would never be decisive. So on January 11, acting on a report of the whereabouts of Scherum's main band, Captain Young, with Lieutenants Jonathan D. Stevenson and Aquila Asbury Reese, Jr., took a column out of Fort Mohave. They arrived at Hardyville that evening. On the twelfth they found a furious storm raging at daybreak, and Dan O'Leary, guide, suggested laying over for better weather. "No," said the captain, "I owe old Scherum a visit, and if I go in a storm, I will be likely to find him at home."

The command marched northeast, crossed the Black Range by Union Pass, and camped. The next day they crossed the high Cerbats and camped in the Walapais Valley. On the fourth morning Captain

[17] *Ibid.*, November 2, 1867. This no doubt is the action at "Truxell" (Truxton) Springs, listed by *Chronological List* as occurring October 25.

[18] *Miner*, November 9, 1867.

[19] Samuel Baldwin Marks Young, although only twenty-eight, had already been brevetted brigadier general. He became a lieutenant general in 1903, was commanding general of the army and died September 1, 1924.—*Who Was Who*.

Young held a war council. It was thought that the Indians must have seen the column by now, and in order to fool them it was split, one portion, under Lieutenant Stevenson, to file off to the southeast as though making for Peacock Springs at the south end of the Peacock Mountains. As soon as they were well along, and no doubt within view of the Indians, Captain Young mounted the remainder of his command and moved northwest, under the shoulder of the Cerbats, "until moccasin tracks became quite plenty." He and his men hid in a ravine that night, careful to light no fire, keep the animals quiet and the men equally so. During the night Dan and Captain Young cautiously reconnoitered and found a trail leading into what was then known as Scherum's Canyon,[20] below the mountain which still shows as Cherum Peak[21] on the maps. About three o'clock in the morning the men were silently aroused, told to saddle up, mount, and form in line, the body then silently picking its way into the mouth of the canyon. Save for the ring of an iron shoe on stone, the jingling of a bridle bit, the creaking of leather, it was still as the ghostly column moved on into the mountain. After a short distance, Captain Young ordered the men to dismount, turn their horses over to one man of four, and proceed afoot. Thirteen enlisted men moved on up the canyon then, with Captain Young and Dan as guides. It was getting light. After a mile the trail turned abruptly and there was Scherum's rancheria, not thirty yards ahead.

The Indians discovered the white expedition at the same time, and pandemonium broke out. With screams and war whoops they took to the rocks, a soldiers' volley splintering around them. More than one hundred warriors took to the steep sides of the canyon. Most were as naked as the day they were born, but they didn't forget their rifles. The soldiers fired three quick volleys with their Spencers and "seven dead Indians rolled down the hill, to climb no more," as O'Leary reported it. The captain himself shot a couple of Indians, and so did

[20] This is probably Vock Canyon, as shown on topographical survy maps. Young called it "Difficult Canyon" in his report.
[21] Scherum's name is also spelled Scerum, Sherum, Srum, and so forth. The 6,978 foot peak is the highest point in the Cerbats.

O'Leary, but his best effort was wounding Scherum badly enough so that he dropped his rifle, though he picked it up again before dragging himself to cover behind some rocks. Now well concealed, the Indians suffered less from the soldiers' persistent fire. Part of the command tried to flank the enemy, but could not do it. Once a soldier turned to Young, who was with his men during the entire fight, and said, "Captain, you are in danger." "Yes," Young agreed, "and so are you." At this moment an arrow whistled down from above and stabbed the ground at his feet. Young plucked it up, looked it over carefully, and coolly remarked, "I had hardly thought of these things." He estimated its source, shoved his carbine forward and patiently waited. Soon an Indian raised his head to find a target, and the captain silenced him for good. Two soldiers, badly wounded, had to be carried from the field, which reduced the already slender party by almost half. After an hour and twenty minutes of fighting, the ammunition was low, and Young ordered a retreat.

Meanwhile, Lieutenant Stevenson had made only a short march and then halted to await events.

After Young's withdrawal the Indians commenced burning their dead, which sent up an immense black smoke, visible for miles and clearly seen by Lieutenant Stevenson. He realized that Young had found the hostiles and engaged them, and that secrecy no longer was necessary, so he turned his command about and hastened for the scene. By three in the afternoon he arrived at the foot of the Cerbats, dismounted his men, and led them into the enemy's stronghold. "He was not decoyed or trapped, but saw his enemies and made for them," O'Leary reported. "The trouble was, there were too many Indians, and they at once overpowered him."

At the first murderous fire Stevenson fell, wounded in six places, including one bullet through the body and another through the groin. His carbine, struck by a bullet, was shattered. His loyal men picked up their valiant officer, carried him from the field, but not without interruption.

"The savages pursued the retreating party for over three miles, the soldiers keeping up a continuous fire as they retreated," according to Dan. "The mountain was rocky and broken, and as the soldiers bore the wounded Lieutenant along over the rocks, the savages would rise up from behind the rocks and fire, and then disappear again like magic. In this way the fight went on until the darkness of night closed the scene." In the pitch blackness a courier was sent to Beale's Springs for an ambulance. "The Lieutenant and men all agreed in stating that this night was the worst ever spent by them," said O'Leary. "They were within hearing of the savages, who were engaged in burning their dead, and now and then a war whoop would make the mountains echo, and then a wail and moan, such as is uttered only by savages, would make a stout-hearted soldier shrink and sicken. . . . Sleep was out of the question; besides a cold north wind was blowing a gale, and the little party dare not kindle a fire."

At daylight the ambulance arrived, the wounded were cared for and sent with a small escort to Fort Mohave, while Captain Young took the balance and struck out for Peacock Springs. Again, it was a feint. As soon as it was night, the captain reversed his course and swiftly made his way back to Scherum's camp once more, surrounded it before dawn, and prepared to level a killing stroke with daylight. But sunup showed that Scherum had flown. He had burned his wickiups and his dead and crept away. On scouring the camp ground, soldiers found saddles, bridles, and other equipment of slain whites. It was calculated that Young's party had killed sixteen hostiles and wounded six; Lieutenant Stevenson's command had killed five.[22]

Peace negotiations with Scherum and Walapais Charley took place in August somewhere in the river country, with Price and Young representing the whites. A notice in the *Miner* on August 31, 1868, said the Walapais had agreed to "give up their arms, remove to the river and remain at peace with the whites. Now for good times. Our country will soon loom up and we will be made joyful." The editor

---

[22] Both the lieutenant and Scherum survived their wounds, the former eventually becoming a captain and dying October 9, 1882. The accounts of this action appeared in the *Miner* for January 25 and February 20. The second, more detailed version, was signed, "Citizen Guide," which from internal evidence, plus the fact that O'Leary was guide for the expedition, seems to have been written by him.

51

cautiously added, "As it was the Indians who first asked for peace, it is barely possible that they may be in earnest."

The peace was less than satisfactory to the Indians, however. They found that they could not live happily in the hot, malarial river bottom, and over a period of six or seven years they periodically left the reservation to escape to the cool, invigorating mountain heights and upper desert country they knew and loved so well. Finally, about 1875, they fled there permanently and were given a reservation on which they have remained to this day.

V

The Hunting of Big Rump

THE TROUBLE with the Apacheria army of the late 1860's was that
there was not enough of it. At the end of the Civil War the
United States was divided for administrative and operational purposes into five military divisions, and these subdivided into nineteen
departments. Two of these divisions were the Military Division of
the Mississippi, commanded by General Sherman, and the Military
Division of the Pacific, commanded by Major General Henry
Wager Halleck. New Mexico was in the Department of Missouri of
the Division of Mississippi, and was commanded by Major General
John Pope during most of the period covered here. Arizona was in
the Department of California, commanded by Major General Irvin
McDowell (and it sometimes took three months to transmit orders
back and forth within it).[1] Thus Apacheria was split into separate
military departments, which were administrative units of separate
divisions. This led to much duplication, lack of co-ordination, and
other difficulties. The Apache problem was not solved until, some
twenty years later, Apacheria came under one operational command,
a makeshift, but it did the job. Each department was split into appropriate military districts. At first Arizona had two of them, at
Prescott, or Fort Whipple, in the north, and at Tucson, or Camp
Lowell, in the south. Eventually these were combined into a single
district, for the same reason Arizona and New Mexico later were
combined operationally into a single department.

But these complications were not all of the story. There also was
rivalry and sometimes even hostility between the military and civil
agencies working with Indians. Occasionally Indian agents were of
dubious honesty, and sometimes the military was imperious, dog-

---

[1] Ogle, *Western Apaches*, 69.

53

matic, and uncompromising. The effectiveness of both of these necessary branches of government was then reduced, and Indian and settler alike were pulled and twisted between rival agencies. The military sought to keep the tribes pacified when sometimes they were starving through criminal malpractice or corruption on the part of certain agents who were supposed to keep them fed as long as they were at peace. Often the agents encouraged the Indians to learn the arts of agriculture and other civilized pursuits while the soldiers sought to confine them closely where they could more easily keep an eye upon them. Nor were disputes within each branch of government always kept locked safely away as internal matters.

For example, in the spring of 1867 General McDowell told General John Irvin Gregg, commanding the District of Prescott and the Upper Colorado, to keep his troops moving and wage effective war against the Walapais. So Gregg issued General Orders No. 4, asserting that all Indians off the reservation—Apaches, Colorado River Indians, even some California tribesmen—would be considered hostile, even if they bore passes from Indian agents. This contravention of the civil agency's authority was too much, and McDowell ordered Gregg to modify his edict, which he did with General Orders No. 12, of June 11, 1867. This time he went too far the other way, declaring even tribes generally hostile were to be considered peaceful "excepting when acting in concert with tribes and confederate tribes in obstructing the roads, and in attacks upon the settlements. Attacks upon trains and travellers and the stealing of stock, by individuals or small parties of Indians, cannot be considered as hostile acts, but as offenses against the common law; the same as if committed by white citizens."[2]

This, of course, made the Arizona settlers furious. William Hardy printed a public notice in the *Miner* asserting that since protection along his Hardyville-Prescott toll road had been "withdrawn," he would temporarily abandon it and "no tolls will be collected . . . until the Indians are declared hostile." Furthermore, he growled, "I will pay a reward of TWENTY DOLLARS to any one passing down said road

[2] *Miner*, July 13, 1867.

that will kill the first red devil of an Indian that undertakes to collect toll in my stead."[3] Aroused by the criticism, McDowell now issued general orders of his own, taking his subordinate publicly to task.[4] It was a discourteous reproof, and the two officers wrangled back and forth for a year while the hostiles killed and civilians became more exasperated.

There were only twenty-seven companies (a company then usually was little larger than a platoon today) in Arizona of 1867, thirteen in the southern district and fourteen in the north, and only one additional company the following year. Garrisoned posts included Fort Yuma, Camp Mohave, Camp El Dorado Canyon, Fort Whipple, Camp Lincoln, Camp McPherson, Camp McDowell, Camp Goodwin, Camp Grant, Camp Bowie, Camp Wallen, Camp Cameron, Camp Lowell and Camp Tubac. Their number reveals how widely the available units were scattered, and how thin was that line of blue that was to defend this vast and potentially rich area, with its growing population of rough frontiersmen whose temper made it inevitable that they would start troubles. In his annual report General Halleck acknowledged that "Military operations would probably be more effective in reducing the hostile Indians if the troops could be concentrated in large posts, so as to have available a greater number for active campaigning in the country. . . . But for this to be done, with the small forces at our command, it would be necessary to withdraw all protection from many small settlements."[5]

Perhaps because of the lack of effective military planning and usefulness, the morale of the troops was low, and desertions were common. The *Miner* reported that sixteen men of one company had gone over the hill and there were nearly forty desertions from General Gregg's command within a month.[6] Desertion was easy and relatively safe, and as a result it was sometimes difficult to keep a unit up to fighting strength, particularly if its officers were not popular or the

[3] *Ibid.*, June 29, 1867.
[4] *Ibid.*, July 27, 1867.
[5] *Ibid.*, February 8, 1868.
[6] *Ibid.*, August 31, 1867.

men lacked confidence in them. The Eighth Cavalry, "a rough sort of regiment . . . had 41 per cent of desertions in 1867," according to one historian.[7] Captain Young reported that he had sent a sergeant, a corporal, and six men to Beale's Springs with orders to patrol from there to Fort Rock, farther east, and they all promptly deserted. His post, he said, was "much embarrassed by the frequent desertions of men on detached duty. Fourteen (14) men of K Company, 8th Cavalry, having deserted during the present month, taking with them all government property in their possession."[8] Yet there was nothing wrong with the courage of the individual soldier and officer who remained loyal. The Arizona service was among the most dangerous in the Army. Men almost daily were being killed or wounded. An enlisted man in the Arizona of the 1860's never knew when he was going to be attacked.

One day in the middle of June, 1868, Sergeant J. Lemon of E Company, First Cavalry, and four privates—two Murphys, one Merrill, and one Theely—were assigned to carry the mail from Camp Reno, in the Tonto Basin, over the high Mazatzals to Camp McDowell. This was prime Indian country. Many of the soldiers, having just been paid, were sending greenbacks in letters home, which accounted for the size of the detachment. Usually mail couriers rode alone. The sergeant, well mounted, took the lead. He was followed by Merrill and the two Murphys, while Theely, who had been in a fight with Indians some months before, warily brought up the rear.

After threading Reno Pass, the sergeant led the party down into rough country on the west of the range. When ascending a hill between a place known locally as Camp Miller and Sugar Loaf Mountain, about fifteen miles east of McDowell, Theely shouted to Lemon that there were Indians ahead—he had seen them raise their heads over a ridge. Lemon spurred into a gallop, perhaps with a view to striking the Indians before they could attack his party. But a murderous volley, fired by an estimated one hundred well-emplaced Indians, poured into the group from three sides. One of the Murphys

[7] McClintock, *Arizona*, I, 193.
[8] Young to AAAG, Camp Whipple, April 5, 1867, Vol. 6, Ft. Mohave.

was killed outright, and the other four men were wounded, as were all the horses. The sergeant, badly hit, kept in his saddle for about four hundred yards, then flopped to the ground and was pounced upon by a huge Indian, but rallied sufficiently to shoot him through the heart. The sergeant's body was later found riddled with bullets and arrows. The second Murphy ran to the top of a hill, where he fortified himself, and made a hard fight, judging by the appearance of the place afterward, but he was overwhelmed, killed, and hacked in two. Merrill's body was found cut to pieces. Theely alone escaped, but barely. He fled to Sunflower Valley at the head of Sycamore Creek and dashed into a stockade built as an outpost of Camp Reno. About twenty Indians pursued him and kept up a desultory fire on the stockade, but without effect. After dark Theely slipped out, somehow made his way back to Reno, and told his tale. A search party found mail scattered all over the scene, most of the envelopes ripped open and the greenbacks gone.[9]

One of the most successful Indian fighters of the period was Captain James Monroe Williams, Eighth Cavalry.[10] In the spring of 1867 word came to Gregg that a large body of Indians was moving through Hell Canyon, a rough gash that joins the Verde River northeast of Chino Valley. Williams was sent out with Companies I and B of the Eighth Cavalry and tough Tom Hodges as guide. He split off a small detachment under Lieutenant William McK. Owens of the Thirty-second Infantry, and on April 10 this patrol surprised a large party of Indians, killing three and wounding others, apparently Yavapais. Six days later a rancheria was struck, about thirty lodges burned, but there was no shooting since the Indians fled. The next day the horses were left in charge of Sergeants Patrick Golden and Terran while the main body clambered up a mountain after the

[9] *Miner*, July 18, 1868.

[10] Williams was born at Lowville, New York, September 12, 1833, and served through the Civil War in the West, becoming a brevet brigadier general of volunteers. Three times he had horses shot out from under him, and he was wounded four times at Elk Creek, Indian Territory, July 17, 1863. He died at Washington, D.C., February 17, 1907.—Information from Recorder J. Truman Swing of the Military Order of the Loyal Legion of the United States.

hostiles, forcing them to abandon their position. This brought the enemy within view of the horse guard. The two sergeants, "encumbered as they were by the horses of the whole command," nevertheless mounted eighteen men and charged the thirty-five or more Yavapais, routing them, killing twenty, wounding others, and capturing livestock and matériel, all without loss to themselves.

Two days later Hodges ferreted out another camp, a general attack was launched, with thirty dead Indians reported.[11] George W. Drummond, a saddler for Company B, was killed and one soldier slightly wounded. Realizing the difficulties in actions of later years of ascertaining the precise number of enemy casualties, one might be somewhat dubious of the round-figure reports of these early expeditions in virtually unknown country. Nevertheless, Williams' successes seem to have been considerable, and the *Miner* printed the triumphant record under a linecut of a thundering cannon and a thirty-four-star American flag.

With this victory for a beginning, Williams continued his successful operations. In the Yampai Valley (now also called Truxton Wash) on June 14, with I Company of the Eighth, he struck a party of Walapais and killed a score, capturing nine. General Gregg joined the command on July 5, and it continued northwest, bivouacking on the ninth at the foot of Music Mountain. In the afternoon Captain Williams and eight men climbed the peak to better inspect the surrounding country. General Gregg went along. But they didn't reach the summit. Indians already were there, and in a resulting fight three were killed, but two arrows near the kidneys marked the end of Williams' Indian-fighting career. A soldier also was wounded. The general, unhurt, with "some trouble" got the wounded men back to Truxton Spring. "Fortunately the Indians did not follow," the *Miner* observed.[12] Captain Williams was rendered *hors de combat* as surely as if an arrow had penetrated his brain. He underwent a painful two-month convalescence before leaving for California, and about a year

[11] *Miner*, April 20 and July 13, 1867. The latter reprints congratulatory General Orders No. 33 from McDowell's headquarters.
[12] *Ibid.*, July 27, 1867.

later returned to Camp McDowell, brevetted major for conspicuous gallantry in his Indian fights. But his wounds never properly healed, and he resigned his commission in 1871. Congress, twenty years later, by special act, retired him as Captain of Cavalry.

Not only the white Indian fighters, but the more prominent Indians became widely known to the pioneers, and none was more famous at this time than Wah-poo-eta, or Big Rump, so named presumably for his most prominent feature. According to the early newspapers, Big Rump roamed an enormous portion of Apacheria, probably because almost any depredation was blamed on any Indian whose name was known, or could be spelled. Such was the price of fame in the 1860's, as it is today. "Camp McPherson was moved in 1868 to a site at the junction of the north and south forks of Date Creek, directly opposite a lofty peak known as Big Rump's Lookout, in honor of the savage and bloodthirsty Apache chieftain and raider of that name," said one story.[13] An undulating valley, several miles broad, somewhere east of the Verde and perhaps along Tonto Creek, was called Big Rump's Valley and was known by reputation as far away as Fort Craig, New Mexico.[14] A gorge up the Salt and east of the Verde was known as Big Rump's Canyon home," and here the troops and Indians, led either by Big Rump himself or Delshay, another noted hostile of the time, had a spirited fight early in July, 1868. It was begun by Pimas.

After scouting "in all directions, over hill, mesas and cactus patches, with the expectation of catching the Apaches fruit-gathering," the Pimas jumped some of their inveterate enemies, killed two, and chased six more into a cave. They hurried to Camp Reno and guided to the cave a troop detachment made up of parts of E Company of the First Cavalry and I of the Eighth, with Lieutenant C. C. C. Carr[15] in command. The troopers halted on the rim of a canyon too steep for

[13] *Ibid.*, April 4, 1868. Big Rump probably was a Yavapai, but to an Arizona pioneer almost every hostile was an "Apache."

[14] Conner, *Joseph Reddeford Walker*, 265n.

[15] Camillo Casatti Cadmus Carr was born at Harrisonburg, Virginia, March 3, 1842, served in the Civil War, and became a brigadier general August 17, 1903. He died July 24, 1914, and served in Arizona three times.—*Who Was Who.*

horses to descend and not feasible even for soldiers, but they shot one Indian, who fell one hundred feet off a cliff before his body smashed onto talus slopes below. The hostiles, however, had their revenge.

About two hundred of them, fifteen mounted, swept up the cattle herd of the camp, even though it was guarded by fourteen soldiers, mounted on mules. All night the hostiles apparently had lain in position. With the dawn a wagon and six men passed directly through the ambush, the Indians allowing it to go unsuspectingly, while awaiting the bawling herd of cattle. It arrived shortly. The drovers let the animals fan out to graze on the dew-freshened grass, posted their lookouts, and took it easy, but not for long. Their reverie was broken by a rattling fire from muskets, pistols, and arrows and the screams from scores of savage throats as the Indians came charging in. The soldiers took cover in nearby brush and it was every man for himself, in thickets sometimes so dense that it was impossible to see more than a few yards. "The mules of the herders acted like mules, and stood still, so their riders had to dismount and hold on to the herd on foot," said a report. Then the mules broke away from the herders, and were captured by the Indians. They were recaptured by the soldiers. The Indians charged once more between the mules and cattle, and drove the mules off for good. The Indian chief went for a herder, shot him off his mule, and was about to mount when the soldier opened fire. A pistol duel resulted, but the chief got the mule and the soldier escaped. Three Indians were said to have been killed and eight wounded, but the hostiles, although pursued for sixty miles, were not caught up with again, and that was the last the herders ever saw of their mules.[16]

Big Rump, whether implicated in this action or not, had about run his luck out. Throughout his adult life his personal war had been not merely against the whites, but also against those perennial foes of the mountain Indians, the Maricopas and Pimas. Often the Apache and kindred tribes raided the settlements of the more sedentary Indians; sometimes the latter raided back.

[16] *Miner*, August 29, 1868.

On one such raid, in the midsummer of 1869, a band of twenty-two Maricopas under their durable old war chief, Juan Chivaria, and an equal number of Pimas, went hunting their traditional enemies, and had fine luck. In the picturesque canyon of Castle Creek, south of the Bradshaws, they spied a camp of enemy raiders, and laid a careful ambush. At a place where the rock walls come closely together Juan's brother, also a noted fighting man, disposed the Maricopas in a matted jungle of brush, and there they awaited the enemy. The Pimas were stationed farther down the canyon, to intercept any hostiles who might escape the Maricopas. Unsuspectingly the enemy filed down the canyon, directly into the trap. The Maricopas, waiting until they were sure of their prey, opened fire. A few of the victims broke and ran back up the canyon, thereby denying the Pimas a chance to get in on the fight. One heavy-set Indian was chased about one hundred yards up the canyon, then up a draw to the north, where he was slain, and there ended the bloody career of Big Rump.

To prove what they had done, the victors told white men about it, and a party headed by Jack Swilling and Lieutenant William Mc-Cleave of the Eighth Cavalry was guided to the scene. McCleave reported that "four of the bodies lay within the space of a few yards of each other, two were amongst the bushes near the trail, but not visible from it." Big Rump's body was found as the Maricopas said it would be, and about it lay many scraps of paper which proved to have been blank muster and pay rolls, while on Big Rump's body were found enough greenbacks to implicate him and his followers in a recently successful attack on the mail near Date Creek, Big Rump's final victory.[17]

The death of a particular war chief, however, did nothing to lessen Indian depredations which sometimes touched Prescott itself. Raiders occasionally ran off stock from the town, and the citizens, usually afoot, rarely could recapture it. Usually they seemed to select animals the pioneers wanted least to lose. The governor had lost five or six favorite saddle horses in a row. When Indians swept down on George

[17] *Ibid.*, September 25, 1869. The fight itself took place the middle of August.

Banghart's Chino Valley place in May, 1867, they took the one cow he valued above all others, for she had become almost part of the family.

George had raised this cow himself upon the River Thames in eastern Canada, and in the spring of 1857 had driven her to Atchison County, Missouri. The next spring she hoofed it over the Santa Fe Trail to New Mexico, then via the Beale route across Arizona as far as Bear Spring, west of the San Francisco Mountains. The party was forced by Indians to retreat to New Mexico, where the cow, which appears to have been nameless, was kept with other livestock for two and one-half years near Fort Stanton. During this time Banghart lost a hundred head of cattle to Indians, mostly Navahos and Apaches, but never this old cow. In 1861 she was driven via the Rio Grande and the southern route through Tucson to Los Angeles County, where she was kept four years. In the catastrophic drought of 1863, she was one of four cattle which survived out of forty-eight head George owned, and although she went blind with thirst, she later recovered her eyesight. In 1866 she was driven to Arizona over the Fort Mohave road and to Prescott from Hardyville. During the whole of her travels, she had given from ten to twenty quarts of milk a day and produced a fresh calf each year. Now the faithful animal was stampeded away by the Indians, her swollen udder banging painfully against her worn hind legs as she managed for a time to keep up with the other stock. Banghart assured Charley Spencer and others in pursuit that "if she could be recovered, he would willingly lose the remainder of his stock."[18] Apparently they failed.

[18] *Ibid.*, June 1, 1867.

VI

Death of Howard Cushing

OFF TO THE SOUTH, beyond the valley of the Salt, there continued the savage battle against Cochise, and rose like a rocket the short-lived career of a young Army officer. Of all the gallant soldiers who served on the Southwest frontier, none was braver, none more admired, no man so relentless or successful in pursuit of the elusive and deadly Indians as Howard Bass Cushing, first lieutenant, Third Cavalry, the Beau Sabreur of the border.

Cushing, with F Company, said Bourke who served with him, "had killed more savages of the Apache tribe than any other officer or troop in the United States Army had done before or since,"[1] and had earned a reputation as one of its most popular figures. His men idolized him. That he was respected by his fellow officers, in a service where jealousy was not unknown, also spoke well for the human qualities of this energetic soldier. In private conversation with a biographer of the famous Cushing brothers, Bourke, whose experience in frontier wars and acquaintance with Indian fighters entitles his remarks to respect, "frankly stated . . . that Howard Cushing was the bravest man he ever saw; and repeated for emphasis, 'I mean just that—the bravest man I ever saw.' "[2] Bravery, like any moral quality, is difficult to account for and even harder to weigh, but whatever its source, and however it be judged, Howard Cushing had it in abundant supply. Two of his brothers, William Barker and Alonzo Cushing, already had come to national prominence by Civil War courage rarely matched.

Howard, himself, had served in much of the Civil War as an artilleryman but, seeking continued action following that conflict, had

[1] Bourke, *Border*, 29
[2] Theron Wilber Haight, *Three Wisconsin Cushings*, 94–95.

63

transferred to the Third Cavalry on September 7, 1867, and was sent to the West Texas Apache country where his company was engaged in punitive actions against the Mescalero Apaches, principally in the Guadalupe Mountains. On one occasion Cushing led a detachment on a two-hundred-mile pursuit and fight with hostiles in which two soldiers were wounded, but the troopers killed and wounded a number of Indians and recovered most of about one hundred and fifty head of stolen stock. About Christmastime of 1869 a Cushing detachment had a fight in which Lieutenant Franklin Yeaton[3] received wounds that ultimately proved mortal. On still another occasion Cushing burned some ninety lodges and killed several savages, besides recovering a sizable herd of stolen stock.[4] When he was sent to Old Camp Grant in southeastern Arizona, his company had already won a reputation for aggressiveness and efficiency.

Grant, at the junction of the Aravaipa and the San Pedro River, was a post for duty at which it is doubtful if any soldier ever applied. Bourke called it "the old rookery," and said it was "recognized from the tide-waters of the Hudson to those of the Columbia as the most thoroughly God-forsaken post of all those supposed to be included in the annual Congressional appropriations."[5] But it was an important Indian-fighting center.

On May 26, 1870, merchandise-laden wagons drawn by straining mule teams swayed and creaked out of Tucson, bound for Grant, fifty-five miles to the northeast. The train belonged to Hugh Kennedy and Newton Israel, proprietors of a ranch and store about a mile down the San Pedro from the camp. The party included two women, some children, and twenty-one men, unfortunately with but four firearms among them. The first the men at Camp Grant heard about the train

---

[3] Yeaton was born in New Brunswick, graduated from West Point June 15, 1869, being sent at once to the Southwestern frontier. He was wounded December 26, 1869, and died August 17, 1872, at Naples, Maine, aged twenty-four. Cullum, *Biographical Register*.

[4] *Miner*, March 19, 1870. *Record of Engagements with Hostile Indians within the Military Division of the Missouri, from 1868 to 1882*, compiled from official records, 25. Hereafter cited as *Record of Engagements*.

[5] Bourke, *Border*, 4.

was when a tattered, exhausted Mexican staggered in with the report it had been attacked.

Without awaiting orders, Sergeants John Mott and Warfield threw saddles on the handiest horses and rounded up the herd. Every available man was put on a horse and rode for the scene, twenty-eight miles distant, where about fifty or sixty Apaches had laid an ambush just as the road topped out on a mesa. It was dark when the troopers neared the scene and then, Bourke reports, from ahead there rose a wail: "Hel-lup! Hel-lup! My God, hel-lup!" In a defile twenty yards from the road they found Kennedy, almost fainting from loss of blood, but still able to describe much of the fight. They would find Israel, he said, next to the body of the Indian who had killed him for, dying, he still had the will to raise his rifle and shoot his assailant. Kennedy had had his left thumb shot off, and when the nearby Mexicans had dropped, he cut free the closest wheeler mule and charged through the oncoming Apaches. They drove an arrow into his chest, and another into his mule, and after he had run the animal a few hundred yards and thought he was clear, a chance bullet had struck the mule in the rump and it bucked him off. He had crawled into the defile where he was overlooked by the savages. The plunderers mistook several cases of patent medicine for whiskey and then, in frustration, fired the wagons.

"It was a ghastly sight," Bourke recalled:

There were hot embers of the new wagons, the scattered fragments of broken boxes, barrels, and packages of all sorts; copper shells, arrows, bows, one or two broken rifles, torn and burned clothing. There lay all that was mortal of poor Israel, stripped of clothing, a small piece cut from the crown of the head, but thrown back upon the corpse—the Apaches do not care much for scalping—his heart cut out, but also thrown back near the corpse, which had been dragged to the fire of the burning wagons and partly consumed; a lance wound in the back one or two arrow wounds, a severe contusion under the left eye, where he had been hit perhaps with the stock of a rifle or carbine, and the death wound from ear to ear, through which the

brain had oozed. The face was as calm and resolute in death as Israel
had been in life.[6]

Kennedy, too, knew his own wound was mortal, even if the troopers
thought not. "No, boys," he said, shaking his head, "it's all up with
me. I'm a goner. I know it was an arrow, 'cause I broke the feather
end off. I'm goin' to die." And he did, at the post hospital the next
night. A four-inch length of arrow shaft was found in his left lung.[7]

With daylight the trail of the marauders was easily followed, since
many of them had gotten drunk on the patent medicine, and Lieutenant Cushing was ordered to take their trail as his first important
scout in Arizona. He was, wrote Bourke "about five feet, seven inches
in height, spare, sinewy, active as a cat; slightly stoop-shouldered,
sandy complexioned, keen gray or bluish-gray eyes, which looked you
through when he spoke and gave a slight hint of the determination,
coolness, and energy which had made his name famous all over the
southwestern border."[8] Cushing, taking his time about making up his
expedition, in order to throw the Indians off their guard, chose Joe
Felmer and Manuel Duran as scouts. The former, post blacksmith,
also ran a small ranch three miles up the San Pedro and was "a Rus-
sian, or a Polynesian, or a Turk, or a Theosophist or something," who
was born in Germany, lived in either Russia or Poland, married an
Apache woman and from her learned the first rule of the frontier:
"When you see Apache 'sign,' be *keerful*; 'n' when you don' see nary
sign, be *more* keerful."[9] Duran was what was called a "tame" Apache,
an Indian at peace with the whites.

The raiders had passed within four miles of Camp Grant while the
troopers were at the scene of the massacre. The command followed

[6] *Ibid.*, 21–26.

[7] *Ibid.*, 28.

[8] *Ibid.*, 30.

[9] Felmer was a member of the California Volunteers, having enlisted at Sacramento August 20, 1861; re-enlisted as a veteran volunteer October 5, 1863; promoted to first lieutenant, Company A, First Cavalry Regiment, June 9, 1864, somewhere in New Mexico.—Richard H. Orton, *Records of California Men in the War
of the Rebellion 1861 to 1867*, 109. After the war he remained in the Apache country and became a scout and prominent pioneer.

the trail easterly, up the bed of Aravaipa Creek and into its gorge where the Apaches had clambered out, and made for the head of the San Carlos River, to the northeast. But that was a blind. The trail vanished, or would have, to any eye less keen than Duran's. He found where the quarry had doubled back toward the mouth of the San Pedro at the Gila. Again they passed Camp Grant, within a dozen miles. They crossed the Gila, worked north over the Dripping Springs Mountains to the head of Disappointment Creek, then crossed the Pinal Mountains at their highest point, Signal Peak. From it the command on the evening of June 4 saw a smoke rising like a dust-devil from a valley to the northeast. During a long, cold night the men crept to the vicinity of the Apache camp, and surrounded it as best they could. The Indians apparently believed they had thrown off pursuit. They seemed to have no thought of danger. They sprawled around their rancheria in and out of rude wickiups, often little more than brushy wind-shelters.

An old man felt cold. He arose to stir the fire. The light played upon his bronzed, muscular form. To get more fuel he stepped toward the spot where Cushing crouched, preparing the signal for attack. The savage suspected something, sensed danger, turned to escape, screaming the warning and stirring pandemonium in the camp. The soldiers yelled and laid a thunderclap volley into the doomed rancheria. No matter where the Apaches sought to flee they ran into a withering fire. Duran saw something rush past him in the gloom and shot at it, killing two at once: a warrior and a boy of five or six being carried to what the elder Apache thought was safety.

McClintock says that ninety-six Indians were killed and a few soldiers wounded,[10] newspaper dispatches said the toll was thirty-five,[11] and General Orders No. 9, based on Cushing's own report, said thirty Indians were killed and mentioned no white casualties.[12] Captured women and boys said the war party was Pinals, just returned from a Sonora raid when they spotted the Israel-Kennedy train.

[10] Bourke, *Border*, 30–33. McClintock, *Arizona*, I, 200.
[11] L.A. Pub. Lib.   [12] *Chronological List*, 23.

Back at Grant the troopers whiled away the tedious hours by stirring up fights between willing armies of red ants and black ants, discussed the killing by an Apache of a Mexican within a thousand yards of the post, or some other sanguinary incident involving hostile activity in southern Arizona. In that era there was no end to such activity; it went on all the time.

One of Cushing's longest scouts was a consequence of an Indian attack on another wagon train, an assault that had the happy result that none of the train's personnel was killed. Bourke referred to this as the Gatchell-Curtis company, but his facts are not clear, and newspapers of the day described an Apache attack of a wagon train led by a Captain John A. Curtis; it is likely that the two events are the same, Bourke interpolating details of some other contemporary event in his account. This would not surprise the honest and conscientious captain for, as he said, "there was so much of that kind of thing going on during my stay at Camp Grant that it is really impossible to avoid mixing up some of the minor details of the different incidents so closely resembling one another."[13] The battle took place on the forty-six-mile trace between Florence and Grant, and lasted exactly one hour.[14]

Lieutenant Cushing was assigned to lead a scout on the trail of the marauders, and he made it up out of his Troop F and Troop K of the First Cavalry. The column crossed the Gila, climbed over the pine-scented Pinals, and camped one night on Pinal Creek, not far from the site of Globe. An ominous cloud hung over the mountains that evening, and Cushing, fearing a cloudburst, ordered camp moved up the hillside. The shift was all but completed when a trooper cried: "Look out! Here she comes!" and a solid wall of water tore down the arroyo, irresistible in its force, inescapable in its mad rush. Cushing was all but swept off of his feet, and had it not been for the oaken arms of Sergeant Warfield and Big Dan Miller, he would surely have drowned. On Pinto Creek the command reluctantly destroyed Indian corn fields, complying with orders though realizing that,

---

[13] Bourke, *Border*, 38.
[14] L.A. Pub. Lib., clipping from *Weekly Arizonian*, July 2, 1870.

having lost this food supply, the Indians must inevitably turn to depredations among the settlers. The command crossed the Salt River, just above the present site of Roosevelt Dam, explored a short distance up Tonto Creek, had a brush or two with the Indians, contacted a column from McDowell, and turned to the east again. Cushing led his men past the mouth of Cherry Creek, then swung more to the south for the upper reaches of the San Carlos River, hard against the Natanes Plateau.

Bourke and a small group one day stood on a rimrock overlooking a cluster of red hills and swales, carefully searching below them for Indian sign, but seeing nothing. The lieutenant gave the order to dismount, so the horses could be led to lower ground when, from a yucca clump not one hundred yards distant, came a crack, a puff of powder smoke, and a bullet plowed along the neck of Bourke's horse. When the animals were quieted, the lieutenant saw two naked Apaches, their heads bound with a camouflage of yucca leaves, scooting for their lives down the valley. Leading their horses, the soldiers skidded and rolled to the bottom, mounted, and thundered down on the Indians, whooping as they came. One of the savages doubled up a side ravine. The other dodged behind a mesquite bush. He proved to have the loaded rifle and fired once, killing a trooper, then bounded out of the bush to meet the whites, swinging his emptied gun like a war club. He knocked Costello cold and smacked the skulls of Sergeant R. Harrington and Trooper Wolf and "would have ended them had not his strength begun to ebb away with his life-blood, now flowing freely from the death-wound through the body which we had succeeded in inflicting," wrote Bourke.

"One horse laid up, three men knocked out, and another man killed was a pretty steep price to pay for the killing of this one Indian, but we consoled ourselves with the thought that the Apaches had met with a great loss in the death of so valiant a warrior."[15]

No one now can tell the number of scouts Cushing led during his meteoric career in southern and central Arizona, but there were many of them. The *Chronological List* mentions some—in 1870 a June

[15] Bourke, *Border*, 40–45.

scout into the Pinals, another into the same region in July, one in August into Skirmish Canyon, into the Pinal Mountains in October, and the Turnbull Mountains in December. In 1871 he led scouts into the Sierra Galiuro, to the Aravaipa Mountains in February, and a hard-fighting expedition to the Sierra Aniba and Apache Mountains in April. The names of the various geographical landmarks have changed with the years, and it would require extended research to follow all of these expeditions, but they involved much travel, exploration, scouting, and, often, fighting. In a Skirmish Canyon area Sergeant Taylor in the forefront of a hot fight, was jumped by a famous Apache chief named Kargé, and was getting the worst of it when Joe Felmer laconically poked his rifle into the Indian's side and blew his heart out.[16] In October, while Cushing's command sought to avenge an attack on an Army paymaster—a campaign into which the boys could well put their heart—mounted Indians savagely attacked men leading their horses to water, wounding three soldiers and losing two killed. Cushing fought them off, captured looted cattle from them, and was chagrined when the warriors counterattacked, recaptured the livestock, and fled to the hills with their plunder. A few days later he joined in pursuit of other Indians who had run off a mule herd a mile and a half from Tucson.[17]

Despite the heroic efforts of the little command to destroy or punish the raiders, the Apaches were more active than ever in the spring of 1871, and Cushing was ordered to Lowell, near Tucson, where he would be closer to supplies. The southwestern army's most successful and energetic Indian fighter, he was ordered to take the field and keep to it; he could roam wherever he thought Indians might be found, and keep after them relentlessly. In point of fact, they were everywhere. So desperate had the situation become that even little Governor Anson P. K. Safford placed himself at the head of Mexicans and veteran Indian fighters, and occasionally took the field. When his party once met a small band of regulars, the governor

16 San Francisco *Alta*, dispatch dated August 11, 1870, from Camp Grant.—L.A. Pub. Lib.
17 L.A. Pub. Lib.

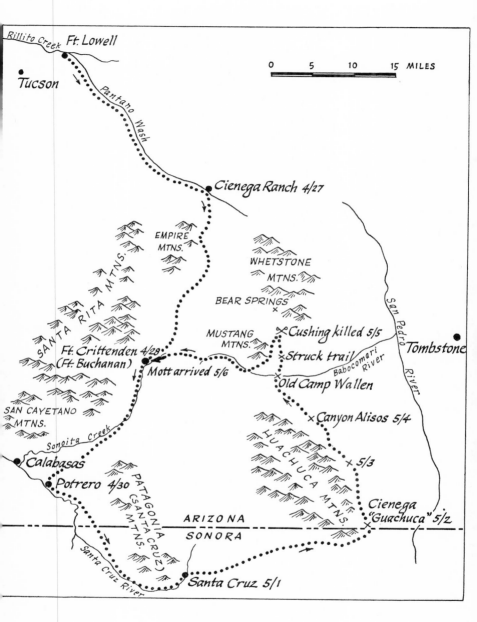

Cushing's Last Scout

even took command. "It seems to me," generously wrote a correspondent for the *Alta*, "that Governor Safford, whatever his motive, deserves credit for going into the field and exposing himself voluntarily to danger, and if he chooses to make an ass of himself by assuming a command over experienced officers and Indian fighters, a good sharp fight in which he will probably be soundly thrashed by the Indians, will do him good in the future."[18] But no one really made much headway against savage hostility in Apacheria, and Cushing came to believe that Cochise was the basic trouble, or a good share of it. He apparently made it his ambition to slay that chieftain, or destroy the fighting force with which he controlled much of the southeastern part of the territory. There would be glory in such a victory. Hard fighting, of course, but Cushing exulted in fighting and its danger. He decided in mid-spring on a long hunt into that enemy-infested southeast corner of Arizona.

The story of that tragic foray is here told for the first time in any book in the words of Sergeant John Mott, who salvaged the remnants of the column. Perhaps the lieutenant's influential relatives exerted pressure to ascertain details of that scout, and it was in response to this that the noncommissioned officer penned his account, now in the National Archives:

Camp Troop "F" 3d Cavalry
in the field near Tucson, A. T.
May 20, 1871

Capt. Alexander Moore
3d U.S. Cavalry
Comdg. Troop "F"
Captain:

In accordance with Special Orders No. 5, dated Hqrs. Troop "F", 3d Cav. in the field near Tucson, A. T., April 26, 1871, Lieut. H. B. Cushing left this place April 27, 1871, with one (1) Sergeant, (myself) one (1) citizen packer, and sixteen (16) privates, for the purpose of scouting the Sonorita and Santa Cruz Valleys, and that portion

[18] San Francisco *Alta*, September 5, 1870.

of the country bordering on the Sonora Line. Marching in a south-east direction, arrived at Cienega Ranch, A. T.,[19] at 5 P.M. same day, on the morning of April 28th left camp at Cienega Ranch and marching due south, arrived at Camp Crittenden, A. T., at 4 P.M.

April 29th laid over to recruit the animals having marched 65 miles the two preceding days.

April 30th left Camp Crittenden, A. T., and marching south-east [southwest] arrived at Portreo [Potrero], A. T.

May 1st left camp at 5 A.M., Mr. Kitchen[20] volunteered to guide the party through that range of mountains lying between the Sonorita and Santa Cruz valleys. At 3 P.M. Mr. Kitchen having concluded to return home, parted with Lt. Cushing. About an hour after Mr. Kitchen had left Lieut. Cushing and myself noticed that the grass was being set on fire and concluded it was done by Indians as a signal to their fellows in the mountains; but I have since learned that when about two miles from the command Mr. Kitchen saw some thirty or more Indians on our trail and burned the grass to warn us; continuing our line of march along the Sonorita and rounding the south-west point of the Santa Cruz mountains, camped at Santa Cruz, Mexico, arriving there at 11 P.M. Lt. Cushing, learning from the commandante at Santa Cruz that there were Indians in the Guachuca Mountains, determined to go there.

May 2nd left camp, marching north-east, camped at the Cienega Guachuca Mountains at 3 P.M.

May 3d, left camp at Cienega, marching due north and at 3 P.M. camped in a cañon on east side of Guachuca Mountains, fresh moccasin tracks clearly indicating the presence of Indians.

May 4th left camp, marching over a broken and rocky country camped in cañon Alisos, grass very scarce owing to the country around having been burning for several days.

May 5th. Left camp at 7 A.M., marching north-west, arrived at

[19] A Butterfield Stage Station was established at the Cienega, thirty miles east of Tucson and three miles west of the community of Pantano. It saw some Apache fighting, but has ceased to exist and the Southern Pacific railroad tracks now run over the site.—Barnes, *Place Names*, 2nd ed., 262–63.

[20] This was Pete Kitchen, a famed and durable Arizona pioneer on whom the literature is abundant. See Frank C. Lockwood, *Arizona Characters*, 48–61.

old Camp Wallen, A. T., at which place Lieut. Cushing intended to camp, but finding the grass all burned off and still burning, concluded to march to Bear Springs, Whetstone Mountains; about two miles north of Wallen struck a trail (one squaw and pony track) going towards the spring; the Lieut. directed me to take three men and follow the track while he followed the main trail with the detachment.

I followed the track about three-fourths of a mile until it entered a cañon which was simply a deep arroya, seeing that the squaw in walking along the sand had taken great pains to make a clear print of her foot at each step, and that she even avoided all stones and rocks in order to do this more effectually, I became convinced that we were being led into a trap and immediately determined to leave the cañon. Scarcely had I reached the top of the left wall, when I found my suspicions had been correct as a party of Indians about fifteen (15) in number were hid in a side cañon joining the one I had just left, and would have intercepted my retreat had I continued following the track. Being at the time well posted I thought I could with two men hold them in check while the third man went off to signal Lt. Cushing back; as we dismounted to be ready for them, I saw a second and much larger party on my left running towards my rear; I then decided it expedient to fall back, but while in the act of mounting, the Indians fired a volley disabling the horse of Private Green and severely wounding Private Pierce. These men started on foot for the rear, closely followed by the enemy, who ran so close on Green as to snatch the hat from his head. The third man who had signaled Lt. Cushing, looking back saw how matters stood and fired into the Indians, who no doubt thought that the main body had come up, as they paused, giving us time to escape. The front line of Apaches (they advanced in two lines) having fired off their rifles did not stop to reload, but kept following us thinking to capture us alive. They could easily have killed us being all around us with breach-loaders and revolvers. Some of the Indians in the second line kept up a brisk but harmless fire.

Lieut. Cushing now coming up having with him Mr. Simpson (a citizen friend) and Pvt. Chapman, I stated to the Lieut. that I thought the Indians would capture Green if we did not go to his assistance, but managed to escape by himself.

74

Moving up at once we attacked them, the rest of the men coming up. Now [we] had about eleven men in line, when a brisk fight ensued, in which we succeeded in driving the Indians to the hills, they leaving at this point five dead in our hands. We had three horses killed. Sending back three men to the pack train, Lt. Cushing gave the command "Forward." I seeing the disadvantage as we stood advancing over open ground to attack an enemy under cover, outnumbering us 15 to 1, said to the Lieut.—"Lieut., do you think it prudent to go farther?" Mr. Simpson, a gentleman of much experience, also counseled him to return, but the Lieut. seemed to think that the Indians were completely routed. Counting our party, he said, "Eight. That ought to be enough"; that was the Lieut., Mr. Simpson, myself and five privates. We advanced about twenty yards when the Indians opened fire, striking Mr. Simpson in the face, the ball passing out back of the head. The Lieut. sent one man to help him out thus reducing our number to six; the Indians seeing our party so small, rushed down from all sides (it seemed as if every rock and bush became an Indian). I was at that time about five yards in advance of Lieut. Cushing, and hearing the words, "Sergeant, Sergt., I am killed, take me out, take me out," turned and saw Lieut. Cushing face towards the horses, clasp his hands across his breast, and fall to the ground; calling to Fichter to assist me, I seized the Lieut. by the right arm, Fichter taking the left, and started for the rear followed by Green who I noticed was very lame. The other two men started to get out the horses. We carried the Lieut. about ten or twelve paces, when he was again shot through the head and fell dead in our arms; we continued to drag the body until we caught up with Yount and Mr. Simpson, when the latter was again shot through the body, killing him instantly. Looking behind me I saw the enemy within thirty or forty yards of me firing as he advanced. Dropping the body of Lieut. Cushing, Fichter and myself turned to sell our lives as dearly as possible, causing the Indians to pause, thus enabling Privates Green and Yount to mount. Acting Corporal Kilmartin now opened fire with his party, thus enabling Fichter and myself to mount, but scarcely had we done so when both horses were shot, two balls striking Fichter's horse in the flank, a third mine in the fore leg, and a fourth killing Private Green. Immediately mounting Lieut. Cushing's horse I detached part of my command (now reduced to fourteen effective men) to move out with the pack train. I keeping the remainder with me to cover the retreat, then commenced a running fight for about a mile until finding I had drawn the enemy from under cover I halted to offer him battle (hoping I could flank him and recover the bodies.) He halted also but declined the gage, evidently having had enough of that kind of fighting, preferring to cut off and ambush me on the trail to Crittenden, which passed the foot-hills within one and one-half miles of his position. I, having to go around the mountains, could strike it in about four miles. Seeing through their design, I crossed the Rio Barbacoma four miles above old Camp Wallen, and continued my retreat over the mesas thus placing the swampy head of the Barbacoma and a half mile of ground between me and the place of ambush and the trail; I had scarcely arrived opposite this place when the Indians uttered yells of savage rage and disappointment, but were powerless to molest me. It was becoming dark, or about 7 o'clock P.M. I continued my route to Camp Crittenden at which place I arrived about one o'clock A.M. on the 6th of May. Four of the pack mules being very weak and poor owing to the scarcity of grass (the country along our route having been burned off by Indians) I had to abandon in my retreat. I succeeded however in carrying off Lieut. Cushing's pistols and Mr. Simpson's Henry rifle.

The Indians were well handled by their chief, a thick, heavy set man, who never dismounted from a small brown horse during the fight. They were not noisy or boisterous as Indians generally are, but paid great attention to their chief, whose designs I could guess as he delivered his instructions by gestures.

I believe I am stating truth when I set down the number of the enemy killed at thirteen (13); it may be more, but that number was seen to fall.

Our casualties were Lieutenant Cushing, Mr. Simpson and Private Green killed, and Private Pierce wounded.

I had four horses killed and two wounded.

The men all behaved well, especially Privates Kilmartin, Fichter, Yount and Miller.

Distance marched on scout—240 miles.

Having submitted the foregoing report for your consideration,
I am, Captain, Very respectfully, Your obedient servant
(Sgd) *John Mott*
Sergt. Troop F, 3d Cavy.[21]

Various writers have assumed that Cochise was the mounted Indian in charge of the native side of the fight, no doubt because he was the best-known Apache leader of the day, and because it makes a better story that way. But we have seen, in Chapter II, that about this time Cochise weighed only 164 pounds, and other contemporaries have described him as "well-formed," certainly not a "thick, heavy-set man," as Mott recalled his antagonist. The Apache war leader who would best fit Mott's description is Juh, a relentless fighter against the Mexicans and an Indian who had little but contempt for white Americans, either. He is often described as "stout," or "heavy," or even "fat." At this date the identity of the warrior who directed the Cushing fight can never be proven, but Juh would seem the most likely nominee.

In a furious letter to the New York *Herald*, Sylvester Mowry castigated the government for undermanning the Army in Arizona and sending such officers as Cushing out with insufficient force. Mowry was a noted Arizona pioneer, celebrated in the history of that state.

"I spent a night in the field with Cushing a few months ago," he wrote from the Union Club on May 15, 1871, "and he was in great hopes and determination of capturing Cachies and his band, and he would have done so had he been properly supported. . . . There is not a hostile tribe in Arizona or New Mexico that will not celebrate the killing of Cushing as a great triumph. He was a *beau sabreur*, an unrelenting fighter, and although the Indians have 'got him' at last, he sent before him a long procession of them to open his path to that 'undiscovered country.' . . . He has left behind him in Arizona a name that will not die in this generation."[22]

[21] Letters Received, District of Arizona, 1871, Civil War Branch, National Archives.

[22] L.A. Pub. Lib.

77

Perhaps not, but his name has assuredly died with subsequent generations. His bones mouldered in a rudely marked grave near Tucson. A street named Cushing Street, in his honor and to his memory, has been changed by some efficient and pragmatic mind to 14th Street, although Simpson Street, named for his perished friend, is the extension of 15th Street and bears its original name for a few blocks. Near Delafield, Wisconsin, and Fredonia, New York, both onetime homes of the Cushing family, there are handsome monuments to the brave brothers, but nothing of that nature in Arizona.[23]

[23] Mayor Don Hummel, Tucson, in correspondence with author, December 19, 1958. Cushing Street was changed to 14th Street "for no apparent reason," according to *Arizoniana*, Vol. III, No. 2 (Summer, 1962), 32. This publication said that Cushing's remains, first buried at Fort Lowell, were removed to the Presidio, San Francisco.

VII

The Whitman Affair

FROM THE PRECEDING CHAPTERS it may be seen that the relationships between the growing white population of Apacheria and its red inhabitants had become almost unremitting conflict in many areas. The 1870 census shows a white population of 9,658, including Army personnel. Of these, 4,348 were of Mexican origin, 686 were immigrants from the United Kingdom and 379 from Germany. The total compares with a white population of 2,421 in 1860, nearly all of whom were of Latin background. Pressure on the native population thus had considerably increased, and as a result of that, and for allied reasons, the carnage mounts and the bloody incidents seem to follow one another in unremitting succession. But they had at least this beneficial effect: they had aroused the country, and many individuals within the nation, to seek some means of settling the stubborn problems in the way of settlement other than by extermination or bloody subjugation and casting aside of the native races. Within the coming few years various individuals were to attempt, in the face of much hostility and disdain from southwestern resident whites, to bring the hostiles into some sort of reservation system as the only practicable solution permitting both whites and redmen to live at peace in the same area. No serious thought was ever given to moving the whites out of Arizona; with its proven and suspected mineral wealth, that would have been considered absurd and unseemly interference with obvious and manifest destiny!

What brought the situation to its real climax was a most unlikely chain of events that now began to emerge. It involved the sensible and not unkindly work of a much-maligned, misunderstood, and controversial Army officer, which resulted more or less directly, however, in one of the most brutal incidents of frontier history. Nevertheless this affair, in turn, led immediately to the assignment to Arizona of a most unusual commander who far more efficiently than his predecessors could wage war against the Indians—but having successfully done so, would then develop the vision, the sense of fair play, and a deep concern for the rights and welfare of the vanquished Indians that would at last make possible a wise and viable solution to the whole puzzle. This complicated chain of events was now to begin, and it was not unrelated to all that went before.

The cruel incident that was a keystone to the whole affair, one that in the words of a representative authority constituted "the blackest page in the Anglo-Saxon records of Arizona,"[1] was a large-scale tragedy that featured a cast of hundreds. It starred four men: a soldier, an Indian chief, an outstanding pioneer, and a leader of Tucson's Mexican community. It was called the Camp Grant Massacre.

The soldier was a first lieutenant of the third Cavalry named Royal Emerson Whitman, a man from Maine with a New Englander's courage and stubbornness and, I think, integrity and inherent democracy of spirit. The chief was Eskiminzin, called Skimmy by the pioneers, and the most controversial Apache in border history. The pioneer was William Sanders Oury, a pillar of Tucson society and a veteran of the Texas war of independence. The Mexican was Jesús María Elías, who occupied roughly the position among his people as did Oury among the North Americans.

Whitman, who became the most vilified man in Arizona, arrived in the territory November 26, 1870, with other officers of the Third Cavalry, the group striking the Arizona *Citizen* as "fine appearing gentlemen [whom] we believe will prove efficient in public duties."[2] He was born on a family farm at Turner, Maine, May 11, 1833, and had a good Civil War record, having risen to the rank of colonel in

---

[1] Lockwood, *Apache Indians*, 178.

[2] December 3, 1870. Interestingly, the *Citizen* chose to ignore the boisterous events by which Whitman and, presumably, his brother officers marked their arrival in Arizona, and which figured prominently in later court-martial proceedings.

the Maine Volunteers.[3] Immediately upon his arrival, Whitman was assigned to Camp Grant, or sentenced to it, as he must have felt. He found Second Lieutenant William W. Robinson already there, but by reason of rank, Whitman assumed command.

Sometime in February, 1871, five old women, hungry, their clothes in tatters and bearing a flag of truce, fearfully came into Camp Grant in search of the son of one of them, taken prisoner along the Salt some months before.[4] The women were courteously treated, fed, and after two days left, having secured permission to return with others of their band. In eight days they were back again, bringing other Indians and some articles for sale, so that they could purchase manta, a type of canvas sold by the yard, with which they desired to cover their nakedness. Again Whitman treated them kindly. They told him that many others of their people desired to come in, and the lieutenant urged that they send in chiefs for a talk. The men, he said, would be protected while on the post and, if no agreement were

[3] Whitman was descended on his mother's side from Governor William Bradford, she being Sally Bradford, born August 17, 1794, and of the sixth or seventh generation after the founding of Plymouth Colony. Royal married three times. His first wife was a third cousin, Lucretia Octavia Whitman, three years his senior. They were married in 1852 and had six children. Royal and Octavia were divorced on grounds of "incompatability," but probably mostly because of long absences caused by his military duties. She "adored him" all her life and taught their children to love and respect him. He next married Harriet Willard of Springfield, Massachusetts, who, being childless, accompanied him to the frontier. When she died he married a widow, Mrs. Mary Blood, at Washington, D.C. There Whitman died of cancer in his eightieth year, on February 12, 1913. He had invented the Whitman saddle, which became quite popular and widely used in the late nineteenth century (a favorite with the Theodore Roosevelt family, for instance), and made considerable money from it. He invested heavily in Washington, D.C., real estate and lost most of his wealth in the financial upheaval of the 1890's, but remained in comfortable circumstances until his death.—Information from Whitman's granddaughter, Mrs. Anthony C. McAuliffe.

[4] Unless otherwise noted, information on Whitman's collecting the Indians comes from his letter of May 17, 1871, to Colonel J. G. C. Lee, Tucson, and Lieutenant Robinson's letter of September 10, 1871, both printed as appendices to a report on the Apache Indians of Arizona and New Mexico by Vincent Colyer: *U.S. Board of Indian Commissioners. Peace with the Apaches of New Mexico and Arizona. Report of Vincent Colyer, member of Board—1871.* (Hereafter cited as Colyer, *Report.*)

reached, might return to the mountains. Once more the Apaches left and in a few days reappeared, about twenty-five in number, with three chiefs, including Eskiminzin, Capitan Chiquito, and Santo, all locally noted Indians. Eskiminzin told Whitman that he was chief of what was left of the Aravaipa Apaches, now a band of about one hundred and fifty, and that he wanted peace. He and his people had no home, he said, and could get little rest since they never knew when the cavalry might pounce upon them. They said that the country along Aravaipa Creek from the San Pedro to the Galiuro Mountains had always been their home, and now they wanted to plant crops along the creek and to be issued tools for that purpose, plus rations until their crops came in.

"I told him he should go to the White Mountains," said Whitman. "He said, 'That is not our country, neither are they our people. Our fathers and their fathers before them have lived in these mountains and have raised corn in this valley. We are taught to make mescal our principal article of food, and in summer and winter here we have a never-failing supply. At the White Mountains there is none, and without it we get sick.' "

Whitman explained that he had no authority to make a treaty with him, or to promise him a permanent home, but if Eskiminzin would go bring in his band, he would feed them, and relay his requests to General George Stoneman, the Department commander. Until he heard back he would issue them a pound of beef and one of corn or flour a day for each adult Indian, and would occasionally give them permission to go out into the mountains to collect mescal. This pleased the Indians. They went to bring in the main band, while Whitman hastily wrote two letters, one dated February 24 and a second the twenty-eighth, to Stoneman, asking approval of what he had done and authority for any further steps. So urgent did Whitman deem his second letter, which was the more complete, that he sent it with a special messenger with instructions to speed it to Sacaton, on the Gila, the first mail station en route to Drum Barracks, California.

The reason for the officer's haste is apparent. He had scarcely settled in his new post when he evidently had in his hands the answer

82

to much of the plaguey Indian problem. If he could get the necessary authority, he might lure more Apaches onto his unofficial reserve and off of the warpath. No wonder he was on edge awaiting a reply!

Meanwhile, more and more Indians came in. About the first of March Eskiminzin arrived with his whole band. Runners had come in from other bands, and to these Whitman offered the same terms. By March 5 there were three hundred Indians at Camp Grant. Before long there were five hundred. None were required to give up their weapons "as they were very poorly supplied with arms," according to Whitman.[5] At first the officer ordered them to camp within a mile of the post, and counted them and issued rations every second day, then every third day, and finally every fifth day. As the season progressed and the Aravaipa dried up, Whitman gave the Indians permission to move their camp five miles into the mountains, where the water still was good, but he did not relax his vigilance. "Knowing as I did that the responsibility of the whole movement rested with me, and that in case of any loss to the Government coming of it I should be the sufferer, I kept them continually under observation," he said. He came to know all of the men and most of the women and children by sight. He stopped other Indians from supplying his garrison with hay, so that he might buy from his newly settled people, who desperately needed cash to buy cloth for clothing. "I arranged a system of tickets with which to pay them and to encourage them," he wrote, "and to be sure they were properly treated I personally attended to all the weighing. I also made inquiries as to the kind of goods sold them and prices." He paid a cent a pound for hay and not only women and children, but also, singularly enough, the men worked chopping and delivering it until in two months they had brought in 300,000 pounds.

There was no evidence of friction between the Indians and nearby ranchers. On the contrary, Whitman had arranged with the whites to hire the Apaches at going field-hand rates when the barley harvest was ready. "At all times," wrote Robinson, the Indians "had behaved themselves in a perfectly orderly manner, and obeyed implicitly the

[5] Testimony of Whitman at the trial of the raiders, as reported in the San Francisco *Alta*, February 3, 1872.

orders of the post commander." Whitman had assured them that they would be protected so long as they behaved themselves. The Indians had even lost "their characteristic anxiety to purchase ammunition, and had, in many instances, sold their best bows and arrows." Clearly they were expecting no fight.

The officer conceded that he had a little difficulty making them understand that by coming in they were at peace not only with Camp Grant, but with all of Arizona as well. He suggested that some of them might be enlisted as scouts in operations against the hostiles, but was flatly turned down. "We are at peace," he was reminded. "We are not at war with those Indians," and, they added shrewdly, they might be ousted from Camp Grant, and how would the hostiles treat them if they had helped the soldiers fight them?[6] However, they might agree to operate against other Indians—if Whitman and his soldiers would accompany them on an expedition against the Sonoran Mexicans. Even Whitman had to grin at that.

At last, six weeks after dispatch of the letter of February 28, an envelope arrived from Drum Barracks. The officer eagerly ripped it open, seeking the long-desired answer that might approve of his actions, to permit the Indians to plant crops and remain with security on their little patches of ground. And what a cruel disappointment it was to withdraw from the envelope his original communication with a curt note from some clerk pointing out that the lieutenant had forgotten in his haste to put a brief note on the exterior describing its contents, a required formality in those days. No answer to his urgent appeal, no authority, no approval, nothing but an example of red tape at its most dense. Or, perhaps it was not stupidity after all. Maybe Stoneman had read the message, using the excuse of the absence of the briefing to return it without making a formal decision?[7]

[6] *Ibid.*

[7] James R. Hastings makes this suggestion in his careful analysis of "The Tragedy of Camp Grant in 1871" in *Arizona and the West*, Vol. I, No. 2 (Summer, 1959), 146–60, with this reference 150n. Stoneman already was harassed by the press and populace of Arizona, knew of the feeding of Indians by Whitman, and issued verbal instructions to Captain Frank Standwood, who was to take over command at the post, to continue it for the time being.

About April 1 Captain Frank Standwood, also a Maine man, arrived to take command of Camp Grant, and so thoroughly approved of what Whitman had done, and his general competence, that on April 24 he took virtually the whole command stationed there on a long scout through the southern part of the territory, leaving the lieutenant with barely fifty men. This was not enough, for it emboldened his enemies, and it led to disaster.

The reasons for the hostility toward Whitman and his experiment are complex. For one thing, Apache depredations south of the Gila were continuing. Nothing very important, but enough to keep the settlers on edge. On March 10 a baggage train had been attacked between Camp Grant and the Pinals. A soldier and a Mexican were killed and sixteen mules captured. Whitman closely questioned his Indians and denied that they could have done this.[8] On March 20 Indians raided Tubac and killed L. B. Wooster, a rancher, carrying off a woman named Trinidad Aggera, or Aguierre. The *Citizen* reported hostiles sweeping up and down the Santa Cruz Valley, and viewers with alarm wrapped these incidents up with others that had occurred since the first of the year as evidence that recalcitrant natives were completely out of hand and threatening to overwhelm the settlers. Oury thus cited the slaying of James Pennington within three miles of Tucson, the killing of the Tubac mail rider within two miles of the city, those of Simms and Sam Brown near Tres Alamos, all in January, and charged that they were done by Whitman's Indians, despite the fact that until late February Whitman had no Indians under his control at all.[9] In addition, there was the common frontier attitude favoring extermination of all Indians, and those at Camp Grant were the handiest and the easiest target for those who would actuate such a policy. It is probably an oversimplification to lay the blame for the affair simply upon border bums, of which Arizona had her share, however.[10]

[8] *Alta*, February 3, 1872.

[9] Tucson *Star*, June 29, 1879. In a two-part article in the issue of that date and of July 1, Oury gave in detail his version of the events leading up to the tragedy, and of the massacre itself.

[10] Paul I. Wellman, *The Indian Wars of the West*, 317, does this. He implies that

More sinister, less easy to prove, and probably more effective was the behind-the-scenes plotting by those vultures of the frontier who made a living out of Army contracts and were unscrupulous about it, and who saw in any successful endeavor to pacify and settle the Indians an economic loss to themselves in a lessened need for garrisons and troops. Their determination to keep the war flames burning is evident right up to the very end of the Indian wars, with perhaps the most flagrant example in the last phase of the Geronimo campaign, as we shall note. But it was always present to some degree, according to contemporaries who were in a position to know. It is highly unlikely that this unholy drive was missing entirely from the affairs that led to the Grant disaster.

"There were staunch and honest citizens in Arizona at that time—but their number was all too few," wrote Lockwood. "On the other hand, there were numerous cruel and depraved men." He notes that a year or so earlier an Army inspector found that one garrison of eighty-six men had lost fifty-four by desertion, most deserters selling their horses and arms to nearby citizens who encouraged the profitable practice. Other people robbed the government outrageously on hay contracts and in provision of needed services. Lockwood quotes Fish: "Of all the contractors of early days, it is hardly possible to find one who remained in the Territory. As soon as they made their money, they went east or to San Francisco to live. Not one of these patriotic fraternity cared a fig for Arizona. The people were taught to oppose agencies where the Apaches worked and were fed. They feared that it would reduce the military force for one thing, and that it would suspend campaigns and lead to an inactive state of war."[11] Ogle, among the most thorough students of the period, is even more explicit: "Subtle intriguers," he wrote, "now proclaimed that the

Tucson's "shifty population of gamblers, 'road agents,' cattle 'rustlers' and loafers" who "hung in a cloud" about the town awaited only the news that most of the soldiers had left Camp Grant before descending in a mob upon the place. The attack was better organized and had deeper roots than that.

[11] Lockwood, *Apache Indians*, 176–78. The reference is to Joseph F. Fish, History of Arizona, manuscript, Arizona Pioneers Historical Society, Tucson.

friendly Indians at Camp Grant were responsible for all the depredations, and that Stoneman's policy of peace was the sole cause of the trouble."[12] This attitude came to be reflected more strongly in the press, which became outspokenly critical of Whitman, referring to him in most intemperate terms. And, finally, the intriguers had their way.

Some of the most dissatisfied of Tucson had formed a Committee of Public Safety to deal with the situation. William S. Oury,[13] the editor S. R. DeLong, J. W. Hopkins, and another were named to visit General Stoneman and urge more protection. The general listened, noted that he had received a memorial from the citizens of the Santa Cruz Valley stating that they spoke for five hundred settlers, and observed that if there were that many there they ought to be able to look out for themselves. Whatever he meant by this, and he probably intended it as no more than an off-hand remark to indicate his disbelief that there were that many concerned, Oury and his deputation later claimed that they took it as a carte blanche to handle the situation as they saw fit. To men of their temperament, in that time and place, only one solution occurred. This became, to them, more imperative when on April 10 Apaches raided San Xavier, south of Tucson, and drove off nineteen head of stock. A punitive party killed a raider and recaptured the stock, but three days later four Americans were killed in an attack and subsequent fight near the San Pedro, and the *Citizen* howled, with no apparent evidence, that the hostiles must have come from Camp Grant.

"The people of Tucson," explained Oury, "were compelled in their desperation, to take matters in their own hands."[14] He con-

---

[12] Ogle, *Western Apaches*, 80.

[13] Oury was a Virginian, born in 1817, who joined Stephen Austin in Texas at the age of sixteen. He was almost caught at the Alamo, but was sent by Travis with dispatches before the place was invested. He was with Sam Houston at San Jacinto, later joined the Texas Rangers, once was captured by Mexicans, but escaped, took part in the 1849 gold rush to California and reached Tucson in 1856.—Hastings, "Tragedy of Camp Grant," *Arizona and the West*, Vol. I, No. 2 (Summer, 1959), 150–51, citing the *Arizona Historical Review*, Vol. IV, No. 1 (April, 1931), 7–20.

[14] *Star*, June 29, 1879. Unless otherwise noted, the description of the organization and the massacre are taken from Oury's two-part account.

tinued: "Frequent excited and angry meetings were held at the court-house, and many valiant but frothy speeches were pronounced, and many determined resolves were resoluted; but nothing definite was done beyond a list being gotten up and signed by some eighty-odd valiant and doughty knights resolved to do or die; but in a few days, with sorrow be it said, the valor of all THESE PLUMED KNIGHTS seemed to have oozed out at their finger ends, and everything was at a standstill."

One night in April, Oury was walking home when he met his trusted friend Elias, and quite an ornate and stilted dialogue took place, according to Oury's account.

"Don Guillermo," said Don Jesús, "what are we to do? The Camp Grant Indians are slowly but surely murdering our people and carrying away our means of subsistence. I have just returned from following a party of them, who stole stock from San Xavier night-before last. We succeeded in KILLING ONE OF THEM, and I pledge you my solemn word that I know him to be a Camp Grant Indian; have seen him there frequently, and know him by his having a front tooth out."

Oury replied: "Well, Don Jesús, let us call our people together at the court-house tomorrow; and lay all of this before them; collect together our eighty-odd doughty knights, and immediately take the war-path."

Elias protested that there already had been too much talk and not enough action. He proposed calling on "our trusty friend Francisco," chief of the Papagoes,[15] to see if he couldn't collect enough warriors to do something, while Elias scoured the Mexican community for recruits and Oury did what he could among the Anglo-Americans. As Oury feared, his countrymen had little stomach for the sort of action contemplated, despite their ferocious declamations, but they didn't object to employing mercenaries to do the work for them, and

[15] This was probably Francisco Galerita, chief of the San Xavier Indians and one of the most influential of the Papagoes, who died December 9, 1879, after having received the sacraments of the Catholic church into which he was born. "He ruled the Indians for many years, and all were obedient to his command and docile to his advices. Nothing was undertaken without his consent."—*Star*, December 13, 1879; *Miner*, December 19, 1879.

contributed a wagonload of arms and ammunition to that end.[16] Be it said to Oury's credit that he had the courage of his convictions and by 1:00 P.M. on April 28 he joined his command of irregulars on the shady banks of the Rillito Creek, which joins the Santa Cruz below Tucson. He and Elias found themselves at the head of a group of 92 Papagoes, 42 Mexicans, and 6 Anglo-Americans, 140 men in all. The party moved up the Rillito to the San Pedro watershed and struck the trail of the San Xavier raiders, following it to where the Apache was killed. The "carcass of the dead Indian" was examined and the march resumed. At 2:00 A.M. the avengers halted to rest, moving into a San Pedro thicket where they lay concealed until just before dark on April 29, when they moved out again.

"To our great surprise and mortification, however, those of us most intimate with the country were mistaken in the distance which yet remained to be overcome," Oury confessed. Instead of fifteen miles, they had about thirty to do, which prevented careful scouting out of the location of the Indian camp they sought. There was, Oury lamented, "no time for anything but a haphazard dash, and kill all we could."

Filled to overflowing with the thirst to murder, the war party had reached the wash of the Aravaipa when word was given and "the Papagoes bounded forward like deer, notwithstanding their night march of nearly thirty miles, and we never witnessed a prettier skirmish [line] in all our military life than was made by those hard-marched Papago soldiers, for about two miles before we struck the rancheria, nor quicker or more effective work after it was struck, for in less than a half an hour not a living Apache was to be seen, save the children taken prisoners, and some seven Indians who escaped by being up and ahead of our skirmish line, so they could not be overtaken without breaking it.

"Thus ended the so-called Camp Grant massacre, denounced as a dastardly outrage by General Stoneman in the killing of about 144 of the most blood-thirsty devils that ever disgraced mother earth."

[16] It is said that the adjutant general of the territory furnished the arms and ammunition.—Ross Santee, *Apache Land*, 175.

What Oury neglected to mention was that all but perhaps 8 of his total of 144 were women and children, ravished, wounded, and clubbed to death, hacked to pieces or brained by rocks.[17] A few, terrified by the assault, attempted to clamber up the sides of the wash to escape, but were shot by the Anglo-Americans and Mexicans and tumbled back into the hands of the Papagoes to be clubbed to death. Not a member of the attacking party was wounded, because there was almost no one to fight back. It was sheer, unqualified murder, with no hand to stay the slaughter. Less fortunate than the slain were almost all of the 27 children taken prisoner, who were sold by the Papagoes into Sonoran slavery.

Lieutenant Whitman was having breakfast when, at seven-thirty that morning, a courier arrived from the commandant of Camp Lowell, informing him that a large party of armed men left Tucson with the avowed intention of killing the Camp Grant Indians. The courier had been delayed by Oury's forethought in assigning sentinels to intercept any such messengers, but Whitman sent a couple of interpreters[18] on horseback to the camp to warn the Indians and bring them to the post. Since he had no cavalry, and no other officer was present, Whitman could not go himself. Lieutenant Robinson was absent on leave, and Captain Standwood had not yet returned from his southerly scout.

[17] The exact number killed is not known. Dr. Conant B. Briesly, post surgeon at Grant, said he saw 21 bodies, but that Apache survivors told him 85 had been killed.—Colyer, *Report*, 34. Miles L. Wood, Camp Grant beef contractor, said he counted 138 dead, but didn't think he saw them all. He added that Eskiminzin lost four wives and five children, "but as he had nine wives he had enough left."—McClintock, *Arizona*, I, 211. It is worth noting that this statement made to McClintock forty years after the event, directly contradicts in imporant particulars Wood's statement a few months after the incident.—Colyer *Report*, 35–36. Whitman reported 125 killed.—Colyer, *Report*, 33. Rais Mendoza, at the trial of the raiders, said there were "sixty or seventy" dead bodies lying about.—*Alta*, February 3, 1872. John P. Clum, who interviewed many survivors, thought 118 had died.—*AHR*, Vol. II, No. 1 (April, 1929), 55.

[18] These were probably Oscar Hutton, former captain of the Volunteers, and William Kness, twenty-six years on the frontier, who, formerly heavily prejudiced against the Apaches, had been convinced by the conduct of those about Camp Grant that they were good Indians. See his statement, Colyer, *Report*, 36.

"My messengers returned in about an hour, with intelligence that they could find no living Indians," Whitman reported.

The camp was burning and the ground strewed with their dead and mutilated women and children. I immediately mounted a party of about twenty soldiers and citizens, and sent them with the post surgeon,[19] with a wagon to bring in the wounded, if any could be found. The party returned in the late P.M., having found no wounded and without having been able to communicate with any of the survivors. Early next morning I took a similar party, with spades and shovels, and went out and buried all the dead in and immediately around the camp.

I had the day before offered the interpreters, or any one who could do so, $100 to go to the mountains and communicate with them, and convince them that no officer or soldier of the United States Government had been concerned in the vile transaction; and, failing in this, I thought the act of caring for their dead would be an evidence to them of our sympathy at least, and the conjecture proved correct, for while at the work many of them came to the spot and indulged in their expressions of grief, too wild and terrible to be described.

That evening they began to come in from all directions, singly and in small parties, so changed in forty-eight hours as to be hardly recognizable, during which time they had neither eaten or slept. Many of the men, whose families had all been killed, when I spoke to them and expressed sympathy for them, were obliged to turn away, unable to speak, and too proud to show their grief. The women, whose children had been killed or stolen were convulsed with grief, and looked to me appealingly, as though I was their last hope on earth. Children who two days before had been full of fun and frolic kept at a distance, expressing wondering horror. I did what I could; I fed them, and talked to them, and listened patiently to their accounts. I sent horses into the mountains to bring in two badly-wounded women, one shot through the left lung, and one with an arm shattered.[20] These were attended to, and are doing well, and will recover.

The Indians, Whitman went on, had shown remarkable understanding and forbearance.

[19] Dr. Briesly.
[20] The latter was the wife of Capitan Chiquito.

"I have . . . been astonished at their continued unshaken faith in me and their perfectly clear understanding of their misfortune," he reported. "They say: 'We know there are a great many white men and Mexicans who do not wish us to live at peace. We know that the Papagoes would not have come out after us at this time unless they had been persuaded to do so.' "[21]

The lieutenant, upon whose shoulders alone rested the hope of keeping these deeply wronged people from the warpath, and to whose dedicated efforts uncounted Arizonans owed their lives during the next few weeks, was reviled unspeakably in those sections of the territorial press which sought with increasing urgency to justify the incident, as horror and revulsion swept over other parts of the country. "You well know," Whitman wrote Colonel J. G. C. Lee at Tucson, "that parties who would engage in murder like this, could and would (and already have) make statements and multiply affidavits without end in their justification." Violent eastern reaction followed. President Grant characterized the attack as "purely murder"[22] and bluntly told Arizona Governor Safford that if the participants were not brought to trial he would proclaim martial law in Arizona. So the five-day perfunctory trial was solemnly conducted, and the jury in nineteen minutes' "deliberation" released the one hundred and more defendants.[23] You couldn't convict a man in Arizona for killing an Apache, whatever the circumstances. At least not before a jury of Arizonans.

Yet the trial and affidavits in connection with it revealed clearly how flimsy was the evidence connecting the Camp Grant Indians with depredations that allegedly had caused the Tucson expedition to be organized.[24] James Lee swore that he and his party had followed and positively identified the trail made by Indians who had raided

[21] Whitman to Lee, Colyer, *Report*, 31–33.

[22] Arizona *Citizen*, June 24, 1871, quoted by Hastings, "Tragedy of Camp Grant," *Arizona and the West*, Vol. I, No. 2 (Summer, 1959), 154.

[23] *Alta*, February 3, 1872, carries the full story of the five-day trial, including testimony.

[24] In these sentences I am following Hastings' careful analysis, "Tragedy of Camp Grant," *Arizona and the West*, Vol. I, No. 2 (Summer, 1959), 155–57.

San Xavier to the Camp Grant rancheria; yet the trail was three weeks old, it followed a well-traveled route, and for much of the journey the Tucson avengers traveled at night when tracking would be impossible. Elias testified that a horse at Camp Grant had been identified as one stolen from San Xavier; this would scarcely be conclusive proof, since a single horse would be the most portable piece of property that could be owned on the frontier. Elias also testified that a captured chief admitted making raids while supposed to be camped at the rancheria; but no adults were taken prisoner. A breast-pin found at the rancheria was "positively identified" as having belonged to Trinidad Aguierre; the pin was hammered out of a $2.50 gold piece, a common practice. No attempt was made apparently to determine how the identification was made so "positively." Elias testified that he could identify the Indian killed at San Xavier as a Camp Grant Indian because of a missing front tooth; but Jose M. Yesques "evidently became confused" at the trial and testified he had talked with the Apache with the missing tooth six months after he was supposed to have been killed.

As Whitman and others at Camp Grant broadcast their own side of the affair by letters to their superiors and other means, the *Citizen* furiously attacked the officer, alleging that he was a drunkard on and off duty, and that his interest in Indians stemmed primarily from a fascination for "dusky maidens." To bolster the latter accusation, the newspaper adroitly extracted passages from a letter complimentary to Whitman, describing his initial attempts to attract the Indians to settle peaceably at Camp Grant. The "dusky maidens" used by the *Citizen*, turned out to be the five old squaws who had first come in to see whether it was safe for others to trade. The charges that Whitman was a drunkard were on equally flimsy ground, although it was incontrovertible that he on occasion could belt a bottle with anyone. But there is no evidence that he ever did so at Camp Grant, or while on duty anywhere. In fact, Lieutenant Robinson wrote:

> Attempts have been made, principally through the columns of the Arizona *Citizen* . . . to make it appear that [Whitman] was a de-

bauched scoundrel and a slave to vice. Among other things, he has been accused of associating with Indian women, and of being a confirmed drunkard. I know little of this officer's history previous to his assuming command of this post, December last, but from the time the Indians came in up to the 11th of April [when Robinson went on leave], and from May 21 to the time they left, to the best of my knowledge he touched not one drop of liquor. The other statement given in the Arizona *Citizen* has not the slightest foundation in truth.[25]

Deep-rooted as the origins and effects of the Camp Grant Massacre were, the most lasting and beneficial result was indirect. For it led to the relief of General Stoneman[26] as commander of the Department of Arizona, effective May 2, 1871, and General George Crook assumed formal command June 4. Although in the specific instance of the Camp Grant Massacre, Crook sided with the citizens against Whitman, he was an officer of integrity, one who could accomplish decisive results and would do so. He was a new type of officer for the Arizona command, one badly needed, and with his coming a new day dawned for the whole of Apacheria.

[25] Robinson to Colyer, *Report*, 38.

[26] Stoneman was a good officer and many of his actions pointed the way toward eventual solution of the Apache problem. Born August 8, 1822, at Busti, New York, he served in the Mexican and Civil wars, retired from the Army in August, 1871, and served as governor of California from 1883–87, a progressive, if controversial, executive.—Cullum, *Biographical Register*.

VIII

Crook Takes Over

CROOK ARRIVED in the unprepossessing, sun-baked, adobe village of Tucson in late June, 1871, accompanied by his aide, Captain Azor H. Nickerson,[1] and Archie McIntosh,[2] his noted half-blood scout, and called at once on Governor Safford, giving him no hint, no doubt, how he hated his new assignment and the embarrassment it was for him. As was his custom he probably listened intently at lunch while the governor supplied the white Arizonan's version of the Camp Grant incident. Certain it is that Crook left Tucson convinced that the citizens had acted, if injudiciously, at least with provocation, and by that time he had developed an intense dislike for Lieutenant Whitman, whom he had not as yet met.[3]

[1] Nickerson, a volunteer officer who remained in the Army after the Civil War, met Crook aboard ship when both were returning to the West. Crook arranged his transfer to his own regiment, whence he joined his staff. Crook once wrote that Nickerson "was wounded 4 times & in the battles of Antietam and Gettysburg was left for dead & his recovery was regarded as almost a miracle. He has now a hole in his chest which you can nearly stick your fist in, & in consequence his health is delicate & at times he suffers terribly from this wound. Notwithstanding all this, his ambition & zeal to do his duty has been . . . great . . . "—Crook to Rutherford B. Hayes, 4 January, 1871. This letter is in the Rutherford B. Hayes Memorial Library of Fremont, Ohio, which has a large collection of Crook documents. Its director, Mr. Watt P. Marchman, has generously given me access to them. Hereafter cited as Hayes Collection.

[2] Archie McIntosh, one of Crook's favorite scouts, had already made his mark in the Northwest, and would also become distinguished in Arizona. For details of his life see Dan L. Thrapp, *Al Sieber, Chief of Scouts*, 88–89n. See also Juana Fraser Lyon, "An Apache Branch of Clan MacIntosh," in *Clan Chattan*, Vol. IV, No. 2 (January, 1960), 15–18.

[3] Whitman, Crook wrote, "had deserted his colors and gone over to the 'Indian Ring' bag and baggage."—*General George Crook: His Autobiography*, 2nd ed., 170. (Hereafter cited as Crook, *Autobiography*.) It is difficult to explain this attitude, since no record now exists of any conversation between the two, although

Upon his arrival orders went out to every officer in southern Arizona to report as soon as possible to the new commander. "From each he soon extracted all he knew about the country, the lines of travel, the trails across the various mountains, the fords . . . the nature of the soil, especially its products, such as grasses, character of the climate, the condition of the pack-mules, and all pertaining to them, and every other item of interest a commander could possibly want to have determined. But in reply not one word, not one glance, not one hint, as to what he was going to do or what he would like to do."[4] Virile, tireless, and intrepid, Crook loved backwoods life and became "more of an Indian than the Indian himself" except in cruelty. Bourke wrote: "There never was an officer in our military service so completely in accord with all the ideas, views, and opinions of the savages whom he had to fight or control as was General Crook. In time of campaign this knowledge placed him . . . in the secret councils of the enemy; in time of peace it enabled him all the more completely to appreciate the doubts and misgivings of the Indians at the outset of a new life, and to devise plans by which they could all the more readily be brought to see that civilization was something which all could embrace without fear of extinction."[5] Yet Crook was never coarsened by his liking for wilderness life. Literate, courteous, abstemious to an unusual degree, never profane or vulgar, considerate of his junior officers while ready to disagree with his superiors, Crook was supremely duty conscious while so averse to ostentation that he rarely even wore the uniform he so thoroughly graced. The *Miner* once told how he was persuaded to have his picture taken and appeared at the studio with a brigadier-general's dress coat rolled up in a bundle. Once the operation was concluded, he hastily slipped it off and folded it away out of sight again.[6]

---

something of the sort must have occurred. It might also be mentioned that Crook's tolerance of the citizens who had perpetrated the massacre paid off, although he did not of course adopt it with that end in view. But long afterward, during his second tour of duty in Arizona, when Crook had come under heavy fire for conditions not of his making, Oury and others who had been involved in the Camp Grant business, came publicly to his support.

4 Bourke, *Border*, 108–109.   5 *Ibid.*, 108–13.   6 *Miner*, March 6, 1874.

From the outset Crook was convinced the Apaches were never
going to be conquered by troops alone, nor by the civilians, nor even
by some combination of troops and civilians. They would have to be
beaten by their own people. The problem was how to bring this about.
He was open-minded enough to try any solution seeming to offer
even the remotest hope of success, and in pursuance of such courses he
sometimes made mistakes. If Albert Banta is to be relied upon, Crook
commissioned him to raise fifty Navaho scouts. Banta said he went to
Fort Defiance to do so, but was put off by the agent and nothing came
of it.[7] It was just as well. On occasion attempts were made to use
Navahos in operations against the Apaches, but never with much
success. They were useful as trackers, but would not close with their
feared cousins; when battle seemed imminent they found some excuse to make medicine until the danger had passed.

In another case, Crook believed Safford and others who suggested
that the "Mexicans were the solution of the 'Apache Problem,' that
they knew the country, the habits and mode of Indian warfare, that
with a little pinole and dried beef they could travel all over the
country without pack mules to carry their provisions, that with ten
days' rations on their backs they could march over the roughest
country at the rate of thirty to fifty miles per day, that they could go
inside an Apache and turn him wrong side out in no time at all, [and]
I hired fifty of their people for scouts."[8] After a short, unsatisfactory
test, he fired them and never used Mexicans again, except individuals
as scouts, even when operating far below the border. It would take
Apache scouts, led by such extraordinary men as McIntosh, Al Sieber,
Joe Felmer, and others like them, to do the job.

[7] Banta, letter to editor of *Arizona Enterprise*, Florence, where it appeared on
May 26, 1892. He had evidently forgotten the incident when he recounted his meeting with Crook in his autobiography; see *Albert Franklin Banta: Arizona Pioneer*,
57–58. Banta, born in Warwick County, Indiana, December 18, 1843, came to
Arizona in 1863, and filled many frontier positions, among others as a self-anointed
oracle on Arizona history. He came to believe he had been a key figure in Crook's
early successes, although a search of the records fails to demonstrate that he had any
part in them whatever. He died at Prescott June 21, 1924.

[8] Crook, *Autobiography*, 163.

Crook selected two of the young officers he interviewed to serve as aides de camp: Lieutenant William J. Ross, a hard-bitten, pleasure-loving, fighting Scotsman,[9] and Lieutenant John Gregory Bourke.[10] On July 11, with Troops B, D, F, H, and L, Third Cavalry, some two hundred men in all, Crook left Camp Lowell and began his first reconnaissance of Apacheria. He arrived at Camp Bowie, near Apache Pass between the Dos Cabezas and Chiricahua Mountains, three days later. The command left Bowie after dusk on the seventeenth, so as not to alert any Indians who might be spying out the place, and camped just southwest of the Dos Cabezas,[11] continued on the next day and found "plenty of Indian signs" which Crook hoped had been left by Cochise, the Apache above all others he hoped to catch. He saw a dust far down the Sulphur Springs Valley and sent Captain Moore, the officer who had sought to avenge Cushing, to a spring in the low range between the Dos Cabezas and Pinaleno Mountains, figuring, correctly, that the Apaches would make for it. Moore, instead of going directly to the spring, where he might have ambushed the Indians, marched in plain view out onto the flats—to cut their trail, so he said; the Apaches, a raiding party returning from Mexico, saw him of course and took flight.

"We thus lost one of the prettiest chances of giving the enemy a severe blow," grumbled Crook, who also became convinced that Moore "lacked one of the most essential qualities of a soldier"—

[9] Ross served in the Civil War and in Arizona, but after Crook was transferred out of the territory he resigned. He did some bookkeeping for various mining camps and once tried, and failed, to secure appointment as Indian commissioner. He died at Tucson July 28, 1907.—Correspondence with Mr. Louis Menager of Tucson, Ross's stepson.

[10] Bourke was born at Philadelphia June 23, 1846, and ran away from home to serve in the Civil War, then went to West Point. He served as aide to Crook for fifteen years and was his Boswell. A wise, witty, urbane man, of a scientific turn of mind, his ethnological writings were published in various journals and had much merit. He died at Philadelphia at fifty on June 8, 1896.—*Dictionary of American Biography.*

[11] In his *Autobiography* Crook says "southeast," but from his contemporary report makes it plain it was southwest.

courage.[12] But there was no help for it. "I saw it was useless running down the horses and men trying to catch them," Crook wrote, so he made for Camp Grant, establishing a bivouac thirty miles up the Aravaipa where there was good grass, water, and wood. Finding no Indians in the immediate vicinity, Crook led his command out of the canyon, probably along the northeastern face of the Pinalenos and Santa Teresa Mountains, to the Gila, down it to the San Carlos and up that river to near the source of its western branch (probably meaning the Blue River), where a band of friendly Apaches was met. Crook struck the Salt below the junction of the White and Black rivers and made directly for Camp Apache, arriving there on August 12. Here he found rancherias of tame Apaches, mostly of the Coyotero and White Mountain peoples, and had long conversations with Capitan Chiquito, who had fled with his company to the lofty mountains after escaping the Camp Grant Massacre, with Pedro, and with Miguel.[13] "I had many long talks" with these Indians, whose bands numbered some five hundred individuals in all, Crook wrote, "and finally got them to join in my plans for subduing the hostiles, which was for them to enlist as scouts and act in conjunction with our troops." One of the first to be enlisted was a young Apache named Noch-ay-del-klinne, who figured in a prominent incident a decade later. Crook regarded their agreeing to the plan as "really the entering wedge in solution of this Apache question." He told them that the scouts would be enrolled as soldiers, receive a soldier's pay and allowances, and observed that there would be a two-fold advantage: use of the Apaches as scouts, and the opportunity to convince the Indians of the benefits of being friends of the whites.

While engaged in these long conversations, Crook noted three

[12] In 1876 during a Sioux campaign Crook again became convinced Moore had misbehaved in the presence of the enemy and had him court-martialed; he was found guilty of "neglect of duty."—*Autobiography*, 192n. Yet Moore had a good combat record in the Civil War. He resigned from the service August 10, 1879, no doubt as result of the court-martial.—Heitman, *Register and Dictionary*, 721.

[13] In his *Autobiography*, 166, Crook refers to this Indian as "Old One-Eyed McGill," but in his report at the time as Miguel.

Mexicans and three Indians ride into camp with a letter from Indian Agent O. F. Piper, of Cañada Alamosa, New Mexico, stating that the party was out to bring in the dreaded Cochise.[14] But, Crook observed, "as two of this party were recognized by several as being Cochise's worst men ... I felt very suspicious they were there in the capacity of spies." However, he continued, there was little of importance they could find out and, besides, he didn't want to interfere with the "Peace Department," that is, the Department of the Interior, so he did nothing about them.

At Camp Apache he organized an expedition composed of three companies of the Third Cavalry commanded by Captain Guy V. Henry, plus the Mexican scouts and some newly enlisted Indians. The command was to scout the country toward McDowell[15] fighting any hostiles they might encounter, and thoroughly testing the capabilities of the Apache scouts. The expedition was a success. Henry reported the combination of Indian and soldier exceeded "his most sanguine expectations; that the Indians were invaluable, and that they enabled him to kill 7 warriors and take 11 women prisoners, under the most unfavorable circumstances."[16] Crook had demonstrated his solution to the Apache problem.

But while this success was in course, Crook continued his survey of the country. With two troops, B and L, he left August 15, probably by way of the north fork of the White River, up past the camps of friendly Apaches busy tending their corn fields, and gained the Mogollon Plateau somewhere northwest of present-day McNary. He took no guide but Archie who, of course, didn't know the country,

[14] This party included Loco, one of the most famous and able of Apache war chiefs, and a Señor Trojero (Trujillo), according to Colyer. The expedition failed, he wrote, "owing to Trojero's having fallen in with General Crook ... and being, as he said, ordered back and forbidden to pursue his errand further."—Colyer, *Report*, 10. This report indicates that the expedition was sent out officially, and was not, as Crook suspected, a party of spies.

[15] McDowell was on the west bank of the Verde River, seven miles above its junction with the Salt. It was founded September 7, 1865. Little remains of it today save the headquarters building and scattered remains.

[16] Crook's *Annual Report* for 1871, Letterbook I, no. 3, pp. 6–9.—Hayes Collection.

having been assured of a plain trail all the way, but found this "pretty much of a delusion." The trail was dim and soon disappeared. The plateau was cut by ridges and cross canyons, some deep and difficult to negotiate. Water occasionally was hard to find. Once only a cloud burst saved the party from a waterless night after a hot, weary day. It was quite a storm, Crook remembered: "The rain came down in torrents. . . . The thunder and lightning were terrific. Trees were crashed to splinters not far from us. Judging from appearances, this country was subject to such storms very frequently, as in places there were acres where most of the trees had been struck by lightning at some time or other. I saw where some trees over 150 feet high had been smashed into fine splinters clear to the ground."[17] The night after the great storm the command found a trail leading them to "a nice spring of delicious water in a little bottom covered with grass," a place named General Springs, after Crook.[18]

Shortly after leaving General Springs the command had its only brush with Apaches. General Crook, Bourke, Thomas Moore, the packmaster, Lieutenant Ross, and Captain Thomas Lee Brent were in advance of the column when a shower of arrows fell upon them from a small party of Tontos, which fled, leaving two of their number poised on the rim of the plateau, "their bows drawn to a semi-circle, eyes gleaming with a snaky black fire, long unkempt hair flowing down over their shoulders, bodies almost completely naked, faces streaked with the juice of the baked mescal and the blood of deer or antelope—a most repulsive picture and yet one in which there was not the slightest suggestion of cowardice." The Indians fired their arrows and disappeared over the edge of the precipice. The whites rushed to see what had become of them and when they spied the savages nimbly leaping down "the merest thread of a trail," Crook fired, wounding one, though both ultimately escaped.[19] Crook's group traveled one more day by compass through the timber and struck the

---

[17] Crook, *Autobiography*, 166.

[18] It marked the site of the later Battle of Big Dry Wash, the last real engagement between hostiles and regulars within Arizona.

[19] Bourke, *Border*, 146–48.

so-called Stoneman Road from the Little Colorado to Camp Verde.[20] In two more days they reached the post and went into camp four miles above it on the Verde River. The route the general had blazed between Apache and Verde became known as Crook's Trail, and two years later he had troops make a formal route of it, though the first wagons did not go over it for another year.[21]

The officer arrived at Verde with a good notion of the general geography of the country and the specific topography of some of it. He now planned five expeditions outfitted like Henry's, with Apache scouts assigned to each, to operate without cessation until the hostiles, whom he estimated at some five to seven hundred warriors, were either driven in or destroyed. But he found himself suddenly forestalled, and his plans held up. "On my arrival at Verde I saw by newspaper accounts that I had been ordered to suspend all operations until the Peace Commissioners visited these Indians," he wrote the adjutant general. So he marched on to Whipple "to await further developments."

In 1867 a Board of Peace Commissioners for the management of Indian affairs had been named at Washington and became permanent in 1869, with the warm support of Grant and other prominent citizens. The movement, designed to protect the Indian from abuses, as well as curb his tendency toward hostility, resulted in "great good throughout the Indian country." Yet in the theory that "the Arizona Apaches could be subdued by kindness or influenced by other motives than those of fear and self-interest, the new 'peace policy' was a sad mistake." The Board had helped in the establishment of several temporary reservations under Stoneman's command, and it now determined to send Vincent Colyer, secretary of the Board, "with full powers to settle the Apache question."[22]

[20] Founded in 1864, Verde was on the east bank of the Verde from its establishment until 1871, when it was moved across the river to the present site of the town of Camp Verde. For many years it was an important Apache-fighting post. It was abandoned in 1890.—Ray Brandes, *Frontier Military Posts of Arizona*, 70–73.

[21] Martha Summerhayes, *Vanished Arizona*, 79–90, graphically describes a wagon train's passage over this route.

[22] The foregoing is from Bancroft, *Arizona and New Mexico*, 560–62. Bancroft

Colyer, who had conferred with some Apache chiefs at Fort Defiance in 1869, returned to the Southwest in 1871 and, after arranging for a reservation for the Warm Springs Apaches in New Mexico, arrived at Camp Apache September 2. He was "received very kindly by Colonel [John] Green"[23] and found, to his "great relief," that Crook had canceled his order to enlist Apaches as scouts.[24] The commissioner conferred with Miguel, Pedro, and other important Apaches, using Corydon E. Cooley[25] as interpreter, designated the surrounding area an Apache reservation, and journeyed to Grant, where he arrived September 13, being "hospitably received" by Lieutenant Whitman and Captain William Nelson, commanding the post to which peaceably-inclined Indians continued to come in. But here Colyer's plans were all but upset by the descent upon the place of about two hundred "armed white citizens from Tucson," who may have intended to re-enact the massacre of a short time previously, or perhaps intended merely to overwhelm the peace commissioner with the militant sentiment of Arizonans toward the Apaches and their

shared the general consensus that Colyer was an "ultra-fanatic," an opinion that was, I think, too harsh. Colyer, born in New York City, September 30, 1824, became an accomplished and highly paid artist. A man of high moral standards, however, he threw aside his career during the Civil War and became colonel of a Negro regiment he had raised. He held many benevolent positions. Under Grant he served as Indian commissioner, visiting Alaska as well as the Southwest. "His character was as noble as his disposition was amiable." He died at Rowayton, Connecticut, July 12, 1888.—*The National Cyclopedia of American Biography*, VII, 541.

[23] German-born John Green served throughout the Mexican and Civil Wars. He subsequently won a Medal of Honor and a brevet rank as brigadier general for heroism in the Modoc Indian war in California. He died in 1908, aged eighty-three. —*Who Was Who*.

[24] Colyer, *Report*, 11.

[25] Cooley, born in Loudoun County, Virginia, April 2, 1836, served with New Mexico forces in the Civil War and came to Arizona as a prospector, marrying two Apache girls simultaneously, it is said, the daughters of Chief Pedro. One soon died, leaving him a monogamist. One of the great figures of the Southwest frontier, he established a ranch at the present site of McNary which was a popular stopping-off place for Army officers and others. He was a noted scout. He died March 18, 1917, and was buried at Fort Apache. He figures prominently in literature of the period. See H. B. Wharfield, *Cooley: Army Scout, Arizona Pioneer, Wayside Host, Apache Friend*.

general contempt for his mission. Whitman and several soldiers dispersed the mission, or whatever it was. The incident resulted in more abuse for Whitman and a rebuke for Nelson from Crook who, from his Fort Whipple headquarters, asserted "Your action in this matter was unwarrantable." Again, Crook's action is inexplicable. From the vantage point of nearly a century later it appears that Nelson had acted with prudence and good judgment, and in accordance with instructions to provide the fullest co-operation with the Colyer mission.

Eskiminzin and Capitan Chiquito, with other survivors of the massacre, took part in councils at Grant, where it was arranged that Whitman, for whom the Indians had deep affection, would remain in charge and a formal reservation established. The Colyer party then moved on to Verde, via the Pima villages and McDowell, where the leader again talked to noted Indians. At Verde the natives were found near starvation, the chief having to be given food and stimulants before he was strong enough to take part in the discussions. "Danger from the whites, ineffective arms for the chase and a general scarcity of game were responsible for the deplorable state to which the band had fallen."[26] A reservation was established for these Apache-Mohaves, and Colyer moved on to Whipple where, for the first time, he interviewed General Crook, who cordially received him.[27] Differences of opinion arose, but Colyer thought most of them were ironed out, and he accepted some of Crook's suggestions in Indian matters.

John Marion, editor of the *Miner*, and other Prescott citizens, urged Colyer to address a public meeting, but he declined, using the opportunity for confronting the pugnacious newspaperman with clippings from the *Miner* in which it had referred to the peace commissioner as a "cold-blooded scoundrel," "red-handed assassin," and a "treacherous, black-hearted dog," among other things. Marion laughed them off and Colyer thought he and the editor, whom he referred to as Merriam, had parted "pretty good friends," but was disabused three days later when the *Miner* assailed him "worse than

[26] Ogle, *Western Apaches*, 93.   [27] Colyer, *Report*, 28.

ever." Shortly he departed for San Francisco, "followed by the curses of Arizonans, but fully convinced that the Apache question was settled."[28]

He arrived back in Washington October 27. He had approved or selected temporary reservations at Apache, Grant, McDowell, Verde, Date Creek, and Beale Springs. In so doing he had established a reservation pattern that would be heavily used by Crook and others.

Yet scarcely had Colyer concluded his busy conferences with Indians and soldiers, than there occurred a tragedy that again shocked the frontier and had lasting repercussions. Known as the Loring, or Wickenburg, Massacre, it took place eight miles west of that mining camp when a stagecoach, with eight passengers, was beset early on November 5, 1871. Six persons were killed outright and another died of wounds. Among the slain were three members of the Lieutenant George M. Wheeler surveying expedition, including Frederick W. Loring of Massachusetts, a young writer of some promise. There was some confusion initially over who had perpetrated the attack, although Indians finally were blamed and, apparently, justifiably. At the outset many thought it was the work of Mexican or white ruffians. Because of this uncertainty, Captain Charles Meinhold was hurried from Camp Date Creek to investigate the tragedy. His report, dated November 9, was addressed to the post adjutant.[29] Its net conclusion was that the tragedy was the work of Indians, probably from Date Creek, and belonging to "the main group of nearly one thousand tribesmen who were being fed" there. When this became generally known, the peace commissioners lost out and a war group got the upper hand. Crook, delighted to hear of the "decapitation" of "Vincent the Good," and fearful lest others "pop up in his place," was eager to get on with his planned campaign, and confident of its entire success.[30] He wrote the adjutant general:

> In my judgment, if these Indians dont soon break out in open hostilities, they will do what is much worse, that is, while their old

[28] Bancroft, *Arizona and New Mexico*, 562.

[29] Indian Bureau, Letters Received, Arizona Superintendency, 1871.

[30] Crook to Rutherford B. Hayes, November 28, 1871.—Hayes Collection.

and decrepit women and children (who are their only encumbrances in the shape of baggage) are living protected and supplied on the reservations, the warriors will with impunity, keep up their bloody work, and when followed, will glide over the rocks and mountains like birds and make their subjugation or punishment next thing to an impossibility. It may not be out of place for me to add . . . if this entire Indian question be left to me . . . I have not the slightest doubt of my ability to conquer a lasting peace with this Apache race in a comparatively short space of time, and a peace which will not only save the Treasury millions of dollars, but will save the lives of a good many innocent whites and Indians.[31]

Once again Crook readied his command. He resumed conditioning of the pack trains, which were his special interest and concern, making them the best in the nation and setting an enduring pattern for the Army as a whole.[32] He selected animals of the proper size, weight, and conformation. He got rid of cruel, drunken, or incompetent packers. He overhauled the equipment, insisting on each mule's being fitted with its own rig, tailored to the individual animal's form to minimize sore backs, and he demanded proper care of the mules.

Crook intensified preparations for a general attack on the hostiles, and in December sent word to the bands that they must be on the reservations by mid-February, to escape chastisement. Hundreds rushed in, to spend the winter fattening on reservation rations and, it was freely rumored, caching supplies and ammunition in preparation for the hostilities they would welcome in the spring.[33] On February 7 Crook announced that after nine more days any Apache still out would be considered an enemy and received only as a prisoner of war. But he was not to carry out this threat, for once more the peace elements at Washington had triumphed. Almost on the very day of hostilities, Washington ordered their avoidance, and informed Crook,

[31] Letterbook I, No. 2, pp. 4–6.—Hayes Collection.

[32] Crook's excellent work in this respect was visible in the Army pack organizations as long as the Army had them. Even so late as World War II, pack troops and companies were used in Burma, China, New Guinea, and elsewhere, and Crook's standards were still in use as this writer, a pack officer during that war, can attest.

[33] Ogle, *Western Apaches*, 102.

via Major General John M. Schofield, commander of the Department of the Pacific, that a new agent of the Department of the Interior would shortly be sent out "to co-operate with the military" in preserving peace.[34]

President Grant fully realized the shortcomings of Colyer, earnest and intelligent enough but afflicted with myopia with respect to some features of the white-Apache problem, so in a new attempt at a viable solution the president and others sent a man of prominence and undoubted competence into the field. The man they selected was Brigadier General Oliver Otis Howard, a fighting Army officer with a good combat record, a Christian who worked at his faith, and a specialist in the field of human relations.[35] Yet tough frontier officers and hardened westerners found Howard's sanctimoniousness, or what they took for that, hard to swallow. To further complicate matters, Howard inadvertently took up the cudgels for Whitman, thereby infuriating Crook who had the controversial lieutenant under arrest awaiting a second—or was it the third?—court-martial for misconduct. The charges were old ones, and seem, upon scanning them today, more funny than serious. But they suggest that there were powers in the Department, to whom Crook lent his support, determined to do away with Whitman at any cost, particularly since he still had influence with the Apaches.

Whitman had been tried December 4, 1871, on two charges and eight specifications, most stemming from the rousing time the young officer had had in the course of arriving at his new post in desolate Arizona. The first charge, of "Conduct unbecoming an officer and gentleman," was a familiar old catchall, still used by ranking officers who desire to chastise their juniors but haven't much to go on. Its specifications in this case included: that Whitman, in uniform, was drunk at the Horton House, a San Diego hotel, on November 5,

[34] *Ibid.*, 103.

[35] Howard was born November 8, 1830, at Leeds, Maine, and was graduated from West Point in 1854. He rose to brevet rank of major general in the Civil War and afterward was commissioner of the Bureau of Refugees, Freedmen, and Abandoned Lands. He was instrumental in founding Howard University. He died October 26, 1909, at his Vermont home.—*Dictionary of American Biography*.

1870, while en route for Arizona; that he was drunk at Point of Mountain, a stage station about eighteen miles northwest of Tucson, on November 24; that he called for drinks for the house at the James H. Toole saloon, Tucson, on December 1, and then didn't pay for them; that on the same day Whitman "did lay drunk in a public saloon," which might explain why he didn't pay for the drinks; that on the same day his fellow officers refused to associate with him because he was too drunk; that at a picnic near Tucson on August 30, 1871, Whitman "did attempt to seat himself in a woman's lap . . . to the scandal of the service of the United States"; and that on September 1 he was still drunk, passed out in the back yard of Lord & Williams, at Tucson. The second charge, of "Conduct to the prejudice of good order and military discipline," contained a single specification: that Whitman, in connection with the September 1, 1871, incident, "being a disbursing officer," sat in on a card game and made bets.[36]

It will be seen that there is nothing very serious in these various charges. On the way to Arizona, which Whitman and his fellow officers must have imagined to be the end of the world, they, or at least he, drank too much, and he did it again a year later at a Tucson public picnic. That is the sum and substance of the charges; they might have been leveled at almost any officer on frontier service, and it would be a mystery why Crook sought to make anything of them except on the basis that he had lent his ear too readily to the Tucson crowd headed by the *Citizen* and Oury. The court accepted Whitman's plea "in bar of trial," and threw the case out, which angered Crook even more. It sustained Whitman's argument that the charges were cumulative, and that they originated with "a citizen Editor of a disloyal paper, abusive of the Army and its officers, influenced by malice."[37]

Crook, in formally disapproving the action of the court, reasoned

[36] *Miner*, January 13, 1872.

[37] John Wasson was editor of the *Citizen* at this time; the paper had been started in 1870. Born in Ohio in 1833, Wasson remained at Tucson a dozen years and died at Pomona, California, in 1909.—Estelle Lutrell, *Newspapers and Periodicals of Arizona 1859–1911*, 100.

108

that it was logical to accumulate counts, "in themselves trifling," as he admitted, but which might together support the charge. In the second place, Crook suggested with reason that it would be more proper to go ahead and prove in court the malice and bad character of the prosecution. Even these, if proven, "in no manner [can] affect the truth or falsity of the charges themselves, which must stand on their own merits." By failing to try Whitman, Crook believed, the court had placed him "in a worse light than he had before occupied," and the court should have gone ahead "so that, if innocent, his honor might be vindicated, and if guilty the service be rid of an unworthy officer."[38]

Whitman was arrested again March 12 and held for another court-martial, this time on order of General Schofield (no doubt at Crook's instigation), charged with disobedience of certain orders. Upon Howard's insistence, he was released from incarceration at Crittenden and met Howard at Camp Grant, where the general had hurried from McDowell in late April, 1872. The Indians there were restive, it was reported, largely because Whitman had been taken from them.[39] Crook accompanied Howard to Grant, and was irritated anew when the envoy, as his first order of business, it seemed to Crook, began "to parade up and down the garrison, arm in arm with Whitman."

What Howard may not have known was that Crook personally was pressing charges against Whitman, and what Crook did not know was that Howard and Whitman were old friends, in fact, relatives by marriage. Their birthplaces were scarcely a dozen miles apart by county road, and there was only a scant three years difference in their ages. Howard had married Elizabeth Ann Waite, a relative of Whitman's first wife.[40] Both Howard and Whitman were intellectually inclined, both were interested in the Indians from a human viewpoint, and so they naturally had much in common. Thus, despite the fact that one was a first lieutenant and the other a brigadier general,

[38] *Miner*, January 13, 1872.
[39] Ogle, *Western Apaches*, 104.
[40] Mrs. Andrew C. McAuliffe, to author, March 23, 1960.

there was nothing out of the way in their "parading arm in arm" while earnestly chatting, but Crook took it as a personal insult. He called Howard on it that evening and so upset the visiting officer that "he could not go to sleep until he found relief in prayer at about three o'clock in the morning."[41]

Whitman was no sentimentalist. He did not share Howard's religious convictions, or at least not to the same degree, and he could even make light of the general's approach. The Indians, he told an acquaintance years later, in describing the Grant meeting,

> . . . were all ready for a council, and I went out with General Howard to the place appointed, and when we got out of the ambulance, and there were the chiefs, all solemnly seated and ready for the talk. He went toward them, and when he came within speaking distance, what do you suppose he did? He got down on his knees and began to pray— out loud! In two minutes there wasn't an Indian to be seen. They scattered just like partridges when they see a hawk. After awhile I caught sight of the old chief [Eskiminzin] peeking 'round the corner of a building and beckoning to me. I went to see what he wanted, and his eyes were fairly blazing. He wanted to know if I'd turned traitor, too!
>
> What did I mean by bringing that man there, to make bad medicine against them? . . . What did I say to him? . . . I burst out laughing in his face. Then I said, "Why, that doesn't mean anything. He always does that when he begins any sort of undertaking—just as you spit on your hands when you go to draw your bow!" . . . Well, in course of time they came back, and met Howard, and the talks was had, and everything went off all right.
>
> Then Howard thought he'd done a pretty good job and he might as well see if he couldn't get a little appreciation. He said to old Eskiminzin, "Now, I think you know that I want to do well by you, and am your friend; could not I come into your lodges at any time— even when you are on the war-path?" You know how wooden an Indian's face can look. Eskiminzin answered perfectly unmoved, "Not unless you want to get killed." Howard was somewhat taken aback at that. "But," he said, "could any white man do it?"

[41] Crook, *Autobiography*, pp. 170–73.

Eskiminzin turned to me—I was in disgrace, you understand, at the time. "Yes," he said, "so long as there is a man, woman or child in the Apache nation who remembers the Camp Grant Massacre, so long *that* man can come among us, by day or night, in war or in peace, and not a hair of his head shall be harmed!" I ask you, wasn't that a rather fine tribute, from an Indian who had had the experience he had?[42]

Howard mollified Crook to some extent by formally agreeing with the Department commander that force was the only recourse in dealing with incorrigible hostiles, and that he should use Apaches to fight Apaches in applying such force.[43] Howard's "peace theories [were] strongly tinged with common sense," according to Bancroft.[44] He consulted whites as well as Indians, and developed some valuable areas of agreement. He made treaties between some Apaches and their Pima and Papago enemies; moved the Camp Grant reserve northward to the Gila, renaming it San Carlos; and, on a second trip to Arizona, late in the summer of 1872, abolished the Colyer reserves at McDowell, Date Creek, and Beale Springs, permitting the Indians to select homes at other reservations. An executive order of December 14, 1872, formally established the San Carlos and the White Mountain, or Fort Apache, reservations.

[42] This is from a typewritten document in the New York Public Library, Acquisition No. 270128A, originating with a Miss L. Lamprey, being received by the Library probably in 1925. She explains: "During my residence in Washington, D.C., from 1892–1904, I came to know Colonel and Mrs. Whitman very well, through my attendance at the Unitarian Church, where the Colonel was one of the founders of the Unity study class. . . . He was then 60 years old. . . . At the time of my acquaintance with him [he] was living in Washington on his pension, and I think he was about the last type of man that anybody who knew him would conceivably regard as a liar. He was quite as frank about anything to his own detriment as he was in stating facts to the detriment of any one else, and decidedly scrupulous in matters of justice and fair dealing even with most insignificant persons. In the matter of these Indians, he felt at the time, and always afterward, that he could not have betrayed their trust in him without losing all respect for himself." Whitman told Miss Lamprey that he was court-martialed three times on account of his pro-Indian stand "and then was not entirely cleared," which was correct.

[43] Ogle, *Western Apaches*, 105.

[44] Bancroft, *Arizona and New Mexico*, 564.

Howard's second mission to Apacheria was aimed specifically at getting some sort of agreement with Cochise, the implacably hostile chief of the Chiricahuas whom white errors had made a blood enemy of the race. In this assignment, Howard was startlingly successful, although the agreement contained a fatal flaw that led to immense bloodshed and expense and war over a period of fifteen more years.

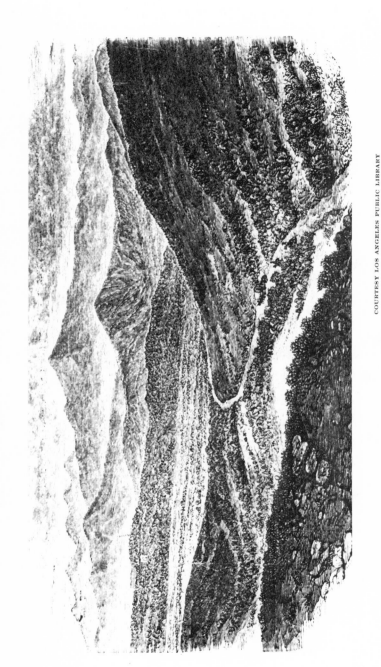

Apache Pass, eastern approaches, complete with emigrant wagon, in the mid-nineteenth century, as pictured by Samuel W. Cozzens in *The Marvellous Country*.

A shaft of sunlight, piercing storm clouds, whitens the ruins of old Fort Bowie until they resemble tombstones in some neglected graveyard. Beyond the ruins, about at the near-edge of the cloud shadow in the right distance, lies Apache Pass and the road through it.

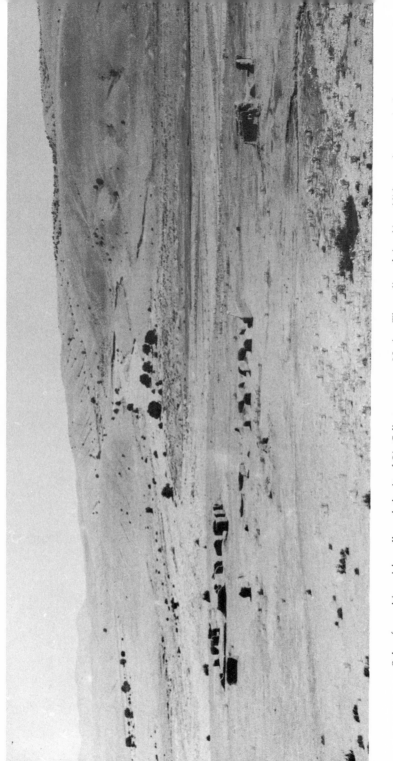

Only a few melting adobe walls mark the site of Ojo Caliente, once the focus for the Warm Springs Apaches in south-central New Mexico. The outline of the old establishment, however, is clear, with the administration building to extreme left.

Stein's Peak, New Mexico, at whose foot lies Doubtful Canyon Pass through the Stein's Peak Range, is now off the beaten path, but once was an important landmark for marauding Apaches and military operations.

Fort Whipple, 1864, one of the few stockaded forts in the West, as pictured in Edmund Wells' *Argonaut Tales*.

Salt River Cave, where the gorge of the Salt River cuts into the southern reaches of the Mazatzal Mountains, was the scene of a bloody battle in late 1872.

The summit of Turret Mountain, center, middle distance, in central Arizona, where some two score Apaches were killed in late March, 1873, in a fight climaxing Crook's first Apacheria offensive.

The only known photograph of Howard Bass Cushing, showing him in Civil War artillery uniform. In 1915 a monument (above, left) was raised at the Cushing Memorial Park, Delafield, Wisconsin, to the three Cushing brothers. The plaque reads as shown below.

ALONZO H.
BORN 1841 - DIED 1863
BREVET LIEUTENANT
COLONEL
FOURTH U.S. ARTILLERY

WILLIAM B.
BORN 1842 - DIED 1874
COMMANDER
U. S. NAVY

HOWARD B.
BORN 1838 - DIED 1871
FIRST LIEUTENANT
THIRD
U. S. CAVALRY

"PERHAPS THE MOST CONSPICUOUSLY DARING TRIO OF SONS
OF ONE MOTHER OF ANY WHOSE EXPLOITS HAVE BEEN
NOTED IN THE PAGES OF HISTORY"

Above: Cochise, Chiricahua Apache leader, mid-nineteenth century, as pictured by Samuel W. Cozzens in *The Marvellous Country*. Courtesy Los Angeles Public Library.

Left: General Oliver Otis Howard, who in the fall of 1872 visited Cochise and sought peace with the Chiricahua Apaches. Courtesy National Archives.

Major General George Crook assumed command of the Department of Arizona in June, 1871, for four years; he again commanded it from 1882–86.

William J. Ross, Crook's aide, was a leader in the Salt River Cave fight; later he tried unsuccessfully to fight Apaches with civilians.

Guy V. Henry, who led the first important scout under Crook's command, later won the Medal of Honor in the 1876 Rosebud fight against the Sioux.

Albert E. Woodson, who fought Apaches in Arizona as a Fifth Cavalry lieutenant, later commanded the Third Cavalry and became a brigadier general.

The Arizona *Star* of Tucson reprints the Mesilla *News's* sardonic editorial "from Victorio," September 16, 1880.

Loco, Warm Springs chief, one of the wisest of Apache leaders, sought peace, but was goaded by other Apaches onto the warpath, where he demonstrated his generalship.

Luis Terrazas, governor of Chihuahua and cousin of General Joaquin Terrazas, the destroyer of Victorio. As governor he directed many campaigns against the Apaches.

Only known photograph of Victorio, Warm Springs Apache leader, whose appearance is tousled because his hair band fell off as he was being held for the camera by two men.

Rare picture of Mike Burns, who was captured by Captain James Burns's command in 1872, and who later became a noted figure in Arizona and wrote of the Indian wars.

Indian Agent John P. Clum, with Diablo (left) and Eskiminzin, at San Carlos in 1875.

Eskiminzin, leader of Aravaipa Apaches, with daughter and son.

Dead Shot, hanged for his alleged part in the Cibicu affair.

John P. Clum and his Indian police from San Carlos in 1876, with Merejildo Grijalba, interpreter, at far left.

Nachez, son of Cochise, along with Geronimo led the 1885 uprising.

Peaches, who deserted Chatto's band in 1883, was Crook's guide in Mexico.

IX

Raids and Punishment

FROM SPIES he had sent among the Indians, and from other sources, Crook soon learned that the Date Creek Indians had been responsible for the Wickenburg Massacre, and he determined to punish them for that incident, as much to warn off other potential raiders as to wreak vengeance on this party itself. After an abortive attempt to confront them in March, 1872, and a long wait while Howard continued his peace missions to the territory, Crook carried out a carefully planned expedition in September that resulted in a wild brawl, perhaps seven Indians slain and several whites wounded, and the escape of many of the raiders into the wild breaks of the upper rivers in the Mohave-Walapais country. After them, late in September, he sent a Fifth Cavalry column commanded by Captain Julius Wilmot Mason, a young officer whose health was poor but whose promise was great, and with eighty-six Walapais scouts under Al Sieber.[1] The expedition was most successful, with about forty hostiles slain and prisoners and loot taken. Most important was the fact that this operation ended forever the resistance of the Indians of western Apacheria to the white man.[2] Crook and his soldiers could now turn their atten-

---

[1] Al Sieber became perhaps the most noted guide and chief of scouts in Apacheria. Born in Germany February 29, 1844, he came to this country as a boy, fought in the Civil War, and served the Army as an Arizona scout for twenty years. He was killed in 1907.—See Thrapp, *Sieber*.

[2] For details of the chain of events starting with the Wickenburg Massacre and ending with Mason's triumph, see Thrapp, *Sieber*, 90–104. See also *Miner*, September 28, 1872; Bourke, *Border*, 166–71; Crook to AAG, Division of the Pacific, September 18, 1872, Hayes Collection; Crook, *Autobiography*, 173–74; and a letter containing an eyewitness account of Mason's fight, Walter Scribner Schuyler to George Washington Schuyler, September 29, 1872, Schuyler collection, Huntington Library, San Marino, California, hereafter cited as Schuyler collection.

tion to the principal enemy, farther east. And here, indeed, there was plenty to do.

Within the single year since Vincent Colyer had entered the territory on his mission of peace, more than fifty raids and forty murders were attributed to the Apaches and other hostiles. As an example, and a sample only, of the sort of depredations plaguing civilians and the military during the torrid summer of 1872, there were these:

✠ Hostiles ran off stock from Williamson Valley ranchers in mid-May, and on the nineteenth Sergeant Rudolph Stauffer[3] of Company K, Fifth Cavalry, along with Ed Clark[4] and Dan O'Leary, led a small punitive force from Camp Hualpai. The raiders were chased one hundred and ten miles east when "considerable of a fight ensued," as Crook dryly reported. Two soldiers were wounded, four hostiles killed, and a single head of stock recovered.[5]

✠ On May 19 raiders drove off the beef contractor's herd from Camp Verde and Captain Robert P. Wilson, officer of the day, and Tracker Jose de Leon[6] chased them. One Indian was killed and thirty head of stock recovered.[7]

✠ May 22 another band of Tontos or Apache-Mohaves swept up two thousand head of sheep, stealing them within a mile and a half of Department headquarters at Fort Whipple after slaying the herder. Nickerson, then in command at Whipple, gathered what men he could and with Archie McIntosh went to the scene, arriving after dark. In a most unusual night pursuit the command followed the

[3] Stauffer was born at Berne, Switzerland, November 27, 1836, and enlisted in the cavalry in 1855, serving until 1878 and winning a Medal of Honor for gallantry. He was a typical, hard-bitten noncommissioned officer of the old cavalry, dying at the Soldiers Home, Washington, June 8, 1918, aged eighty-one.

[4] Walapais Ed Clark was born February 7, 1849, at Primrose, Wisconsin, and died at Hermosa Beach, California, February 5, 1924. He figured largely in the conquest of Apacheria as a scout.

[5] Mason to Nickerson, May 23, 1872, Indian Bureau Record Group 75, National Archives.

[6] Jose de Leon was important in early Apache campaigns. Captured by the Indians he had learned their language and was an expert tracker and guide. He was drowned during a scout in January, 1874.

[7] Captain Robert P. Wilson to Post Adjutant, Camp Verde, May 24, 1872, War Department Record Group 98, National Archives.

trail, broadly cut by eight thousand sharp hooves and made out by a young bugler with the eyes of a cat, and caught up with the raiders eighty miles east of the post. Most of the Indians escaped and $20,000 worth of sheep recovered.[8]

⚔ Early in June Indians again stole stock, mules this time, from near Prescott, and Second Lieutenant Thomas Garvey took some men, with Archie and Bill McCloud as guides, and pursued through several skirmishes to the foot of Bill Williams Mountain, then southeast again to an "immense canyon" where they found the mules, dead and being aired, had a fight, and returned to base.[9]

Not always were the soldiers triumphant. On August 27, Second Lieutenant Reid T. Stewart, twenty-two and newly arrived in the territory, and Corporal Joseph P. G. Black left Crittenden for Tucson, where Stewart was to have a role in a general court-martial. The officer, in a hurry to get there, over-ruled the corporal, a man of considerable Indian experience,[10] who urged him to await nightfall before entering Davidson's Canyon,[11] the most likely place for an ambush. Stewart and Black started off in a buckboard drawn by swift little mules, and soon left behind their escort, Corporal James Brown, four enlisted men, two invalid soldiers, and Banta, who was weakened and suffering from dysentery. By the time they reached the canyon, the lieutenant and Black were an hour ahead of the others.

[8] A. H. Nickerson, "An Apache Indian Raid, and a Long-Distance Ride," *Harper's Illustrated Weekly*, Vol. XLI, No. 2116, July 10, 1897, 693–94. Crook to AAG, Military Division of the Pacific, Indian Bureau Record Group 75, May 28, 1872; *Miner*, May 25, 1872. Cremony, *Life*, 282, wrote that sheep could be driven faster than cattle, which is difficult to believe. He said the Apaches (probably speaking of the Mescaleros) arranged stolen sheep in a parallelogram with the strongest sheep on the edges and "in this manner the Apaches will run a flock of twenty thousand sheep fifty to seventy miles in one day."

[9] Garvey to Commanding Officer, Fort Whipple, June 13, 1872, Indian Bureau Record Group 75.

[10] Black, of Company F, Fifth Cavalry, had carried the mail between Tucson and Crittenden for three years, making the trip four hundred times, according to McClintock, *Arizona*, I, 203, but passed through the dangerous part of the country at night, when Apaches would not fight.

[11] This canyon, between the Empire and Santa Rita Mountains, now holds Arizona Highway 83. It was named for a pioneer who also was killed by Apaches.— Hinton, *Handbook*, 232.

At the top of the divide the escort found the nude body of Stewart, with a bullet through his forehead, another through the body, and four lesser wounds. His clothes, gun, watch, and ring had been taken, the buckboard was upset a few yards from the road, and the mail bags, mules, and their harness were missing. So was Corporal Black. But his tracks, surrounded by those of bare feet and moccasins, showed that at the first attack he had leaped down, perhaps wounded, and run for his life. He was, unfortunately, not swift enough, and had been captured. Just beyond the bend the little escort party found a far more ghastly sight. On a hillside above the road, and in full view of it, Black was tied to a dead tree which already was afire, and even as they watched he was being tortured to death. Brown's party charged up the hill toward the scene, according to the report, but was vastly outnumbered.

When Brown saw fifteen Indians bearing down on him from another direction and three from still another, he said he was forced to abandon the attempt to rescue Black. Banta, who gives a sarcastic eyewitness version of the action, said "we could have whipped that fight easily if those dough boys had been any good," although he admitted that Brown was a cool, hardened fighter himself. The soldiers placed Stewart's body in the wagon and continued on toward Tucson, one bullet smashing through the vehicle but no one being wounded. Brown later was made sergeant and received the Medal of Honor. Black's body, when recovered, showed at least one hundred punctures where knives, lances, and firebrands had been driven into him, some perhaps before he died.[12]

That same bloody day three Mexicans were killed by Apaches only eighteen miles from Crittenden and four more Mexicans slain between the Santa Cruz and Sonoita valleys, at the foot of the Santa Ritas. "Since April last, in the little valley of the Sonoita, with a population of only about thirty, thirteen have been brutally murdered; the wounded . . . are to be seen in almost every cabin, and

[12] W. P. Hall to AGO, Washington, August 29, 1872, Indian Bureau Record File 75; L.A. Pub. Lib.; McClintock, *Arizona*, I, 203; Banta, *Arizona Pioneer*, 59–62.

destitute women and orphan children fill the land with their lamentations," mourned the *Citizen*.[13]

Crittenden, as much as Prescott, was a center for Indian depredations all during 1872, it seemed. About 11:00 A.M. on September 30 a courier reported to Second Lieutenant William Preble Hall, commanding, that Indians were even then attacking a Mr. Hugh's ranch only two miles distant. Hall mounted up a dozen men and galloped to the scene, but found the savages had fled after killing a Mexican and stealing three horses. They were then in "a strong position in the mountains, south from the ranch a mile. There appeared to be some sixty or seventy Indians, and they were very anxious for my party to attack them," he wrote in his official report. He thought the Apaches were too strong for his small party, and sent Sergeant George Stewart with five men toward other ranches, warning the citizens that hostiles were prowling the countryside. Stewart fulfilled the task, and on his return, within four miles of the post, "his party was fired upon by about fifty Indians, who were lying in a little ravine, two feet deep and not more than fifteen paces from the road; the place was very open and it would seem almost impossible for them to have been concealed in such a place."

Almost instantly Stewart and Privates Andrew Carr, William Nation, and John Walsh were killed. Private Larkin, fifty yards in the rear, wheeled his horse and fled. Bugler Kershaw, who was beside Stewart at the first fire, clapped spurs to his horse, and drove ahead with Indians whooping and shooting at him at every leap for about a quarter of a mile before he lost them. This event, concluded Hall, "and many others that have occurred during the past two months show that these Indians are as well armed as the soldiers, and are getting bolder all the time, and gaining confidence in themselves every day."[14] And he was exactly right. The *Chronological List*, which is incomplete, shows thirty-three actions involving Army per-

[13] *Citizen*, August 31, 1872.
[14] Hall to AAG, Department of Arizona, October 1, 1872, Indian Bureau Record Group 75.

sonnel and hostiles in 1872 in Apacheria up to November 15 when Crook's offensive got under way. In these at least twenty-six civilians and ten soldiers lost their lives, not counting those killed in strictly non-Army fights during the same period. Truly there was no easing of hostilities, and just as certainly Crook's counteraction was overdue.

Even the people back East were now convinced of this. Crook had been patient. He had co-operated fully with Colyer and Howard, even though in his heart he believed their missions were largely futile. Their failure had not been complete, however. Many hundreds of Indians had been placed on the various reservations they had helped establish. There remained, nonetheless, thousands of Indians who had not come on any reservation, and would not willingly do so. Most westerners and most military men, too, shared the conviction that "no warlike Indian ever submitted to reservation restrictions until he had been whipped,"[15] and to administer this beating Crook was now prepared. In his annual report for 1872 he said that "I think I am justified in saying that I have fully carried out that portion of my instructions which required me to co-operate with the agents referred to, and believe that humanity demands that I should now proceed to carry out the remainder of my instructions, which require me to punish the incorrigibly hostile."[16]

[15] Dunn, *Massacres*, 626.
[16] Crook to AAG, Division of the Pacific, September 21, 1872.—Hayes Collection.

X

The Offensive Begins

THE THIRD CAVALRY and Twenty-first Infantry had been ro-
tated out of Arizona, and the Fifth Cavalry and Twenty-third
Infantry, both veteran Indian-fighting outfits, had arrived and become settled at the sprinkling of forlorn little military posts. Crook's
pack trains were at a peak of efficiency, as were his wagon units, draft
oxen and mules, and communications network. His Indian scout companies, including Apaches, Walapais, Yavapais, or Apache-Mohaves,
Paiutes, and others, were at full strength. To such white scouts as Mc-
Intosh, Sieber, Felmer, Merejildo Grijalba, and McCloud had been
enlisted other, equally able frontiersmen: O'Leary, Jack Townsend,[1]
Gus Spear,[2] Ed Clark, Lew Ellit, Mason McCoy, down from the
Oregon country where he had served Crook's cause before, and Willard Rice.[3] As a legal basis for his offensive, Crook used his General
Orders No. 10, issued a year earlier, November 21, 1871, which said
in part that all roving bands of Indians would have to go at once to
reservations or "be regarded as hostile and punished accordingly."
Word of this order had penetrated by means of spies and captured
Indians turned loose for the purpose, to all the recessed canyons and
secluded forests of Apacheria. There was no excuse for any Indian
not to know of it.

Crook's plan was to launch preliminary columns at outlying haunts
of the savages, smash those who could be found, and so stir up and

[1] John Townsend, born July 24, 1833, in Tennessee and reared in Texas, was
a former Confederate soldier who became one of the most successful Indian killers
of central Arizona. He in turn was slain by them in September, 1873.

[2] Augustus A. Spear in later life was a rancher northeast of present-day Needles,
on the Colorado River.

[3] Rice, among the greats of the scouting trade, was born at Greensboro, Vermont,
October 22, 1832, and reached Arizona in 1863. He died at Prescott January 2, 1899.

batter the remainder that they would withdraw toward their inner sanctum, the Tonto Basin. He would then drive home enough columns to lace up completely that rough and scarcely known area, criss-crossing it with hard-fighting, highly mobile units until the enemy would be beaten. Only then would important elements of the hostiles surrender, he believed. The general would send out these columns while he himself moved incessantly from point to point around the narrowing perimeter. While leaving the tactics to his dependable junior officers, he would co-ordinate their movements. Since winter would not only minimize the problem of watering his commands, but also make it impossible for Indians whose homes and food supplies were burned to survive in the high mountains, he established D-Day as November 15, 1872. The enemy would be starved and frozen as well as fought into submission. Crook's plan was ruthless, but at the same time humane. He saw the apparent cruelty of it, and planned it that way, but made clear that only by a brutal, sledge-hammer offensive could he force the hostiles to their reservations where kind, if firm, guidance could show them the only way by which they could survive the white tide engulfing their homeland. The Indians would discover that Crook was their best friend, but they must be bloodied and broken before they came to this realization.

Crook's final instructions to his columns was terse and pointed: If the Indians could be made to surrender, accept. . . . where they prefer to fight, give them all the fighting they want, and in one good dose, instead of many petty engagements. . . . in either case hunt them down until the last hostile is killed or captured. . . . avoid killing women and children, and prisoners of either sex should not be abused in any way. . . . enlist prisoners as scouts if possible, the wilder the better, because the wild ones would know best the nature and retreats of those still out. . . . no excuse will be accepted for abandoning a trail; if the horses play out, follow the enemy afoot as long as your men can stand. . . . no sacrifice to be avoided to make the campaign short, sharp, and decisive.[4]

[4] Bourke, *Border*, 182.

November 16 three columns pushed out from Camp Hualpai, each composed of a company of cavalry and thirty to forty Indian scouts, with the mission to scour the Chino Valley, headwaters of the Verde, the vicinity of the San Francisco Mountains, and thereafter to operate out of Camp Verde. Crook also ordered organization of two columns with Date Creek Indians as scouts. Then he, Bourke, Ross, and a small escort including McCoy and probably McIntosh, left for Apache by way of the high and cold Mogollon Plateau. They left Verde November 20 and arrived at Apache the twenty-ninth, leaving there December 3 and reaching Grant the seventh. Here he organized an expedition under command of Major William H. Brown, to include Bourke and other officers and to scout along the southern edge of the Tonto Basin. "I am afraid we shall miss much of the fun as the other Comd's being in the field earlier than we, may have all the work to themselves," lamented Bourke, in his diary. He needn't have fretted.[5]

The three columns from Hualpai had varying luck. They were commanded by Captains Emil Adam, Mason, and Robert H. Montgomery, and guided by O'Leary, Clark, Spear, McCloud, and possibly Sieber. Adam, whose scouts were the Apache-hungry Paiutes, had the best luck, striking an unwary band of hostiles in the Red Rock country on the east side of the Chino Valley, killing eleven warriors and capturing three women and a child. Montgomery's command destroyed several rancherias, killed two warriors, and captured three individuals. Mason, suffering heavily from persistent rheumatism, directed the destruction of rancherias and winter supplies, but had to leave his command when it reached Verde, turning it over to First Lieutenant William F. Rice. The columns all suffered terribly from lack of water, and the Indian scouts suffered more than the troops. When they reached Verde on November 30 they were all for going home and to hell with white man's fighting, but finally agreed to stay for another fifteen days. After that the snows came, and it wasn't so bad.

[5] The original of Bourke's diary, more than 120 volumes of it, is in the library of the United States Military Academy at West Point. Much of it has been filmed

Nickerson, left in charge at Whipple and assigned to organize operations from there, McDowell, and Verde, met the columns at the latter point with new instructions that started them out after only three days to refit. He had also organized two more detachments at Verde: Captain Carr with Company I of the First Cavalry, and Lieutenant Albert E. Woodson, with Company A of the Fifth. These units, with a few Indians as scouts and with Willard Rice and Walapais Charley Jaycox as guides, were directed to help the other three scout thoroughly the Black Hills and part of the Red Rock country, the whole lying in a semicircle from northwest to southwest of Verde. To do this all five columns left Verde on December 3, this time heading westerly, Woodson on the extreme left. North of him, in succession, were Carr, Adam, Montgomery, and Rice on the extreme right. Nickerson, meanwhile, hurried back to Whipple to clean up what headquarters business had accumulated and left almost immediately for Townsend's Ranch on the Lower Agua Fria. Here he was to meet Captain George F. Price, coming in from Date Creek with E of the Fifth Cavalry and about thirty-five Date Creek Indian scouts. Price would scout easterly, and contact Woodson, thus extending the line considerably to the south; Price would scout almost as far down as McDowell. The whole vast operation, of course, was to clear the hostiles from west of the Verde, drive them east, into the Tonto country.

"If not successful in killing the Indians," reported Nickerson, the commands would "at least make them move, and keep them moving."

After instructing Price, Nickerson pushed on to Verde, where he met his five columns returning for re-rationing on December 18. All had destroyed rancherias and supplies, but only Rice had struck hos-

---

and is in the library of the University of New Mexico, where it was used by Lansing R. Bloom for a series of excerpts on the Southwest in the *New Mexico Historical Review*, Vol. VIII, No. 1 (January, 1933), intermittently through Vol. XIII, No. 2 (April, 1938), which, though it concludes with "To Be Continued," was never taken farther. For detailed information on the diary, and on Bourke himself, see Bloom's introduction to the series in Vol. VIII, No. 1, pp. 1–10. My excerpts from the diary are taken from the New Mexico file.

tiles. "The Indians on leaving the Black Hills were crossing into the Red Rock country, and not expecting anything from that direction," Nickerson wrote. "Lieutenant Rice struck them with his command as they were going into camp, killing thirteen warriors, capturing three squaws and destroying everything they found." Then, the very day that Rice's rations were exhausted, his scouts struck a large band of Indians, entrenched on a mountain, and lost a Walapais scout in trying to storm the place. He came on into Verde where Nickerson hastily had him rationed and sent him back with Carr's command and that of Woodson to re-engage the Indians, "and if they could not surprise, at least drive them out and make them move." Price meanwhile had returned to Townsend's from where he reported that he had bitten off too much. He reported "finding more country than he could cover and plenty of Indians." He captured nine women and an old man of a band that was raiding down on the Gila and in the Wickenburg country "and from whom we have since heard, as they stole a lot of stock about the same time Price captured their rancherias and squaws."

Scarcely had the commands returned to Verde when Nickerson sent them out again; they left the evening of December 23. Captains Adam and Montgomery were to operate southward in conjunction with Price. The columns under Carr, which included his own and those of Rice and Woodson, also went south, then crossed the Verde, separated and ranged through the northern Tonto Basin as far as the Mogollon Rim, returning to Verde from the east. Price, Adam, and Montgomery were also to cross the Verde as soon as they had completed their southerly scout, and work out the East Fork and Fossil Creek in time to return to Verde by January 8.[6] All of these operations were based on Verde, but they were only part of the big offensive.

Crook had found the Indians at Apache and elsewhere "a little

[6] This reconstruction of the first phase of Crook's offensive is drawn principally from his field report to the adjutant general, U.S.A., dated Camp Grant, December 13, 1872, Hayes Collection; Nickerson's report from Prescott to AAG, Military Division of the Pacific, December 26, 1872, Indian Bureau Record Group 75; and the *Miner*, December 7, 1872.

feverish and afraid [but] when I asked them to help me punish the bad ones who were out, more volunteered than I wanted."[7]

He said in his autobiography that he found the Indian Bureau people "very indignant at me, and hinting around that I would soon have my comb cut for transcending my authority." One thing that irritated the civilians was an Army officer's count showing only eleven hundred Indians at Apache while the Indian Bureau had been issuing rations to fourteen hundred, and at Grant the discrepancy was more marked.[8] Yet, said Crook, "I had made up my mind to disobey any order I might receive looking to an interference of the plan which I had adopted, feeling sure if I was successful my disobedience of orders would be forgiven [and] . . . if I was again stopped, I would lose my head anyway."[9]

From Apache, Crook had sent an expedition led by Captain George M. Randall of the Twenty-third Infantry, Crook's own regiment, to scout westerly along the Salt and across the lower Tonto Basin to McDowell. The command's Apache scouts were led by Cooley, who had mastered their difficult language. The party reached McDowell about December 16, reporting some little success. Lieutenant Tom Garvey, with eight soldiers and twenty scouts, had made a most difficult thirty-mile march afoot at night to strike Delshay's band, a key hostile clique, at nine in the morning on Bad Rock Mountain, north of old Fort Reno. After a stubborn two-hour fight he won the field, but missed Delshay, although killing fourteen hostiles. The command was reunited and "while marching in the evening the bark of a dog was heard," being readily distinguished by these veteran woodsmen from the yipping of a coyote. As a result, Lieutenants Peter S. Bomus and W. C. Manning "with a detachment of men and Indians struck another large rancheria, eleven Indians were killed and six squaws and children captured."[10]

Brown's expedition from Grant was a strong one, including two

[7] Crook to Adjutant General, December 12, 1872.—Hayes Collection.

[8] *Ibid.*

[9] Crook, *Autobiography*, 177.

[10] Captain J. L. Smyth, Twenty-third Infantry, to Crook from McDowell, December 16, 1872, Old Army Records, Record Group 98, National Archives.

companies of the Fifth Cavalry and thirty Apaches, and Archie, Joe Felmer, and Antonio Besias as guides while it scouted through the Mescal, Pinal, Superstition, and Mazatzal mountains, also bound for McDowell. The expedition, rationed for thirty days, planned in the Superstitions to contact a McDowell expedition under Captain James Burns, commander of that post. Brown was ordered to make a special effort to seek out Delshay and another notorious chieftain, Chunz, and destroy or neutralize them.

Bourke's diary shows the winter campaign to have been arduous, although less so than had it been made in the summertime. Most of the enemy contacts, at least early in the operation, were made by scouts. They worked from twelve to twenty-four hours ahead of the white soldiers, the idea being that they would scout an enemy position, then await the troops, who would take care of it. The trouble with this theory was that the Apaches couldn't forgo a fight, and by the time the soldiers arrived, it usually was all over. Thus on December 15 a party of scouts, with McIntosh and Besias, ran upon a rancheria and exchanged shots, wounding an Apache who got away in heavy brush, however. Chunz's camp was struck by the scouts at daylight the following day, but the hostiles "fled, leaving everything behind—our Indian allies pursued for (5) five miles, but were unable to overtake the flying enemy." Bourke thought the operation thus far was very successful because "at the present season these incorrigible devils must feel keenly every deprivation, and more that they are without an article of clothing, a particle of food, or any necessaries, the bitter winter winds will cause them to perish upon the tops of the Mountains." On the night of the seventeenth the Indians regaled the camp with a mighty war dance, "a few singing in concert, although not in harmony, supplied the necessary music."

On Sunday, December 22, the scouts had a short fight with another party on Raccoon Creek, on the south slope of the Sierra Anchas, killing several and capturing three. But there were no important actions. The troopers wandered along the gorge of the Salt and climbed at last into the Superstitions, where they contacted Burns and his McDowell command on Christmas Day. Burns had about a hundred Pimas and had been out six days, during which he had struck a rancheria in the high Four Peaks area of the Mazatzals, killing six or seven and capturing two. One of the captives, a woman, was sent to McDowell, but the other, a bright-eyed, ingratiating boy of six or seven, was named "Mike Burns" and brought along.[11] Years later Mike told Bourke that his father and all his other relatives were slain in the fight which now was pending.

With Burns' column, Crook now had in the field nine expeditions, "which I propose to keep operating until the Indians are subjugated."[12]

It grew increasingly apparent that the success of the troops depended on the scouts. Without scouts, the troops couldn't find the enemy; with scouts they rarely missed. It was as simple as that. Mike Burns tells how once that winter "the soldiers passed right by a camp of Indians on a thick flat of cedar; it was snowing and the wind was blowing right into the soldiers' faces. They never looked down on the ground to see if there were any tracks of the Indians, and went right on by." He added that, but for the assistance of Indian scouts, "the soldiers were worth nothing."[13] Bourke wrote, "The longer we knew the Apache scouts, the better we liked them. They were wilder and more suspicious than the Pimas and Maricopas, but far more reliable, and endowed with a greater amount of courage and daring. I have never known an officer whose experience entitled his opinion to the slightest consideration, who did not believe as I do on this subject."[14] Crook gradually came to depend almost entirely on the Apaches for his scouts. The Paiutes are not heard of after the earliest expeditions; the Navahos never amounted to much; the Maricopas

[11] Mike Burns was born about 1864, as nearly as he could calculate, and considered himself an Apache-Mohave. Army officers saw to it he received the rudiments of an education, and he was assisted to further learning through the Indian Rights Association, General Crook, and General Wesley R. Merritt. He wrote an autobiographical account which is valuable because it gives the Indian version of some famous fights, often quite divergent from the white narratives. Burns died at Fort McDowell, I think in the 1930's.

[12] Crook to Adjutant General, December 13, 1872.—Hayes Collection.

[13] Farish, *History of Arizona*, III, 325.

[14] Bourke, *Border*, 203.

were sent home as worthless; and the Pimas lasted longer, but were ultimately replaced, too. The Yavapais were most valuable in the country they knew best, and as commands worked farther eastward, they gradually were replaced by Tontos and other Apaches.

The combined Brown-Burns command, two hundred and twenty men, bivouacked December 27, perhaps in the deep canyon of Alder Creek or some canyon west of there, at the base of Four Peaks. Brown held an officers' call and informed the men of their prospects for trapping Indians at what he called "Delshay's stronghold," although that war leader did not, in fact, operate in this area. Bourke's picturesque description of the succeeding events is rather well known; a fresher version is that which he penned in his diary and which is used here, in part.

All singing, &c is strictly forbidden and indeed no precaution is omitted tending to secure the secrecy of our movements. Every preparation is being made for a night march on foot. Each man looks to his weapons, sees that his cartridge belt is full—inspects his clothing—rejecting all that is not absolutely essential to protect him from the cold—provides himself with rations to do for a day or two, and a few matches. . . . The sky has become overcast with clouds—*Maj Brown* has accordingly allowed the Indians to stew the mule which died to-day and whose remains the noble red men brought along. We are to start when a *certain star*, known to the Indian [the scout, Nantje, who had been a member of the party in the hidden redoubt], rises to its position in our meridian.

8 P.M. our Indians moved out in front, then *Burns'* Co, then [Lieutenant Jacob] *Almy*, [Captain Alfred B.] *Taylor* and finally the *Pimas*, under their old chief, *Antonio*; after marching nearly due W about 3 miles, passing (2) two prominent sandstone buttes of considerable altitude on our R . . . our general direction becomes S. . . . About 12:15 the next morning we were at the summit. . . . We now rested for nearly an hour every man closing up to his proper position in the ranks and then lying prone to the ground. *Apache* scouts were soon sent ahead, who soon returned with the information of fires being discovered in the cañon below. We now advanced one man at a time until we reached the edge of a gloomy abyss, how

deep it was I could not then discover, and upon this edge we waited in the cold piercing night air without blankets or overcoats until the morning rays beamed upon the surrounding hills." [No evidence of the enemy was seen, a bitter disappointment, wrote Bourke.]

Most of the command being fatigued sat down to rest but *Joe Felmer* and a few others started down the trail towards the Rio Salado [Salt River] not with any expectation of finding hostile Indians but rather from a disposition to examine into the nature of the country. About 300 yds from where they left us, in a secluded spot, was found a recently abandoned rancheria of (3) or (4) huts. Passing on rapidly, upon descending the mountain somewhat farther, a drove of fifteen horses and mules was encountered and almost immediately afterwards a rancheria was seen in an almost impregnable position. . . . This handful of our comrades, with a gallantry that cannot be too highly extolled, at once charged the Indians, killing (6) six and driving the remainder into the cave at whose entrance the rancheria was situated. Word having meantime reached *Maj Brown*, the main body was pushed forward as fast as our tired legs would permit, the enthusiasm of the men rising again at the prospect of a fight. . . . The rancheria was situated in a small, elliptical nook. Upon the crest of the bluffs which here enclose the *Rio Salado* was a small cave or depression in the rocks which overhung this nook by at least 500', the bluffs first mentioned being 1000 or 1200' above the *Rio Salado*. In front of the cave, a natural rampart of sandstone 10' high afforded ample protection to the *Indians* altho the great number of boulders scattered in every direction screened our men in turn from the fire of the besieged.

Our policy was obvious—the incorrigible *Apaches*, at least a portion of them, were now entrapped beyond possibility of escape. . . . Orders were given to make no charge upon the works, to pick off every Indian showing his head, to spare every woman & child, but to kill every man. Twice the besieged were asked to surrender their families, promises being given that no harm should befall them but, confident in their ability to repel us, their only answers were yells of defiance. These shouts of scorn were soon changed into groans of despair as our shots began to fall with deadly accuracy about them, reckless attempts at escape being made but in each case resulting in the death of those who tried to run our gantlet of fire. One splendid looking Indian over 6 feet, most beautifully proportioned but with a very savage countenance, did indeed succeed in breaking through our front line and making his way down the arroyo, full of large rocks, upon one of which he sprang with a yell of defiance, bravado or joy, I cannot say which. Twelve of use, concealed at this point, levelled our rifles and fired. Every shot must have hit him as he fell dead, riddled from head to foot. . . . A volley was now directed upon the mouth of the cave, & for (3) three minutes, every man in the command opened and closed the breech-block of his carbine as rapidly as his hands could move. Never have I seen such a hellish spot as was the narrow little space in which the hostile Indians were now crowded. . . . The bullets striking against the mouth of the cave seemed like drops of rain pattering upon the surface of a lake.

I must not omit to state that *Capt Burns' Co G, 5th Cav* had succeeded in gaining a position upon the crest of the overhanging bluffs, whence they discharged deadly volleys upon the wretches fighting below. Not content with the deadly efficacy of bullets, they resorted to projecting large masses of rock which thundered down the precipice mangling and destroying whatsoever they encountered.

A charge was now ordered and the men rushed forward; upon entering the enclosure a horrible spectacle was disclosed to view—in one corner (11) eleven dead bodies were huddled, in another four and in different crevices they were piled to the extent of the little cave and to the total number of (57) fifty-seven [seventy-six altogether were killed in the fight] and (20) twenty women and children were taken prisoners. The spoils, very considerable in quantity, were destroyed. We found mescal, baskets, seeds, hides, skins and the material usually composing the outfit of these savage nomads. Our captives were nearly all wounded, more or less severely, but by good fortune we succeeded in bringing them off in safety. One of our *Pima* allies was killed, but with this exception, no losses occurred. . . . *Nanni-Chaddi*, the chief, had been in to McDowell last year talking with that spawn of hell, *Vincent Colyer*, from whom he received presents of blankets and other necessaries, promising in return to comply with the demand of the lawful government and obey its orders. He had also visited *Grant* where in conversation with *Col* [William B.] *Royall*, he boasted that no troops ever had found his retreat and none ever would.

Six young women and one old one had escaped the slaughter, being away from the cave when the fight began, and long years later Bourke heard how one other Indian, a warrior, had escaped. He had been badly wounded by a bullet through his leg when the fight began. Before the troopers stormed the place, he crawled under a slab of stone, and bodies of the dead gradually accumulated over his hiding place. When the soldiers had gone he fashioned crutches from broken lances, and worked his way out of the canyon and over to Tonto Creek, where he turned back an approaching band of hostiles and went with them to another retreat of his people on Turret Mountain.

The column with its eighteen prisoners, mostly wounded, made its way to Sycamore Creek and down that to the Verde and thence to McDowell, to which couriers had been sent notifying the post that injured were en route.[15]

Results of the fight were far-reaching. For one thing, it totally annihilated Nanni-chaddi's band of raiders who had been making life unendurable for settlers along the Gila and the Salt. But the shock went deeper than that, for it proved that the troops, properly guided, could penetrate to the heart of Apacheria, ferret out the most secluded retreats, destroy the enemy no matter how well protected he might be in his natural fortifications, and demonstrated anew the bulldog persistency with which Crook's campaign was to be carried on.[16]

[15] The first official report, sent as a telegram from Nickerson to AAG, Military Division of the Pacific, January 11, 1873, reported fifty-seven warriors killed and that is the figure in the *Chronological List*. It is possible that slain women and children made up the difference. Two wounded prisoners died before the column reached McDowell.

[16] Significant as the fight was, it was forgotten soon enough. Thirty-four years later the cave was rediscovered by a cowboy, Jeff Adams, later sheriff of Maricopa County. His account of a mysterious cave full of human bones stirred considerable interest until McClintock printed an error-strewn account of the battle in *Sunset Magazine* (February, 1907), 340–43.

XI

The Offensive Concludes

THE SALT RIVER CAVE BATTLE, sharp as it was, failed by any means to end resistance elsewhere, in part due to the fragmented nature of Apache society in which the experience of one band was of no immediate concern to others. So Crook's offensive was forced to continue until other groups had felt the iron weight of the Army's ire, until no band felt safe, no camp secure, no spot unreached by the sharp justice of a leaden missile. Scarcely had Major Brown's command brought the haggard prisoners to McDowell than the units were ordered out again to comb the Superstitions and clean the hostiles out of its massive upthrust. Again Bourke went along. The use of the five companies of the Fifth Cavalry, with ten officers, three guides, and thirty Indians, suggests that Crook wanted this column to end hostile resistance below the Salt, as other efforts were directed at eliminating it from west of the Verde.

After one small skirmish January 15, the expedition continued its work until on the eighteenth, Bourke recorded in his diary, it

> . . . sent out Indian scouts to capture or kill some [hostile] Apaches who were seen on hill to our L., heard halloing at us. After a short time, an Apache boy came down the mtn side and joined us. Maj. *Brown* told him to go back and bring in his band—a pass was given him to ensure his safety. These people report being very much frightened at the sight of such great numbers of troops in their country." Later a woman came in; she too was fed and sent back; then an old man was similarly treated. Eventually contact was made with a sizable band whose leaders promised to surrender by the time the command reached Grant.
>
> As we drew nigh to the site of the post, it seemed as if from behind clusters of sage brush, giant cactus, palo verde or mesquite, along the

trail, first one, then another, then a third Apache would silently join the column with at most the greeting of 'Siquien' [my brother]. When we reported to General Crook again at the post . . . there were one hundred and ten people with us, and the whole business had been done so quietly that not one-half of the command ever knew whether any Apaches had joined us or not.[1]

The campaign for the Superstitions was concluded, and Crook enlisted twenty-six of them as scouts. A new enemy now threatened the offensive however, an "epizootic," a sort of horse influenza which swept the country like a storm and in Arizona caused the death of thousands of animals.[2] But even dismounted, the troops carried on. Rations, blankets, and equipment on their own backs, they struggled through the wilderness, hunting the enemy, surprising him when they could, fighting whenever opportunity offered.

The soldiers, with their red allies, were everywhere that winter. First Sergeant William L. Day of Company E, Fifth Cavalry, a broad-shouldered Kentuckian, had a good season. About the turn of the year he was with Captain Price's command, which was guided by Lew Ellit and Jack Townsend. The command had scoured the country southeast of the Bradshaws, around the old beaver dams on the Agua Fria and below Black Canyon, and Day was sent on a side scout across the Agua Fria toward the south. At the mouth of Baby Canyon his detachment surprised a party of eight warriors, killing five.[3] On the other side of the river another warrior was killed and one wounded and nine women and children captured.[4] On January 19, to the northwest, Day, again in command of a small unit, ignored signal smokes that said the hostiles knew of his presence. He led his

[1] Bourke, *Border*, 207.

[2] This epizootic, although primarily a disease of horses and mules, may have extended itself to the Indians, particularly those weakened by malnutrition; see William F. Corbusier, "The Apache-Yumas and Apache-Mojaves," *The American Antiquarian* (September, 1886), 277; see also *Miner*, November 9, 1872, and Crook, *Autobiography*, 178–79.

[3] Baby Canyon cannot today be positively identified, but it may be the canyon of Little Squaw Creek, joining the Agua Fria at Gillette.

[4] *Chronological List*; *Miner*, January 11, 1873.

little party rapidly down a trail "to the bottom of one of the deepest canyons of the east branch of the Verde River," found a rancheria and slew five.[5] Like Sergeant Rudolph Stauffer, he earned a Medal of Honor that winter.

The *Miner* of February 22, 1873, listed a number of actions newly reported, not all of those under way, by any means, but a representative sample. Lieutenant Frank Michler, en route from Camp Verde to Grant, had surprised a sizeable rancheria of Tontos on Tonto Creek. In a charge Private Hooker of K Company, Fifth Cavalry, was the first man into the camp, and was killed,[6] but the enemy lost seventeen fighting men. One night Lieutenant Woodson's command was fired into and a horse killed; it was a rare instance of Apaches making hostile overtures after dark. On February 6 Captain Thomas McGregor killed two Indians in Hell Canyon and returned to Whipple after a hard trip through the mountains where the men had to wade much of the time through deep snow. But despite the activities of the troops, the Indians had not ceased their depredations.

On March 11 a band of Indians slaughtered three men, at least one by livid torture, and thereby set in motion the best organized punitive operation in the history of the region, and bringing to a climax Crook's offensive. The white victims were John McDonald, George W. Taylor, a twenty-one-year-old Scot, and Gus Swain, an old Indian fighter of wondrous experiences. He was one of ten men who had established a settlement at Walnut Grove and all of the others, one by one, had been killed by Indians, until only Gus was left, and in the end, he, too, succumbed.[7] Taylor was captured alive

[5] George F. Price, *Across the Continent with the Fifth Cavalry*, 675. Hereafter cited as *Fifth Cavalry*.

[6] "I regret his loss exceedingly, as he was an excellent soldier, brave and trustworthy," reported Michler.—Price, *Fifth Cavalry*, 675. Hooker, born at Frederick, Maryland, received a posthumous Medal of Honor.

[7] A. C. Swain, a Georgian of about forty, came to Prescott very early, although he apparently was not a member of the Walker Party. Once prospecting with several others on the Verde they were attacked by Indians. Swain shot what he thought was their chief, dashed through a hail of bullets to scalp him, and emerged unscathed but with his clothing riddled. However, as Conner dryly put it, "I will venture to say that this Indian was killed, robbed, and scalped in less number of minutes than any

and tortured. He had come to Arizona with his parents, his father becoming superintendent of a mine not far from Wickenburg, and one evening he said he would "walk up the cañon and call upon a neighbor. . . . He took no arms."

Now it transpired that a band of these Tonto-Apache cut-throats were hidden in the rocks overlooking the cañon, waiting to plunder the Arizona and California stage coach. . . . [They] saw this young man . . . [and] concluded to amuse themselves meanwhile with him. Quietly they dropped down from their hiding places and, as they are the most expert stalkers of game, whether it be man or beast, in the world, they soon had this young man surrounded and captured him alive.

They then took him up to a sheltered spot among the rocks, stripped him of his clothing, tied his hands behind him, fastened his feet together and commenced to torture him by shooting arrows into his naked body, taking care not to hit a vital spot.

I visited the place where this young man was thus cruelly put to death, immediately after the ghastly deed had been consummated, and the ground where the victim had laid was all matted down as he had rolled over and over in his awful agony, breaking off the arrows as he rolled until over one hundred and fifty of these cruel missiles had been broken off in his body. And then, when by reason of the loss of blood, he could move no more, they finished him in a manner so excruciating and beastly that I could not, if I would, shock my readers with a hint of the method of his final taking off.[8]

Crook ordered punitive efforts everywhere redoubled, and the Indian casualty list mounted sharply. Messengers reached Department headquarters at Whipple on March 26 with fresh reports that showed:

Major Brown's command had killed fifteen warriors and captured

---

other had ever been in the Rocky Mountains." The scalp wound up in Editor Marion's custody, and he tacked it to the front door of the *Miner* where it remained for years.—Conner, *Joseph Reddeford Walker*, 227–28; *Miner*, March 14, 1866.

[8] A. H. Nickerson, Major and Assistant Adjutant General, U.S.A., "Major General George Crook and the Indians," unpublished manuscript, Huntington Library, Schuyler collection.

eight women, one of whom reported their warriors had just returned from a raid in which they had killed three whites. Lieutenant Woodson's company killed fifteen warriors and captured two women. Lieutenant Michler's command killed five men and captured as many women in the Mazatzals. Captain Alfred Taylor's men killed three warriors and captured two women. Lieutenants Almy and Bourke continued hard scouting near the Bradshaws. Lieutenant Rice was near Granite Wash where with Dan O'Leary he was trying to work out the trail of the slayers of the trio of white men. Captain Randall also was supposed to be searching for the hostiles with an expedition from McDowell.[9] And Randall found them.

Lieutenant Rice had tracked the raiders until sign indicated that the McDowell command had cut them, when he took his party into Whipple. Randall, meanwhile, stubbornly working out the trail, had pushed on through Bloody Basin and its incredible maze of arroyos, chaparral, buttes, and rolling lowlands, in a generally northeasterly direction toward the forks of the Verde. As the country roughened in the vicinity of the forks, his scouts ran into fresh Indian sign, much fresher than the trail he was following. Randall became "very discreet in his movements, moving his column after night, and watching during the day while the best of his scouts slipped through the tangled brush, spying out enemy sign and trying to locate the hostile encampment" they were positive was in the vicinity.

This might have continued for some time had not some of his mules strayed, as mules will do. Here, however, it was dangerous, for the creatures fell into the hands of hostiles, who excitedly sent up signal smokes, alerting bands for scores of miles. But so carefully did Randall conceal his men and their movements, that the hostiles couldn't find him any more than he could locate their rancheria. Randall's scouts now captured a woman whom they "intimidated," as Crook put it, into guiding her captors to her people. She warned that the march would be rough. Before starting out the soldiers wrapped their booted feet and knees with gunny sacks to muffle their movements. After dark word was passed there could be no smoking, no

[9] *Miner*, March 29, 1873.

talking, no cursing when one's ankle turned or a man slipped and drove a Spanish bayonet into his hand. The column, silent as wraiths, filed out.

With the woman for a guide the soldiers floundered down the Verde for a distance, then turned west across a brush-girt wilderness of broken ground. They came at last to an incline of broken chunks of lava, split off and tumbled through the ages from a dimly discernible cliff above them, black as the night itself and massive enough to cut off much of the night sky. This was mysterious Turret Mountain. The sharp, angular boulders of all sizes made climbing through the pitch darkness perilous as well as arduous. At length the ghostly column arrived at the foot of a palisade, finding, on the river side, a single way to its top, through a notch formed where a piece of palisade had broken away. On their hands and knees the men worked through, inching on their bellies under a huge rock athwart the opening. Just before daylight they gained the summit, an acre or two of fairly level ground, seamed by cracks resulting when the lava which formed this nearly circular peak had cooled. They crawled close to a compact rancheria on this most unlikely retreat.

"Just at dawn of day our people fired a volley into their camp and charged with a yell," wrote Crook. "So secure did [the hostiles] feel in this almost impregnable position that they lost all presence of mind, even running past their holes in the rocks. Some of them jumped off the precipice and were mashed into a shapeless mass. All of the men were killed; most of the women and children were taken prisoner."[10]

If the mountain now known as Turret Peak is that so identified in 1873, and I suppose it is, one may doubt that many Apaches leaped wildly into space as the charge developed, although there are other

[10] Crook, *Autobiography*, 178. I have followed Crook throughout in the description of this approach and fight; I have been unable to locate in the archives or anywhere else any other account of this famous engagement. Randall's original report has not been found. Turret Mountain, which I climbed one hot August day, is more confined on top than I expected and in other respects does not quite match Crook's description. However, he had not seen the top.

accounts of such panic among Apaches.[11] While part of Turret Mountain is rimmed by an escarpment, at other points ready access to the summit may be had, even though the slopes are very steep.[12] It seems probable that most of the Indians who disappeared over the rim slipped and scurried down into the brush and, if so, lived to fight another day.[13] Nevertheless, Randall's men, carbines in hand, swung down from that mountain now reeking of death, and although they could not then know it, they had effectively broken the back everywhere of Apache resistance.

Until this time about the only captives taken were collected after sharp fighting, but now a strange thing began to happen. For the first time in the history of Apacheria, bands of Indians, small groups at first and then larger, drifted in to the various military posts with offers to surrender. "In the first week of April," wrote Bourke, "a deputation from the hostile bands reached Camp Verde, and expressed a desire to make peace; they were told to return for the head chiefs, with whom General Crook would talk at that point. Signal fires were at once set on all the hills, scouts sent to all places where they would be likely to meet with any of the detachments in the Tonto Basin or the Mogollon, and all possible measures taken to

[11] For example, there is a steep escarpment above Superior called Apache Leap because it is said about seventy-five Indians, cornered by troops, leaped off in panic. Barnes, *Place Names*, 22, says there is "no historical basis for this story," and the second edition, p. 289, says "no official reports of this incident have been located." Yet Mrs. Woody, best informed of local historians, affirms that the tale "is not a myth; it really happened."—Woody to author, September 9, 1959.

[12] Claude Wright, veteran mountain lion hunter of the Bloody Basin country, told me he had once ridden a mule to its summit. The claim, which I accept, is evidence of the climbing qualities of a mule, and does not indicate that scaling Turret Mountain is anything but rugged, however.

[13] There is a wide discrepancy as to how many Indians died and were captured on Turret Mountain. The *Chronological List* shows 33 killed and 13 captured, but 10 of those were killed and 3 captured in a mysterious action two days earlier, March 25, "near" Turret—"mysterious" because there is no other reference to this incident except in Price, *Fifth Cavalry*, 676. The *Miner*, April 5, 1873, reported 47 killed and 7 captured. Ogle, *Western Apaches*, 116, says Randall captured "the entire group including some one hundred and thirty-six souls."

prevent any further hostilities, until it should be seen whether or not the enemy were in earnest."[14]

The various commands congregated at Verde, coming in one after another, riding down the white stone benches in long, swinging columns, working their way up the Verde or down it, down Beaver Creek, West Clear Creek, Oak Creek, or the other streams. From the points of the compass they came, "and a dirtier, greasier, more uncouth-looking set of officers and men it would be hard to encounter anywhere," Bourke recalled. "Dust, soot, rain, and grime had made their impress upon the canvas suits which each had donned, and with hair uncut for months and beards growing with straggling growth all over the face, there was not one of the party who would venture to pose as an Adonis; but all were happy, because . . . we were now to see the reward of our hard work."[15]

The full story of Crook's offensive can never be told now, could not have been fully told even in 1872 or 1873. But Crook and others gave hints now and then of what took place. From the General's annual report for 1873 we get such a clue:

> The officers and men worked day and night, and with our Indian allies would crawl upon their hands and knees for long distances over terrible canyons and precipices where the slightest mishap would have resulted in instant death, in order that when daylight came they might attack their enemy and secure the advantage of surprise. . . . There is hardly a space of 10 miles square in the country operated over that has not some terrible lava bed or precipitous canyon with fortified caves, which the Indians could have held against all odds and with terrible loss of life, had the enemy been approached in daylight and assailed when they were on the alert. . . . The examples of personal exertions & daring among the officers and men if all told would fill a volume.

When the Indians finally sued for peace, he wrote, they complained that every rock had turned into a soldier "and that they were sprung from the ground, as was literally true in several instances

[14] Bourke, *Border*, 211.
[15] *Ibid.*, 212.

when the troops crawled down into caves to come up in the rear of the position between the Indians and the entrance to the caves in which they expected to take shelter in case of attack."

The first reward was the timid approach of an Apache-Mohave chief named Cha-lipun, whom white Americans, in their thick-tongued way, nicknamed Charley-pan. Representing some twenty-three hundred Indians, he surrendered them unconditionally, explaining they gave up not because they loved Crook, but because they were afraid of him. The Americans alone never frightened him, but now there were his own people, as well, to fight. Cha-lipun said his people could not sleep at night because they feared a murderous dawn attack. They could not hunt because a rifle's crack would bring soldiers. They could not cook mescal because the flame and smoke would draw the enemy. They could not remain in the valleys, and when they withdrew to the snowy mountaintops the troops followed them there. They wanted to surrender to the Gray Fox.

Crook shook hands and told him that "if he would promise to live at peace and stop killing people, he would be the best friend he ever had." The Indians killed had been slain through their own folly. They had refused to come in, and so "there was nothing else to do but go out and kill them until they changed their minds." Crook added that it was useless to argue about who began the war; there were bad Americans just as there were bad Indians and bad Mexicans, but now was the time to establish peace. The Indians must remain on the reservation, submit to a daily count until all the bad Indians had been killed or captured so the whites would know who was bad and who was good. The Indians must change some of their ways, such as cutting off the noses of unfaithful wives, but, on the other hand, they would gain, for the Army would keep bad white men away and protect the good Indians and teach them to live as the whites did, with hard work and full bellies.[16]

---

[16] In the above I have followed Bourke, *Border*, 212–14, and have done so at length because this discussion was typical of the General's approach to all surrendering Indians, against whom he was a merciless fighter, but humane, wise and just, and devoted to their best interests once they gave up.

Crook cautioned those of his officers who would deal with the surrendered Indians that the natives "should not be judged harshly for acts which in the civil codes would constitute minor offenses," but that "care should also be taken that they do not succeed in deceiving their agents and the officers in matters of greater import, being careful to treat them as children in *ignorance*, not in *innocence*."[17]

With the surrender of Cha-lipun and other leaders, organized enemy resistance was broken, but could not be entirely ended until the worst of the Tonto Basin warriors, Delshay, was taken. Randall continued hunting him through the brushy jungle of the Mazatzals, but the Indian was wily. He had plenty of reason to distrust, not to say, hate, the white man. Probably a Tonto, he was born perhaps in the Mazatzal region about 1835 or 1840.[18] In his maturity he was described by one who knew him well as a heavy-shouldered individual who "sort of lumbered along" in a half-trot, rarely walking, and always wearing an ornament in his left ear. He wore nothing in his right ear because, he would explain, it would interfere with the operation of a bow or gun. And that activity was more important to him than decoration.[19] Old Camp Reno was established in early 1867 to end the depredations his band allegedly perpetrated. The following year troops stationed there had captured a dozen Indians, including Delshay's brother, a fine-looking man named Rising Sun who was shot dead "while trying to escape," as the expression went.[20] In 1870 Delshay himself was wantonly shot and seriously wounded by the post physician for no reason ever revealed, the Indian by then coming and going freely about the camp.[21] Major Andrew Jonathan Alexander earlier had shot Delshay also, hitting him, the Indian

[17] General Orders No. 13, Department of Arizona, April 8, 1873.

[18] *Miner*, August 23, 1873, said that the Indian at that time, although called "Old Del-che," is a "young man, not over 35, but said to have the most devilish expression of countenance."

[19] William T. Corbusier, son of Dr. William H. Corbusier, Camp Verde physician who once treated Delshay for tapeworm, in interview with author.

[20] *Miner*, June 13, 1868.

[21] *Ibid.*, January 29, 1870. A shooting which might be this one is told, with some variation of detail, by Mike Burns in Farish, *History of Arizona*, III, 299–300.

said, with thirty shots, which perhaps was another reason Crook always referred to him as a chronic liar, but perhaps the major had used a shotgun.[22]

Delshay was high on Vincent Colyer's agenda, but they did not meet. Colyer wrote that he was informed that Delshay "has been at McDowell several times during the past few years, and that on two occasions he has been dealt with very treacherously; at one time shot in the back, and at another time attempted to be poisoned by a post-doctor." However garbled his information, it was true in tenor. Various officers sought to bring Delshay and his people in to talk with Colyer; each time they were about to succeed he was frightened off, perhaps by the white soldiers, or perhaps by rumors, spread by Mexicans or others, that the Pimas or Maricopas—his deadly enemies—were coming in force to massacre him and his party. On one occasion, when he and his group appeared almost destitute, Delshay told Captain W. McC. Netterville at Sunflower Valley: "I don't want to run over the mountains any more; I want to make a big treaty . . . I will make a peace that will last; I will keep my word until the stones melt. . . . I will put a rock down to show that when it melts the treaty is to be broken. . . . I promise that when a treaty is made the white man or soldiers can turn out all their horses and mules without any one to look after them, and if they are stolen by the Apaches I will cut my throat."

But Delshay made conditions. He didn't want to be moved to McDowell, where the rations were insufficient and there was little food the Indians could secure for themselves. He wanted seeds sent to him, the white commander to come whenever sent for, just as he would come in when the whites asked that he do so. He was afraid of neither whites nor Mexicans, but feared the Pimas and Maricopas, "who steal into my camps at night and kill my women and children with clubs," and he wanted them kept away from him.[23]

---

[22] *Miner*, February 19, 1870; Crook, *Autobiography*, 180.

[23] Colyer, *Report*, 22–27. This includes correspondence and reports from Colyer, Netterville, and other officers, and considerably more detail than I have gone into here. I have merely summarized the incidents reported.

Then, after a visit to McDowell to sign the "big treaty," the Indians bolted, presumably on receipt of word that their traditional enemies were coming. And now he had to be tracked down again, and made to surrender.

Randall's scouts kept probing in ever-narrowing circles about the Mazatzals and environs for the elusive Indian. They crowded him and his people from their traditional range across Tonto Creek and at last, farther east, cornered him in the upper reaches of Canyon Creek, which flows southward from the Mogollon Rim toward the Salt. On April 25 Randall's command surrounded Delshay's camp and at dawn started firing into it. They had loosed scarcely twenty bullets, however, when Delshay hoisted a white flag and asked permission to surrender. Randall objected. Too often had Delshay surrendered, he growled, only to break his word; the soldiers had lost confidence in him.

> Delshay commenced crying and said he would do anything he would be ordered to do. He wanted to save his people, as they were starving. Every rock had turned into a soldier, and his people were hunted down as they never had been before. He had nothing to ask for but his life. He would accept any terms. He said he had had one hundred and twenty-five warriors last fall, and if anybody had told him he couldn't whip the world, he would have laughed at them, but now he had only twenty left. He said they used to have no difficulty in eluding the troops, but now the very rocks had gotten soft, they couldn't put their foot anywhere without leaving an impression by which we could follow, that they could get no sleep at nights, for should a coyote or a fox start a rock rolling during the night, they would get up and dig out, thinking it was we who were after them.[24]

Randall hesitated as long as seemed appropriate, then accepted Delshay's unconditional surrender, and the Indian band humbly followed the Army column to the White Mountain Apache Reservation.[25] Delshay found, however, as soon as his fears had vanished, his stomach filled and his people rested, that he didn't like the White

[24] Crook, *Autobiography*, 180.
[25] *Miner*, May 10, 1873.

Mountains any better than McDowell, so once more his band fled, this time to turn up at Camp Verde. Delshay told Lieutenant Walter Scribner Schuyler, in command at the time, that "he was abused at [Camp] Apache by other Indians and could not stay there, and that he will behave himself at Verde."[26] He was permitted to stay.

On April 9, 1873, Crook issued his famous General Orders No. 14 commending his successful command upon virtual completion of the arduous operations which, he told his men,

> ... entitle them to a reputation second to none in the annals of Indian warfare. In the face of obstacles heretofore considered insurmountable, encountering rigorous cold in the mountains, followed in quick succession by dire extremities for want of water to quench their prolonged thirst; and when their animals were stricken by pestilence or the country became too rough to be traversed by them, they left them and carrying on their own backs such meagre supplies as they might, they persistently followed on, and plunging unexpectedly into chosen positions in lava beds, caves and canyons, they have outwitted and beaten the wiliest of foes with slight loss, comparatively, to themselves, and finally closed an Indian war that has been waged since the days of Cortez.

General Schofield, from the San Francisco headquarters of the Military Division of the Pacific, added his accolade in General Orders No. 7: "To Brevet Major-General George Crook, Commanding the Department of Arizona, and to his gallant troops for the extraordinary service they have rendered in the late campaign against the Apache Indians, the Division Commander extends his thanks and his congratulations upon their brilliant success. They have merited the gratitude of the nation." The *Miner* considered Crook "the Napoleon of successful Indian fighters."[27] He was the hero of the hour. The first telegraph line to penetrate the territory was soon to reach Prescott. Its first message informed Crook that he had been promoted, over the heads of scores of officers who never forgave him, from lieutenant colonel to brigadier general.[28]

[26] *Ibid.*, August 9, 1873.
[27] *Ibid.*, March 29, 1873.   [28] Crook, *Autobiography*, 183n.

XII

Lieutenant Almy

B ROWN'S COMMAND ALONE, in its several detachments, had killed 500 Indians, Bourke calculated, and had marched a total of 1,200 miles in a space of 142 days since the offensive began. That drive now was all but concluded, most soldiers thought, and only mopping up remained. Probably few of them would have predicted that this would take almost a decade to accomplish, but it did.

And then there was the problem of Cochise. This Indian chieftain bothered Crook, although the two had not come to blows, and there was no firm indication that they would do so. But Cochise was specifically eliminated from Crook's Apacheria assignment as an Indian to cool off, because he had come to terms with General Howard, terms that Crook could never learn anything definite about. Although it was not specifically spelled out, this may have been because the Cochise-Howard agreement perhaps was never written down. At any rate, General Crook's many attempts to get a "copy of this treaty," as he put it, were unfruitful. While he was prevented from carrying the war to Cochise, for the moment, at least, the Chiricahuas, he was convinced, continued raiding into Mexico, bringing depredations and uneasiness south of the border. This, Crook felt, must stop.

In his autobiography, Crook writes that after the Tonto Basin offensive:

> I moved all these commands to where New Grant was being constructed, intending to iron all the wrinkles out of Cochise's band of Indians who were then in the Dragoon Mountains. I already had my spies in his camp and intended moving on him with my whole force after night, and surrounding him by daylight in the morning and give them such a clearing out that it would end him for all time to come, as his band was recognized as the worst of all the Apaches.

... Just then General Howard made a treaty of peace with Cochise. ... This treaty stopped all operations against them by me. It had a bad effect on my Indians as they thought I was afraid of Cochise ...[1]

The general, however, was slightly confused in his chronology, since Howard had made his pact with Cochise in the autumn of 1872, Camp Grant was moved on December 19, 1872,[2] Crook's offensive did not get under way until mid-November, 1872, and virtually concluded with the surrender of Cha-lipun in April, 1873. Cochise had then only about one year to live. Yet it seems clear that Cochise occupied much of Crook's thoughts, and even plans. How much of this was due to the actual unrest caused by the great Apache's Indians, and how much to Crook's inherent competitiveness and unwillingness to brook a rival in his Department, can only be surmised at this date, but at any rate, the two did not clash.

However, Crook did send a mission to Cochise in January and February of 1873. Headed by Brown, the party also included Thomas Jeffords,[3] agent for Cochise's band, as interpreter; George H. Stevens,[4] acting San Carlos agent; Lieutenants C. H. Rock-

---

[1] Crook, *Autobiography*, 176–77.

[2] Brandes, *Frontier Posts*, 37.

[3] Thomas Jonathan Jeffords was a remarkable man of the southwestern frontier. Born in 1832 in New York state, he came west as a mature man, was a dispatch bearer and scout in the Civil War and after the war drove a stage and operated a line through Cochise's country. Cochise was then at war with the whites, but Jeffords made a pact with him, became his friend, and they remained friends until Cochise died. Jeffords died February 19, 1914, and is buried at Tucson.—Farish, *History of Arizona*, II, 228–40; McClintock, *Arizona*, I, 217; Lockwood, *Apache Indians*, 110–29.

[4] Stevens was born at Southwick, Massachusetts, in 1844 and came to Arizona in 1866. He married an Apache woman named Francesca, variously reported to have been a daughter of Cochise, Victorio, or Geronimo or of some unnamed "White Mountain Apache chieftain." Stevens was a scout for Crook, started several ranches, was elected a member of the territorial legislature and later sheriff of Graham County, of which he was at one time the only white resident. He was called "Little Steve" by many Arizonians. He is reported to have left the territory under unexplained circumstances and in 1906 was reported running a gambling house at Victoria, British Columbia.—Arizona Dictations, Graham County, HHB, P-D 12, Bancroft Library; Bancroft, *Arizona and New Mexico*, 628n.; Barnes, *Place Names*, 424; APHS notes, information from Mrs. Clara T. Woody, Miami, Arizona.

well and John Bourke; and Archie McIntosh, who was sent along no doubt to get an idea of the lay of the land in case of eventual hostilities.

In his diary for February 3, Bourke writes that the group met Cochise "and his family with a few young warriors" in a Dragoon Mountains canyon:

Cocheis is a fine looking Indian of about (50) winters," wrote Bourke, "straight as a rush—six ft in stature, deep chested, roman nosed, black eyes, firm mouth, a kindly and even somewhat melancholy expression tempering the determined look of his countenance. He seemed much more neat than the other wild Indians I have seen and his manners were very gentle. There was neither in speech or action any of the bluster characteristic of his race. His reception of us was courteous, altho' he said but little in the way of compliment. He expressed his own earnest desire for peace—said that in the treaty made with *Howard*, it was understood that soldiers could pass over the roads on his reservation, but could not live upon it, nor were citizens to settle there. In reference to the *Mexn*, he said he considered them as being on one side in this matter, while the *Americans* were on another. The former had not asked him for peace as the latter had done. He did not deny that his boys were in the habit of raiding on *Mexico*, but this he could not prevent as it was no more than was done from all the Reservations.[5]

At the end of this volume of his diary, Bourke gives a transcript of the interview,[6] but it does not differ materially from his summary.

Elsewhere in Arizona, meanwhile, "as soon as the Indians . . . became harmless the Indian agents, who had sought cover before, now came out as brave as sheep, and took charge of the agencies, and commenced their game of plunder," as Crook later put it. One such agent, he charged, left after a short stay in Arizona with $50,000 "as his share of the spoils."[7] On some reservations profiteering and greed led to rations so reduced as to cause actual starvation. The Army

[5] Bourke, Diary, Vol. I, pp. 130–32.
[6] *Ibid.*, 178–84.
[7] Crook, *Autobiography*, 184–85.

shared with civilian agents the running of the major reservations, and Crook chose with care the officers he assigned this task. Schuyler was sent to Verde. Brown was assigned to Fort Apache, and to San Carlos the general sent First Lieutenant Jacob Almy, an able, Quaker-reared officer from New Bedford, Massachusetts, then thirty-one. Already difficulties were arising at San Carlos, where there had been jammed Indians of different tribes and bands, subject to mutual rivalries, jealousies, and inherited hatreds. There had been three agents in the last months that many of these Indians had been at Camp Grant and during the first few months they had been at San Carlos: Ed C. Jacobs, George Stevens and Dr. R. A. Wilbur. Of these Stevens was the best and Wilbur easily the worst.

"The difficulty in finding a satisfactory agent for the . . . Indians is shrouded in deep mystery," noted Ogle.[8] Underground political machinations no doubt played a part. They apparently inspired "a malicious sergeant of the First Cavalry" to write a scurrilous letter against General Howard and pass it off as the work of Stevens,[9] and before the forgery was detected, Stevens was relieved and a Major Charles F. Larrabee of Maine, recently mustered out of the service after a good record of several years, appointed to succeed him. Since it would take months for Larrabee to reach San Carlos, Dr. Wilbur of Tucson was named interim agent, and no more unfortunate choice could have been made. Wilbur was, to put it generously, a crook. It is impossible to escape the conclusion, on the basis of the record and his own admissions, that he was more or less directly responsible for the murder of Lieutenant Almy and that he expected, and tried to incite, a great deal more bloodshed. He was, in large part, responsible for an extension of Crook's military operations for another full year, and it was only due to great good luck, and the heroism of a few soldiers, plus the good sense of Eskiminzin and Capitan Chiquito, that the events set in motion by the supremely greedy and sinister Dr.

[8] Ogle, *Western Apaches*, 138.

[9] *Ibid.*, 138n. Major Brown, in a report, considered Stevens "the only reliable and honest man" in charge of the Indians and said he was "the victim of a base plot . . . charged with writing a letter, which letter was a forgery and summarily removed without a chance for defense."

Wilbur did not wash the territory in blood. He was willing to perpetrate such an atrocity upon his fellow citizens apparently for the sole purpose of restoring his position at the San Carlos trough.[10]

Major Larrabee arrived at San Carlos early in March, 1873, and took over from Dr. Wilbur "who had probably made arrangements for a much longer stay in office, and who, being summarily ousted, did all that a thoroughly bad man could do under such circumstances," as a board of investigation put it later.

Larrabee found his charges divided into two more or less hostile factions, each vying for the favor of the agent and ready to warn him of the other's evil intentions. One faction was headed by Eskiminzin and Capitan Chiquito, and included the Aravaipa Apaches and their kin who had been moved to San Carlos from Grant. The other element was more turbulent and dangerous. It was headed by the outlaws Chunz,[11] Cochinay, and To-mas, or Ba-coon. The worst were the former two. When Larrabee arrived, Wilbur had two immediate objectives: to retain his influence with the Indians and those who held lush contracts to keep them fed, and to prevent Larrabee's obtaining any such influence. All else was secondary. When Concepcion, the Apache-Spanish interpreter, told him that an Indian had reached the agency with the grim purpose of killing William Cox, the agency farm instructor, Wilbur bruskly told him to advise the Indian "to wait until I get out of here, and then he can do as he pleases." He made a point of calling on Elijah Stout Junior, whom everyone knew

---

[10] For the killing of Almy and circumstances surrounding it, involving the various principals, I depend upon the report of the Board of Investigation and testimony before it, all sent to the Division of the Pacific by Crook July 3, 1873, and Major Brown's official report to Crook, dated June 15, 1873. All these documents are on Indian Bureau microfilm, National Archives, Record Group 75. The Board of Investigation was headed by Captain Sanford C. Kellogg, Fifth Cavalry, as president. Witnesses included Corporal Charles L. Essick, Privates Frank Butcher, John Golden, W. H. Elliott, and Joseph Reuter; Guide Joe Felmer, William Cox, George H. Stevens, Larrabee, Elijah Stout Junior (whose last name was Junior), and Merejildo Grijalba.

[11] Chunz was a murderer whom the military had outlawed after he wantonly split the head of a Mexican boy with an axe at Grant the year before.—McClintock, *Arizona*, I, 211. Apparently he had made peace with civilian Indian agents.

as Black Jack Junior, the agency representative for the beef contractor, and with syrupy arguments try to influence him. "Jack," Wilbur told Junior, his arm thrown around his shoulder, "I cannot get along with Major Larrabee [who had scarcely yet unpacked his bags] and you know that any man that cannot get along with me is in fault." He confided that Larrabee had said he would accept no beef on the hoof, but only on the block, which, although he did not say so, both men knew to be a means of making more certain that correct weight was delivered. "I would advise you, Jack," Wilbur continued, "to go over and put a head on him."

A day later Wilbur resumed his conversation with Junior, telling him that Concepcion was a man whom the Indians would always believe, and that Wilbur had told him to tell the red charges that Black Jack was "a good man," and they should come to him, instead of to Larrabee, for council. "In case anything happens," Wilbur concluded with a sly wink, "Concepcion will notify you in time so you will have a chance to get away." The agent urged Junior to write the beef contractor that he could not get along with Larrabee, and urge him to contact Wilbur for details.

"I thought at the time," Junior told the board of investigation, "and I think so still, from Dr. Wilbur's language, manner and actions, that he meant to, or had at the time, used his influence with the Indians by false representations, etc., to have all the white people at this, the San Carlos Division, White Mountain Reserve, massacred after his departure therefrom."

Larrabee learned at once of the general situation and on March 4 sent an Indian to the mountains to summon Chunz, Cochinay, and Ba-coon[12] in for a talk. They drifted in the following day and settled down about one hundred yards from the agent's quarters. Concepcion told Larrabee that "not for ten thousand dollars" would he stroll alone into that hawk's nest for a talk, as the agent suggested. Larrabee

[12] Ba-coon, or To-mas, was killed in a quarrel with another Indian April 2, 1873, and was buried "like a soldier," as he requested.—Captain James Burns to Crook, April 23, 1873, Indian Bureau Microfilm, Record Group 75, National Archives.

told the interpreter then to follow him and led the way. Black Jack came along. They found Wilbur already talking with the surly outlaw chiefs. Larrabee then addressed them. "The agent told the chiefs that he had been sent here by order of the President to do all he could for their benefit," Junior told the board, "that he was going to tell them the truth and expected them to tell him the truth." The talk was long, and eminently unsatisfactory. The Indians would not believe Larrabee. Ne-zhar-titte,[13] a Tonto, bluntly told the agent he had seen Larrabee with "too many" soldiers, and that proved he was no friend of theirs. "Dr. Wilbur was sitting by the side of the chief Chunz," reported Junior.

> When the Tonto chief said to the agent that he had seen him with the soldiers, I saw Dr. Wilbur nod his head several times and laugh, signifying his approbation, and when this chief added that he did not believe the agent was their friend, I distinctly saw Dr. Wilbur nod his head and smile, embracing and hugging at the same time the murderer chief, Chunz. I saw the Indians sitting behind get up on their feet, put cartridges in their guns and form a hollow square around the agent. All the Indians became then very restless, insolent and threatening in their actions. I ran hastily to the agent's quarters, where my rifle was, as I expected the Indians intended to massacre the agent and all his employees.

But Larrabee remained outwardly unruffled and continued his talk. After a long time he came to his quarters and said, "Jack, I want you to issue a beef to Ba-coon's party right away, for they are very hostile, I assure you." Junior quickly ordered up a beef, and no sooner was it in sight than the Indians loosed their emotions upon it, shooting it full of holes and lancing it into fragments as soon as it fell, washing their faces in its warm blood while making the night "hideous with their yells and outcries, war dances, &c."

"I was given to believe," Black Jack concluded, by Dr. Wilbur and

---

[13] This Indian, a "prophet" and of wide influence, was considered by the whites a trouble-maker, and the Board recommended that the military get rid of him. Whether this was done is not reported, but he is never heard from again.

others, "that Major Larrabee's presence would not long be tolerated here; that he would either be killed or driven off before very long."[14]

Larrabee's intentions obviously were of the best, but he lacked experience in handling such implacably turbulent spirits as these Apaches, and he had nowhere to turn for sure guidance. As Crook said following his own investigation some months later, "if the Agent had pursued the policy of punishing the bad and protecting the good, any disaffection would have been checked in its incipiency, and no two parties could have arisen." But the rather sinister Wilbur intervened and "disaffection gained ground until the Indians thought they had the [new] Agent thoroughly cowed."[15]

Larrabee promised concessions to the outlaw and his followers, but found that the more he offered them the more surly and insolent they became, and at length he applied for military assistance. Major Brown, the military commandant of Camp Grant and the reservation, arrived at San Carlos May 8 and found a situation that left him aghast, with the Indians practically running the place and the agent virtually beleaguered, while the two major divisions, "separated beyond hope of reconciliation," snarled at each other. One band under Eskiminzin, was camped on the San Carlos and the other on the Gila, about five miles distant. The latter group was in two parts, one under Chunz and the other under Cochinay. Larrabee rejected Brown's impassioned plea that Chunz be arrested and dealt with by military law and explained his promise to seek a pardon for him, and finally Brown told the agent that "I would support his policy although I differed with him utterly." Brown remained for seven days. He called a council of chiefs to which Larrabee was invited.

Brown talked earnestly with the Indians, and convinced most that Larrabee was there by authority of the president and must be obeyed.

[14] Wilbur virtually confessed his complicity in all this in a letter to Larrabee from Tucson, March 27, 1873. The letter was inspired by Larrabee's denunciation of Wilbur in a communication to Dr. Herman Bendell, superintendent of Indian Affairs for Arizona.—Almy records, Indian Bureau Microfilm, Record Group 75, National Archives.

[15] Crook to AAG, Division of the Pacific, July 3, 1873.—Hayes Collection.

Had the agent then sided with Eskiminzin, his troubles would have been over; however, Larrabee apparently thought that his big problem remained Chunz, and if he appeared to favor him, it might win over that recalcitrant. Brown's remonstrations were fruitless. Finally he said, "The day is coming when you will need me and my soldiers. Send for me. I will come, but I fear I shall only arrive in time to bury your dead body." He prepared to depart. Archie McIntosh, "whose judgment is infallible where Indians are concerned," urged him to stay to avert trouble, but reports of Indian outrages along the San Pedro called him away. But before leaving, Brown, who planned to leave Almy and a detachment to serve as Larrabee's muscle, if needed, called the lieutenant aside and "talked long and earnestly with him."

"I saw the evil was coming," he wrote later, "and I endeavored to prepare Lieut. Almy to meet it promptly and effectively. I urged upon him the necessity of vigilance. I told him while it would be unfortunate to be whipped, it would be disgraceful to be surprised. It was necessary to act vigorously and strike a blow in case he was called upon to act. I cautioned prudence and directed in case he was compelled to use force, to make himself so secure by numbers as to avoid the possibility of defiance."

So portentous was the situation that Capitan Chiquito took his people to the White Mountains and Eskiminzin his to the wilderness. But to keep touch with events, he sent spies in to San Carlos to report. One of them was his son. May 27 was ration day, which came each five days, and more than one thousand Apaches thronged the stony, dusty flat before the agency headquarters, chatting, gambling, or quarreling as the mood struck them. About four hundred of the men were armed, as was their custom. Major Larrabee, at headquarters, worked out the necessary documentation that accompanied the issuance of rations, and he was bothered, in addition, by a sullen, short, and blocky Indian named She-shet or Chan-deisi, a discharged scout belonging to Cochinay's band, who sought ration tickets to which he was not entitled. Larrabee refused his request and continued with his work. The Indian "stood around there for about three quarters of an hour, during which time he repeatedly asked for rations. I told him he could not have them until he complied with my regulations . . . He then raised his lance or spear at me in a threatening manner when he was pushed aside . . . by an Indian named To-mas." To-mas, or Ba-coon, the erstwhile outlaw, had saved the major's life, and, incidentally, probably his own, since his action removed him from the recalcitrant ranks. Larrabee continued with his work, but the nagging thought kept recurring that he could not drop this matter. He had had enough of Apache belligerency. About five minutes after the incident, he dashed off a note to Almy asking military help in arresting Chan-deisi.

Meanwhile, unknown to the agent, Eskiminzin's son, lurking around the rear of the agency headquarters, overheard Chunz urge Chan-deisi to kill the agent and everyone else he could, and then flee to the mountains.

Within twenty minutes a guard of seven men, headed by Corporal Charles L. Essick and Merejildo Grijalba as interpreter, trotted up to the south end of the agency, where Larrabee met it and told it to wait until he had found the Indian. Almost immediately thereafter Almy hurried up, asked if the Apache had been caught and when told he had not, hastened on toward the Indians, despite being unarmed. Why he did this foolhardy thing in direct violation of Brown's instructions would be a mystery were it not that there was later found among his effects letters from his mother and friends at New Bedford, urging upon him the Quaker philosophy of dealing with Indians and this, as Brown later thought, must have influenced him to attempt to solve this explosive situation peacefully, even at the risk of his own life. Or perhaps he simply underestimated the gravity of it. Larrabee, from the corner of his eye, saw Almy disappear toward the milling throng of Indians. Suddenly shooting started. One thousand Apaches boiled over at the first shot, and all was confusion. The small guard of soldiers leaped forward and commenced firing indiscriminately as soon as they saw Almy stagger toward them, his hands pressed to his sides, and moaning, "Oh, my God!"[16] They saw him shot again, a bullet shattering his skull, and he fell, dead.

Firing by the soldiers had little effect. Concepcion had shouted, "Don't shoot!" and struck up the rifle of Private William Elliott as the soldier drew a bead on an Indian he said he had seen shoot at Almy.[17] For this Concepcion came under suspicion, but the board of investigation cleared him of complicity, although it urged his discharge. Despite the firing, Almy was the only immediate casualty. Lieutenant Charles H. Watts, who succeeded Almy in command of the company at San Carlos, took men out on the trail of the outlaws, but couldn't catch them. Both good and bad Indians fled into the mountains in the heady confusion, but most of the former, including Ba-coon, soon filtered back, apologetic for their behaviour.

Crook was furious. He ordered that not one of the renegades would be permitted to surrender until they brought in the arch-criminals—Chunz, Cochinay, and Chan-deisi (or John Daisy, as Crook wrote it)—dead or alive, and left no doubt which he hoped it would be.

Larrabee, in a short note to Brown dated June 18, indicated he had had enough. He said he thought that his "continuance here will tend only to aggravate affairs," and asked that the officer take over the agency, as he was resigning. Crook then ordered Lieutenant Rice to assume Almy's post and urged upon Brown and Rice a "firm and decided" policy of "impartial justice to all who do well, the olive branch to all who desire to be at peace, but certain punishment to the wrongdoers."

"Let no Indian profit by his own misdeed," Crook concluded, "but let it be unprofitable to the last degree to the wilfully persistent wrongdoers."[18]

Schuyler, and his chief of scouts, Al Sieber, at Verde, meanwhile were also in the midst of turbulent, undependable hordes of Indians,

[16] Price, *Fifth Cavalry*, 522, says he cried, "My God! it has come at last!" but there is no recorded testimony to confirm that.

[17] Identified by Merejildo Grijalba and others as Chan-deisi, although it was not certain who had fired the second shot at the wounded officer.

[18] Nickerson to Brown from Prescott, July 3, 1873, Brown report, Indian Bureau Microfilm, Record Group 75, National Archives.

and the worst of the lot was Delshay, though many others caused concern. Schuyler wrote to his father:

> The Tontos act well enough as they have been well whipped, but the Yumas & Mojaves have not been thoroughly punished and . . . are the very worst bands in the country. . . . They can be ruled . . . only with a hand of iron, which is a manner of governing totally unknown to the agents of the Indian Bureau, most of whom are afraid of the Indians and are willing to do anything to conciliate them, thereby making them lose all respect and confidence in him and only sowing the seeds of insurrection. I am afraid of them myself, but have seen enough of them to know that the only way to ensure my safety and their future civilization and prosperity, is to make them afraid of me. An Indian . . . only know[s] two emotions, fear and hate, and unless they fear a person they despise him, and show in every way they can their contempt for his authority.[19]

Gradually there clustered around Delshay the more unruly Indians, causing the whites no little uneasiness. By late summer Schuyler wrote of his fears to Crook, who promptly replied: "By all means arrest Delché & send him with a strong guard to Camp Verde [from his rancheria west of the post]. . . . Get sufficient men from the post so as to prevent a collision & do your utmost to prevent one, but should one unavoidably occur, have your men so posted that they can kill all the ring leaders. . . . I shall feel very anxious about you until I hear from you again . . ."[20] The word arrived too late, however, for Delshay already had sprung the trap. He and his men swiftly surrounded the whites, obviously planning to massacre them, but the loyal scouts and Indian police, no doubt rallied by Sieber, upset their plans and forced the rebels to flee.[21] Thus, by late 1873 there were loose in the Apacheria wilderness four of as vicious renegade leaders as ever ravaged the countryside: Chunz, Cochinay, Chan-deisi, and Delshay, and Crook must make plans for operations against them. The offensive of 1874 was an effort only slightly less than that of 1872–73, but it was to be as successful.

[19] Schuyler to Schuyler, July 6, 1873, Schuyler Collection, Huntington Library.
[20] Crook to Schuyler, September 15, 1873, Schuyler Collection, Huntington.
[21] For details of this incident, see Thrapp, *Sieber*, 121–25.

XIII

The Renegades Destroyed

O NCE MORE Crook organized several commands, to be dispatched from the various forts and camps and criss-cross the Tonto Basin and surrounding ranges, fighting the enemy wherever he might be found. The situation had somewhat worsened by the rigorousness with which Major Randall, who had succeeded Brown at San Carlos, dealt with the essentially democratic Apaches. On January 1, 1874, he had arrested Eskiminzin, for reasons that are obscure but which the Indians did not feel were justified.[1] Within three days the chief escaped, fled to the mountains, and was followed by several bands, most of which soon filtered back to the agency. Because of an unusually hard winter, they were permitted to erect lodges on high ground across the Gila. Its rising waters soon cut them off from the agency.

The outlaws Chunz and Cochinay took advantage of this isolation to slink into camp and reassert their leadership. Drunks followed the gulping of quantities of tiswin, a fermented corn beverage, and on the last day of the month, while the Gila was still impassable, intoxicated warriors attacked freighters camped near the rancheria, killing two of them, while most of the Indians fled in fright. "For a short time," wrote Crook, "these renegades held high carnival, the weather prevailing after the outbreak and continuing for weeks being the most inclement and rigorous ever experienced in Arizona since the American occupation. The whole country was flooded and streams

---

[1] Crook wrote to the adjutant general April 10, 1874, that "I mistrusted the Head chief Eskiminzon, who I saw was not acting in good faith [and] the military officer in charge was obliged to order his arrest," implying Eskiminzin was somehow involved in the slaying of the teamsters, who were killed instead by his enemies.— Crook to AAG, April 10, 1874.—Hayes Collection.

ordinarily attenuated brooks, changed into swollen torrents impassable by troops. Rain & snow so softened the ground our pack trains could not advance one step." When the weather moderated columns were made ready, although "fortunately for the Apaches, only a few commands were available for pursuit."[2] But depredations had continued. About fifty of the most vicious hostiles had raided as far as Tempe, killing after shocking torture a family of six.

One expedition was sent from Verde into the Basin, and another from Whipple. A third, from Lowell, was to comb the Superstitions again. Randall led a column northward out of Camp Grant, being joined by Camp Apache White Mountain scouts and with McIntosh as guide, and with elements of six Fifth Cavalry companies. This large expedition was dispatched after word was received that a large enemy camp had been located atop the almost unassailable Pinals. Marching only at night the command reached a point fifteen miles from the Pinals, but a renegade guide said that an intervening canyon would make it impossible to move directly on the position, and led the way by a twenty-five-mile roundabout route on another approach.

"The country was one mass of broken rocks, and canyons with almost precipitous sides crossed the trail at frequent intervals," wrote General Wesley Merritt some years later of this approach and fight:

All night long they stumbled, struggled, scrambled forward. . . . The briefest of halts for rest were made; for should daylight come before the crest was reached, discovery, repulse and death to many must follow. Before the glimmer of the dawn appeared it was apparent that they were climbing up the side of the last and highest ascent. . . . From the almost precipitous face of the ridge sharp rocky spurs ran out at intervals in the direction from which the troops advanced. The attack was made in three parties, each ascending by one of these natural scaling ladders. So well timed was the operation that when, just at the first streak of dawn, the White Mountain scouts on the right opened fire, and with shouts charged the startled hostiles, the troops had gained the top of their rocky spurs, and the fortified camp

[2] Crook, *ibid.*; Ogle, *Western Apaches*, 143.

which, warned of the attack, could have repulsed a brigade, was carried in three places.[3]

The chief renegades, Chunz, Cochinay, and Chan-deisi, escaped, but many of their comrades did not, there being a dozen killed and twenty-five captured, while the troops did not lose a man. Randall was brevetted colonel.

On Pinal Creek, April 2, Lieutenant Alfred B. Bache had another big fight, killing thirty-one of the enemy and capturing fifty. His scouts having located the rancheria, Bache laid his plans during the night for a dawn attack. About midnight he sent twenty-four soldiers and fifteen White Mountain scouts under Lieutenant Ben Reilly and Archie up Pinal Creek to get on the far side of one of the hostile camps by daylight, then to open fire. A squaw had been captured the day before and impressed as guide. Bache, meanwhile, would take the rest of the men and attack a smaller rancheria. He gave Reilly the honor of striking the larger "as we were officers of nearly the same rank, and as it was Mr. Reilly's first experience in Arizona and he was most anxious to distinguish himself."

Bache and his party descended to a creek, crossed it, and ascended the other side, so steep "that the Indians were obliged to pull us over the rocks. Exhausted and worn out we at last reached the top of the ridge where we lay for two hours shivering with cold waiting for daylight." Reilly meanwhile was getting into position. The hike through the Pinal Creek gorge was a "laborious one," as he admitted, "all my command being obliged to march in the bed of the Creek (the water being quite high) and reached the mountaintops thoroughly drenched from the knee downwards, when they were exposed to a cold and piercing wind." But the tough veterans accepted this as routine, and the summit was reached an hour before daylight. The men crept cautiously into position on a ridge, "in full view and quite close to the Indian fires," but not close enough for warmth. Reilly sent McIntosh with fifteen Indians to the extreme left "to cut off the retreat" of the enemy. Just at daylight a shot was heard on the right.

[3] The preceding account is based on an article by General Merritt in *Harpers*, April, 1890: "Three Indian Campaigns." The general saw no Arizona service.

Thinking that Bache had opened fire, or that the troops had been discovered, Reilly opened fire himself, rousing the panic-stricken enemy from their brush huts. "After firing a few rounds I ordered an advance upon the rancheria, which order was obeyed with great alacrity," the men dashing among the hostiles, "seemingly fresh and with great cheerfulness," despite their night of hard work. Bache also had opened a deadly fire on his rancheria, "and as the Indians were caught between two fires, it is wonderful that any escaped."

Reilly's men collected prisoners and destroyed camp equipment of the hostiles. He found seventeen dead warriors, but none of the renegade leaders, nor did Bache, whose men had killed thirty-one, find any of those most wanted. "I regret to say," the latter reported, "that many women and children were unavoidably killed during the heavy fire." The action led to the conviction that Chunz, Cochinay, and Chan-deisi were not north of the Gila at this time.[4]

Lieutenant Schuyler and Al Sieber returned to Verde after a three-month scout which had taken them all the way to the Aravaipa Mountains, east of Grant, and on which, in a series of skirmishes, they had slain at least eighty-three hostiles and taken twenty-six prisoners, one of the longest and most successful scouts in Apacheria records. But they missed the main renegades, too. Eskiminzin and his band surrendered late in April at San Carlos. Delshay still was lying low somewhere in the breaks below the Mogollon Rim. Chunz, Cochinay, and Chan-deisi were reported here, there, and everywhere. Their followers were picked off one by one, but they themselves remained unscathed. It seemed uncanny.

"These Indians were so encamped with their followers that in almost every case of attack by the troops and allies who were constantly in pursuit, the blow fell upon the followers and the leaders got away, until these followers began to see that they were the great sufferers, after which desertions to our side became more numerous,

---

[4] Reilly's report to Bache, and Bache's report to Randall, of April 11, 1874, incorporating also a report from Captain John M. Hamilton, who led out another expedition from Camp Grant, are the bases for this account; see AGO 2112, 1874, Record Group 94, National Archives.

and it was through these desertions that we were finally enabled to get the ringleaders," Crook reported.[5]

At long last Cochinay was killed by a small band of scouts who reportedly caught him within three miles of Tucson, "awaiting a chance to depredate." His head was borne proudly into San Carlos. A month later Crook wrote Schuyler that "Recent telegram from [Lieutenant John B.] Babcock says that John Daisy's [Chan-deisi's] head was brought into Camp Apache the other day, which leaves now only Chunz's head on his shoulders." He urged Schuyler to "Start your killers as soon as possible after the head of DelChé & Co. The more prompt these heads are brought in, the less liable other Indians, in the future, will be to jeopardize their heads."[6]

Chunz, most elusive of all, had about run out of followers, and also out of luck. His demise came about, not primarily through efforts of the whites, however, but those of Desalin, either a White Mountain war leader or a Tonto, who had surrendered April 1 after a hiatus in the mountains. Since then he had brought in Chief Pedro, a wanted Indian, now was to bring about the death of Chunz, and later was to share the credit for slaying Delshay. Then Desalin, himself, was to be killed tragically at San Carlos within a year.

However, now he had tracked Chunz to his hiding place, about fifteen miles from Tucson "in the precipices of the Santa Caterrina [Santa Catalina] Mountains," reported the *Miner*:

Chuntz had with him a small body of desperadoes who showed fight to our Indians and held them at bay for an entire day. . . . During the night, Chuntz and his band sneaked off through the rocks, leaving behind one of their number, badly wounded. The Indians from San Carlos then returned to that point, where they arrived on [July 15], almost at the same time another of Chuntz's party, badly disabled in the conflict, surrendered himself . . . and offered to conduct the detachment to the place where Chuntz had hoped to find safety and where he had cached a large quantity of ammunition. Thirty Indians were at once dispatched with this Indian to hunt Chuntz down. On

[5] Annual Report for 1874.—Hayes Collection.
[6] Crook to Schuyler, June 23, 1874.—Huntington, Schuyler Collection.

that night [the night of the sixteenth] another of Chuntz' party gave himself up, and the next morning still another. This last arrival reported he had left Chuntz in the canyon about thirty-five miles west of the Agency, and that all his party had abandoned his fortunes except three, who with him, despaired of being able to elude pursuit and were running from rock to rock in frantic terror.[7]

Many volunteers joined the expedition that trapped the doomed Chunz in his final lair. Apparently they found a half-dozen followers with him, instead of three, for they secured seven heads. On July 31 Babcock wired Crook that the head of Chunz and of six other outlaws had been brought in July 25 and neatly arrayed on the parade ground.

So Delshay was left.[8] Crook had offered a small reward for his head, and scouting parties were sent out both from Verde and San Carlos. Both were successful. Three Tontos from Verde, under Schuyler's orders, swore they killed Delshay July 29 near Turret Mountain, and brought in a scalp and an ear to prove it. Desalin, out of San Carlos, brought in a head he claimed to be Delshay's.

"When I visited the Verde reservation, they would convince me that they had brought in his head," wrote Crook, "and when I went to San Carlos, they would convince me that they had brought in his head. Being satisfied that both parties were in earnest in their beliefs, and the bringing in of an extra head was not amiss, I paid both parties."[9]

[7] *Miner*, July 31, 1874.

[8] For speculation that Delshay was in contact with renegade whites during his last hegira, see Thrapp, *Sieber*, 156–57.

[9] Crook, *Autobiography*, 181–82; *Miner*, August 21, 1874; in a letter, August 26, 1874, to the commissioner of Indian Affairs, Agent John P. Clum said that a scout of twenty-five warriors under "Dis-a-lin" left San Carlos twenty days earlier seeking Delshay, "a most desperate and troublesome Indian." He added: "Said scout returned [to San Carlos] this A.M. having taken the head of 'Del-Chay' and left same with the Commanding Officer at Camp McDowell, A. T. 'Dis-a-lin' also brought with him seventy-six captives and thirty-nine members of his own band who have not been on the Reservation since the outbreak." In a letter of October 30, 1874, also to the commissioner, Clum noted that the scout from Verde had brought in only a scalp and an ear while "Dis-a-lin" brought in a head, generally recognized as Delshay's, and had been paid the reward.—Indian Bureau Record Group 75, National Archives.

John Clum Takes Over

WITH THE SECOND Crook offensive completed, the military and civilian Indian agents could settle back to major wrangling over minor issues as was their custom. Jealous of their prerogatives, proud of their respective branches of government, convinced that only their particular way would attain the end that both factions desired, small differences of opinion were magnified out of proportion. But, it should be stated, not all difficulties were manufactured.

At Verde the troubles began when Dr. Josephus Williams, an agent with whom Crook and his officers could work, became insane and was succeeded by his clerk, Oliver Chapman who, Crook admitted, "is probably not as bad as some of the others,"[1] but who lacked the imagination and resourcefulness his position would seem to have required.

Of more immediate moment were the difficulties developing at giant San Carlos, which was to become the key reservation in the Southwest and the focal point for all the Indian difficulties to come. Whether coincidence or not, the difficulties seemed to coincide with the tumultuous Apache career of one agent in particular, John Philip Clum.[2] Clum, on his arrival August 8, 1874, as agent at San Carlos, made it known that he was a figure to be reckoned with. Not quite

[1] Crook to Schuyler, November 9, 1874.—Huntington Collection.

[2] Clum, born September 1, 1851, near Claverack, New York, secured a position with the U.S. Signal Corps' newly organized meteorological service as an observer at Santa Fe in 1871. A member of the Dutch Reformed Church, at that time charged with supervision over the Apaches, Clum accepted the position of agent at San Carlos, to date from February 27, 1874. He arrived at his new post August 8. After leaving San Carlos in 1877 he was an editor and, among other papers, ran the Tombstone *Epitaph*, which he founded May 1, 1880, and became mayor and post-master. He was a postal inspector in Alaska during the 1898 gold rush and died at Los Angeles at eighty-one of a heart attack May 2, 1932.—Woodworth, Clum,

twenty-three, physically short though agile and strong, he was presumptuous, belligerent, cocky, and cantankerous and apparently had an ingrained contempt for officers and the military in general. The typical reaction toward him of the territory's frontiersman was succinctly put by the *Miner*: "The brass and impudence of this young bombast is perfectly ridiculous."[3] But Clum also was intelligent, thoroughly honest, able, willing to assume authority and responsibility alike, and utterly fearless.

He was also about as loquacious an individual as ever landed in Arizona, and much of his time seems to have been spent in penning stinging letters to and about his widening circle of enemies—and friends. When he concluded his Indian work in the territory, he employed his writing talents in composing memoirs that are impassioned, often wildly inaccurate, and always good reading.[4]

John Clum arrived at San Carlos as extensive upheavals in Indian management were imminent, and he was just the man for them to center about. Arizona, the Apaches, and soldiering in the Southwest would never be the same again, once he had imposed his solutions for the big new problems. En route to the San Carlos Agency, Clum stopped for the night at new Camp Grant where he encountered Eskiminzin in chains, he having been brought there from San Carlos after his spring surrender. With George Stevens as interpreter, the new agent and the Indian leader had a chat and reached an area of mutual respect.[5] From that time forward there was affection, even high regard, between the two, and "Skimmy," as Clum called him, became the agent's most dependable ally. Their friendship lasted as long as they both lived. As further indoctrination into the ways of the Apacheria Indian wars, Clum was greeted, the morning after his arrival at San Carlos, by the row of Indian heads on the parade

Apache Agent; *Los Angeles Times*, May 3, 1932; Lutrell, *Newspapers*, 79; *Arizona Historical Review*, April and October, 1932.

[3] Clum, *Apache Agent*, 254, attributes this to the Miami *Miner* of June 15, 1877, but since there was no Miami *Miner*, the reference must be to the Prescott paper.

[4] This is not to imply that they are not prime historical source material, for they are, but they should be used with caution.

[5] Clum, *Apache Agent*, 129–30.

ground, Chunz's among them and presumably in disreputable condition, having been collected two weeks before.

Clum found that his major problem initially was in asserting his authority, not over the Indians, but the military. As he read it, his instructions were to take over entire control of the agency, but Major Babcock thought differently. Clum could scarcely see the officer's viewpoint, but civilian control had been directly responsible for the murder of Almy and the great *émeute* which sent several hundred Apaches roving and depredating over central Arizona; Crook had instructed his officers to make sure that nothing of a similar nature reoccurred. But Clum saw in the situation nothing but military arrogance. This stirred his easily aroused ire. The situation was a standoff for three weeks, while much behind-the-scenes negotiating went on, in Arizona, at Washington, and on the reservation itself. Babcock then informed him that the military would concede Clum entire supervision of Indian affairs at San Carlos.

Already the new agent had made considerable progress in improving the agency and the Indians' lot. He urged them to keep their living quarters and villages clean, to avoid sickness. He counted the adult males daily and all Indians each Saturday, when rations were distributed. He urged the chiefs to name four Indians to be policemen. He organized a high court, with himself as chief justice, to try ordinary infractions of law and discipline. Most important, he persuaded the Apaches to turn in their arms; if one wanted to go hunting, he checked out a rifle for that purpose and returned it after use. He forbade the manufacture of tiswin, and personally led at least one raid with his policemen to destroy its clandestine manufacture. He found work for his Indians, principally in building an agency compound with a main building, living quarters, blacksmith and carpenter shops, harness and tool rooms, a wagon shed, and corral. During the course of all this, a husky, red-headed Irishman named Martin Sweeney, who had been fifteen years a cavalry sergeant, was hired as clerk and majordomo.[6] Clum, years later, wrote that Sweeney was a great help to him. "Honest, industrious, good-

6 Banta, *Arizona Pioneer*, 70–71, 78–79, says Sweeney was a "New York ex-

natured, fearless, he carried out my instructions almost before I issued them. His military training, plus his sympathetic understanding of Apache character, enabled him to teach military tactics to the Indians so that they not only learned how to drill, but enjoyed it, and became excellent soldiers." Clum was to organize his expanded Apache police later into a quasi-military outfit, not only to keep peace on the reservation, but chase renegades outside it.[7]

The real reasons for Clum's success with the wild Apaches are not far to seek. He trusted them, and they appreciated his trust, and returned it. He respected them as individuals and as a people, and they returned respect. He considered them adult enough to govern themselves in internal affairs, and they proved him right. He liked them, and they returned his affection. He was a violent partisan of theirs in all disputes with other whites, and they, in turn, were willing to fight for him. Clum realized that they were an energetic, lively people, and if he didn't find something worthwhile for them to do, they would spend their energy in more reckless pursuits. So he employed them, at a salary, on his building projects and in other ways, and they proved themselves industrious, hard-working people, and capable of becoming excellent craftsmen. He worked out a program that, while not so successful as he believed, yet was far more successful than anything done by and for Apaches in the past. He had his seven hundred or more charges well in hand by the time new and greater problems were thrust upon him.

Washington officialdom had embarked upon a "removal policy" which had, as one of its objectives, the concentration on San Carlos of virtually all the western Apaches and associated tribes in Arizona and New Mexico. Many writers have discussed this program, most of them concluding that it was promoted and abetted by evil men, composing the various so-called "Indian rings"—contractors and others standing to profit one way or another by the policy. Whether

prize fighter," and reported Sweeney later was killed at Tombstone by a badman named Oliver Boyer (Jack Friday).

[7] Clum's account of his first days at San Carlos is summarized in *Apache Agent*, 132–39.

this was true or not, a study of the record for succeeding years would force one to conclude that the concentration policy was unwise, at least with the minimum of psychological preparation that accompanied it. There can be little doubt that it led more or less directly to the Victorio war, or that it was mainly responsible for the Loco and Geronimo campaigns that followed, or for the corollary Nana and Chatto-Chihuahua raids that rattled the southwestern peace the policy was supposed to promote.

The first phase of the concentration policy to be carried out in Arizona was removal of almost fifteen hundred Indians from the Verde Reservation to San Carlos. This was done under direction of special commissioner L. Edwin Dudley, former Indian superintendent in New Mexico, starting February 27, 1875. It was accomplished with a minimum of bloodshed, although one battle between Tontos and Apache-Mohaves and Apache-Yumas was barely stopped in its earliest phase by Guide Al Sieber.[8] Clum triumphantly escorted the new arrivals to a camping ground safely removed from the San Carlos Indians and over a matter of days, using ration tickets as a lever, managed to get them to give up their arms.

Meanwhile things were far from tranquil at Camp Apache where a typical dispute between the military, represented by Major Frederick D. Ogilby, and the Indian service, represented by Agent James E. Roberts, had resulted in the military's forcibly occupying the agency buildings and taking over management of the place. The trouble apparently was no one's fault. Several severe epidemics had ravaged tribesmen, and the survivors turned to tiswin drunks to relieve their distress and fears. Disorders resulted, including slayings and even depredations upon whites. Ogilby felt that Roberts could not control the situation; Roberts believed the military was usurping his authority. The result was that the agent hurried to the nearest telegraph, told Washington about it, and then rode to San Carlos to inform Clum. The Indian commissioner wired Clum to take charge of Apache, and Roberts and Clum rode toward that place, encountering Ogilby with escort en route. The agent showed the officer his

---

[8] For details on this hazardous move, see Thrapp, *Sieber*, 156–69.

166

telegraphic orders, and the latter determined to return to Apache and fight the matter out.

Bickering between the factions reached a new high, or low, as each sought to gain some advantage. In the absence of Roberts, Ogilby had placed the camp doctor over the agency; Clum arrested him for opening Roberts' mail. Clum ordered a count of the Indians, and Ogilby ordered a military count of them at the same hour, threatening to attack those who responded to Clum's demand. Clum rode his horse over to confer with the beef contractor at the fort, and the officer of the day tried to arrest him for riding too fast on the parade ground. Clum insisted that all Indians should be under his control, so Ogilby released all guardhouse prisoners, including two murderers Clum wanted held. The officer also commanded military forces to refuse any request Clum might make for assistance.

John Clum returned to San Carlos after ten days, went to Washington, and reported to the commissioner, who thought it best to move the White Mountain and Coyotero Apaches from Camp Apache to San Carlos. Back in Arizona the little agent took Stevens, Eskiminzin, and about sixty other Indians to Apache and attempted to persuade the natives there of the advantages of San Carlos. Most of the Indians agreed to move, although Chief Pedro's band, and perhaps others, refused. The transfer was effected without incident, and Clum now had forty-two hundred Indians under his direct control.[9] He wanted Al Sieber as his chief of Indian police, but couldn't get him and settled for an excellent second choice, Clay Beauford.[10]

His Indian police concept received its greatest test following a *faux pas* in which the ebullient youngster attempted to advise the flinty warrior Desalin, who had two wives, how he should treat them.

[9] The story of the removal of the Camp Apache Indians to San Carlos is told in more detail in Clum, *Apache Agent*, 155–63, and Ogle, *Western Apaches*, 126–32.

[10] Beauford, or Buford, whose real name was Welford Chapman Bridwell, was born in Maryland in 1848 and at fifteen fought with Pickett at Gettysburg. After the Civil War he enlisted in the Fifth Cavalry, winning a Medal of Honor for heroism. He was with the San Carlos police for several years, subsequently married, and established ranches and became a man of some prominence. He died at Los Angeles on February 1, 1905.—Barnes, *Place Names*, 66–67; Clum, *Apache Agent*, 163; Price, *Fifth Cavalry*, 673, 674, 680; Tucson *Star*, February 19 and 22, 1882.

Desalin tried to kill him and was slain instead by his brother, Tauel-clyee, a policeman who, of course, regretted the incident but was convinced, so he said, that it was his duty. Clum had reason to be grateful for this sample of his policemen's loyalty, for he soon had need of them on a most dangerous expedition to the south, to collect and bring to San Carlos such of the Chiricahua Apaches as he might. They had thought themselves secure on their vast reservation, bordering handily on Old Mexico, and they had remained there following Cochise's pact with General Howard several years earlier. This agreement, or, possibly, treaty, was arranged by the general and the chief after they had met through the assistance of Jeffords, one of the few white men Cochise would trust. But Cochise had demanded that if he were to accept a reservation, Jeffords would be named Indian agent for it. This was done, against the white man's wishes, it was reported, and on his terms.

"He was to be absolute boss upon the reservation, admitting no one on [it] unless with his consent, and taking absolute control and authority over the Indians. . . . Thereafter no soldier or civilian, or official of any kind, came upon the reservation without Jeffords' consent, and for the four years that he was Indian agent, there was never any trouble with the Chiricahua Apaches."[11] Jeffords was bonded for $50,000, while most Indian agents were bonded only for $10,000, but when his accounts were audited at Washington, his bondsmen were released within three months, "something unheard of in the history of the administration of Indian affairs in Arizona."[12] Criticisms developed over the way in which he ran what came to be considered his barony in southeastern Arizona, but how far they were justified it is difficult to say. There were charges that Jeffords sold ammunition to the Chiricahuas,[13] and these may have been true, although since the Indians at this time plotted no general uprising, the significance is not clear, but it may have been more apparent to citizens of Sonora. Governor Safford wrote Crook March 31, 1873,

[11] Farish, *History of Arizona*, II, 235. This was not literally true.
[12] *Ibid.*, 239.
[13] Ogle, *Western Apaches*, 107n.

sending him a copy of a communication from Governor I. Pesqueira of that state, listing twenty or more depredations occurring between October, 1872, and March, 1873, involving many murders and other outrages, allegedly committed by Apaches.[14] Safford added that "so far as the people of Arizona are concerned, I believe that Cachise has kept his word with us," but any attempt to halt Chiricahua raids on Mexico might touch off renewed hostilities against Americans.

Cochise died of some malady on June 8, 1874,[15] and was succeeded as chief by Taza, his son. This was the situation as it existed when John Clum took over at San Carlos. It was complicated, however, by the fact that the Warm Springs Apaches from New Mexico wandered back and forth, visiting their blood brothers, the Chiricahuas, and perhaps raiding and depredating en route. The Chiricahua reserve, moreover, was a refuge for renegades from both sides of the border, as well as for wilder spirits from the White Mountain and San Carlos reserves. Adding to the difficulties, Jeffords' supply of beef was cut, perhaps by orders from Washington, and it was impossible to ration his own Indians properly, let alone the visitors. So he told his charges that they would have to supplement their issued food by hunting, and a portion of the tribe moved to the Dragoon Mountains. There a quarrel arose, and three Indians were killed. Most of the remainder, under Taza, returned to the vicinity of the agency. One leader, Skinya, with a dozen followers, sullenly remained in the Dragoons, others raided into Mexico, returning with loot, including some gold dust and silver.

A stagecoach station attendant named Rogers, and his assistant, Spence, offered the Apaches whiskey at ten dollars a bottle, in order to get their booty. Pionsenay, Skinya's brother and one of his most devoted followers, bought some liquor, became drunk, wanted some more, and when Rogers refused to sell it to him, killed both Rogers and Spence, stole the whiskey, plus arms and ammunition, and re-

[14] Safford to Crook, from Tucson, March 31, 1873, including translation from the Mexican document headed "Apaches in Sonora," the whole from Record Group 94, National Archives.

[15] For a delineation of Cochise's character and added details about his last years, death and burial, see Lockwood, *Apache Indians*, 124–30.

turned to camp. A few outlaws the next day, still drunk, killed another white man and stole some horses. Troops, with Jeffords, cornered the renegades in the Dragoon crags, but couldn't dislodge them. A month later, on May 3, Clum received telegraphic instructions to go to the Chiricahua Reservation, suspend Jeffords, and, "if practicable, remove Chiricahua Indians to San Carlos."

Agent Clum waited until the entire Sixth Cavalry was deployed in southeastern Arizona, to take care of eventualities, and then moved on the reservation with fifty-six San Carlos police. He arrived at Sulphur Springs June 4, 1876. That same day Skinya and his outlaws slipped into Taza's camp and tried to persuade the chief's Indians to swing out on the warpath. When they refused a fight developed in which Skinya and six of his men were killed and two were wounded, one of them Pionsenay. Clum arrived at Apache Pass the next day and talked with Taza, who agreed to go with his band to San Carlos, while a messenger soon arrived from Pionsenay who, apparently thinking his wound was mortal, wanted to come in and die. Twenty scouts under Tauelclyee were sent to bring him in.

The young agent left Apache Pass for San Carlos June 12 with three hundred and twenty-five Indians, about one-third of those supposed to be on the Chiricahua Reservation. The worst of the lot, some four hundred under the doughty recalcitrants Juh, Geronimo, and Nolgee, fooled Clum and fled into Sonora, and perhaps two hundred others slipped off and made their way to the familiar New Mexico stamping grounds. The wounded Pionsenay, too, escaped, after being turned over by Clum to the sheriff of Pima County to be tried for murder. Clum's police reached San Carlos with this small and relatively inoffensive portion of the Chiricahuas, including only sixty warriors, on June 18, but the agent, in his memoirs, writes as though he had brought in the entire band.[16] Most, and the worst, were in a

[16] Most histories of the region describe the transfer of the Chiricahuas, but my main reliance has been Clum's own account: "Geronimo," part I, *New Mexico Historical Review*, Vol. III, No. 1, (January, 1928), 7–26. See Lockwood, *Apache Indians*, 214–18: Ogle, *Western Apaches*, 166–68; Dunn, *Massacres*, 637–38; Bancroft, *Arizona and New Mexico*, 567–58n.; Wellman, *Indian Wars*, 361–63; Clum, *Apache Agent*, 170–84.

more threatening position than ever, securely based in the Sierra Madre. In fact, twenty whites were slain by these Indians and at least one hundred horses stolen north of the border within two months. One historian wrote:

> The removal of the Chiricahua Apaches from their reservation was the crowning folly of the Indian Bureau. Not only did the Chiricahuas dislike the region of San Carlos; not only was it already overpopulous with tribes averse, or even hostile to each other, held there against their will; but the Chiricahuas were keenly aware of the fact that their own reservation had been taken away from them, not because of the disloyalty of the Chiricahuas as a people, but as the result of the misdeeds of a small, violent faction arising directly from the wicked greed of a white man placed in their midst.[17]

With these successful transfers, if they may be called successful, Clum had now concentrated at San Carlos virtually all of the western Apaches—save the Warm Springs and Victorio, and their time had almost come.

Victorio, probably a Mimbres Apache,[18] was the last of the really

[17] Lockwood, *Apache Indians*, 217–18.
[18] C. L. Sonnichsen, *The Mescalero Apaches*, 159, says there is a "tradition in northern Mexico and the border country that he was a Mexican captive, who came into the tribe as a little boy and rose to eminence by sheer personal force and fighting ability." He adds that some Chihuahuans believe he was taken as a child from the Rancho del Carmen of Luis Terrazas. Mrs. Eve Ball of Hollywood, New Mexico, who has spent many years interviewing innumerable descendants of Warm Springs and other Apaches, does not believe this. Her informants frankly told her, "If it had been true, we would have been told," and they were not told. It is noteworthy that Geronimo and Mangas, to name but two, also were rumored to have been white, or part white, tales probably equally untrue. Carlysle Graham Raht, *The Romance of Davis Mountains and Big Bend Country*, 271, says "Victorio has often been called a Mescalero Apache, but he was a Chiricahua Apache." Frederick Webb Hodge, *Handbook of American Indians North of Mexico*, I, 64, 282, says he was a Chiricahua, although leading Mimbrenos, Mescaleros, Mogollones, and others. Ogle, *Western Apaches*, 56, considers him a Mimbreno, and so does Wellman, *Indian Wars*, 253–54. Carl Coke Rister, *The Southwestern Frontier: 1865–1881*, 185n., says simply he was a "southern Apache." Lockwood, *Apache Indians*, 222, and Clum, "Victorio," *NMHR*, Vol. IV, No. 4 (October, 1929), 11, say simply that he was chief of the Warm Springs band. Sonnichsen himself, p. 159, admitted that Victorio "passed for a Mimbres or Gila Apache."

great war leaders of that people, judging from his record. Various attempts had been made to settle the Warm Springs on various reserves, but with indifferent success. At last they had been permitted to settle at Warm Springs, or Ojo Caliente as it also was called, in southern New Mexico,[19] from where continuing depredations, persistent hostility toward them of white settlers, and other factors, finally persuaded the Interior Department that they should be removed to San Carlos. John Clum was charged with the transfer, and he stepped with engaging enthusiasm into this challenging project. His orders, from the commissioner of Indian Affairs, dated March 20, 1877, read: "If practicable, take Indian Police and arrest renegade Indians at Southern Apache Agency; seize stolen horses in their possession, restore property to rightful owners, remove renegades to San Carlos and hold them in confinement for murder and robbery."[20] The orders were precipitated when First Lieutenant Austin Henely of the Sixth Cavalry espied Geronimo in the vicinity of Las Palomas and believed he was making his headquarters at the Southern Apache, or Warm Springs, Agency; word of it reached the commissioner.

The agent, eager to embark on "one of the most important and exciting campaigns I have ever undertaken," ordered Clay Beauford to take his police company, bolstered by the enlistment of forty more Indians, and start for Ojo Caliente, several hundred miles from San Carlos by wagon road. General Edward Hatch, commanding the Department of New Mexico, ordered eight companies of the Ninth Cavalry to co-operate and planned a rendezvous with Clum April 21 near the agency. But the cavalry didn't arrive on time, and the agent determined to use only his own force of 102 Indian police, and Beauford. He had learned from a spy that there were from 250 to 400 "well armed, desperate Indians" there, and that Geronimo, with 80 to 100 followers was camped within three miles of the agency. Clum

[19] Ojo Caliente, or Warm Springs, was eighteen miles north of Winston, which is thirty-seven miles by road northwest of Truth or Consequences, New Mexico, and on the Alamosa River. See James W. Abarr, "Fort Ojo Caliente," *Desert Magazine*, Vol. XXII, No. 4 (April, 1959), 19–21.

[20] Clum, "Geronimo," *NMHR*, Vol. III, No. 1 (January, 1928), 26.

pushed ahead with 22 police, ordering his chief of police to follow the next day with the balance.

Situated on a dusty bench and circling an assembly ground, the adobe agency has long since ceased to exist, but its outlines can still be seen from the heaps of half-melted walls here and there. At that time it was a busy, thriving place. Clum sent a courier under cover of darkness to Beauford, with orders to bring in his police and conceal them in the commissary building before dawn. And at dawn, the little agent sent a messenger to Geronimo, telling him to bring in his important men for a talk. "They came quickly—a motley clan, painted and equipped for a fight," Clum recalled. "Supported by a half-dozen of my police I took my position on the porch of the main agency building over-looking the parade ground. . . . The reserves were instructed that at a signal from Captain Beauford their sergeant would swing wide the great commissary doors and then race eastward along the south line of the parade ground, and they were to follow hot on his trail at intervals of about two paces—every man with his thumb on the hammer of his gun."

Defiantly the renegades[21] gathered in a compact group in front of Clum, and the agent stepped forward to address them, saying "if they would listen to my words 'with good ears' no serious harm would be done them." Geronimo promptly retorted "that if I spoke with discretion no serious harm would be done us."

"This defiant attitude convinced me it would be useless to continue the parley," Clum wrote. "The crisis had arrived. The hour had struck. . . . On either side were the most determined of men. . . . The situation demanded action—*prompt action*, and very promptly the signal was given. Instantly the commissary portals swung open and Sergeant Rip started his sprint along the south line of the parade grounds. As if by magic the reserves came swarming out from the commissary, and, in single file, leaped after their sergeant at top speed with intervals that left room for the free use of their weapons." Half a dozen hostiles started to flee, but Beauford raised his rifle and ordered them back.

[21] Ogle, *Western Apaches*, 173, says they included Geronimo, Gordo, Ponce, Francisco, and thirteen others.

"There are always a few belligerent squaws who insist upon intruding whenever a 'war-talk' is in progress," Clum noted, "and one of these athletic ladies had stationed herself close by our stalwart chief of police. With a wild yell she sprang upon Beauford and clung to his neck and arms in such a manner as to draw down his rifle. . . . I had been keeping my two eyes on Geronimo, but with the echo of that genuine Apache yell, I turned just in time to appreciate Beauford's expression of profound disgust when he discovered that he had been captured by a squaw. Then he swung that great right arm to which the lady was clinging and she landed ingloriously on the parade ground—and at a respectful distance."

Clum ordered Geronimo to the guardhouse. "He did not move," the agent wrote. "Then I added, 'You must go now.' "

Like a flash he leaped to his feet. There was a picture I shall never forget. He stood erect as a mountain pine, while every outline of his symmetrical form indicated strength and endurance. His abundant ebony locks draped his ample shoulders, his stern features, his keen piercing eye, and his proud and graceful posture combined to create in him the model of an Apache war-chief. There he stood— GERONIMO THE RENEGADE, a form commanding admiration, a name and character dreaded by all. His eyes blazed fiercely under the excitement of the moment and his form quivered with suppressed rage. From his demeanor it was evident to all that he was hesitating between two purposes, whether to draw his knife, his only remaining weapon, cut right and left and die fighting—or to surrender? Instantly Sergeant Rip sprang forward and snatched the knife from Geronimo's belt, while the muzzles of a half-dozen needle guns . . . pressed toward him—their locks clicking almost in unison as their hammers were drawn back. With flashing eyes he permitted himself to indulge in a single swift, defiant glance at his captors. Then his features relaxed and he said calmly: "In-gew" [all right]—and thus was accomplished the first and only *bonafide capture* of GERONIMO THE RENEGADE.

Shackles were riveted to his ankles, irons that were not removed as long as Geronimo remained in Clum's custody. Other Indians, including Ponce, also were ironed. By the time the military arrived, April 22, the principal renegades had been shackled and were in a makeshift guardhouse, the corral, guarded by ten policemen. Clum retained twenty-five picked police and sent the remainder home under Beauford with instructions to intercept if they could small bands of hostiles raiding between Ojo Caliente and Dos Cabezas mountains. Hardly had that force marched out, however, than he received new instructions from Washington.[22] He was directed to take all the Ojo Caliente Indians, whether renegade or not, to San Carlos, "if, upon consultation with the military authorities, such action was deemed desirable." General Hatch thought it was a great idea, taking the southern Apaches out of his department, so Clum called a second conference, this time with Victorio as the principal Indian, noting that he was "the recognized chief of the Warm Springs Indians." A lengthy talk ensued, as Clum reports it, and the Indians agreed to remove to Arizona. By sundown 434 individuals, Victorio among them, had been collected. The total later reached 453 men, women, and children, of whom 110 were Geronimo's following and the remainder Victorio's.[23] May 1 was set as the departure date, but on that day Clum was disturbed to see an Indian sitting on a step, head in hands and loose hair tumbling about his face. When spoken to, the Indian moaned. The agent was aghast to discover that the Apache had smallpox, but he found a policeman who had had the disease and who agreed to drive the victim in an ambulance at a discreet distance from the column.

The Ojo Caliente Indians, Victorio among them, arrived at San Carlos May 20 and the shackled Geronimo was offered to the Pima County sheriff, but no legal action was taken against him. Victorio was added to the reservation's council of judges, but the New Mexico

[22] It is difficult to determine the sequence of events from Clum's accounts. In one place he says that his talk with Victorio occurred on the same morning as the Geronimo capture; in another he says that he received instructions to take Victorio to San Carlos after Beauford left. The latter seems likely.

[23] Lockwood, *Apache Indians*, 222. For most of the preceding information on removal of the Warm Springs, I have used Clum, "Geronimo," *NMHR*, Vol. III, No. 1 (January, 1928), 26–40, checking it against other accounts.

Indians remained restless, unsettled, unhappy.[24] The multitudinous depredations of the renegades still out did nothing to resign the Warm Springs Apaches to their fate, either.[25] Not only was there mutual hostility and distrust between the various Indian bands crowded onto San Carlos, but the ceaseless civil-military bickering between Indian Service and Army officials must have seeped into the

[24] "In every instance," wrote Lockwood, *Apache Indians*, 225, "the removal was a breach of good faith ... of the Government, was contrary to the best judgment of Army officers ... , and was in opposition to the desire of the Indians. Nor was the transfer ... completely effected. Many ... refused to come along, and ... the best fighting men ... slipped away." Dunn, *Massacres*, 641–43, examines the national concentration police and excoriates it even more bitterly. It is extremely difficult to correlate the various writers on the removal of the Warm Springs bands, particularly after Victorio broke out. Clum of course, was sanguine in his view, but Bourke, *Border*, 444, wrote: "The 'Warm Springs' Apaches were peremptorily deprived of their little fields and driven away from their crops, half-ripened, and ordered to tramp to San Carlos; when the band reached there the fighting men had disappeared, and only decrepit warriors, little boys and girls, and old women remained." In much of that he is correct. Wellman, *Indian Wars*, 366, says that "at the time Clum arrested Geronimo and Pi-hon-se-ne, he had a talk with Victorio, who told him he would far rather die than go to San Carlos." Clum did not arrest Pionsenay at this time, for the latter was raiding in Mexico, and it was two years later that Victorio voiced violent opposition to a return to San Carlos. Dunn, p. 639, says, "None of the Indians wished to leave Ojo Caliente, but there was no chance for resistance. Very few escaped, the principal party being some 40 warriors led by Victorio," implying that Victorio never went to San Carlos, but he did. McClintock, *Arizona*, I, 229, implies that Loco and Nana were in the Warm Springs contingent; they were not. Hodge, *Handbook*, I, 64, is hopelessly confused: "The police [of concentration] was applied to the Ojo Caliente Apaches of New Mexico ... but when the plan was put in action only 450 of 2,000 Indians were found, the remainder forming into predatory bands under Victorio." Lockwood, *Apache Indians*, 218–23, is most lucid, and Ogle, *Western Apaches*, 172–75, is probably as accurate.

[25] Samples of the activity: a Brayton scout in the Tonto Basin from January 9 to February 5, 1877. Lieutenant John Rucker with his Sixth Cavalry unit and three companies of Indian scouts struck hostiles in the Leitendorf Range, New Mexico, January 9. Ninth Cavalry units clashed with renegades January 23 in the Florida Mountains of New Mexico, and five days later in Old Mexico. March 7 there was a fight near Fort Davis, Texas, with roaming Apaches. Lieutenant Frank West with two companies of the Sixth Cavalry had a fight near Camp Bowie late in May, after two mail carriers had been killed near the post. Lieutenant T. A. Touey's command was defeated by hostiles in the Las Animas Mountains shortly after. August 29 Lieutenant G. E. Overton and a Sixth Cavalry unit captured thirteen hostiles near Black Rock, Arizona. Most of these are reported in the *Chronological List*, 41–42.

Apache consciousness. The Indians could not have known the details, but neither could they have been unaware of it in substance. John Clum resigned as agent in a huff, effective July 1, 1877, and H. L. Hart was appointed to succeed him. Insufficient supplies, either because of inefficiency in distribution or cupidity on the part of reservation officials, now added to the difficulties, and an explosion clearly was in the making. It came early in September.

Pionsenay, fresh from Mexico and burdened with loot, slipped into the reserve on the night of September 1. He wanted his women and the families of his band, and he boasted of his successes below the border, and in New Mexico and Arizona as well. This was the spark the disenchanted Mimbres and Chiricahuas needed, and under Victorio and Loco they made their break. Three hundred and ten men, women, and children dashed eastward, into the jumbled ranges of eastern Arizona and western New Mexico.[26] They swept up loose horses and mules belonging to the White Mountain Apaches, who swiftly notified the agent, and before dawn a mixed posse of police, scouts, and volunteer Apaches were hot on the trail. They collided with the hostiles at the foot of Natanes Mountain, pinned against a sheer wall. Victorio's people defended themselves, but couldn't hold on to their animals and lost not only those they had stolen from the White Mountains, but their own as well. The posse then let the hostiles escape.[27]

Later the pursuit was resumed and the enemy again met near Ash Creek. A few hostiles were killed, about thirty women and children captured, and the soldiers then camped for the night. They awakened, no doubt relieved to find Victorio gone, and went home themselves, their only casualties "the skinned up agency mules." Victorio's party scattered northward into the broken country south of Fort Wingate, among the lava beds, broken buttes, peaks, and arroyos. Not yet hungry enough to surrender, they killed at least a dozen ranchers, running off a hundred or so horses, and engaged in sharp clashes with

---

[26] It is noteworthy that Geronimo, who had been freed by Hart, did not go with them.—Ogle, *Western Apaches*, 184.

[27] Tucson *Star*, March 29, 1880.

the military from New Mexico and Arizona as well as police elements.[28] After losing 56 persons in scattered fights, 190 hostiles surrendered finally at Fort Wingate, southeast of present-day Gallup, and 50 came in later.[29]

What should now be done with them? They could not be at once returned to San Carlos, because it would turn the whole reservation into an uproar. Nor could they be left at Wingate, for a variety of reasons. Pending some better solution they were returned to Warm Springs, General Hatch promising them that "if they would prove themselves to be good Indians, he would do what he could to have them remain there," according to one contemporary.[30] They worked hard to prove themselves "good Indians," and so well did they succeed that "the Rio Grande settlers were secure in their persons and property; the various valleys in the mountains were being settled up and peace reigned throughout that region. Prospectors, travellers and freighters went unmolested. From Fort Wingate to Fort Stanton, and from Fort Union to Fort Bliss, Texas, all was quiet and peace; not a head of stock was stolen by the Indians."[31]

At San Carlos, meanwhile, there was continued unrest, probably spurred by Victorio's temporary success. In December Juh and Nolgee captured a wagon train in the Stein's Peak area, killed several men, and scoured the countryside for loose stock. They fled toward Mexico, but Lieutenant John Anthony (Tony) Rucker, coming home from a scout below the border, stumbled onto their camp in the Animas Mountains December 18, 1877, attacked it with eighty

---

[28] Ogle, *Western Apaches*, 183. It will be observed that these depredations do not seem comparable to the bloody ones later, and it would seem that Victorio used restraint, stealing horses merely as remounts and killing whites only when it was unavoidable.

[29] It is possible Victorio was not among them. With a handful of followers he may have fled to Mexico, surrendering voluntarily in February, 1878, at Ojo Caliente. Only in a newspaper summary, printed in 1880, have I found it stated that Victorio did surrender at Wingate.

[30] Letter signed, "Palomas," in Tucson *Star*, April 6, 1880. The writer refers to himself as "no Indian lover," the better, no doubt, to stress his objectivity, but he was apparently acquainted with details of Victorio's story.

[31] *Ibid.*

men, and killed fifteen hostiles, capturing one, retaking sixty animals and much plunder. Rucker's Mexican scout was under an agreement revoked by Mexico the following spring, permitting a command from either side to cross the border when in "hot pursuit."[32]

Victorio took little interest in these operations. He and his band continued to live at Ojo Caliente while the Interior Department deliberated over their fate. The Army grew increasingly weary of its chore of guardianship while Indian Service specialists mulled over whether to return Victorio to San Carlos, leave him where he was, or move him entirely out of the Southwest, even perhaps to Fort Sill, Oklahoma, as was for a time under consideration. Finally Generals William Tecumseh Sherman and Philip Sheridan, commander of the U.S. Army and of the Division of the Missouri, respectively, threatened to turn Victorio loose altogether.[33] Interior then asked the War Department to deliver the Mimbres group once more to San Carlos; "in an evil hour," the concentration policy was reaffirmed.[34] Captain F. T. Bennett of the Ninth Cavalry, with two companies of troops and scouts, reached Ojo Caliente on October 8, 1878, to effect the transfer.

"Victorio told him that his home was here, that his people had been born here, that they loved their home, and, further, that not a buck of his band would go to San Carlos." When Captain Bennett said that he had to obey his orders and that Victorio would have to go to San Carlos, the Indian reportedly replied: "You can take our squaws and children in your wagons, but my men will not go!" and with a yell, he and his band broke for the mountains, "where they are yet."[35] About eighty Indians bolted, and seventeen others followed shortly; all efforts to track them proved fruitless, because autumn storms obliterated their trail.

---

[32] Ogle, *Western Apaches*, 186n.

[33] *Ibid.*, 193.

[34] Tucson *Star*, April 6, 1880.

[35] *Ibid.* This is by the reckoning used here. The chronology may be open to question, but it is difficult to correlate the events any other way. The various authorities seem to confuse 1877, 1878, and 1879 completely and to ignore their own obvious discrepancies.

A mixed group of 169 Indians, noncombatants for the most part, remained, were loaded into wagons, and taken in December, 1878, on a miserable trip through mud, rain, and snow to Fort Apache. Dr. Walter Reed, of Spanish-American War fame, stationed at Apache at the time, adopted a little Indian girl who had suffered severe burns during a campfire accident on the trail.[36] Storms had closed the San Carlos trail to wagon traffic, but the bedraggled and half-frozen prisoners were turned over to Dan Ming,[37] veteran frontiersman and then chief of police at San Carlos, and with forty scouts he conducted them as humanely as possible to that post where they were closely guarded in anticipation of probable efforts by Victorio to free them.

Victorio wintered in the soaring country of southern New Mexico, where savage weather made for difficult times. By February, 1879, he had had enough and with twenty-two men he cautiously approached Ojo Caliente, pleading that they be permitted to surrender and stay there, or anywhere but San Carlos. They preferred to die, they said, rather than return to San Carlos among their enemies.[38] Lieutenant Charles W. Merritt, Ninth Cavalry, listened sympathetically and promised to do what he could for them. He sent a message to his commanding officer, and Hatch relayed it to Washington, and again there was the problem of what to do with this troublesome chief who so loved his homeland. Rumors came to Victorio that he was to be taken to the Mescalero Reservation, at Tulerosa, and sud-

[36] Ogle, *Western Apaches*, 194n.

[37] Daniel Houston Ming, born near Louisville, Kentucky, February 23, 1845, in 1872 helped bring a herd of two thousand Texas cattle to Arizona and became a prominent stockman. He was a packer in the Philippines in 1899 and died November 12, 1925, at San Francisco. He won local fame with a prayer he delivered at an 1866 cattlemen's meeting called to consider a drastic drought: "Oh Lord, I'm about to round you up for a good plain talk. Now Lord, I ain't like these fellows who come bothering you every day. This is the first time I ever tackled you for any thing and if you will only grant this I'll promise never to bother you again. We want rain, good Lord, and we want it bad, and we ask you to send us some. But if you can't or don't want to send us any, for Christ's sake don't make it rain up around Hooker's or Leitch's ranges, but treat us all alike. Amen."—Interview with Bud Ming, Ray, Arizona; Barnes, *Place Names*, 279.

[38] Pope to Adjutant General Edward D. Townsend, Washington, D.C., February 13, 1879, Record Group 75, National Archives.

denly he didn't want to go there, either. So he and his warriors once more took to the mountains, this time in April and springtime. But by early summer they had again had their fill of the fugitive life. The whites had said they must go to the Mescaleros—all right, they would go. On June 30, 1879, they appeared before the agent there who agreed to take them if they would promise to raise corn and stop raising trouble. As an added inducement, he offered to urge that their wives and children be sent them from San Carlos. Victorio readily agreed.[39]

All might have been peace, save for one of those curious coincidences that sometimes cause difficulty. In July an indictment was brought at Silver City charging Victorio and others with murder and horse stealing. Somehow word of it reached the Indians and made them uneasy. In late summer a hunting party rode through the reservation, and Victorio recognized among them a judge and prosecuting attorney, and thought they were after him.[40] Panic ensued. In a passion, Victorio jerked the agent's beard, whistled in his horse herd, ordered the women into action, hurriedly packed his ponies, and with his fellows scampered toward the westward mountains once more.[41] It was September 4, 1879.[42] They were through with reservation life; from now on forever it would be war. With him rode what Southern Apaches were at hand. Within a few months they were to be joined by three hundred and fifty Chiricahua and Mescalero raiders from Mexico, the Davis Mountains, and the Mescalero Reservation, and perhaps some Comanches.

[39] Lockwood, *Apache Indians*, 229.

[40] *Ibid.*

[41] Sonnichsen, *Mescalero Apaches*, 161–63, gives interesting details of Victorio's final break, drawn from A. N. Blazer, "Beginnings of an Indian War," *New Mexico*, Vol. XVI, No. 2 (February, 1938), 22ff.

[42] Again chronology is a question. Newspapers use this date.

XV

Victorio!

Victorio's bloody work began at once. At Temporal Canyon his warriors killed two sheepherders and stole their horses. They swept down on the horse herd of Company E, Ninth Cavalry, killing the five soldiers and three civilians on guard and stealing forty-six head of Captain Ambrose Hooker's stock.[1] Freshly mounted, they made for the inaccessible reaches of the Black Mountains to the west, ravaging the countryside and striking widespread terror as they went. Major A. P. Morrow, in command in southern New Mexico, ordered every available trooper into the field. Commands from west Texas to central Arizona were put on the alert. The military in southern Arizona was prepared to take the field on short notice. A board of officers that was to have convened at Fort Lowell was ordered to postpone the meeting, the members to hasten back to their respective posts.[2]

Second Lieutenant Charles Baehr Gatewood with fifteen soldiers and twenty men from Company A, Indian scouts, was ordered out from Fort Apache to "intercept Victorio, should he attempt to go near San Carlos," where the families of the hostiles were still quartered.[3] Company D, Indian scouts, was sent with a Sixth Cavalry

[1] *Chronological List*, 47.

[2] Tucson *Star*, September 9, 1879.

[3] Gatewood, given twenty-four words by Heitman, was a West Pointer from Woodstock, Virginia, born in 1853. His services during his short lifetime were almost without parallel. "Commanding a company of Indian scouts, and on other duty connected with the management of the Apaches," he wrote, he "took part in all the campaigns against them from 1879 to 1886." Charles B. Gatewood, "Campaigning Against Victorio in 1879," *The Great Divide* (April, 1894), 102–104. His middle name is spelled Bare in Army records, but Baehr in Gatewood, "The Surrender of Geronimo," *Proceedings of the Annual Meeting and Dinner of the Order of Indian Wars of the United States* (January, 1929).

detachment under Lieutenant Guy Howard to scout the country east of Camp Huachuca. Lieutenant Augustus P. Blocksom took a detachment with Company C, Indian scouts, into the field from Bowie. Captain Tullius C. Tupper was sent from Grant to scour the surrounding hills. General Eugene A. Carr hurried to Fort Lowell, Tucson, to take active command of the Sixth. Thus patrols under energetic and experienced officers threw up a screen against Victorio's hostiles along the southern Arizona-New Mexico border, and Victorio left them alone. But not so the troops of New Mexico, pushing toward the heart of his stronghold, near the headwaters of the Animas, twenty miles above Hillsboro and forty south of Ojo Caliente.

Victorio laid a skillful ambush with about one hundred fifty of his fighting men early on September 18, 1879. It was done so well that Captain Byron Dawson and forty-six Navaho scouts and men of the Ninth Cavalry were "hardly aware of their immediate presence before [he] found he could not extricate himself without heavy loss and perhaps utter destruction."[4] The hostiles loosed a withering fire from both sides of a rocky defile. The troopers dove for cover, abandoning their frightened horses, but the Indians covered most available shelter. A courier was sped back for help. About ten o'clock a shout went up from those troopers farthest down the arroyo, signaling the approach of fifty-two more men, many of them citizens from Hillsboro under Captain Charles D. Beyer. However, "owing to the constant and galling fire of the savages, and the utter impossibility of dislodging them from their commanding position, Captain Beyer could do no more than afford Captain Dawson all possible aid, in the hope of extricating him and his men from their perilous position."[5] The fight continued all day. Many acts of heroism were performed.

[4] Silver City, New Mexico, *Herald*, reprinted in the *Star*, October 1, 1879; Selected Documents, relating to the activities of the Ninth and Tenth Cavalry in the campaign against Victorio 1879–80, Adjutant General's Office, Letters Received, Record Group 94, National Archives and Records Service (hereafter cited as Victorio Papers with serial number), 6236, Morrow to McDowell, September 25, 1879, and 6323, Pope to Sheridan, September 25, 1879.

[5] Silver City *Herald*, October 1, 1879.

Second Lieutenant Matthias W. Day rescued and bore off a wounded soldier across two hundred yards of open space, every foot of it under heavy fire. For this he was awarded a Medal of Honor and narrowly missed a court-martial.[6] Dr. Kennon, a contract surgeon, scoured the hostile positions with field glasses until a rifle ball smashed them in his hands.

At dusk Captain Beyer decided to withdraw, leaving the field to Victorio. Eight men, including Jack Hagan, a citizen, and two Navaho scouts, were killed, and two enlisted men seriously wounded. Fifty-three government horses and mules were abandoned, thirty-two reportedly killed, and the hostiles captured the baggage of most of the officers and much other booty.

Lieutenants Blocksom and Gatewood, with their scouts, had been ordered to Fort Bayard, near Silver City, to strengthen Morrow and as soon as word of the debacle reached the post, were sent over the Mimbres Mountains to the site, while strong cavalry elements rounded the mountains by road in support. The third or fourth day out the scouts struck the hostile trail, according to Gatewood.[7]

> Cutting loose from our pack trains we followed that trail for three nights, each man carrying his rations and equipments. We laid over in the daytime. It rained every minute of the time, and as we dared to build only very small fires to do our cooking by, there was no chance to dry our clothing and the few blankets in the party. The only part of the little we had to eat not spoiled by the rain was the bacon. The second day we found some jerked horse meat and the third an old abandoned government mule. From the time his throat was cut by a scout till a stew of bacon and mule was simmering very few minutes elapsed. By the fourth day we were far into the Black Range. It had ceased raining.

[6] Gatewood wrote of this that Day "declined to retreat and leave his wounded behind, but carried a disabled soldier away under a heavy fire, for which offense the commanding officer, Byer, wanted to have him tried by court martial, and for which the Congress of the United States gave him a gold medal."—Gatewood, "Victorio," *The Great Divide*, 102.

[7] *Ibid.*, 102–103; see also Victorio Papers 6324, Pope to Sheridan, September 26, 1879; 6528, Sheridan to Sherman, October 4, 1879; 6536, Sheridan to AGO, October 8, 1879; 6718, Hatch to AG, Division of the Pacific, October 7, 1879.

Just before sundown our scouts in advance located Mr. Victorio and his "outfit" encamped in a deep canyon. They saw each other about the same time, and the fun began. The firing, of course, brought up those in rear "double quick." From the small number of scouts first seen, the hostiles thought themselves already the victors and became quite saucy and facetious, daring them to come closer and even inviting them to supper. My first sergeant, Dick, answered, "We are coming," and when old Vic's braves saw forty odd scouts and as many soldiers come tumbling down the side of the canyon into their camp, they stayed not on the order of their going. Darkness aided their flight. Result: two bucks and a squaw on their side; on our side, nothing. They managed to drive their stock away.

Early next morning, as we had just finished breakfast, a single shot rang out down the canyon, then a volley, suddenly increasing into more shots and more volleys, with sounds of command, all doubled and trebled in reverberations up the valley, until it was one roar of pandemonium that was enough to set a nervous man wild. I didn't believe there was a sane man in the country, except the Corporal, who cooly informed me after awhile that I was sitting on the wrong side of a rock and pointed out to me the folly of protecting a rock.

Confused fighting centered on Morrow's camp, a mile distant from that of the scouts, who hurried to join the fray.

When the scouts began to appear, it was impossible for us to tell whether they were hostiles, but when we heard the fog-horn voice of Sergeant Jack Long bellowing, "Mucho bueno! God d—n, come on!" we knew them for scouts. It was useless to try to follow the impertinent rascals into the high and rocky fastnesses, though occasionally a few would appear on peaks and precipices, shake breechclouts at us and otherwise dare us over into their back yard. So we returned to our camp. Apache Indians seldom make an attack on troops so bold and daring as this one. They never tried it on that column again.

Several soldiers, however, had been killed, although an unascertained number of hostiles were wounded. Yet the enemy was not quite through with the command. Trying to extricate its stock from the canyon, the soldiers again came under fire, but escaped.

Many actions transpired of a similar character, most of them indecisive. In one action Major Morrow lashed into Victorio's camp and retook sixty horses and mules, including a dozen taken from Hooker's outfit near Ojo Caliente.[8] A score of volunteers from Mesilla went hunting Indians, and regretted it. On October 13, in the Black Range, they spotted three horses and rode after them, right into an ambush. Indian fire killed five Mexicans and an American, W. T. (Bill) Jones.[9] The Apaches let them escape, then, to turn on two wagon trains near a ranch, burning vehicles, pitching the wounded and the dead into the flames, slaying in all eleven men, and capturing a woman and child. Then they faded southwest, into the Florida Mountains, fat with loot and happy with memories of bloodletting. One report indicated that the latter raid may have been perpetrated by Apaches under Juh, fresh up from Mexico, and not by Victorio's men at all.[10]

Yet the situation seemed desperate to the people of the Southwest. They knew that "a large and murderous band of Indians are scattering death broadcast," as the *Star* put it. "Southwestern New Mexico is virtually in the hands of the Apache. The people are up in arms; the military is in close pursuit."[11] The alarm seemed justified. October 22, 1879, the *Star* reported that Lieutenant Blocksom's Apaches had a hard fight with Victorio, losing seventeen scouts and two enlisted men, a report that was probably exaggerated, if not entirely false,[12] but it added to the unrest. Victorio now, however, apparently had had enough of New Mexico for the time being, and turned to the south, with Major Morrow following, pushing hard. Lieutenant Gatewood, commanding Company A, Indian scouts, was with him

---

[8] Victorio Papers, 6752, Hatch to AG, Division of the Pacific, October 7, 1879.

[9] Gatewood, "Victorio," *The Great Divide*, 103, says they killed a posse of fourteen men; Victorio Papers, 6728, Pope to Sheridan, October 16, 1879.

[10] Victorio Papers, 6782, Pope to Sheridan, October 18, 1879.

[11] *Star*, October 17, 1879.

[12] *Ibid.*, October 22, 1879. This fight is not listed by *Chronological List.*

and from his pen we learn what this cruel, punishing march was like[13]:

[From Palomas Lake] we marched in the broiling heat all day in a southeasterly direction, and about dark found a small tank of water in the rocks near the foot of the Goodsight Mountains, which furnished perhaps half a pint to each man and animal. There we camped for the night. All next day the command plodded along through the sand and heat, across the desert north of the Guzman Mountains. The trail wound among sand hills and lava beds, tending generally southward. Horses and mules began to grow leg weary and suffer from thirst and the heat, and for every horse that was shot by the rear guard a soldier was placed on foot. About 9 o'clock we found a pool of mud in an alkali flat, and camped. It had been a pool of impure water, but the hostiles that day had driven their horses through it and it had been so thoroughly stirred up that it was about the consistency of thin mortar. Men and animals tried to drink it, but not with much success. In the two days' march fully seventy miles had been covered. An unknown country still lay ahead, but the hope of overtaking the enemy spurred the men on to extra efforts. The next morning march was resumed. The number of animals killed by the rear guard increased, the sun seemed to beat down hotter and hotter. There was no singing, no joking, no conversation, no smoking in the column, and the banjo of a colored soldier that used to enliven the men was silent. The Indian scouts, who always marched on foot, were more used to hardships, but even they began to show the effects. Several times we passed places where the wily savages had laid in ambush, but abandoned them. In the afternoon we found a tank of clear and cool water, but alas! a coyote had been killed and disembowelled in it, and it had been otherwise disgustingly poisoned. It was difficult to keep many of the men from drinking it. After dark we entered the projecting ridges of the Guzman Mountains, twenty miles perhaps from Janos. Here the very plain trail ran between two parallel ridges, covered with bushes and rocks, and a line of warriors in each ridge waited for us to come within easy range. But our scouts were not deceived. The full moon had just arisen, and in that clear atmosphere

[13] Again this account from Gatewood, "Victorio," *The Great Divide*, 103–104, somewhat abbreviated.

one could see a man at considerable distance. Some of our scouts succeeded in getting to the rear of one of the lines and a volley, followed by the advance of dismounted soldiers, caused a precipitate evacuation of their strong position. They rallied on a higher ridge, a few hundred yards further on, but the Apaches can't stand close quarters; they broke and ran, as they always will. Our men steadily advanced into a rougher and more broken mountain region. The Indians seemed to have plenty of ammunition and the whole top of the mountain was a fringe of fire flashes. Nearer and nearer to the top of the ridge approached the flashes from our Springfield carbines and the reports from their Winchesters above were so frequent as to be almost a continuous roar. Suddenly the firing ceased; the rumbling and crashing of large stones down the mountainside could be heard; the line had run against a palisade of solid rock, twenty feet high or more, which had not been noticed. The hostiles were rolling heavy stones down among our men, but luckily none were hurt, though several had been killed and several more wounded during the heaviest fusillade.[14] Unable to reach the enemy, Morrow withdrew behind a small ridge.

A flanking operation to the left was undertaken, with Gatewood and six of his scouts in the advance. But it failed to surprise the enemy who savagely counterattacked, driving Gatewood's men pell-mell back to the main command.[15]

The men were too exhausted from thirst, fatigue and want of sleep to do any more climbing. When they halted, every man lay down, and most of them went to sleep. The Colonel concluded the best thing was to take his command to water. It was now about 2 o'clock in the morning and very cold, being the 28th of October. Officers were ordered quietly to wake up their men and conduct them

[14] The *Chronological List* says one enlisted man was killed and two wounded in this fight. Its figures, however, are not necessarily correct. *Record of Engagements*, 92, says the slain man was a scout.

[15] Victorio Papers, 379–1880, Morrow to AAAG, District of New Mexico, November 5, 1879, says Gatewood held his position until out of ammunition. This very lengthy report gives a good summary of Victorio operations to and after the drive into Mexico. Morrow said his command totaled eighty-one enlisted men and eighteen scouts on this campaign.

to the rear, where our animals had been left. This was not easy. Many men showed symptoms of that wild insanity produced by great thirst. It was [still] dark when we reached the [water]. Some of the scouts had gone on in advance, and had built large fires along the little stream that ran from the spring. White, colored and red men, horses and mules, all rushed pell-mell for the water. They drank of it, they rolled in it, and they got out of it and returned to it. They wept and cheered and danced in it, and the mud they made seemed to make no difference in drinking. In seventy-six hours, from Polomas to [this stream], they had marched 115 miles on the small allowance of water indicated, besides making the fight at night in the Guzman Mountains.

Watered at last, the command turned north and reached Bayard November 3.[16]

A party of fifty-two frontiersmen, according to one unsupported account, crowding in where Morrow had left off, was ambushed in the Candelaria Mountains by Victorio's forces and although they fought bitterly for ten hours, were all but wiped out. Thirty-two were killed and eighteen wounded, it was said. The survivors escaped to their New Mexico homes.[17]

Newspapers reported the hostiles back in the territory by early December, but it was not Victorio, but Juh and Geronimo, anxious to surrender, at least for the winter. Their capitulation, if it may be called that, was brought about by Archie McIntosh, Tom Jeffords, and Captain A. S. Haskell, aide-de-camp to brevet Major General Orlando Willcox, and they turned up at the White Mountain Reservation with 108 followers. Geronimo, Ponce, Francisco, and several other noted renegades had fled San Carlos April 4, 1878, for Mexico,

[16] Morrow, *Ibid.*, gave Blocksom and Gatewood and "their invaluable Indian scouts" the "entire credit of Victorio's expulsion from the country as I know that without the assistance of Indians the command would never have been able to follow Victorio's trail."

[17] This story no doubt was based on the celebrated incident in the Candelaria Mountains of Chihuahua when two parties of Mexicans, totaling twenty-nine individuals, were slain to a man by the Apaches. For complete details from an officer who examined the ground while the bodies still were there, see Victorio Papers, 277–1880, George W. Baylor to AG, State of Texas, December 3, 1879.

but no official report of their departure was made.[18] They united with Juh and Nolgee in the Sierra Madre and soon "established a heavy traffic in stolen goods with the citizens of Janos."[19] By July, 1879, it was learned where they were. Late in that year, Jeffords, depending upon his personal acquaintance with them, Archie, Haskell, and several friendly Indians came into communication with the hostiles. But, it will be noted, they never resumed their relationship with Victorio.

By January 1, 1880, Arizona, commanded by Willcox of the Twelfth Infantry, included in the department thirteen posts and two military depots. It was garrisoned by the Sixth Cavalry, Twelfth Infantry and two companies of the Eighth Infantry, plus four companies of Indian scouts. Brevet Major General Edward Hatch, colonel of the Ninth Cavalry and commanding the District of New Mexico, ordered his entire regiment to the southern part of the territory and took personal command, assuring himself of unrivaled abuse from territorial newspapers which expected military miracles. Troops and scouts under Gatewood, Major Anson Mills, and Captain Curwen B. McLellan, a dour Scot, reinforced him from Arizona.[20]

With the new year Victorio again came north, killing an occasional prospector, ripping down telegraph wires, fighting whites here and there. "The hell-hounds are again at work in New Mexico," sighed the *Star*.

Mexican General Geronimo Trevino, who launched an operation with four hundred men against Victorio on December 28, was credited with driving him across the line, but the Indian's raid probably had no such origin. He was often pursued, but rarely driven. Major Morrow was supposed to be the stone wall against which Victorio would smash himself, and General Carr had concentrated forces at Fort Bowie for the kill, if any. "General Carr and Major Morrow have the renegades about where they want them," announced the *Star* on January 8. But Victorio's fighters whiffed past

[18] Ogle, *Western Apaches*, 198n.
[19] *Ibid.*
[20] Lockwood, *Apache Indians*, 230.

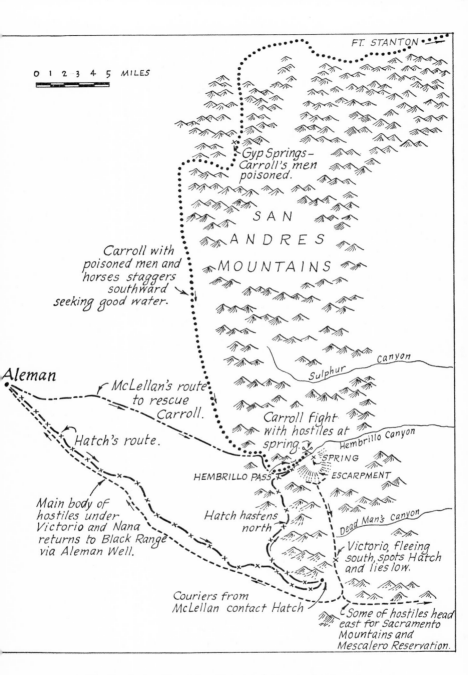

The San Andres Mountains: Victorio's fight and related events

like shadows and two days later were reported in the Blacks once more, Morrow with five companies of cavalry in pursuit, "twenty-four hours behind the Indians."[21] Then, on the upper Rio Puerco, on January 12, Morrow caught up, and a sharp fight resulted, lasting from about two in the afternoon until dark. Several Indians were thought to have been hit; Morrow conceded the death of Sergeant Gross and the wounding of two others.[22] The hostiles then broke for the San Mateo Mountains, northeast of Fort Bayard, where they were overtaken within a week. In this fight, Lieutenant J. Hansell French, Ninth Cavalry, was killed and two Indian scouts wounded.[23]

Once more the hard-riding major and his campaign-wearied troopers pushed on along Victorio's trail, across the Rio Grande, and again they caught up, this time on February 3, 1880, in a canyon northeast of Aleman's Well on the Jornada de Muerte near the San Andres Mountains. Parts of five companies plus Indian scouts ran into the hostiles, who had been placed "in squads of fifteen or twenty men upon the sides of the canyon." Major Morrow drove them from ledge to crevice, but the task was hopeless. As soon as one enemy unit was routed, others opened up. The following day the fight was resumed in a desultory fashion, but then Victorio broke off, and this time the troops did not pursue. Morrow's men had shot their bolt. They were utterly worn out, ammunition low, supplies about gone.[24]

A single unit was left to pursue Victorio into the San Andres, a company under Captain L. H. Rucker that chased the enemy for two days, coming "suddenly upon them strongly fortified in a narrow and rough canyon" of the mountains, said a Silver City dispatch printed by the *Star*. "The troops were received by a heavy fire, under which several horses and men fell. Perceiving their advantage, the Indians charged the troops, who gave way, and retreated in pell-mell order; the Indians in turn became the pursuers and drove the troops across

[21] Victorio Papers, 238–1880, Pope to AAG, Chicago, January 12, 1880; 259, Whipple to Sherman, January 14, 1880; 280, Pope to Whipple, January 9, 1880.

[22] *Ibid.*, Pope to Whipple.

[23] *Ibid.*, 414, Morrow to Townsend, January 20, 1880.

[24] *Ibid.*, 828, Pope to AAG, Chicago, February 3, 1880; 928, Pope to AAG, Chicago, February 7, 1880.

the river. In the retreat rations and bedding were abandoned, which the Indians secured."[25]

Two more companies of the Ninth were hurried south from Santa Fe, and Hatch again hastened into the field. Newspapers called for "not less than a thousand men" to be sent against the Indians, and it is a matter of record that the number of scouts and soldiers surpassed that figure, but the nimble enemy remained free. This was assuredly not due to lack of diligence on the part of the troops. In a lengthy report, Hatch from Ojo Caliente on February 25, described their work and the miserable conditions under which it was performed. The terrain, he explained, made the "well-known Modoc Lava beds a lawn" by comparison.

Major Morrow's command shows that the work performed by the troops is most arduous, horses worn to mere shadows, men nearly without boots, shoes and clothing. . . . When following the Indians in the Black Range the horses were without anything to eat five days except what they nibbled from Piñon pines. Going without food so long was nearly as disastrous as the fearful march into Mexico of 79 hours without water. . . . Morrow deserves great credit for the persistency with which he has kept up the pursuit. . . . The Indians are certainly as strong as any command Major Morrow has had in action. . . . The Indians select mountains for their fighting ground and positions almost impregnable usually throwing up some rifle pits where nature has not furnished them and skilfully devising loop-holes. . . . The Indians are thoroughly armed and as an evidence they are abundantly supplied with ammunition their fire in action is incessant, and nearly all the horses and mules they abandon on the march are shot. It is estimated they have killed from 600 to 1,000 since the outbreak. When the animal becomes too foot sore to go further the Indians shoot him . . .[26]

Casting about for some means of curtailing the hostile activity other than by exhausting pursuit and occasional skirmishing, the mili-

[25] *Star*, February 17, 1880.
[26] Hatch to AAG, Fort Leavenworth, Victorio Papers, no serial number, February 25, 1880.

tary by early January were casting speculative eyes over the huge Mescalero Reservation at Tulerosa. Here were hundreds of armed, well-mounted Indians who supplied, officers became convinced, not only moral support but many recruits for Victorio, and these Indians, they reasoned, should be disarmed and dismounted. Plans were formulated to bring this about.[27]

Reports of depredations spread rapidly. Not all were caused by Victorio, of course, nor in all probability were all caused by Indians, but Victorio was blamed for most of them. When he first bolted he is said to have slain between seventy-five and one hundred civilians before slipping into Old Mexico. Now that he was back, outrages increased.[28] Hatch, far from idle, began preparations for a major blow against the chief. He laid his plans carefully.[29] By March 31 everything was ready. Hatch had learned that Victorio and his main band were camped in Hembrillo Canyon,[30] a large defile on the eastern side of the San Andres Mountains, about fifty miles east of Cuchillo Negro, now, as then, a scattering of adobe structures along the shallow Cuchillo Negro River.

There Hatch had assembled three companies of Apache scouts, including some from Arizona, a pack train, three troops of the Ninth Cavalry with two more on the way, and one troop of the Sixth, commanded by Captain McLellan. Secrecy was enforced, although Hatch had learned that the "damned Chillacagoes," as the scouts called the hostiles, knew of the planned operation. Two troops from Fort Stanton,[31] under Captain Henry Carroll, were to march west across

[27] See, for example, Victorio Papers 280, Pope to AAG, Chicago, January 9, 1880; Interior Secretary Carl Schurz to Secretary of War, 1065, February 13, 1880.

[28] A list of recent depredations and murders was published by the Mesilla, New Mexico, *News*, April 1, 1880.

[29] For this account and subsequent events, see Thomas Cruse, *Apache Days and After*, 70–77; Victorio Papers, 1567, General Field Orders No. 1, with endorsements up to Sherman, February 25, 1880; Hatch, Special Field Orders No. 18, no serial number, April 5, 1880.

[30] Cruse makes this Memtrillo Canyon, but there is none of that name. For a description see Henry James, *The Curse of the San Andres*.

[31] Stanton was midway between the Rio Grande and Pecos rivers. It was established in 1855; Farmer, "New Mexico Camps," Museum of New Mexico.

the almost impassable malpais, or lava country, and reach the northern end of the San Andres northwest of Three Rivers, by April 6, and block all movements by Indians north from San Nicholas Springs. The next day Carroll was to move south toward Victorio's camp. McLellan, meanwhile, was to take his command from Aleman's Well, west of the San Andres, and move eastward by a night march, reaching the canyon at daylight on April 7. Hatch was to take four troops southeast from Aleman's Well, plunge into the San Andres and cut all trails leading southward toward Old Mexico. Then he would wheel to face north and work up the range to close in on the hostiles. Brevet Major General Benjamin Henry Grierson, colonel of the Tenth Cavalry and a famed Civil War raider, was moving up from west Texas and would smash any hostile attempt to flee into the broken country southeast of the San Andres.

Had these commands been fighting anyone but Victorio, and any Indians but Apaches, the plans probably would have worked to perfection. It was an unfortunate incident involving Carroll's column that wrecked them, although had he had Apache scouts with him the campaign might have been saved. On the evening of the fifth, Carroll camped at Malpais Spring, where the water flowed clear and inviting, but was dangerously charged with gypsum. Men and horses, unaware of this, drank heavily and by next morning were in pitiful shape, deathly ill, scarcely able to go on. But they moved into the mountains, seeking a spring Carroll remembered from the autumn before. However, it had been a dry winter, and the spring had vanished.

The weakened command staggered southward and, about six o'clock, crept into Hembrillo Canyon where there was water—and hostiles. The sudden appearance startled the Indians, who fled into the rocks but, discovering something wrong with the whites, seized favorable positions between them and the water, and fought back viciously. It was nearly dark, but Carroll and several of his men were wounded, two mortally, in trying to reach the spring. Some daring soldiers managed to slip down to it and secured a few canteens full, but most of the men and all of the stock went without. Early in the morning the Indians became more aggressive, apparently believing that the command was alone and done for, and surrounded it, shooting in from every direction. Fortunately most of them were atrocious marksmen.

No imaginary drama could have been more thrilling than the rescue that followed.

McLellan, just at daylight, had reached the westerly cliff above the canyon and was startled by crashing volleys of rifle fire. He ordered Lieutenant Timothy Touey and Gatewood to take scouts and twenty troopers and spy out the valley. In a few minutes a courier dashed back reporting that the Indians had white men trapped, and the entire command was flung into the canyon, establishing contact with Carroll's men. By nine o'clock the Indians had been driven back from the waterhole. Touey and Second Lieutenant Thomas Cruse led a charge that cleared the Indians from sites overlooking the springs, while Gatewood and his scouts turned the hostiles' flank and forced them back into rough country where they could not be followed.

Hatch, meanwhile, was crossing the plain from Aleman's Well south of the fight, but totally unaware of it. Two couriers from Mc-Lellan caught up with him, just as his column was at the point of entering the range. Hatch, thinking that disaster faced the other detachments, led his men back from the mountains and northward at their best speed along the foot of the range, in doing so missing an opportunity to settle with Victorio and end the campaign. For the Indian, slowed by his women and children, was coming south through the mountains along the very trail Hatch had intended to follow northward. The entire band was weary, almost out of ammunition, and would have been easy prey for the soldiers. Years later old Nana, a chief with Victorio in this fight, said that Victorio saw Hatch and his command coming toward the trail, and had a bad fifteen minutes until the soldiers passed a short distance away. A reconnaissance subsequently showed how closely the trails paralleled, Victorio's going south, Hatch's north. Scouts reported that the hostiles, leaving the mountains, split into two bands, one heading eastward to the Sacramento Mountains and the Mescalero Reservation, and the other southward for fifteen miles, then vanishing. Victorio was with the latter, and as soon as Hatch was out of sight, led his party back up the soldiers' trail to Aleman's Well, where he broke padlocks on top of the troughs and watered his ponies and people. Range cattle had obliterated their trail by daylight. There was nothing to prove they had not gone into Old Mexico when, in fact, they recrossed the Rio Grande and gained their favorite summer haunts in the Black Range.[32]

The flight of Victorio's band easterly added evidence, if any more were needed, that part at least of them had come from Tulerosa, and Generals Hatch and Grierson now converged upon the Mescalero Reservation to disarm and dismount its Indians. Grierson had left Fort Concho, at present-day San Angelo, Texas, about the middle of March with 280 men and officers of the Tenth Cavalry and Twenty-Fifth Infantry, moving westerly and so disposed as to cover a strip of country about fifty miles wide. The command, constantly gaining evidence that hostiles were coming from the Mescalero Agency, reached the Tulerosa April 12, being informed by Agent S. A. Russell, whom Grierson admitted was "an honest man," that the "Indians encamped in the mountains adjoining the Tulerosa were there by his direct order and authority; that they were good, quiet, peaceable Indians, who should not be molested." Yet Grierson believed that "the Agency [had] become, virtually, a supply camp for Victorio's band." He contacted Hatch, coming in from the west, and, believing Hatch's "power supreme . . . or at least sufficient to enable him to dispose of the Mescalero Apaches, and put them where they could do no further harm," placed his command at Hatch's disposition.

The Indians had been called to the agency for the disarming, and about three hundred twenty had arrived. On the sixteenth, however, Lieutenant Gatewood and his scouts intercepted a party of Mescaleros they thought were running off stock, and killed two of them.

---

[32] Victorio Papers, 2207, Sheridan to AG, Washington, April 10, 1880; 3993, McLellan to Post Adjutant, Fort Bowie, May 16, 1880; 2207, Sherman to Sheridan, April 12, 1880.

Russell claimed that the Indians "were sent out after the animals" and were innocent of wrongdoing. This incident perhaps helped precipitate the resulting fiasco. The troops moved that same day to disarm the Indians. A fight ensued in which several warriors were killed, thirty to fifty of the Apaches escaped, a few firearms were taken from others, and about four hundred animals were seized. Grierson believed that "about one-half of the Indians who escaped will soon return to the agency; and that the others will join Victorio, or, in small parties, continue to raid into Texas, or elsewhere, as heretofore." Grierson then pulled out, returning to his headquarters by May 8.[33] But the storm raised over the "disarming" of the Mescaleros long endured.

However, it was a significant factor in the eventual curbing of Victorio's activities. If he had not won every engagement, he at least had lost none, and he probably inflicted more casualties than he suffered. But the whites could stand to lose men more than could the Indians. Victorio's band was wearing down. He had no ready source of supply. He had secured some arms and ammunition, and perhaps livestock from the Mescaleros, but now this avenue was closed. His ammunition could come only from the whites he killed, and that was at best a haphazard source. He lay quiet for a time, but then the depredations began again, with thirteen Mexican sheepherders slain and thousands of sheep scattered through the Black and Mogollon ranges.

Thus far Victorio had left Arizona alone, but in early May newspapers warned that "Victorio is coming toward San Carlos," and for once were correct, at least in that some of his Indians were making a sweep. About forty attacked Cooney's Camp on Mineral Creek in the Mogollons. An all-day fight had left Cooney and two others killed, several wounded, and twenty-five horses taken. Only a couple of Indians were thought to have been slain. Most of the Arizona troops

[33] *Ibid.*, 2261, Sheridan to Sherman, April 13, 1880; 2320, Sheridan to Townsend, April 17, 1880; 2341, Pope to Sheridan, April 20, 1880; 5012, Grierson to AAG, San Antonio. In a lengthy exchange of missives, the latter, Grierson's very lengthy full report, is the most valuable.

that had been sent to New Mexico had by now returned and were sent into the field. Of most immediate attention was a raid by fourteen well-armed warriors under Washington, said to be a son of Victorio, toward San Carlos, apparently to kill and destroy, although their exact purpose is not clear, and they may have intended to reach relatives living on the Arizona reservation. They apparently skirmished with the "peaceful" Indians of the Juh-Geronimo group, had a sharp fight with troops and swung away, taking time to pillage a wagon train along the Gila, dropping into the Burro Mountains, scattering to foil pursuit, and rejoining Victorio's main camp twenty miles south of Hillsboro without losing a man.[34]

"Other Indian tribes are beginning to go over to Victorio," warned the Silver City *Southwest*. "An Indian, thickset and stout, was killed a few days ago, who was proven to be a Comanche; from the various signs about his person, the probabilities are that he was a sub-chief, and if this is true he had certainly joined Victorio with a large following of his tribe. The number of the Indians on the warpath cannot be estimated, but Victorio can now certainly command a larger force than General Hatch." The *Southwest* reported that seventy-eight persons had been killed by the hostiles in May, and suggested that "most of the small settlements west of here will be abandoned."[35] However, Brevet Major General John Pope, commanding the Department of Missouri, termed reports of depredations "greatly exaggerated."[36]

But they were increasing, it seemed. Mimbres and Chiricahuas traditionally had spared the isolated herders and others in the remote recesses of the frontier, depending upon these people for supplies and liaison with white settlements. The Mescaleros and Comanches, however, had no such scruples, and they murdered and pillaged at will. No one was spared.

Among the tough Indian fighters serving under Hatch was a chief of scouts from Fort Bayard named "Captain" H. K. Parker, in

---

[34] For details of this raid, see Thrapp, *Sieber*, 216–17.
[35] Reprinted in the *Star*, May 29, 1880.
[36] Victorio Papers, 3218, Sheridan to Townsend, May 22, 1880.

charge of from sixty to seventy-five Indians. His immediate commanding officer was Major Morrow and when, on May 17, Hatch's command was on the Fresco River, his stock worn out, Parker approached the major and asked permission to take his scouts and chase Indians. "You see the condition we are in," Morrow reportedly told him. "I have no orders to give you. Go do the best you can." Parker took eight pack mules and four days' rations, and started off into the mountains. When the weakened mules gave out, Parker and the scouts went on alone. The fourth day they found Hatch and his command, still recuperating at Ojo Caliente. "Go out and kill one or two Indians," Hatch was said to have told him. "We have got to keep things stirred up until I can get the troops in shape to continue the pursuit." Parker cooked three more days' rations, packed them on the scouts, and started off once more, in a southerly direction, as the *Southwest* told it.

On the second day his scouts cut sign, and the command slipped into the timber, lying low until the hostile camp could be located. Just at sunset on May 23 the scouts reported they had spied out the enemy on the canyon headwaters of the Palomas River. Parker "ordered Sergeant Jack Long to take twenty of the scouts and cautiously go around to the other side of the camp." Sergeant Jim was ordered to take thirty men and move up immediately above the hostiles, while Parker took eleven picked shots and crept up to the exposed side of the camp. He had instructed Long not to fire until the Indians came down the canyon, and Jim to open fire at daylight.

> The Indians had a sentry out on the side next to Jim's position, and Jim selected a man to kill him, while the balance fired down into the camp. According to orders, Sergeant Jim opened fire at daylight, and the hostiles broke up [to] the position held by Captain Parker. A galling fire sent them back into the canyon, and they ran down it, gathering together as they ran, when they came plumb upon Sergeant Jack Long's command and received a fire that drove them pell mell back to their camp. The hostiles then commenced fortifying, supposing that they were surrounded, being fired upon from all sides;

those who got into the fortifications fought desperately until night. Many were killed before they could reach the fortifications.

Once the scouts shouted to the squaws to come out and surrender, that they would not be hurt. Derision greeted them. Scouts reported having struck Victorio himself in the leg early in the fight; later a woman, screaming imprecations at them, cried that if Victorio died "they would eat him, so that no white man should see his body."

Parker, knowing he had Victorio bottled up, sent his Mexican packer to Hatch, asking more ammunition and outlining his position. Late in the afternoon, with no response as yet, he found his ammunition was down to five rounds per man; he ordered them to conserve it, unless they were charged. Still there was no reply from Hatch. By evening, convinced that his courier had been killed, and all but out of ammunition, Parker reluctantly pulled his men back five miles to water and camped there two nights and one day, vainly awaiting assistance. His rations were gone, and he killed two horses for food. No word from Hatch. At last Parker gave up and moved his command to Ojo Caliente. Hatch wasn't there. No one knew why ammunition had not been sent him. His courier had arrived safely and reported to Hatch and then had been ordered to duty with a pack train at Camp French on the Canada Alamosa, where Parker went. He found his courier and was told that the urgent message had been delivered to Hatch who, the *Southwest* reported, had accepted the news, hurried to Fort Craig on the Rio Grande, "and there telegraphed that celebrated message, 'that his COLUMN with the scouts as an advance guard, had struck the Indians,' etc." The newspaper cited the fact that other officers knew of the fight, but were unable to assist Parker on their own responsibility, and fumed, "Is Hatch an imbecile?" and commented, "General, the blood of over five hundred of our citizens slain by the merciless Apache within the last twelve months, calls for vengeance; bombastic dispatches do not satisfy."[37]

[37] *Southwest*, reprinted in the *Star*, June 5, 1880; *Record of Engagements*, 95; *Chronological List*, 50; Victorio Papers, 3334, Pope to Sheridan, May 27, 1880; 3669, Hatch to AAG, Chicago, May 27, 1880; 3662, Hatch to AAG, Fort Leavenworth, May 31, 1880.

The exact extent of Parker's victory cannot now be ascertained, but it must be accounted one of the decisive battles of the Apache wars. Official records state that fifty-five of the enemy were killed, Parker himself estimating his kill at about thirty. Cruse noted that some estimates ran as high as sixty, but figured the actual count was "probably ten or twelve," which seems too low.[38] But, Cruse added, "whatever the number actually killed, it was a deadly blow to Victorio, as he lost some of his best men and was himself wounded." Parker also captured seventy-four horses, and lost no men. Victorio's wound evidently was not serious enough to incapacitate him, but discouraged him from fighting in the north. At least half of his band melted away after the Parker encounter, disappearing among the peaceful Indians on the various reservations, while Victorio and the others headed south for Mexico, pillaging as they went. He must have seemed to Hatch and others indestructible. They were being pressured constantly anew to terminate the unrest and pacify the country, as much so the Southern Pacific railroad, then being pushed across southern New Mexico, could progress as for the sake of the isolated settlers and prospectors.[39]

Hatch was being given a hard time by the territorial press. Abuse was heaped upon him. One dispatch gives the tenor of many:

SHAKESPEARE, N.M., June 17.—A negro deserter from Hatch's 9th Cavalry passed through camp last night. When questioned as to the cause of his desertion, he replied that he could not longer stand the disgrace of serving under Hatch, so he had waltzed off. His truthful wit rendered his escape from here very easy.[40]

Derided as they were, the troops remained doggedly on Victorio's trail until he crossed the border. On June 5 Major Morrow with four troops of the Ninth struck the hostiles in Cook's Canyon, not far

[38] Cruse, *Apache Days*, 84.

[39] Victorio Papers, no serial number, Sherman to McDowell, San Francisco, May 28, 1880. Neill C. Wilson and Frank J. Taylor, *Southern Pacific: The Roaring Story of a Fighting Railroad*, 77, report that the line was building eastward from Tucson across southern New Mexico at this time. It reached Lordsburg by mid-October and Deming by December 15, 1880.

[40] *Star*, June 22, 1880.

from Fort Cummings,[41] killed ten and wounded three, capturing much livestock. One of the dead was said to have been the raider Washington, Victorio's son.[42] But greater things were planned. Southeastward, along the Rio Grande, the greatest manhunt in the history of the Southwest was being prepared as Victorio established himself in a favorite sanctuary.[43] This time many hundreds of Mexican regulars were to be added, along with Texas Rangers, civilian posses, and other elements.[44]

The Denver *Tribune* reported July 1 from El Paso that the Apache had attacked San Lorenzo and an establishment of the governor of Chihuahua, shooting more than one hundred horses. Thirty-nine miles west of San Carlos they captured another hundred horses and killed some Mexicans. Although the governor personally took the field, leading some two hundred federal troops and volunteers, the Indians continued their depredations. They circuited Chihuahua City, thirty miles to the north, and finally camped some forty miles southwest of Amilyos, from where they occasionally went into Gallegos to trade.[45] For the moment they stopped killing people, according to word received by Hatch, who however predicted they would eventually cross into Texas below Fort Quitman, which they did.[46]

---

[41] Cummings, according to Cruse, *Apache Days*, 63, "was one of the few walled stations I ever saw in the West. . . . Many a time . . . the stage would come rushing in with arrows sticking in it and with tales of narrow escapes from Apaches." If it was walled, no trace of that structure now remains.

[42] Victorio Papers, 3528, Pope to Sheridan, June 8, 1880.

[43] *Ibid.*, 3889, Pope to AAG, Chicago, June 3, 1880; with respect to negotiations for a mutual crossing of the border when in "hot pursuit," see 4233, Pope to AAG, Chicago, with endorsements, June 14, 1880; 3787, Hatch to AAG, Chicago, with Sherman's second endorsement, June 14, 1880; 5691, State Department report of negotiations, with enclosures, September 8, 1880; and permission finally granted, 6369, Valle to Hatch, August 9, 1880.

[44] Victorio's effective fighting force at this time was estimated at 160 men, among whom were two Comanches and no San Carlos Indians; see Victorio Papers, 3939, Pope to AAG, Chicago, June 21, 1880.

[45] Victorio Papers, 4380, Hatch to AAG, Fort Leavenworth, July 14, 1880.

[46] Fort Quitman was on the Rio Grande, due west of Eagle Springs, which was on the southern slope of the Eagle Mountains, about one-third of the distance from El Paso to Presidio.

General Grierson wired from Fort Davis in late July that Colonel Adolph I. Valle of the Mexican army would take the field shortly with about three hundred twenty cavalry and two hundred fifty infantry against Victorio, "with authority from Washington to cross into the United States" if in hot pursuit. Grierson sent his offer of "hearty co-operation." Almost at once there was a skirmish between the hostiles and the Mexicans at Ojo del Pino, about forty or fifty miles below Eagle Springs. Six Mexican soldiers were killed and two hundred took up pursuit of the Indians.[47] A sizable body of hostiles slipped across the Rio Grande, making for waterholes to the north, and attempting to pass near Fort Quitman. Grierson, on patrol with six men, spotted the Indians and sent for all available troops from Quitman and Eagle Springs. His order was misunderstood, however, and only a light escort was sent him. He sent more couriers demanding anew that every man who could bear arms be rushed up. The Indians meanwhile had spotted Grierson, and he sent Lieutenant Leighton Finley with fifteen men to charge the superior force. The junior officer gallantly held the hostiles at bay for about an hour when relief from Quitman and Eagle Springs forced them across the river again. It was a narrow escape for Grierson, and a checkmate for Victorio, who lost about seven killed compared with one killed and four wounded for the soldiers.[48]

Grierson promptly threw out his scouts between Van Horn's Wells and the Rio Grande, around the eastern side of the Eagle Mountains. But by August 4 the Indians slipped through, after a brief skirmish, and moved north.[49] Grierson rapidly moved up parallel with them, taking care to keep a range of mountains between him and the hostiles to shield his movements. He left his camp south of Van Horn at three in the morning, and marched until the following midnight, arriving then at Rattlesnake Springs, having covered sixty-five miles in less than twenty-four hours. He found himself far enough in

[47] Victorio Papers, 4633, Ord to AG, Chicago, July 25, 1880; 5747, Grierson to AAG, Chicago, August 1, 1880; 4845, Platt to AAG, Chicago, August 3, 1880.

[48] Many of the Victorio Papers refer to this action, but Grierson's summary is in 4805, Ord to Sheridan, August 2, 1880.

[49] Victorio Papers, 4865, Ord to AG, Chicago, August 4, 1880.

advance of the Indians to lay an elaborate ambush. Two companies under Captain Charles Delavan Viele were placed on either side of the ravine, above the waterholes, and lay quietly, awaiting the arrival of the enemy.

The straggling column of Indians approached about two in the afternoon. Eager soldiers withheld their fire until it seemed evident that the Indians would approach no nearer, then cut loose with the first of eight volleys. Surprised by the crashing fire which, however, was from too great a range to do much damage, the savages scampered into the rocks and clambered upward. They soon learned the small size of the force opposed to them, and launched an attack of their own, desperately seeking control of the waterhole. Before the hostiles could make much headway, H and B companies under Lieutenant Thaddeus Winfield Jones swarmed to the rescue, sending a volley from a new direction into the Indians and flushing them from the scene once more. They concealed themselves on the rugged slopes of the canyon, beyond reach of fire. Neither soldiers nor Indians had the strength to renew the fight at once. For two hours there was an undeclared truce.

Then, about four o'clock, a supply train escorted by Captain J. C. Gilmore and elements of the Twenty-fourth Infantry, rounded a point of the mountains some eight miles to the southeast, heading for the waterhole. Apparently the train's personnel was unaware of the fight in progress. Most of the escort was riding in the wagons, hidden from view. The prospect of loot seemed irresistible to Victorio, and a warrior party swarmed down on the inviting target.[50] They were startled when uniformed soldiers tumbled out of every wagon and

[50] Apparently the fight at Rattlesnake Springs in early August, 1880, is the same described by Raht, *Davis Mountains*, 262, as occurring at "Fresno Springs" in August of 1879; Raht was mistaken in the date. He also erred in believing that the soldiers had not yet sprung their trap when the wagon train hove in view, asserting that the Indians, unaware of the proximity of the troops, laid an "ambush within an ambush" for the train, forcing the soldiers to come to its protection, and destroying their opportunity to annihilate Victorio's band. Many writers have followed Raht in this, probably because it makes a better story. Unfortunately it is not the true story, which is recounted by Rister, *Southwestern Frontier*, 212–13.

met them with fire which killed one and wounded others. A second Indian party, slipping down a side canyon, also was repulsed.

Beaten four times, baffled on every front, and probably desperate for water, the hostiles straggled off toward the Carrizo Mountains, between the Diablos and the Blancas, northeast of Quitman. It had been a bad day for Victorio. Grierson reported it was impossible to tell how bad, because the Indians "carried off their dead and wounded," which, as most Army men knew, was a euphemism for, "We don't know whether we hit any of them, but at least we hold the field."

Grierson now sent columns to most of the mountain waterholes: Captain Nicholas Nolan to the Carrizos, Captain Thomas Coverly Lebo to scout the country between Rattlesnake Springs and Sulphur Springs, Captain Louis Henry Carpenter with three companies to Sulphur Springs itself. The only unit with any luck was that of Captain Lebo, which struck Victorio August 9, capturing camp equipment, twenty-five head of cattle, and other supplies.[51] The Indians, now broken into smaller bands and obviously dispirited, turned back to the Rio Grande, seeking sanctuary in Mexico. The Denver *Tribune* reported August 13 that half of the band crossed the river in one group and the remainder later that day.

Fearing Victorio might swing westward, Hatch urged that Arizona units make a protective sweep into Mexico, which was done, but they found nothing.[52]

After crossing the Rio Grande, Victorio's Indians dropped sixty miles into the interior, made an idle pass at Santa Maria, a tiny village where they killed two Mexicans and stole a few horses, probably for food. Colonel Valle was off in southern Chihuahua fighting a revolution, and for the moment there were no forces to oppose the Indians.[53] Only bronchos troubled the Southwest, but they continued to be a

51 Rister, *Southwestern Frontier*, 214. Both the *Chronological List* and *Record of Engagements* place this action August 3, before the Rattlesnake Springs action.

52 For details, see Thrapp, *Sieber*, 217–19.

53 Victorio Papers, 6211, Hatch to AAG, Chicago, August 18, 1880; 6271, Pope to AAG, Chicago, August 19, 1880.

constant nuisance, making "travel on all roads between Socorro, Silver City, El Paso and vicinity very unsafe."[54] Early in September such a party waylaid and wrecked a stagecoach sixteen miles west of Fort Cummings, killing Alexander Le Beau, the driver, and two passengers, Emery S. Madden and Isaac Roberts. Madden, nineteen, was the son of Captain Dan Madden of the Sixth Cavalry. Pursuing soldiers overtook the Indians and had a short fight, in which one soldier and two Indian scouts were killed and two scouts seriously wounded. The enemy escaped.[55] On another occasion Indians attacked a stage near Fort Quitman, mortally wounding Brevet Major General James J. Byrne, a Civil War veteran now employed by the Texas Pacific Railroad.[56] These were but two incidents in an endless series.

While Victorio was recuperating with little interference in Mexico the press had not slackened its caustic criticism of the Army and sarcastic references to the Indian as the real lord of the Southwest. The Tucson *Star*, on September 16, printed a front-page satirical editorial presenting "Victorio's Compliments to President Rutherford B. Hayes." But the Army again was not as idle as settlers feared. A final major campaign to wipe out Victorio already was under way.[57]

Several American columns crossed the Rio Grande and entered Mexico about September 10. They headed for the Candelaria Mountains, where Victorio was reported to have been in camp in mid-August. This report had been brought out by Charles Berger, a white scout, who went south across the border accompanied by Lipan and Pueblo scouts to locate the hostiles.[58] Berger reported that the Mexicans had given Victorio a clear passage westward, perhaps in the hope that he would cross the line and move up into his former sum-

[54] Cruse, *Apache Days*, 54.

[55] Victorio Papers, 6829, Hatch to AAG, Fort Leavenworth, September 10, 1880.

[56] *Ibid.*, 5344, Ord to AG, Chicago, August 26, 1880; 6391, Grierson to AG, Chicago, August 25, 1880; James B. Gillett, *Six Years with the Texas Rangers*, 181–82.

[57] Victorio Papers, 6801, Grierson to AAG, Texas, September 7, 1880; 7079, Pope to Sheridan, September 20, 1880.

[58] Rister, *Southwestern Frontier*, 215.

mer ranges.[59] Scouts subsequently reported that Victorio had moved his camp to Corral de Piedras, and the Mexicans seemed to have determined that, since he was not going north, he must be exterminated. The Chihuahua government raised the price on his head from $2,000 to $3,000, American, it was said, and General Joaquin Terrazas was dispatched with about one thousand troops to track down the marauders. He was to be joined by token American units: sixty-eight Chircahuas under Captain Charles Parker; Lieutenant James Maney of the Fifteenth Infantry, with twenty Negro troopers, and Colonel George W. Baylor with hard-riding Texas Rangers.[60]

With the pursuit closing in from all sides, it became apparent that the hostiles' days were numbered. The Indians were holed up in a range of hills called the Tres Castillos, ninety-two miles northward of Chihuahua City. One account says Victorio was camped in a box canyon; another that he was on a saddle between two peaks, but in any event, he was trapped. Before the encircling elements could close in on the Indian position, Terrazas bluntly informed the Americans that they could go home. He gave as his reasons that he did not trust the Chiricahua scouts, many of them related to Victorio's people, and that he had received orders from his superiors to instruct Americans to leave Mexican soil. The Americans had no recourse but to accede, and they turned homeward. They had traveled but a day, however, when a courier overtook them and told them that it was all over.

On the afternoon of October 14, 1880, he said, Mexican troops overtook and surrounded Victorio's band, and at daybreak on the fifteenth the fight was ended. Victorio, repeatedly wounded, was finally finished off by a Tarahumari scout, Mauricio, who was pre-

[59] "There seems to be a tacit understanding between Victorio and many Mexicans, that so long as he does not make war upon them in earnest, he can take whatever food and other supplies he may need for his warriors."—Grierson report, 1880, District of Pecos, 6602, Old Records Section, AGO, and quoted by Rister, *Southwestern Frontier*, 215.

[60] Baylor, a son of John W. Baylor of Civil War fame, was born August 24, 1832, at Fort Gibson, Oklahoma, and became one of the great Texas Rangers; see Gillett, *Texas Rangers*, 142–44.

sented a fancy nickled rifle by the grateful state of Chihuahua, in recognition of his feat, in addition to the reward money. It is said that Mauricio later used this rifle to kill Captain Emmet Crawford, in January, 1886.

In the great slaughter, Terrazas messaged Hatch, he slew seventy-eight Apaches, including Victorio and sixty warriors, plus a number of women and children, and captured sixty-eight women and children and two hundred horses and mules. Terrazas losses were only three killed and as many wounded, showing that the Indians were almost completely out of ammunition. The result was a massacre, rather than a battle.[61] About thirty Apaches escaped, Nana among them.[62]

The Mexicans, however, did not get off quite so lightly. On November 16 thirty or forty Apaches ambushed Mexican troops on the high road between Chihuahua and El Paso, south of Carrizal, and nine Mexicans were killed outright. Among them was a sergeant who was mounted on Victorio's saddle and carrying a few trinkets from the body of the famed chief. The sergeant's corpse was slashed into tiny pieces by the Indians. General Terrazas himself was attacked and, of his escort of ten men, only one escaped with the officer. The raging Apaches lashed out far and wide, it was reported, and dozens of Mexicans were reported slain and "mutilated most horribly."[63]

One curious fact remains. No eyewitness account of the death of Victorio is known to exist, from the white side. No American is known to have visited the site of the battle, or to have seen the bodies of the slain. Cruse always insisted that Victorio was killed through treachery, not in battle, and told it this way:

"Victorio and his band . . . ventured into the vicinity of Santa Rosalia to buy ammunition and supplies. They seemed to have plenty

[61] *Star*, October 21, 24, 1880; Victorio Papers, 6488, Pope to Sheridan, October 22, 1880; 6513, Buell to AAG, Fort Leavenworth, October 19, 1880; 6835, State Department to Secretary of War, November 9, 1880; 6583, Buell to AAG, Fort Leavenworth, October 23, 1880; Gillett, *Texas Rangers*, 183–89.

[62] Gillett, *Texas Rangers*, 187; Nana, according to other information, was scouring the countryside for ammunition, and thus escaped.

[63] *Star*, December 2, 1880.

THE CONQUEST OF APACHERIA

of money . . . but the Mexicans sent a courier to General Joaquin Terrazas," asking him to slip into Santa Rosalia. "Then they staged a big fiesta. . . . When the 'celebration' was over Victorio and his band had been summarily exterminated."[64]

[64] Cruse, *Apache Days*, 85–86.

XVI

Nana's Raid

VICTORIO WAS DEAD. For the first time in decades the border country could breathe easily, with no strong bands of Apaches in a position to spread terror and destruction, or so it was thought. Apacheria was growing up. Arizona had fourteen weekly newspapers and four dailies, and they could now turn to mundane affairs. For example, the *Star* one day noted that "Henry D., usually known as 'Hank' Williams, who has been preaching a temperance crusade through the streets of Tucson for several weeks . . . says he is about to sober up and lead an exploring expedition." In a fit of public concern the newspaper called for more hitching posts. "At present," it said, "where there is a store on the corner, a customer goes in one door and generally sees a horse saying how do you do at the other." When the animal walks in, it added, "considerable difficulty is experienced in ejecting him without smashing showcases, or having him go through the dried apple barrel." The newspaper noted, too, that the city's morals were not all they should be. Introduction of hordes of Chinese workmen by the railroad company, far from causing the moral tone to collapse, could only have a beneficial effect because "it would be impossible to make the morals of Tucson any worse than they are."

Tucsonians entered the year 1881 quietly enough, according to the *Star*, which reported, January 1: "Everybody swore off from drinking, gambling and all kindred vices." January 18: "The pledges and reform promises of New Year's are forgotten." February 25: "Distressing dullness in criminal affairs." March 8: "Frank Chapman mopped the floor with a cowboy." March 20: "Escapes occurring. New jail needed." March 25: "Fifty prisoners in jail." March 26: "Prisoners in jail attempt to escape by a tunnel." April 18: " 'Johnny-behind-the-deuce' escapes from jail." May 1: "Prisoners in the jail saw off their shackles." May 12: "Attempt to break jail frustrated by Ike Brokaw." August 27: "Great Feast of San Augustin commenced at Levin's Park." September 1: "Safe robbed at the feast grounds and $900 stolen." And so it went.

But not all was as quiet on the Indian front as Southwesterners had hoped. The spectacular, if brief, raid of old Nana clearly demonstrated this. A Warm Springs Apache, Nana, who now was perhaps seventy winters in age, was given to such idiosyncracies as wearing a heavy gold watch chain, stolen of course, in each of his wrinkled old ears, but he was no fool and as a raider has few peers in frontier history. Perhaps he learned something from Victorio, but he already was a veteran warrior when Victorio was a toddler barely old enough to learn the delights of torturing such small birds and animals as fell into his clutches. Nana had been wounded many times in his countless fights with the white-eyes, and perceptibly limped. Some believed his great raid was in vengeance for Victorio's death, but of course it wasn't that. It was a normal Apache outbreak, a dashing adventure that developed with no plan and proved more successful than the Indians had any right to hope.

Fifteen warriors rode with Nana when he crossed the Rio Grande toward the east and entered New Mexico in July of 1881. Word of his coming had spread, and he was joined by about twenty-five Mescaleros, bored with reservation life and eager for excitement and plunder. The report of their bloody work occupies but a scant two pages, 99 and 100, in the *Record of Engagements*, and is largely relied on here.

The Apaches moved boldly by day to the northeast, their alert black eyes missing nothing, noting tracks, distant dust whorls, the smokes, traces of wandering prospectors, travelers, stockmen. Without deviating to right or left they made their way into the Sacramento Mountains where, in Alamo Canyon on July 17, 1881, they came unexpectedly upon two men of a small Ninth Cavalry detachment commanded by Lieutenant John F. Guilfoyle, and hastily laid an ambush. It wasn't much good. They wounded Chief Packer Burgess and captured three mules, but they stirred up the cavalry, and Guilfoyle was to pursue them doggedly almost to the end of their developing raid.

Nana, no doubt hearing that the mountains before them were alive with soldiers, drew back and headed west by northwest. His band slipped down through Canyon del Perro, and on the edge of the White Sands they found and killed two Mexicans and a woman. They were jumped at the scene by Guilfoyle's cavalrymen, but a skirmish resulted in no loss for either side. Nana pushed westward. Guilfoye followed. The hostiles made for their old haunts in the San Andres, but the troopers gave them no rest. On July 25 Guilfoyle again attacked, and this time his Negro soldiers captured a couple of horses, twelve mules, all of Nana's camp supplies, and believed they had killed two hostiles. The strange flight and pursuit continued toward the west, the Indians apparently making for the San Mateos.

Crossing the Rio Grande six miles below San Jose, old Nana stopped long enough to slaughter two miners and a Mexican, then fled toward the high mountains, killing another four Mexicans in the foothills on July 30.

The white settlers were up in arms over the free-swinging raid. They organized posses of reckless, Indian-hating horsemen to sweep the breaks and lower ranges. One such group of thirty-six riders moved into the San Mateos without spotting a trace of the elusive warriors. Having no notion that Apaches were about, they worked up brush-choked Red Canyon all morning, and nooned at a freshwater spring where there was good pasturage and shade. It was hot. They left a guard or two to loose-herd the stock. The rest of the manhunters lazed under the cottonwoods, talking, smoking, dozing. But their reverie was shattered by unearthly screeches from a dozen wild throats and mounted hostiles popped out of the brush, shooting as they came and slashing at the air with fluttering blankets to stampede the mounts. It was all over in seconds. Nana left in his wake eight fallen whites, one dead, and not a horse for even the wounded to ride. He had made off with thirty-eight head, enough to remount all his band and leave a few horses for meat. He killed a Mexican on his way out of the canyon and rode on.

But Guilfoyle was not far behind. On August 3 he struck them again, this time at Monica Springs in the San Mateos, and once more the lieutenant was sure his men had hit and wounded at least two hostiles, captured eleven head of stock, some saddles, and other equipment. But wily old Nana, his main band intact, slipped away. On August 11 Guilfoyle found where two Mexicans had been killed and two women carried away by the raiders near La Savoya.

Colonel Hatch had now ordered every available soldier into the field, assuming personal command. Altogether eight troops of cavalry, eight companies of infantry, two companies of Indian scouts scoured the mountains, the plains, the canyons, and the wild range country for the hostiles. But the enemy could not be brought to a conclusive fight, preferring to dart down from a hideout, strike and melt back into the wilderness again. Day after weary day the soldiers kept after their elusive quarry; no troops ever campaigned harder, with less result.

Guilfoyle, his equipment worn out and his men as well, was forced to withdraw for refitting, but many others kept to the trail. Captain Charles Parker, veteran of the Victorio campaigns, struck the enemy August 12 about twenty-five miles west of Sabinal. A sharp fight ensued among the chaparral and bayonet cactus, and it was a bloody one. Parker lost five men, one of them killed, another missing, and three wounded, but thought he had killed four Indians before they had "drawn off" as they always did. Four days later Nana's band was forced into still another fight, this time with I Troop, Ninth Cavalry, and again it was sharp. Lieutenant Gustavus Valois figured there were about fifty Indians opposing him in this action along the Cuchillo Negro River, and he can be excused for overestimating a bit. The Indians struck like a whirlwind. Lieutenant George R. Burnett was twice wounded while saving the life of an enlisted man, and was rewarded with a Medal of Honor. Two other enlisted men were killed and six horses slain. Nana disengaged and galloped westward, toward the Black Range where with Victorio and Mangas Coloradas he had summered during eventful years gone by, but it wasn't the same, now. Too many troops combed the country. Scarcely had he pulled away from Valois when he ran into another Ninth Cavalry detachment, commanded by Lieutenant F. B. Taylor who gobbled up some of the hostiles' loose horses, recaptured some stolen property, while Taylor lost a few horses killed, but no men. Nana withdrew once more and plunged into the Blacks, Taylor in close, but slowing, pursuit.

Ten fights in less than a month had probably taken its toll of even the Apaches' seemingly indestructible belligerence, and Nana, convinced that his notion of spending a season or two plundering through his old haunts was impracticable, turned toward Mexico, but he was not to get away without a flaming sendoff.

Fifteen miles from McEver's Ranch, in Guerillo Canyon, the raiders clashed with Lieutenant G. W. Smith and a Ninth Cavalry patrol of twenty men. The official summary of these engagements says that the hostiles "were defeated after a very severe fight," but does not explain on what grounds it concludes this. On the record the decision was the other way around. Lieutenant Smith was killed as were four of his men and George Daly, a civilian member of a posse which joined the fight. Three other troopers were wounded, which amounted to about 50 per cent casualties and left the raiders in command of the field, scarcely a resounding victory for the soldiers! But it was the last time the troops would engage Nana, on this raid. He and his dusty, indestructible band slipped across the border "where, under positive orders from the government, the chase was abandoned," said the summary, with relief.

Nana's raid was legendary, in truth. In something like six weeks the rheumatic old man led his handful of warriors over more than a thousand miles of enemy territory, sometimes pounding seventy miles or more in a single day. During this campaign they foraged on the countryside, fought a dozen skirmishes with troops and won most of them. They killed from thirty to fifty Americans and wounded many more, captured two women and not less than two hundred horses and mules, eluded pursuit by a thousand soldiers and several hundred civilians, and did all this with a band that numbered fifteen at the start and probably never counted more than forty. From the Indian viewpoint it was a grand adventure and might well have been the finale for the superannuated old brave's career. But it wasn't even that.

XVII

Cibicu

A MONG THE APACHES now coming prominently to the forefront of Arizona concerns was an ascetic, slight medicine man, almost a dreamer, named Noch-ay-del-klinne, five feet, six inches tall and weighting only 125 pounds. His complexion was so pale as to seem almost white. As early as 1871 he had appeared as "a kindly White Mountain herb doctor," of twenty-six, and was a member of a small delegation of Apaches sent to Washington that year. "When he came home," wrote Cruse, "he had not only the big silver medal given him by the President, but a supply of amazing stories and the power to tell them," of the wonders he had seen in the East. Naturally his listeners could not understand these things. Eventually the mystic was sent to Santa Fe to attend school. There he "absorbed but hardly understood the elements of the Christian religion. He was particularly impressed by the story of the Resurrection and when he went back to his own people it was to think about the withdrawal of Christ for meditation."[1] He went into the mountains periodically to fast and pray and speculate upon religion,[2] and within a decade had become widely known as a healer and mystic, although not considered a dangerous one. He had also engaged in more earthy pursuits. He was said to have been one of the first Apache scouts enlisted by Crook.[3] He reportedly had come under Geronimo's baleful influence.[4]

But mostly he was a rustic who dreamed his way into the subcon-

---

[1] Cruse, *Apache Days*, 93–94.

[2] It was a commonplace to say that the Apache "had no religion," but this was far from the truth as Bourke makes clear in his "Medicine-Men of the Apache," Bureau of American Ethnology, *Ninth Annual Report* (1892), 449–603.

[3] John G. Bourke, "General Crook in the Indian Country," *Century* Magazine, Vol. XLI, No. 5 (March, 1891), 654.

[4] Ogle, *Western Apaches*, 204.

scious of his people, arousing them to a fervor of devotion and trust. By June of 1881 he had become the center of revival-type Apache gatherings, and the authorities, fearing the sort of unrest which eventually culminated in the ghost-dance craze that swept northern reservations beginning in 1888, became concerned. Noch-ay-del-klinne, as other prophets before and after him, centered his appeal on resurrection of the dead and the return of better times.[5] It was reported that he had predicted the whites would soon be driven away. He taught his followers a peculiar new dance in which the sacred meal, hoddentin,[6] had a place, and he promised to restore to life two chiefs killed shortly before. This caused great excitement.

San Carlos Agent J. C. Tiffany, whose business it was, as General Carr noted, "to keep informed of the doings and temper of his Indians and to sound the alarm if necessary,"[7] called some of the head men to him and remonstrated with them, but the excitement grew, as did tension among Arizona whites. When, about the first of August, there occurred a large gathering of the medicine man's followers at Carrizo Creek, some eighteen miles above Fort Apache, Cruse, then in command of Company A, Indian scouts, sent Sam Bowman, his chief of scouts, up to have a look.[8] Bowman returned, strangely

[5] James Mooney, "The Ghost Dance Religion," Bureau of American Ethnology, *Fourteenth Annual Report* (1896), 704–705.

[6] Hoddentin, the most sacred of Apache medicine substances, was the pollen of the tule or, sometimes, of corn; it was yellow and resembled corn-meal, and had immense powers for good, and was offered on many occasions. Bourke, "Medicine-Men of the Apache," BAE, *Ninth Annual Report* (1892), 499–549.

[7] The following account of the Cibicu affair is based, unless otherwise specified, on two basic accounts: 970AGO1883, Department of Arizona, March 1, 1883, "Official history of operation under Gen. Carr in and leading up to Cibicu affair," dated from Fort Apache, November 2, 1881, which is Carr's full report, and Cruse, *Apache Days*, 93–133. Cruse is somewhat unreliable on names, but his facts check closely with Carr's, the general paying tribute to Cruse's "great activity, energy and bravery on all occasions, his position being a most precarious one." Although the name is spelled Cibecue today, most contemporaries, including General Carr, spelled it Cibicu, which spelling is used here. See Barnes, *Place Names*, 2nd ed., p. 237.

[8] Bowman was a noted frontier figure during the latter-day Apache wars, although perhaps because he was illiterate, very little has been preserved about him. He was part Negro and part Choctaw, brave and reliable. He was said to have been murdered; see Thrapp, *Sieber*, 400.

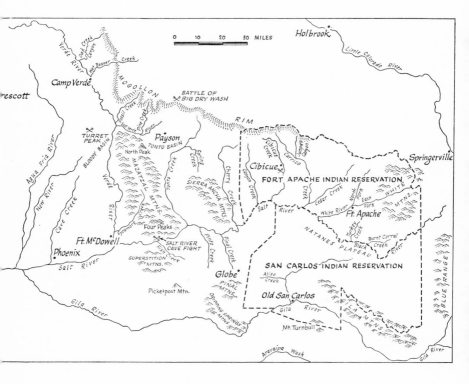

Tonto Basin Country

moved, and told Cruse he wanted to quit. Nat Nobles, chief packer, later told the officer Bowman had informed him that "that kind of dance always meant trouble, and he didn't want to get mixed up in it." When the Apache moved his meetings closer to Fort Apache, Cruse himself went to observe.

"As I looked at the swaying, engrossed figures, moving like automations to the thump of drums, I was amazed at the fraternizing between tribes and elements which had always held for each other the most deadly aversion," he wrote.

The Prophet, as Noch-ay-del-klinne came to be called, then moved his meetings to Cibicu, forty-six miles from the fort. Scouts heretofore thoroughly loyal became infected with wild enthusiasm. They demanded passes so that they might attend the dances. They overstayed their time. When they did return they were exhausted, surly, insubordinate, unfit for duty, grumbling that this was Indian country, not the whites'. Tiffany sent his Indian police to arrest the medicine man, but they returned without their arms and sulked about the agency. When the agent denied passes, hundreds of San Carlos Indians went without permission, and when he sent the police to bring them back, they said they were helpless to do so. The whites became convinced that the movement was assuming a military nature, and that a general outbreak was forming. On August 6 Carr telegraphed Willcox that the Dreamer was telling the Indians their dead chiefs could not return "because of the presence of the white people; that when the white people left, the dead would return, and the whites would be out of the country when the corn was ripe."[9] On one occasion, as Cruse many years later was informed, the Prophet and others conjured up a vision of departed Indians who told them to live at peace with the white man.

The factions interpreted the dream to suit themselves, Cruse wrote. "To no more than a handful was it a command to remain at peace," and of course the war faction was what interested the military.

Noch-ay-del-klinne refused an invitation to call upon Agent Tiffany at San Carlos and upon General Carr at Fort Apache, and

[9] Lockwood, *Apache Indians*, 236.

August 15 the latter received a telegram from Tiffany saying he wanted the Prophet "arrested or killed or both." Carr consulted with his officers, some scouts he believed loyal, and certain civilians and, when the medicine man refused a fresh invitation to come in, Carr "determined to start with what force I could muster to arrest him." He left the fort Monday, August 29, with 117 men, including 5 officers, a surgeon, 79 soldiers, 23 scouts, a guide, George Hurle, or Hurrle, interpreter, Nobles and 5 assistants, Carr's son, Clark, fifteen, and 9 civilians, a list of whom is not known to exist. The first day's march was about twenty-nine miles, camp being made in the gorge of Carrizo Creek. "Ammunition had for two or three weeks been kept from the Indian scouts and their arms kept in the orderly room," Carr noted, the scouts having been deemed untrustworthy because of the influence of the medicine man. "After supper, ammunition was issued to the scouts. . . . I had to take chances. They were enlisted soldiers of my command for duty; and I could not have found the Medicine man without them. I deemed it better also that if they should prove unfaithful it should not occur at the Post," where there were many women and children.

"I called them around my tent and had a long talk with them, told them I had sent for the Medicine man to talk to him about the reports that he had said the whites would leave the Country when the corn was ripe, &c. [Sergeant] Mose manfully defended his friend," but finally gave in to the idea that "When there is a misunderstanding between friends they should talk it over." Carr said that "now I was going to bring him [in]. That I was not going to hurt him, but to show him that he must come when sent for," and added that the whites indeed were going to stay in the country. Mose suggested he might go ahead and tell Noch-ay-del-klinne that the whites were coming, and Carr told him to do "as he pleased." He went ahead. Chopeau, another sergeant, remained with the company, and Carr depended upon him to point out the Prophet.

About two in the afternoon on August 30 the column entered the broad valley of the Cibicu, a pleasant expanse, wooded along the water course, grassy, and spotted with small meadows and corn fields, now as it was then. It lies between parallel ridges, low, bony with exposed formations and yellow sand, and speckled with scrub mesquite and other bushes. Here and there is a peach orchard.

"Upon approaching within about two miles of Cibicu Creek we found two forks of the trail, one of which, the main Verde trail, led directly across and the other diagonally up the valley," wrote Carr:

> I sent word to Lieut. Cruse to take the most direct route. . . . Noch-ay-del-klinne lived two or three miles above the Verde crossing. I think perhaps the Indians were prepared to fight at the regular crossing and were disconcerted that I turned up the valley . . .
>
> A chief called Sanchez . . . came out with his face painted red, which does not with this tribe mean war in particular, riding a nice white pony; he shook hands with me and told the Interpreter he was going home; rode down the line to the rear, no doubt counting our numbers. . . . It was my policy to show no distrust.
>
> When we approached the crossing the scouts wanted me to camp on this side . . . but I told them I had come a long distance to get the Medicine man and I was going to get him before camping.

Cruse awaited the arrival of Carr at the Prophet's lodge, a brush and canvas affair. The cavalry rode up and wheeled into line facing the wickiup, a long blue row of tanned troopers, warily alert on their California horses.

Carr told the medicine man, with Hurle interpreting, "what I had come for. This was told in the presence of the other Indians [crowding around], in their language, so that all should understand. There were fifteen or twenty male Indians around, besides the scouts. . . . He made excuse for not coming before that he had a patient to attend . . . but said he had cured him . . . and he was now ready to go with me." Carr appointed Sergeant John F. MacDonald and a small guard to bring the Prophet along, and told the Indian he would be killed if he tried to escape or if there were an attempt at rescue. Noch-ay-del-klinne smiled at this, and promised that neither eventuality would take place. "This talk was all in presence of other Indians, purposely to reassure them, and make a good case in their minds," wrote Carr. "Mose at times repeated and explained when he did not seem to catch the meaning of Interpreter Hurle."

"We had been watching, listening, during the colloquoy," Cruse commented. "When Carr's ultimatum was understood by the Apaches, I could actually *feel* the stiffening in that crowd, Indian by Indian. I thought that the clash was coming then. The soldiers tensed in their saddles. They felt the strain too." It is likely that some misinterpretation occurred at this point. About ten years later, in a newspaper interview, Al Sieber charged that this fight was caused by "misinterpretation through ignorance, the interpreter not knowing enough of the Indian language." Sieber, himself, probably was not at Cibicu.[10] Sergeant Mose and other Indians, sensing the crisis, stepped over to Noch-ay-del-klinne and reassured him, speaking loudly so that his followers might hear. "I saw them relax, and I drew a breath of relief," Cruse recalled.

The column then prepared to return to Camp Apache. Carr and First Lieutenant William H. Carter, adjutant, led, followed by Captain Edmund C. Hentig and his command of forty-six soldiers and the pack outfit. First Lieutenant William Stanton, with thirty-three troopers, and Cruse's scouts waited for the medicine man, who was to precede them. The first section rapidly disappeared around a bend in the trail, but the second detachment was held up while the Prophet was eating. Stanton and Cruse became increasingly uneasy, and the former at last ordered MacDonald to bring the prisoner along.

"There was a rustling among that crowd of watching Indians that reminded me of the buzzing of a rattlesnake aroused," wrote Cruse. When they went forward, hordes of heavily armed Indians surged after them. Cruse rode with Stanton.

"We nearly caught it back there," he told his companion. "It looked like a fight." "I thought so, too," Stanton agreed, "and I passed word to the troop very quietly to get ready."

Carr, several miles along, had selected a camp site. "I sent for Capt. Hentig to come up. We congratulated ourselves on the result, tho't it had come out right. I said to Capt. Hentig that I was rather

[10] *Arizona Enterprise*, Florence, May 12, 1892.

ashamed to come out with all this force to arrest one poor little Indian. Capt. Hentig put on his saturnine expression and said little, but evidently considered it a case of great cry and little wool. We cantered forward together, laid out the Camp."

The second section crossed the stream and entered the camp site. Carr directed the guard with the prisoner to camp in an enclosure of packsaddles and cargo, and Cruse came up seeking orders.

"It looked pretty scaly for a while, as we came along," Cruse said. "Those Indians—" "What are you talking about?" Carr demanded. "You're always using words I don't understand. Scaly! Scaly! Now, what does that mean?" Cruse explained, "Well, the Indians kept pouring into the trail out of every little side canyon. They were all stripped and painted for fighting. It looked to Stanton and me like an attack at any minute." Cruse indicated the Indians crossing the ford toward camp, and Carr ordered Hentig, the officer of the day, to clear them out. Hentig moved toward them, waving his arms and calling "Ucashay," by which he meant, "Go away."

"Lieut. Carter was just then directing the scouts where to camp," wrote Carr:

Dead Shot, 2nd Sergeant, said, "Too much anthills." Lieut. Carter then said, "Then go beyond the ant hills," when the scouts dropped their guns in the position of load, and loaded; an Indian at the head of those mounted and armed, also one of the scouts, Dead Shot, gave war whoops, and the scouts and all commenced firing. Sanchez went for the herd, and drove it away, killing Pvt. John Sonderegger. Capt. Hentig was killed at the first fire; a scout called Dandy Bill [Cruse calls him Dandy Jim] and another Indian being seen to fire at him.

Captain Hentig's orderly, Private Edward D. Livingstone, was killed by eight bullets through his body at the same instant.

"The Indians, as soon as they fired—which was at once returned by all of D Troop, and all about Hd. Qrs., who could seize their guns—dodged into the brush and weeds, and got behind the trees &c. in the creek bottom, and poured a murderous fire into camp. It was then that Privates Wm. Miller and John Sullivan were killed and

Privates Henry C. Bird, Thomas F. Foran, and Ludwig Baege, wounded (the two former since died)." Stanton was sent with E Company to sweep out the bottom with skirmishers. When the shooting commenced, the medicine man began crawling, apparently to join the hostiles, and MacDonald, although himself shot in the leg, and Trumpeter William O. Benites each fired at him, dropping the Prophet for good. The enemy drove off about half of the command's horses and mules.

"It may be thought that I might have been more particular in keeping them out of the vicinity of Camp, guarding my horses &c.," Carr reported, "but I stopped them the moment I knew of it. I did not allow enough to get in to overwhelm us, or in fact to do any harm if the scouts had not been traitors." He added that "the firing continued till dark, we arranging breastworks of packages, rocks &c. My tent was struck a number of times, one box of canned stuff in a breastwork was riddled and the cans set leaking."

Cruse and a sergeant saw five of the expedition's animals grazing about two hundred yards from their sector, which was quiet, and slipped out to recapture them, but instead the animals ran toward the hostiles who opened a heavy fire on the adventurous pair. "I was never so 'thoroughly surrounded' by bullets in my life," Cruse confessed. He estimated that the Indians, who had numbered three hundred at the start of the fight, totaled about eight hundred by dark. He thought about eighteen Indians had been killed, including six mutinous scouts. "I have always believed that if the hostiles had owned one leader of consequence they would have annihilated us," he said.

Others were not so sure. Many thought that the Indians had not sought the action, did not desire it, and only decided to pursue the matter when they realized how deeply they had become involved. "I learned to my own satisfaction," wrote Crook, later, "that the Indians are [so] firmly of the belief that the affair . . . was an attack premeditated by the white soldiers . . . that I am convinced any attempt to punish any of the Indian soldiers for participation in it would bring on war. . . . I have no doubt from what I know of the Indians and the country in question, that if the Indians had been in earnest not one of our soldiers would have gotten away from there alive. Of course afterwards, it was perfectly natural for the Indians who had lost friends and relatives to commit the depredations which they did in the vicinity of Fort Apache."[11]

A onetime Mexican captive of the Apaches and now considered almost a chief, Severiano, and Notzin, an Apache of Pedro's band, hearing of the fight, hastened ahead of the command into Fort Apache with the report that Carr and all his men had been massacred, and word was flashed across the nation where, so soon after the Custer incident, it was widely believed. The New York *Times* carried columns about the affair on September 4 and 5. "The newspapers simply rewrote the story of Custer's Last Stand," commented Cruse, dryly, which "as everyone knows, is a thrilling story."

Back on the Cibicu, meanwhile, Carr hastened preparations to pull out. "I directed a broad grave to be dug under my tent. The bodies were carefully marked. . . . When all was ready, I said over them as much of the service as I could remember, and had Taps sounded. This served for 'good night' for them and also to indicate to Indians we were going to sleep." Nearly a month later, on a return to the scene, salutes were fired over the graves. Carr denied that arms, ammunition, or anything else of value to the Indians was abandoned, although he was short pack animals. He particularly rejected a report that he had left five thousand rounds of ammunition for the hostiles, but admitted that a lost mule load later presented them with three thousand rounds. At 2:30 P.M. the following day the command filed into Fort Apache, to the immense relief of the worried civilians and others at the post. Loose bands of Apaches scoured the countryside. They ambushed and burned four Mormons almost within sight of Fort Apache. They killed three troopers eight miles distant. The next afternoon, while men were digging a grave at the cemetery, about six hundred yards east of the post, Indians appeared and chased them into the fort which, of course, was only a scattering of structures, and

[11] Crook to AAG, Division of the Pacific, written "In field, Camp near San Carlos Agency, A. T.," September 28, 1882.—Hayes Collection.

not a "fort" at all, in the architectural sense. They besieged it in one of the extremely rare instances of an Indian attack on a post in western history. First Lieutenant Charles G. Gordon, Sixth Cavalry, was shot seriously in the leg and, as he crumpled to the ground he wise-cracked, "Well, I got my billet and bullet the same day!" referring to the fact that with Hentig's death he had become commander of Troop D. The Indians set fire to some buildings but were driven off, and during the night most of them left.

The Indian participants of course wrote no account of the fight from their viewpoint, but Mike Burns, in passing, commented on the Apache's side of this incident. He told how the chiefs had died and that "in the camp there was a medicine man" who called the people to dance for their resurrection, the dance lasting nearly a month:

> Some trouble maker made a report to the Indian Agent and to the Post Commander, saying that the Indians at Cibicu had called all the other Indians together to make a raid on the soldiers at Fort Apache. The agent and the soldiers believed the stories and sent out some detachments of soldiers to Cibicu to arrest all the Indians engaged in the dances, and to bring them to the fort, especially the medicine man . . . who was brought in in irons. . . . One morning the Indians saw the soldiers coming over the road by column. There must have been about ninety soldiers or more, and about twenty-five Apache scouts. When the soldiers reached the camp they went right through to the great wigwam where the medicine man and the singer were seated. . . . The medicine man was dressed in eagle feathers, and his body was painted with all kinds of paints, as was also the man who sang for the dancers. Most of the Indian men left the wigwam, and got their guns, and went up on the foothills, the women and children having gone farther on the tops of the hills. No one was left in the medicine lodge but the great medicine man, and when the soldiers came there they took him over to the camp. He had warned the young men not to shoot any of the soldiers, saying that if they took him away they would only put him in the guardhouse for a few months or a year, and he would not be killed because he had not done any wrong. He was taken by the soldiers and a guard put over him, and while he was seated on a rock some of the young Indians tried to get close enough

to him to speak to him, but the soldiers pulled out their guns and pistols and drove the young men back three times. The fourth time the Indians were mad, and came right down, not minding the threats of the soldiers, and shot down all the soldiers who were there and then they ran off to the hills. The medicine man was still sitting on the rock with his wife and child, but when his wife tried to get him to go away over the hills to where the rest had gone, he told her to go alone; that there was no use for him to go anywhere after there had been so much killing on his account, as they would kill him no matter where he went, and it was just as well for him to meet his fate where he was. Just then one of the soldiers who had hidden among some saddles came out, pulled out his pistol and shot the medicine man through the head while his wife had her arm around him. The soldier, however, did not try to kill the woman and child.

In the meantime a sister of this medicine man, who was on a fast horse, rushed in and rounded up the whole herd of the soldiers' pack mules, which were loaded with ammunition and so on, and drove them all off through the hills. The Indian men came over to the dead soldiers and took off their arms, so that they were well prepared for war. The twenty-five Apache scouts, who were the bravest Indian bucks there were, and who were well armed and trusted by the government for their honesty and reliability as guides for the soldiers, this time turned upon them, killing nearly all of them. The Indians took the horses and pack mules with the loads of ammunition and were ready for war. Some of the Indian women went over to the soldiers' camp, and finding everybody dead, they took everything off them.[12]

Despite understandable discrepancies, this account agrees in certain points with the white version, except that it presents the facts from the Indian viewpoint. Obviously Noch-ay-del-klinne was widely revered by the Apaches, whose thoughts were on his teachings and their aspirations. Because the egocentric whites could not understand this, and failed to see how the Indians could be emotionally aroused by anything except a desire for violence against the whites, bloodshed and tragedy resulted.

[12] Farish, *History of Arizona*, III, 335–39.

In addition, Arizona Department Commander General Willcox was so dissatisfied with the handling of the Cibicu affair that he preferred charges against Carr, although there is reason to believe that the dispute between the high-ranking officers had other origins.[13] At any rate, he charged Carr with neglect of duty and, as specifications, listed his allowing the command "to become separated and thereby putting it in great and unnecessary peril" on the return from the Prophet's lodge; camping "in a negligent manner" and failing to take necessary precautions with resulting disaster; and, finally, arming the Indian scouts of dubious loyalty and taking them along.[14] Carr demanded a court of inquiry to investigate the charges and one court, with Hatch as president, reviewed the entire case, deciding that Carr selected his camp with good judgment and took proper precautions, acted wisely in the matter of the Indian scouts, but was responsible for the gap between the commands in the column, although because of brush and for other reasons he was unaware of it, because he was the "responsible officer." "The court is of opinion that the errors . . . seem to have been those of judgment only," it decided.[15] However, President Chester A. Arthur, reviewing the case, expressed himself as "not satisfied with the condition of affairs in the Department of Arizona" and directed that the general of the Army "properly admonish" Carr.[16] This was done.

The fighting did not end with the attack on Fort Apache and depredations in the environs. Up near Pleasant Valley, about thirty miles from the Cibicu, was the Middleton ranch, circling a tiny log building with a detached milk house, corral, and other structures. Here the large and growing Middleton family lived.[17] Mrs. Middleton with

[13] The long and involved dispute between Willcox and Carr is treated in some detail in James T. King, *War Eagle: A Life of General Eugene A. Carr*, 193–226.

[14] 668AGO1882 in Document File 4327–1881, Apache Troubles 1879–1883, National Archives Record Group 94; hereafter cited as AT with code number.

[15] AT no serial number, General Orders No. 125, Headquarters, AGO, Washington, October 21, 1882.

[16] AT 668AGO1882 Headquarters of the Army, Washington, February 13, 1882.

[17] William Middleton, the father, was born in Kentucky, went to California in 1849, then to Arizona. He raised nine children and was drowned in Pennell Creek,

Cliff, five, Della, nine and Lee, seven, was at the milk house when Indians suddenly opened fire. She fled to the main building. Hattie Middleton, sitting on the front porch between George L. Turner, Jr. and Henry Moody, saw them both killed and lost a lock of hair to a bullet, but escaped into the house. Henry Middleton was struck above the heart, but lived. Others of the family had narrow escapes. The Indians ran off about seventy-five head of horses, and under cover of darkness the family fled to Globe.[18]

General Willcox, as soon as the Cibicu report reached him, rushed troops to the Fort Apache–San Carlos area. Soldiers swarmed everywhere. So impressed were the Indians that they surrendered in droves. Five of the alleged mutineers gave themselves up September 20, and sixty other wanted Indians came in during the following week. Not all of the mutineers were apprehended; some remained bronchos in the wilderness, but on November 11 the five who had surrendered were court-martialed at Fort Grant for mutiny, desertion, and murder. Two were dishonorably discharged and sentenced to long terms at Alcatraz, then an Army prison. The other three, Sergeant Dandy Jim, accused of shooting Captain Hentig, Sergeant Dead Shot, and Private Skippy, were sentenced to hang. On March 3, 1882, at 12:30 P.M., the scouts were led from their cells to the gallows, before ranks of troops at attention, gathered in case of trouble.[19] Dead Shot's wife is said to have hanged herself the same day.[20]

---

at Globe, during a cloudburst. One son, Eugene, was badly shot in the Apache Kid outbreak; see Thrapp, *Sieber*, 337–41.—Interview with Lee Middleton, another son, July 13, 1958, at Phoenix.

[18] Hattie Middleton's account of this harrowing experience appeared in the *Frontier Times* for June, 1928. It was reprinted in *True West*, Vol. XI, No. 4 (March–April, 1964), 28, 48, 50.

[19] *Star*, March 3, 4, 1882.

[20] Barnes, *Place Names*, 95.

XVIII

Loco

Tの HE AFFAIR AT CIBICU had unnerved a good part of the Southwest, and those who thought the Apache wars won. Troops were sent to San Carlos and other areas from many places. "General Willcox . . . telegraphed to the east and to the west for reinforcements," wrote John Clum, many years later, "with the result that twenty-two companies of troops—eleven from New Mexico, and eleven from California (which included three batteries of artillery) were rushed into Arizona."[1] He charged that so many troops milled over the reservations by late September that all of the Apaches were edgy, and the ever-suspicious Chiricahuas and Warm Springs bordered on terror.

With the surrender of Juh and his band in January, 1880, practically all of the western Apaches except Victorio's band had been concentrated at San Carlos. There had been no troops on the reservation proper since the relocation of the Chiricahuas there in June, 1876. But now the reservation was crisscrossed by marching columns and their presence, admittedly, had persuaded many Cibicu recalcitrants to surrender, but it had the reverse effect on the wary Chiricahuas. On several occasions they demanded assurances of Tiffany that troop movements were not directed at them in retribution for their former raids from Mexico. On September 20 they sent their important men to the agent once more to learn "what was going on, and what so many troops meant about the agencies."[2] Tiffany said he told them that the maneuvers were not directed against them, that

<hr>

[1] John P. Clum, "Apache Misrule," *New Mexico Historical Review*, Vol. V, No. 2 (April, 1930), 141.

[2] *Ibid.*, Vol. V, No. 3 (July, 1930), 228. In this two-part article, Clum of course places most blame on the military, but also charges that weak and vacillating Indian Bureau personnel compounded the situation.

peaceful Indians would not be molested, and urged them to return home. Delightedly the Indians shook his hand and did as he asked.

"Then, about a week later, without apparent necessity or cause—and without the slightest warning—three troops of cavalry came galloping down from Camp Thomas and halted in battle array at the very threshhold of their crude camps," reported Clum. What had happened was this: the White Mountain Apaches under George and Bonito were encamped near the sub-agency of Camp Thomas, with the wild Chiricahuas nearby. Indians suspected of having had a part in the Cibicu affair had been ordered to surrender, and these two bands did so, being released on parole. Five days later, General Willcox decided to terminate their parole and "unnecessarily, stupidly and fatally," as Clum put it, sent the cavalry to effect it.

It was ration day and Ezra Hoag, the only white man present (who had been sub-agent since 1875), was busily distributing beef, flour, and other supplies. George and Bonito, not wanting to miss their rations, sent word they would voluntarily surrender later, but Major James Biddle, commanding the expedition, declared this would not do. He deployed his troops, advancing on the throng. The inevitable happened. Seeing this hostile array, the most nervous of the White Mountains fled to the Chiricahuas, blurted their version of the situation, and "so alarmed them that during the night seventy-four . . . fled from the reserve,"[3] all under fat old Juh and Nachez, a son of Cochise.[4]

---

[3] Lockwood, *Apache Indians*, 244.

[4] Although the record is confused, I believe Geronimo was with this fleeing party, although he is not specifically mentioned in most accounts. Bancroft, *Arizona and New Mexico*, 569, says Juh and Nachez made the break, followed next April by Loco and Geronimo, and Hodge, *Handbook*, I, 65, reprints this statement, almost unquestionably in error. Dunn, *Massacres*, 644, mentions Juh and Nachez, but not Geronimo. But Ogle, *Western Apaches*, 208–209, says that Juh, Geronimo, Chatto, and Nachez made the break; Clum, "Apache Misrule," *NMHR*, Vol. V, No. 3 (July, 1930), 224, said that the "wild Chiricahuas, under Ju (Hoo) and Geronimo . . . fled toward Mexico," and adds in another place that George also went. Cruse, in a letter to Britton Davis of October 8, 1927, said that "Geronimo and Juh made the break, tried to get Loco, but couldn't persuade him." In his book, Davis, *The Truth About Geronimo*, 6, consequently says that Geronimo and Juh made the break. The Loco outbreak is better documented than this one, and if Geronimo had been a

No one accepted blame for this disaster. The military blandly insisted that the Indians fled "for some unexplained reason,"[5] though Willcox, with more imagination, said it was because "the reservation authorities did not help them take out a water ditch." Lockwood believed the cause lay in the abysmal corruption on the reservation.[6] Clum, of course, blamed the military, and Hoag agreed that "the Indians were literally scared away."[7] Whatever the deep-seated motives, it seems likely that the troop demonstration at least provided the spark. Bourke, in his dry manner, suggested that profound dissatisfaction contributed:

The Chiricahuas . . . led a Jack-in-the-box sort of existence, now popping into an agency and now popping out, anxious, if their own story is to be credited, to live at peace with the whites, but unable to do so from lack of nourishment. When they went upon the reservation, rations in abundance were promised for themselves and their families. A difference of opinion soon arose with the agent as to what constituted a ration, the wicked Indians laboring under the delusion that it was enough food to keep the recipient from starving to death. . . . To the credit of the agent it must be said that he made a praise-worthy but ineffectual effort to alleviate the pangs of hunger by a liberal distribution of hymn-books among his wards [various churches supplied many of the agents of this period]. The perverse Chiricahuas [were] not able to digest works of that nature.[8]

Only the rear guard of the fleeing Indians clashed with soldiers near Cedar Springs, at a ranch on the west side of the Pinalenos, about sixteen miles from Camp Grant on the road to Thomas. Mrs. Mowlds, forted up in the stone ranch house with two men, saw the hostiles savagely attack a wagon train from Tucson, shoot her husband and six other men, loot the train, and be interrupted while hav-

---

part of it, he surely would have been mentioned. That he does not figure more prominently in the Juh-Nachez outbreak testifies to the minor role he played in Apache affairs to this time.

[5] William Harding Carter, *The Life of Lieutenant General Chaffee*, 92.

[6] Lockwood, *Apache Indians*, 244.

[7] Clum, "Apache Misrule," *NMHR*, Vol. V, No. 3 (July, 1930), 236.

[8] John G. Bourke, *An Apache Campaign in the Sierra Madre*, 8.

ing "a good time generally," by the arrival of troops, G of the First, A and F of the Sixth Cavalries, a detachment of the Eighth Infantry and Company D, Indian scouts, all under command of Willcox himself. This sizable force pitched into the Indians, who hastily withdrew into the rocks and taunted the soldiers to come get them. The whites tried to oblige, losing a sergeant and two men killed and as many wounded, while not claiming to have hit a hostile.

Just before dark the Indians made a sharp attack on the soldiers' positions, firing seven volleys and carrying the attack forward until the opponents sometimes were within ten feet of each other; yet it was a bluff, to permit women, children, and cattle to be escorted away. During the night the Indians slit the throats of their dogs and light-colored horses and slipped away to Mexico, stealing $20,000 worth of Henry Hooker's horses on their way.[9]

Once more the Southwest could brace itself for raids. It was inevitable that the lure of plunder and adventure would prove irresistible to young men of the reservation camps, and that they would contact the wild Indians to the south. And the southern hostiles had friends on San Carlos, and would spare no effort to lure them to the warpath. Prime target was Loco and what was left of the Ojo Caliente warriors who had followed Victorio, though Loco was reluctant. The Apaches, being individualists, were difficult to generalize about. General John Pope thought them "a miserable, brutal race, cruel, deceitful and wholly irreclaimable,"[10] but Crook, who knew them better, and others thought them a superior people. Probably it depended in part upon the viewer. There were brutal, unreliable Apaches, just as there were whites who could be so characterized, and there were men of justice and honor and wisdom among them, too.

Loco, who knew war well, was a wise man, and in his wisdom he saw no future in war with the white man. One might wonder what he saw in peace at San Carlos for his people, either, but an old man searches for something different than a young man, and Loco was well into middle age. He had lost an eye as a young man to a grizzly

9 Barnes, *Place Names*, 84–85.
10 Victorio Papers, 280AGO1880, Pope to AAG, Chicago, January 9, 1880.

bear,[11] but despite the resulting deformity, his was not an unkindly countenance, nor was its appearance misleading. There were more flamboyant Apache leaders, but few with more influence, more listened to in council, more respected by red and white alike. Loco did not join Juh and Nachez in the September bust-out, and the thought of seven hundred Warm Springs and Chiricahuas remaining on the reservation rankled the Sierra Madre independents.

About the middle of January, 1882, messengers from the south filtered into Loco's camp, a mile or more from the sub-agency, which was eighteen miles from San Carlos toward Thomas. They said they had come from Juh and Nachez, which Loco already knew, and warned that within forty days the hostiles were coming on a raid, and would force Loco and his people to return with them to the Sierra Madre.[12] Loco grunted, and kept his counsel. But others talked. By the middle of February Al Sieber had heard of it. He, Lieutenant John Y. F. (Bo) Blake, and ten scouts searched the Dragoon Mountains for hostiles, but found none.[13]

Tiffany scoffed at the report of contact between reservation and Mexico Indians, and told General Willcox that he was sure of his control over the agency Apaches.[14] Willcox was not so sure. To be safe, he sent two cavalry troops to the border. All posts and commanders were ordered to be on the alert. In New Mexico Colonel George Alexander Forsyth, a celebrated Indian fighter, was in the field with six troops of the Fourth Cavalry, patrolling the Southern Pacific Railroad from Separ to beyond Lordsburg. Sieber was sent with some scouts toward the end of March to scour the Stein's Peak mountains, on the Arizona–New Mexico border, and at last he struck hostile sign, but it was too late. He found traces of Chiricahuas coming up from the south to force the Warm Springs Indians to leave San Carlos.[15] But before he could warn Willcox, the break came. On April 18 the renegades struck.

[11] Jason Betzinez, *I Fought With Geronimo*, 33.

[12] Lockwood, *Apache Indians*, 246–47.

[13] *Star*, February 22, 1882.

[14] Lockwood, *Apache Indians*, 247.

[15] Sieber to Willcox, June 8, 1882, AGO, Letters Received 2924, Department of Arizona, 1882.

The raiders, under Chatto, Chihuahua, Nachez, and possibly Geronimo[16] cut the telegraph wire west of the sub-agency and, without disturbing Loco at once, made for San Carlos, perhaps intending to spread havoc there. Only the courage and persistence of one man, Ed Pierson, the sub-agency telegraph operator, forestalled them.[17] In the dark he found and repaired the wire break, then sat at his instrument through the night, sending over and over a warning to San Carlos where it finally was received by the awakened operator, who called Chief of Police Albert D. Sterling[18] and sent him galloping off toward the sub-agency with a single Indian policeman, Sagotal. Somewhere between San Carlos and Loco's camp the pair ran into the hostiles, and lost their lives, although they forestalled an attack on the agency. According to one account, Sterling's head was played with like a football by the foes who hated him.[19]

The wild band now swirled back into Loco's camp and so stirred up his people that he reluctantly agreed to move out on the long warpath. Some say he did so only at rifle point. Several families, not wishing conflict, fled north to join the Navahos, but were arrested and held at Fort Union.[20]

Now outlaws anyway, the Indians jumped some wagons eight miles from the sub-agency, the freighter Gilson, his son, and a hired man abandoning the vehicles and somehow escaping with their lives. Indians looted the wagons and destroyed what freight they did not want.[21] A white force, hastily organized under Dan Ming, lost the trail after ten miles, and as the hostiles went murderously on, the press screamed for miracles. Of miracles there were none, but of

---

[16] Cruse said that Chihuahua and eight men composed this party—Cruse to Davis, October 8, 1927, Letters Collection of Davis' correspondence with former Army colleagues, owned by Mrs. J. F. Connor; hereafter cited as Davis Collection.

[17] McClintock, *Arizona*, I, 235.

[18] George A. Forsyth, *Thrilling Days in Army Life*, 79, considers Sterling "a splendid young fellow, fascinated with Indian life." Betzinez formed a "fast friendship" with Sterling and said it was the "warriors," that is, the Apaches from Mexico, who killed him.—Letter to author, November 10, 1959.

[19] L.A. Pub. Lib.

[20] Crook to AAG, Division of the Pacific, July 11, 1884.—Hayes Collection.

[21] L.A. Pub. Lib.

courage there was plenty, as the story of Felix Knox attests. Knox was a gambler, and rumor had it not a too scrupulous gambler, at Globe, but at this time was returning with his family from their Gila River ranch. The party ran into Apaches and Knox heroically gave up his life that his family might be saved, leading historian Sharlot Hall, in commemoration, to pen a verse which said, in part:

> *Knox the Gambler—Felix Knox*
> *Trickster, short-card man, if you will;*
> *Rustler, brand-wrangler—all of that—*
> *But Knox the man and the hero still!*[22]

The Apache route led them close to Thomas where Lieutenant Colonel George W. Schofield within an hour mounted two companies of the Sixth Cavalry and rode in pursuit.[23] They pursued the Indians eastward "until they made them scatter in all directions," and came upon the still-warm bodies of three prospectors, after which they returned to the post, short of rations, it was reported. A few miles beyond the hostiles killed ten more whites. They swept up what loose stock they could find at George H. Stevens' ranch, including about $5,000 worth of sheep which they took only after slaying all the people they could find, including seven men, one woman, and two children, one of whom was roasted alive and the other tossed screaming into a nest of needle-crowned cactus. A San Francisco newspaper carried a vivid account of the Stevens tragedy in a Safford report via a Tucson dispatch:

Little Stanislaus Mestas, aged nine years [reported that] the Indians attacked our camp whilst we were all asleep. My father and five other men . . . attempted to get their guns, but were too late. The Indians rushed in from all sides and overpowered them before a shot could be fired. . . . An Indian put the muzzle of his gun against the head of one man and fired, blowing his brains against the floor and

[22] McClintock, *Arizona*, I, 236–37.

[23] George W. Schofield was of an inventive turn of mind, a Smith & Wesson revolver being named after him for design improvements he suggested. On December 18, 1882, he committed suicide; he had been in poor health.—*Star*, December 19, 1882; see John E. Parsons, *Smith & Wesson Revolvers*, for details of his inventions.

walls. I saw them kill my mother and two little brothers by beating their brains out with stones. They took my father and tortured him most dreadfully. He begged them to spare him, but they only tortured him the more. When they were tired of torturing him one of them split his head with an axe. An Indian squaw, wife of one of the four friendly Apache herders who worked with us, saved my life by holding me behind her and begging them to spare me. . . . They soon were sorry that they spared me, for they sent a party back to the house to kill me, but the squaw begged so hard for me that they said they would go back and tell the chief that they could not find me. . . . [The correspondent continued:] The face of little Stanislaus is indicative of great suffering. Horror is depicted upon his every feature.[24]

A flood of news bulletins, interlaced with military dispatches, crowded the telegraph wires, revealing a growing list of victims and a state of complete confusion, as the fighting area spread eastward.

"The count at San Carlos shows all the Warm Springs out," chattered a message from Tucson. "Grave doubts are entertained regarding the White Mountain Indians and there would be no surprise to hear of their leaving the reservation." A Lordsburg report said that "A courier just arrived from Clifton reports that the Indians attacked an O. K. Smythe & Babcock freighting firm train, killed five teamsters four miles west of Clifton and ran off sixty head of mules." On the morning of April 21, wrote a correspondent from Clifton, a party including John P. Risque, a Silver City lawyer, Sam Eckles Magruder, Captain John Slawson, mining superintendent, a Captain Frink, and H. L. Trescott pulled out of town despite warnings of old timers, to inspect mines to the west. Two hours later came word that Risque, Trescott, and Slawson had ridden into an ambush and were killed, although the other two "saved their lives by making good use of their heels, as the Indians failed to hit them at the first fire."[25] On the morning of the twenty-second came word that the Indians attacked a train of twelve ox wagons driven by a dozen Mexicans, killing the whole outfit. "How long, oh! how long is this thing to last!"

[24] L.A. Pub. Lib.
[25] *Ibid.*

wailed a correspondent. A Silver City burial team reported interring thirty victims during the first week of Indian fury, and the total dead by this time was fifty.[26] Loco probably was not entirely to blame for these bloody depredations, but rather it was Juh—and the need to arm and feed some seven hundred fleeing individuals.

The savages, for their part, had missed their biggest game. Despite the obvious threat, General William Tecumseh Sherman and a small party, engaged in an inspection of the Indian country, "missed the Chiricahuas by the narrowest of margins," while enroute to Camp Grant. Will C. Barnes, as telegraph operator, had an unrivaled opportunity to learn of the situation, and recalled later that "the military authorities at Whipple and Grant spent some mighty anxious hours until he was reported safe into Grant."[27]

Most of the hostiles apparently now plunged up West Doubtful Canyon toward the crest of Stein's Peak Range, although a small group swept south along the Southern Pacific right-of-way, killing a track walker before rejoining the main band. Twenty-five Ojo Caliente warriors worked north of the Gila, burning the ranches, sweeping the country bare of stock, and killing six or eight men. Fears were felt for prospectors and miners on the San Francisco River. A company of fifty mounted volunteers grimly left Shakespeare,[28] near Lordsburg, headed for the Gila and San Francisco rivers. The papers continued to wax sarcastic.

"Troops are in pursuit," ran a typical account, "but, as usual, well in the rear."[29] Another said, "No effectual obstruction has been placed in the pathway of the fleeing Apaches to-day, and they still continue to wade through slaughter towards Mexico. The military in this, as in former outbreaks, have proved entirely inadequate to the occasion,

[26] *Ibid.*

[27] Barnes, *Place Names*, 85. Barnes says this incident occurred during the Juh outbreak the previous September, but Ogle, *Western Apaches*, 216, says it was in April, 1882, and so does Clum.

[28] Shakespeare at this time was a booming mining town. It began in Civil War years as a stage station and surged to prominence in 1872 with a San Francisco banker's ill-fated promotion scheme.—*Service Record World War I and II, Hidalgo County* (Lordsburg, New Mexico, 1949), 117–18.

[29] L.A. Pub. Lib.

and much dissatisfaction is felt and expressed on all sides."[30] An editorial note in a San Francisco newspaper commented: "The military are not in high favor in Arizona. It is generally believed in the Territory that the officers are not doing their duty, and that they think more of their comfort and scalps than they do of any plan of speedily suppressing an outbreak."[31] But the soldiers were not idle. Forsyth and his six companies were cutting for sign along the Southern Pacific tracks east of the New Mexico line. Other units were in the field; more headed for the danger zone.

The country was unusually dry this spring. Forsyth figured that the hostiles would follow the Gila and then head for Mexico via the comparatively well-watered Burro Mountains, or the Stein's Peak Range, farther west, and he moved his men west from Separ to Lordsburg.[32] There was no water to be had at Steins, west of Lordsburg, so he ordered a tank car sent from San Simon to Steins, and as it had not yet arrived the night of the twenty-second, his troopers made a dry camp. They groomed their horses at 3:20 A.M., and by four the tanker arrived. The parched horses had to be watered from camp kettles, because there were only two spigots on the tank. By six, however, all were in the saddle, moving northeast, away from the railroad and toward Richmond.[33]

The command intended to keep well clear of the Stein's Range, moving northeast to cut the Richmond Road and follow it to the Gila. But realizing that the Indians quite possibly were in the mountains to the westward, Forsyth sent an Indian-fighting first lieutenant, David N. McDonald, with six mounted scouts and two enlisted men to cut for sign along the southeastern bulge of Stein's mountains. At McDonald's request he included in the detachment Yuma Bill, "our most reliable Apache scout," who spoke English very well. Forsyth sent also six other scouts along the base of the range, but farther out

---

[30] *Ibid.*

[31] *Ibid.*

[32] The following account, through the Garcia incident, is based unless otherwise specified, on Forsyth, *Thrilling Days*, 79–121.

[33] Richmond's name was changed to Virden on Christmas Day, 1915. It is eight miles up the Gila from Duncan, Arizona.—*Hidalgo County*, 52.

Left: Mangus, son of Mangas Coloradas, was the only important Apache actually captured in the field, in 1886.

Right: Nana, whether aged seventy or ninety, was one of ablest Apache war leaders, died unreconstructed and incorrigible.

James Cook (probably Long Jim Cook), with pack mules and packers, at San Carlos sub-agency in 1883.

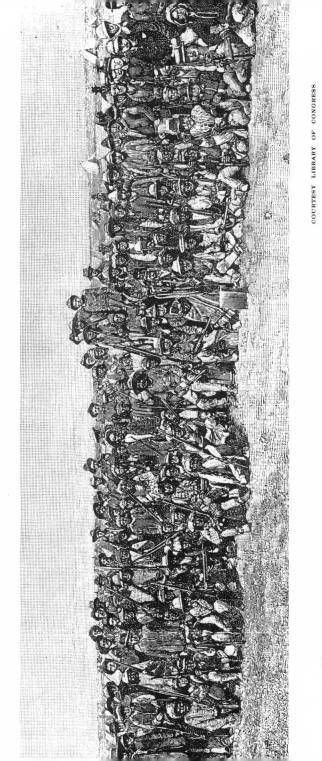

The original legend reads: "General Crook's Apache Campaign.—Crook's Command of White Mountain Apache Scouts and Cavalry-men, now in pursuit of the Apaches in Mexico. From a photo. by Chas. S. Baker, taken at Willcox, Arizona, April 22d [1883]." This is from the only existing photograph of the 1883 Mexican expedition.

General George Crook, mounted on Apache, his noted mule. This rare photograph was made in 1885 in an arroyo in Apache Pass, near Fort Bowie, Arizona.

Sam Bowman, chief of scouts (top), and Lieutenant Charles B. Gatewood (in big hat, just below Sam), and scouts.

Micky Free, interpreter and scout, lower left, and Chatto, foreground, Britton Davis's first sergeant, with scouts.

Albert Payson Morrow, as a major chased Victorio, later was named colonel of the Third Cavalry.

General Orlando B. Willcox, commander of the Department of Arizona, 1878–82, was succeeded by Crook.

Wirt Davis, in many Indian fights, including Geronimo campaigns, later became colonel of the Third Cavalry.

Colonel S. B. M. Young, in charge of operations against the Walapais, later became a lieutenant general.

Middleton Ranch, Sierra Ancha Mountains, about 1880, where George Turner and Henry Moody were killed by Apaches and where, about 1888, the first fight of the Pleasant Valley War took place.

Photograph taken in Mexico in 1886, showing Geronimo and his warriors while still hostile. Nana is mounted; Geronimo is in front and to the left of the horse.

COURTESY GEORGE S. SCHAEFFER

Hostile Chiricahuas in 1886, with Geronimo standing at center.

General George Crook (center) and some of his officers and scouts about 1886.

Standing: seventh from left, with white goatee, Charles M. Strauss, mayor of Tucson; tenth from left, Lieutenant William Ewen Shipp; eleventh from left, behind Crook, Lieutenant Samson Lane Faison; twelfth from left, Captain John G. Bourke; fourteenth from left, with large white hat, dark shirt, and suspenders, Al Sieber.

Sitting: fifth from left, in white shirt, Tom Horn; sixth from left, Lieutenant Marion P. Maus; seventh from left, Captain Cyrus Swan Roberts; eighth from left, Charles D. Roberts, son of Captain Roberts; ninth from left, General Crook; tenth from left, "Interpreter," possibly Corydon E. Cooley.

The late General Charles D. Roberts, son of Captain Cyrus Roberts, was most helpful in identifying these people. The other men shown cannot now be identified.

General Crook's conference with Geronimo, March, 1886, in Canyon de los Embudos, Mexico: A—Lieutenant William Ewen Shipp, B—Lieutenant Samson Lane Faison, C—Nachez, D—Captain Cyrus Swan Roberts, E—Cayetano, F—Geronimo, G—Concepcion, H—Nana, I—Noche, J—Lieutenant Marion P. Maus, K—Jose Maria, L—Antonio Besias, M—Jose Montoyo, N—Captain J. G. Bourke, O—General Crook, P—Charles D. Roberts, Q—Tommy Blair, R—K. W. Daly, S—Josanie, T—Chihuahua, U—Tom Moore, V—Martin Foster (?), W—Mayor Charles M. Strauss of Tucson. Others cannot now be identified.

Lieutenant Charles B. and Mrs. Gatewood. One of the unsung heroes of the Apache wars, Gatewood commanded Indian scouts for many years, engaged in countless fights with hostiles, and in 1886, near Fronteras, in Mexico, talked Geronimo into finally surrendering. Gatewood died in obscurity, plagued by crippling injuries.

General Nelson A. Miles and staff at Bowie Station, September 8, 1886. Left to right: Surgeon Leonard Wood, Lieutenant Robert F. Ames, Lieutenant Wilber Elliot Wilder, Captain Henry Lawton, General Miles, Captain W. A. Thompson, Major A. S. Kimball, Lieutenant J. A. Dapray, and Lieutenant Charles Clay.

G Troop, Tenth Cavalry, taking Indian prisoners to U.S. Court at Tucson.

Apaches leaving Fort Bowie for Florida.

toward the plain. It was very hot. Forsyth's alkali-dusted column moved in a sweating, grimy formation northward. They had gone scarcely three miles when they received word from McDonald that he had struck a twelve-hour old trail, leading north. This no doubt was of the party that had killed the track walker and now sought to re-establish contact with the main band, but Forsyth thought it was a minor grouping fresh out of Mexico, a deduction he later regretted. McDonald plunged into the barren, sun-baked peaks following the trail.[34] It ran through the worst of the mountains, where the threat of an ambush was so apparent the lieutenant with difficulty persuaded his scouts to continue. For twelve miles the advance continued, until they found their way barred by a rock wall, pierced by a narrow gorge, beyond which rose a whisp of smoke, so faint that McDonald could barely distinguish it even when his eagle-eyed scouts pointed it out. The only way forward was through the defile, but the scouts to a man refused to enter it, so certain were they that an ambush awaited them.

"As neither force nor persuasion would avail, I taunted them as cowards and squaws," wrote McDonald. He dismounted, handed his reins to one of them, instructed the scouts to back him up as well as they could, but if he should be shot, to work their own way back to the command. He then cocked his carbine and "with a great show of boldness I struck out on the trail." He soon lost sight of his scouts. The defile was narrow and twisting; he could see only a few yards on either side. "Constantly expecting to hear the sharp crack of a rifle, I tried to see in front, behind, and above, lest a hideous Apache should quietly poke his gun over the edge of the chasm and shoot me in the back," recalled the officer. Creeping from point to point, he came eventually to a circular opening or basin, with several still-smoking Indian campfires on the floor. A twig cracked behind him, and he whirled with weapon raised. But it was Yuma Bill, his hand upheld in

[34] McDonald's own account, written at Forsyth's request, is printed in the latter's narrative. McDonald, a Tennesseean, had already performed frontier duty in Texas and the Indian Territory. He resigned from the Army in 1888 and returned to Carthage, Tennessee.—Cullum, *Biographical Register*.

warning, who "had become ashamed" and bravely followed the lieutenant up a trail which he must have been certain would lead only to his death.

Collecting the other scouts, the little party pushed on along the trail, eventually reaching a summit from which could be seen the trail leading northeasterly toward the dark gash of the Gila, and toward the plain which the main command was then crossing, although out of sight. But the sign, after all, did not continue in that direction. McDonald's dogged party found that it kept well within the foothills, leading northerly toward the mouth of East Doubtful Canyon. Before they had progressed far, they saw men off to the right and plunged from the trail to cut them off. They were two burro-equipped prospectors, terrified of the scouts whom they took for hostiles.

"To say that they were cowards and frightened almost out of their senses would not convey any idea of their condition," McDonald wrote. "These two men ran in circles, with their hands, jaws and apparently the very skin of their bodies shaking and quivering, the guns in their hands oscillating like the hands of a palsied person. Perspiration in huge drops ran down their faces, hair and beard, and they were utterly incapable of making the slightest defense. Although I stood before them in my uniform and spoke to them, telling them who we were, it was several moments before they seemed to realize they were not to be massacred." Yuma Bill and the scouts thought it uproarious. "White man heap scared; no catchum news!" Bill chuckled.

Again seeking the trail, Bill guessed the enemy must have swung back toward the mountains. He pointed to a rock shelf, several hundred feet long, at the base of a spur to the left, and predicted the trail would be somewhere near its base. McDonald moved in that direction. They found the trail again, "so obscure that we were only a few feet from the rock when Bill pointed it out," the officer wrote. Looking to the right, then, Bill called out: "Two Indians!"

Everyone saw them at once. The McDonald party bunched and swung in close to the rock, knees touching, horses straining forward, the men with their bodies hunched, looking to the right where the two Indians walked, apparently oblivious to the pursuit, half a mile distant.

All this happened in a few seconds, and as the horses' heads reached the rock it brought us five abreast. It then seemed to occur to Yuma Bill that he had not looked over the rock; or he may have heard some noise, for he jerked his face so quickly to the front that he came near striking it against mine as I was leaning, looking to the right. I believe the portion of a second that I gained in suddenly jerking my face out of the way . . . saved my life, for in a flash I saw poked over the rock a thick array of gun barrels, with twelve or fifteen Indian heads and faces showing behind them. At the same moment Bill shrieked: "Watch out, Lieutenant McDonald!" Throwing myself forward on my horse's neck, I grasped the reins close to the bit on each side to turn him away, and then came the volley, and with the smoke in my face and eyes, I threw my horse's head to the left-about, over the bodies of the three dead Yumas, that had been riding on my left, and had now fallen under his feet. I knew, from an exclamation, that Bill had been struck, and somehow was conscious that he had not fallen from his saddle. I heard the corporal, who, being a little behind and lower down the slope, had not been exposed to the volley, wheel to the rear and call, "Come on, Lieutenant," and I galloped after him, the three troop-horses that the dead scouts had ridden whirling and running abreast of me, as they had been drilled to do in the troop.

McDonald reined in his plunging horse fifty yards from the ambuscade, wheeled him, getting a bullet through his hat and another singeing his jaw as he did so, and fired at the Indians. As he turned he glimpsed a sight he would never forget.

Yuma Bill had stopped and turned almost simultaneously with myself. As his horse halted, facing the foe, he rose upright in his stirrups, standing straight as an arrow, every nerve and muscle at full tension, his big eyes blazing, and his long black hair floating behind him, even his horse standing with the glory of battle on him, with arched neck and fiery eyes, in an expectant attitude, ready to leap. I saw Bill's long rifle come up swift and steady, but I saw no more. I was closing the breech-block of my carbine and raising it to my shoulder. I heard the report of Bill's gun, and then a heavy volley from the Indians.

It was time to wheel now, and as I closed in my second cartridge I turned to the right-about looking for Bill. There stood his horse with his neck distended and blood pouring from several wounds, Bill still in the saddle, but drooping forward, his head turning downward by the side of his horse's neck. I saw his head touch the tip of the horse's mane, which was towards me, and I suppose he fell on his head, but I did not see him leave the saddle, for my horse turned and again dashed to the rear.

McDonald sent a courier after Colonel Forsyth and, with his remaining men, stood off the Apaches, about one hundred and fifty men, apparently Loco's full force. Later in the day, when things looked their grimmest, swept up a welcome sight, "six splendid cavalry troops in beautiful order *en echelon*," coming to the rescue. McDonald concisely reviewed the situation. Forsyth moved his men toward the enemy, who fired the grass and brush, creating an enormous smoke cloud as screen to their movements.

Colonel Forsyth found the hostiles "strongly intrenched on the left side of Horse Shoe Cañon, and also in the middle of it." He divided his command to form two flanking parties, of two troops each, left another with the horses, and began to assault the Indian position frontally with his last company. Major Wirt Davis opened the attack, charging through the blazing grass and bushes, and rounding up a number of the hostiles' ponies.[35] The firing became general. "In about an hour we compelled them to abandon their position and fall back," wrote the colonel. "They then took up a second strong position, which we again flanked them out of, and gradually drove them back into the cañon and up among the high peaks of the range, some of them firing at us from points eight, twelve, and even sixteen hundred feet above us. I never saw a more rugged place." At last the whites could no longer reach the enemy. "The air was suffocatingly hot in the cañon, and we were weary and very thirsty. On one side of the cañon, near its head, was a small spring trickling into a pool in

[35] *Star*, May 2, 1882.

the rocks, and no sooner was it discerned than it was surrounded by men with canteens, while others drank from the brim of their campaign hats, and again others threw themselves flat on their faces and lapped up the water. . . . Like a flash came the crack of five or six rifles, and bullets seemed to strike everywhere around us, but no one was hit. The way that thirsty crowd broke for cover was astonishing." A second volley was sent into the white positions, but that was all. "It was impossible to do more," reported Forsyth to General Ranald S. Mackenzie. "The canyon was the worst I ever saw."[36] The battle of Horseshoe Canyon was over.

Forsyth maintained, though not very confidently, that the whites had won the engagement, but the southwestern frontiersmen, Al Sieber and others, rose wrathfully to deny it, to argue faint heartedness on Forsyth's part, and to accuse him of having no stomach for a battle, once he had the Apaches cornered. He had lost, in addition to McDonald's slain scouts, Private Kurtz, killed outright; Sergeant Morby, mortally wounded; Lieutenant J. W. Martin and three other privates, all wounded. Thirteen enemy horses were slaughtered to prevent their falling once more into hostile hands, and Forsyth thought he had killed at least two of the enemy.

He now withdrew his command to the Gila to water his horses and freshen up his troopers—while the hostiles mustered their own people, and slipped across the wide San Simon valley, undisturbed, to the precipitous upthrust of the gloomy Chiricahuas. There they took a quick swipe at Galeyville, a short-lived mining camp on the eastern slope, killed a deputy sheriff and ripped down some tents, and disappeared down the valley once more in a southerly direction. But they were not to escape scot-free. A column commanded by Captain William Augustus Rafferty and Captain Tullius C. Tupper, and with Sieber as chief of scouts, swung down off the Chircahuas on their trail, not to abandon it until contact was made.[37]

[36] L.A. Pub. Lib.

[37] The account of Tupper's important pursuit and fight with Loco is based on several records. Al Sieber wrote, or at least was by-lined, on a detailed description and analysis of the campaign: "MILITARY AND INDIANS: Al Seiber Tells What He Knows About the Late War," in the *Prescott Weekly Courier*, May 27, 1882. In

The punitive command followed the broad trail through the night at a trot and gallop for about thirty miles until the Indians scattered, waited until daylight, picked up the sign again, and crossed the Peloncillo Mountains, following along all day until forced to camp north of Cloverdale at 6:00 P.M. Here the pack trains caught up and fresh rations were distributed. At 4:30 A.M. on April 27 they resumed their pursuit, tracking the enemy across the Animas Valley, southward along the San Luis Mountains (for they now had entered Old Mexico, although no treaty permitted this), crossed the range and by ten that night were working down a broad valley on the eastern slope of the mountains.

Sieber, believing the Indians camped not far ahead, urged Tupper to halt the column while he and three scouts investigated. In half an hour he found their camp. "One of the scouts crawled up to the camp and discovered they were making medicine. As soon as I familiarized myself with the location, I went back and reported to Captain Tupper." As calm a narration of as daring a feat of reconaissance as will be found in Indian war annals. Tupper ordered two scout companies to gain a main range of mountains about two miles distant, placing themselves on a rocky hillock, about fifty feet above the hostile camp and some four hundred yards distant. With his two companies of white troopers, the officer would move on down the valley and attack the enemy frontally from a distance of eight hundred to a thousand yards. The hostiles were camped in what is known today as the Sierra Enmedio, near the present community of Los Huerigos. During the remaining hours of darkness the attack forces moved up, while the hostiles made their medicine, celebrating a safe arrival in Mexico, or so they thought.

The action was precipitated by an unforeseen circumstance. While the scout companies were easing into position, four of the enemy, including Loco's son, left camp and climbed directly toward the waiting scouts, hunting mescal in the pre-dawn light. Since discovery was

---

addition to Sieber's and Forsyth's accounts, Captain Rafferty's diary was printed in the *Star*, January 22, 1884; and there is a further account in Tom Horn, *Life of Tom Horn: A Vindication.*

inevitable, the scouts shot them down and continued firing into the camp, delivering about eight hundred rounds in four minutes, while across the basin eager cries of charging cavalrymen told the enemy that the border no longer marked a safe sanctuary for him. Losing six men killed at once, the hostiles kicked their fires out and dove for cover behind the rocks, returning the whites' shots. "If the hostiles had kept cool, there would have been no chance at all," Sieber reported, "and every man would have been shot down. As it was they fired too high, and the bullets passed over our heads every time."

The whites dashed to within almost rock-throwing distance, but realized that since they could not dislodge the Indians, they would be lucky to get away with whole skins, and under the heaviest bombardment they withdrew, losing one man killed and another badly wounded. Lieutenant Bo Blake, ordered to drive off what enemy horses he could from in front of the hostile positions, took his troopers at a pounding gallop along the Apache front, receiving close fire at every step but capturing seventy-four animals and virtually dismounting Loco.

By 11:30 A.M. it seemed apparent that a withdrawal was necessary. The command had fired almost all its ammunition, leaving an estimated three rounds per man. The officers didn't know there was another command within one hundred and fifty miles. They had done their best, and it wasn't enough, so they pulled out. Sieber and others estimated that the whites and their Indian allies had killed about seventeen warriors and seven squaws along with fifteen ponies in addition to those captured. Loco himself had been wounded, although they could not know that.[38] The wretchedly tired, dirty command was pulled back nine miles and went into camp about eight that night, seeking its first rest in more than thirty-six hours.

The command had no more than finished a belated and tasteless meal when with a great clatter and uproar what seemed an immense army rode into camp. It was Colonel Forsyth, now commanding seven companies of cavalry and two or three of scouts, having picked up Captain Charles G. Gordon's Sixth Cavalry command and Beak

[38] Betzinez, *Geronimo*, 69.

Gatewood's scout company which had been following the hostiles independently. Now Forsyth "gobbled" Tupper, Rafferty, and their exhausted units. Forsyth was chagrined to think he had missed the fight, and the veterans were even more unhappy to realize that with relief so near, they might have held the hostiles for a massive pummeling. With his huge and unwieldy command, Forsyth had been unable—or unwilling—to move as swiftly as the hostiles or the smaller Tupper command, and had backed and filled along the trail until after the battle at Enmedio. Now he was all eagerness and wanted the tired troopers to join him that very night in a fresh push on the enemy camp, but Tupper told him his command must have rest and sleep—to go ahead and his men would catch up next day. Forsyth thought it over and "went into camp for the night with his small detachment of 400 soldiers and fifty scouts," wrote Sieber. When camp was broken at six the next morning and moved to the scene of the fight, it was found deserted. The Indians had gone, deeper into Mexico.

Forsyth decided to continue into Mexico, where he had no legal right to be. About ten miles farther on the command captured a wounded woman who told them, or so Forsyth understood her, that the band had lost six men killed in the Tupper fight and thirteen at Doubtful Canyon. These figures should almost certainly be reversed. General Crook, in an official report about a year later, said:

> From repeated conversations with their relations at the San Carlos reservation and from other reliable information I learned that when the Chiricahuas broke out from their agency last April they numbered all told 175 fighting men. . . . Their losses have been as follows: Killed in fight with Capt. Tupper, 6″ Cavy, 14 men. In fight with Lt. Col. Forsyth, 4″ Cavy. one man. . . . To guard against any possibility of mistakes, intentional or unintentional in this story, I examined the relatives several times one by one, without shaking their testimony in the slightest. Their story was so circumstantial that they gave me the name of every male Indian who was killed and where and how.[39]

[39] Crook to AAG, Division of the Pacific, March 28, 1883.—Hayes Collection.

Crook's honesty and experience, and his care in employing only the most skilled interpreters, militate in favor of his estimates.

Considerably deeper into Mexico, Forsyth encountered Colonel Lorenzo Garcia of the Sixth Mexican Infantry, who informed him that he had ambushed the fleeing Loco band the day before and killed 78 Indians, losing 3 officers and 19 soldiers killed and 3 officers and 13 men wounded of his 250-man force. Most of the Indians slain were women and children who had been at the head of the column while their fighting men guarded the rear against the Americans, unaware of the Mexican threat ahead.[40]

The commands parted amicably after an exchange of written protests and replies regarding the "invasion" of Mexico by the American command, and Forsyth returned to New Mexico, sending his Arizona units to their bases. No official report of the Forsyth-Garcia meeting was ever filed in this country, nor, so far as is known, in Mexico. General Mackenzie, realizing the diplomatic furor that might follow revelation of the action, courteously returned Forsyth's report, informing him that "it was not unlikely I might find myself in trouble for my action. However, if the Mexicans did not make a direct complaint to the State Department, he should not take action, as the result justified the end; but the less said about it the better."[41] Rafferty, in his diary published in the *Star*, May 17, 1882, frankly reported the operation in Old Mexico, but apparently this account went no farther than Arizona, and the full story was not revealed until Forsyth's book was published in 1900.

Southwesterners were most caustic in their comments on Forsyth's

Forsyth said Mexican captives confirmed the figures given him by the wounded squaw, but Lieutenant Francis Darr, present when the prisoners were questioned, asserted that "it was agreed that 17 bucks and 7 squaws were killed in Tupper's fight, and that 16 of those killed by Garcia had wounds received by Tupper's command."— *Star*, May 26, 1882.

[40] Cruse said the Mexicans had camped at or near the Corralitos River, and were breaking camp when Loco's band was sighted.—Cruse to Davis, October 8, 1927, Davis Collection. Betzinez, *Geronimo*, 68–75, graphically recounts the Indian side of the Tupper and Garcia fights.

[41] For a more extended description of the Tupper campaign and fight, and the Garcia action, see Thrapp, *Sieber*, 225–43.

conduct of the campaign, and loud in praise of Tupper and Garcia. The latter was formally presented a handsome sword by North American residents at Hermosillo on November 9, 1882,[42] in commemoration of his notable feat. But in his analysis of the campaign, bitterly worded in part, Al Sieber probably spoke for many border men and, in predicting that the escape of the ringleaders among the hostiles would lead to much further action, he spoke no more than the grim truth. That Washington was convinced by the Loco exodus that Apache affairs once more were out of hand was demonstrated by the prompt reappointment of Crook to command the Department of Arizona and reassignment of Willcox to the Department of the Platte, a transfer welcomed by Arizonans.[43] It is likely that Willcox's dispute with Carr had little or nothing to do with the transfers.[44]

[42] *Star*, November 10, 1882.
[43] The assignment was made in July, although Crook did not assume command of the Department of Arizona until September, 1882.—*Star*, July 13, 15, 1882.
[44] That the dispute figured in the transfer appears to be implied in King, *War Eagle*, 226.

XIX

Dry Wash and Crook Again

U NHAPPY WITH THE MILITARY'S apparently ineffective thrusts against the Indians, and sure that rough-and-tumble civilians could do better, Tucson merchants enrolled about fifty hard-riding frontiersmen under Captain Bill Ross,[1] sending them into the field May 10, 1882. The expedition had no Apache guides and hadn't a ghost of a chance to do any good. The men returned disarmed, dusty, bearded, and sullen on June 17, glumly conceding their trip had been a fiasco. Ross reported first to the businessmen, gathered at Hooper & Co.'s mercantile establishment, and then gave the *Star* reporter a review of his humiliating venture. He repeated it in a formal testament sent to Washington in an effort to forestall diplomatic difficulties because of the unauthorized penetration of Mexico.[2]

In order to make the operation as legal as possible, Ross was made a deputy sheriff for Pima County and equipped with warrants for the arrest of certain Indians for murder. Other members of his "Tucson Rangers" were to be his posse. Ross further was "duly commissioned as Captain of militia of the Territory of Arizona," and his men were "enrolled as a company of militia." There is reason to doubt that the territorial government ever heard of its newly formed "militia" company, however; surely it failed to foot the bill for it. Ross's sworn statement admits that his "company were mounted and furnished

---

[1] William J. Ross was the officer who had saved General Crook's life in 1872, and participated in the Salt River Cave fight in December that year. Born in Scotland he served in the American Civil War. He resigned from the Army, October 18, 1875, did bookkeeping work at various mines, and died at Tucson in 1907.—Louis Menager, a step-son of Ross's, to author, October 28, 1960, from Tucson.—Heitman.

[2] This half-baked expedition is rarely mentioned in histories of the period. This account is based on the *Star's* interview with Ross, printed June 20, 1882, and Ross's sworn statement, printed in the *Star*, June 30, 1882.

with arms by said county of Pima, there being no money in the treasury of the Territory for such purposes."

The early part of the march passed without incident. On May 28 they met a twelve-man detachment from the Sixth Cavalry who told Ross that the Mexican troops had the Indians "surrounded" near Casas Grandes, in Chihuahua, "and that the commander had requested the troops to cut their line in the rear, as his [the Mexican's] line was thin in places and he did not know whether or not he could hold them." It is difficult to determine what action this refers to, for the Sixth had pulled out of Mexico long before and had not reentered the country, or if it had, no record remains. It may be that Ross met some scouts operating across the line, and heard a garbled version of the Garcia fight. At any rate, on June 2 they encountered Indians who fled into the "Cretta" Mountains. The rangers, glad of a fight at last, galloped after them and, it is said, killed thirty-seven, mostly women and children, and all of whom they hoped were hostiles. The next day the Tucson men ran into a seventy-man company of Mexicans under a Captain Ramirez. The quick-triggered rangers saw this party at a distance and, supposing them to be Indians, dashed in pursuit, fortunately discovering their mistake before opening fire.

For a couple of days, Ross claimed, his party operated with Captain Ramirez (the Mexican secretly dispatching to his superiors a query as to what he should do with the intruders) "in guarding the rear of the Mexican troops to prevent said Indians from breaking back." To give added respectability to his mission, Ross sent a courier to General Joaquin Terrazas, the Victorio-slayer commanding Mexican forces in Chihuahua, "offering his forces in any capacity he might see fit to employ them." But before he could hear back, the Ross-Ramirez camp was engulfed by a regiment of infantry and squadron of cavalry under General Bernardo Reyes and Colonel Garcia, who had intercepted Ross's courier and also captured some men sent into nearby Janos to purchase supplies. Ross and his party now were prisoners, and were very nearly executed. Ross protested that he and his men were not a United States Army detachment on a subversive mission, but civil authorities engaged in the pursuit of fugitives. Reyes countered by solemnly reading aloud a three-year-old Army register listing Ross as a commissioned officer, and "it was hard to convince the officer of the change in position that had taken place since then," Ross wryly conceded to the reporter. The perspiring American argued fervently to convince the Mexican and save the lives of himself and his comrades. He succeeded, but believed "that if he had not been able to produce his commission as a deputy sheriff . . . they would all have been shot."

General Reyes was perplexed. This was the third American "invasion" of his country in a few weeks, as Garcia could attest, and for four days the troops and rangers camped side by side, each warily keeping the other under surveillance, but maintaining the fiction of military courtesy, Ross and the Mexican commanders messing alternately in each other's quarters. Finally, on the fifth day, Reyes informed Ross he could go, but he must immediately return to his own country—and that "his troops would be relieved of all their arms." It was a bitter pill, but Ross had fifty men and the Mexicans six hundred and fifty, so the Arizonans turned in their weapons. To save face Ross demanded a receipt. The Mexican tersely obliged:

> I have taken from Capt. J. Ross, commander of Tucson Volunteers, fifty-eight rifles and five carbines, Springfield pattern, for having come with his company into Mexican territory, from which I have caused him to return to the United States.
>
> *Bernardo Reyes,*
> General

Ross must now guide his party homeward across nearly three hundred miles of hostile-infested country, and with utterly no weapons with which to defend themselves, although they did retain their ammunition, now useless. The resourceful officer had each man cut a short pole and lay it across his saddle horn, "thus giving the appearance at a distance of a musket." The ruse was a success, and the comic-opera party returned without incident.

North of the border, meanwhile, a new crisis was building in

Apache affairs. Many of the Cibicu insurgents were restless, and they at length found a leader in the person of Na-ti-o-tish, who had fled from arrest the night before Juh and Nachez broke out, in September, 1881.[3] On July 6 he and some followers ambushed John L. (Cibicu Charley) Colvig,[4] who had succeeded Sterling as chief of police at San Carlos, and three Indian policemen, and killed them. Buggies driven by Charles T. Connell and trader Rube Wood[5] were approaching the scene and were warned away by an Indian who opposed the hostile faction. Connell and Wood hastened to Globe with the news, and from there it was flashed across the country by telegraph.[6]

Na-ti-o-tish's warriors, gathering adherents until they numbered about fifty-four fighting men, whooped up the beaten trails to slash at McMillen, ten miles northeast of Globe, where they wounded a man named Ross, swept on to the Salt and down it to Tonto Creek, swinging north up that well-remembered route into the Tonto Basin country where, no doubt, the ghosts of Big Rump and Delshay rose to join them. But the band was hotly pursued. Their uprising had curled the hair of the frontier as not even Loco had done, and civilians, soldiers, and even other Apaches swarmed out to intercept and destroy them. Eight chiefs, according to the *Silver Belt*, warned that "if this band was not stopped and cleaned out every Indian who had done a bad thing would join them . . . and if some white man would go with them they would get volunteers out of their own bands

[3] AT97oAGO1883, "Report of Operations in District of Apache Under Command of Colonel E. A. Carr, 6th Cavalry, September 1 to October 20, 1881," Carr to AAAG, from Ft. Apache to Willcox, November 4, 1881.

[4] Colvig, nicknamed "Charley the Mail Carrier," or "Charley the Bar Keeper," had been a mail rider between Fort Apache and Thomas and a civilian packer for the Army. He had been at Cibicu for the fight.—AT97oAGO1883, Carr to AAG, Whipple Barracks, November 2, 1881.

[5] Connell was a onetime chief of scouts and later worked for the Immigration Service. In his later life he wrote articles for newspapers describing early events in the territory of which he had personal knowledge. Reuben Wood was trader at San Carlos for a time.

[6] The report caused "the wildest excitement" at Globe because it was that all whites had been killed at San Carlos and a general uprising was under way, according to the *Silver Belt*, July 8, 1882.

and hunt them down." Dan Ming, new San Carlos chief of police, offered to go along. Even Washington was alarmed and, besides speeding the last of the veteran Third Cavalry from Fort D. A. Russell at Cheyenne to Arizona, it had reassigned Crook to the Department of Arizona, although he did not arrive in time to influence the developing campaign. Within hours of the outbreak fourteen companies of troops were in the field, moving toward the scene from several points, ringing the hostiles with a narrowing band of iron. Nor were the civilians entirely idle. The glowering Globe Rangers, eleven men under Captain D. B. Lacey, took the field, "well primed with the best brand of whiskey and carrying an ample supply with them."[7] At Middleton's ranch they were reinforced by four other men but, taking a siesta, their horses were all stolen by the hostiles, and they were forced to trudge back to Globe afoot.[8]

The successful military campaign concluding with the fight at Big Dry Wash, or near General Springs on Chevelon Fork or East Clear Creek, has often been described and need be only summarized here.[9] It is noteworthy principally because it was a classic example of efficient military concentration and effectiveness, and because it was the last major action between military and hostile Apaches in Arizona. "This fight was more than a victory," wrote Ogle. "It was the end of an era in Apache affairs. Never again . . . with the exception of the Chiricahuas, were the Apaches violently to oppose governmental control."[10] The hostiles lost perhaps a score killed (the *Chronological List* said sixteen) and many wounded, and the troops two killed and several, including an officer, wounded. Destruction of the Apache band, however, was complete, the survivors filtering away through

---

[7] Davis, *Geronimo*, 27, described the rangers as "an organization of barroom Indian fighters," but there were men of character among them, including the Middleton men and others.

[8] Eugene Middleton was slightly wounded in the incident; *Star*, July 19, 1882.

[9] See, for samples, Cruse, *Apache Days*, 158–76; Davis, *Geronimo*, 11–28; Thrapp, *Sieber*, 244–57.

[10] Ogle, *Western Apaches*, 215.

the wilderness and slipping back onto the reservations as they could. Na-ti-o-tish was said to have been among those killed.

Crook returned to Arizona September 3, 1882, to find that "no military department could well have been in a more desperate plight."[11] At least two severe fights had taken place within months, and in addition, more than fifty whites had been killed in Arizona and New Mexico from the time of Victorio's slaying until Crook's return. Across the line were more than six hundred Chiricahuas, "the tigers of the human species," to use Crook's own phrase,[12] and among them were at least one hundred and fifty warriors and boys of fighting age. That they would raid again across the border was a certainty; where and when they would attack no white man could say. Desperate, too, was the situation on the reservations, and by September 11 Crook was in the saddle aboard faithful old Apache, his famous mule, headed for the Indian country. Those Apaches not on the warpath already, he found, were "in such a sullen, distrustful state of mind that it would have been better in some sense had they all left the reservation and taken to the forests and mountains," as Bourke put it.[13] At Fort Apache Crook councilled with such of the Apaches as could be induced to come in, Alchise,[14] Cut-Mouth Moses, Chile, and others. He immediately discovered that outrageous crimes had been perpetrated against the Apaches to keep them dependent upon government largesse, and hence upon the "Indian ring" of crooked contractors and agents. The ring, wrote Bourke,

> was determined that no Apache should be put to the embarrassment of working for his own living; once let the Apaches become self-supporting, and what would become of "the boys"? [Agreements

[11] Bourke, *Border*, 433.

[12] George Crook, The Apache Problem (typescript), Arizona Pioneers' Historical Society Library, taken from *Journal of the Military Service Institution of the United States*, Vol. VII, No. 27 (October, 1886), 14.

[13] Bourke, *Border*, 433.

[14] Alchise, a noted White Mountain Apache generally considered an able leader and good friend of the whites, had fled in panic after Cibicu and was captured September 18, 1881, at Cooley's ranch, forty miles from Fort Apache.— AT970AGO1883, "Report of Operations in District of Apache," Carr to AAAG, November 4, 1881.

which the Indians respected] were all swept away like cobwebs, while the conspirators laughed in their sleeves. They had only to report by telegraph that the Apaches "were uneasy," "refused to obey the orders of the agent," and a lot more stuff of the same kind, and the Great Father would send in ten regiments to carry out the schemes of the ring, but he would never send one honest, truthful man to inquire whether the Apaches had a story or not.[15]

A classic suggestion of the deplorable state of affairs complained of by the Indians is the report of the Federal Grand Jury of Arizona, published in the Tucson *Star* of October 24, 1882, and the more noteworthy since it was an indictment of white men by white men, a rarity indeed in frontier-Indian relations. In part the scathing document read:

The investigations of the Grand Jury have brought to light a course of procedure at the San Carlos Reservation . . . which is a disgrace to the civilization of the age and a foul blot upon the national escutcheon. . . . We feel it our duty . . . to express our utter abhorrence of the conduct of Agent [J. C.] Tiffany and that class of reverend peculators who have cursed Arizona as Indian officials, and who have caused more misery and loss of life than all other causes combined. . . . For several years the people of this Territory have been gradually arriving at the conclusion that the management of the Indian reservations in Arizona was a fraud upon the Government; that the constantly recurring outbreaks of the Indians and their consequent devastations were due to the criminal neglect or apathy of the Indian agent at San Carlos; but never until the present investigations of the Grand Jury have laid bare the infamy of Agent Tiffany could a proper idea be formed of the fraud and villainy which are constantly practiced in open violation of law and in defiance of public justice. Fraud, peculation, conspiracy, larceny, plots and counterplots, seem to be the rule of action upon this reservation. The Grand Jury [opened] a Pandora's box of iniquities seldom surpassed in the annals of crime . . .[16]

[15] Bourke, *Border*, 437-38.
[16] It is but fair to point out that although Tiffany was accused of sundry abuses, he was never, I believe, convicted of any misdoing, and that this famous, if intem-

In a letter to United States District Attorney J. W. Zabriskie, Crook said that a policy of preventing outbreaks before they occur could "only be successful when the officers of justice fearlessly perform their duty in proceeding against the villains who fatten on the supplies intended for the use of Indians. . . . Bad as Indians often are, I have never yet seen one so demoralized that he was not an example in honor and nobility to the wretches who enrich themselves by plundering him of the little our Government appropriates for him."[17] In a canyon of the Black River, Crook listened while one hundred Apaches reported on

> the general worthlessness and rascality of the agents . . . ; the constant robbery going on without an attempt at concealment; the selling of supplies and clothing intended for the Indians, to traders in the little towns of Globe, Maxey, and Solomonville; the destruction of the corn and melon fields of the Apache, who had been making their own living, and the compelling of all who could be forced to do so to depend upon the agent for meagre supplies; the arbitrary punishment inflicted without trial, or without testimony of any kind; the cutting down of the reservation limits without reference to the Apaches. Five times had this been done, and much of the most valuable portion had been sequestered.[18]

The Indians complained also that the rations were not sufficient: a single shoulder of a small beef issued to twenty people for one week, a cup of flour to each adult to last for seven days, hoofs, horns, and

---

perate, report was published when the territorial press indulged in the most outrageous calumnies upon rival newspapers, editors, and political figures as a matter of course. There was much opposition to the Indian "policy" of whatever administration happened to be in power. This skein of diatribe, rhetoric, and abuse has not to this day been satisfactorily unraveled. Reporting Tiffany's death July 14, 1889, at Deming, New Mexico, the *Silver Belt* asserted he had been "a square man, and for that reason made war on those, who for fees, caused his indictment and prosecution for alleged defrauding the government [after] . . . approval of his accounts by the Indian department." The *Silver Belt*, incidentally, was said by Crook to be "considered by many people who profess to know the organ of ex-agent Tiffany."—Crook to Secretary of the Interior H. M. Teller, March 27, 1883.—Hayes Collection.

[17] Bourke, *Border*, 445.
[18] *Ibid.*, 441.

intestines divided up as part of the ration. "The rottenness of the San Carlos Agency extended all the way to Washington, and infolded in its meshes officials of high rank. It is to the lasting credit of Hon. Carl Schurz, then Secretary of the Interior, that when he learned of the delinquencies of certain of his subordinates, he swung his axe without fear or favor, and the heads of the Commissioner of Indian Affairs, the Inspector-General of the Indian Bureau, and the agent of San Carlos fell into the basket."[19]

After listening to the Indians, Crook called in his officers and heard them, one by one, while they told their version of events. "Several of us were abruptly ordered to report to the Commander's tent," Cruse recalled. "We went pretty stiffly, for the General's aloofness had made us feel that we lay under his disapproval. When one by one we were ushered into his tent, to face his statue-still face and utter silence, while Captain Bourke cross-examined like a prosecuting attorney, our uneasiness increased."[20] But Cruse might have relaxed. He had been given a clean bill of health before his appearance. "Crook was interested only in getting the whole situation clear in his mind—the legitimate grievances of the Apaches, the real character of their leaders, the best method of returning all Apaches to their reservations."

By September 27, Crook could wire Division of the Pacific headquarters that he had "arrived at a thorough understanding" with all the disaffected Indians, and "there is not now a hostile Apache in Arizona."[21] The Chiricahua threat from Mexico remained, however, and he laid plans to cope with it, as well as to better the conditions of Apaches who had remained on the reserves. "I have but very little doubt that in a very short time there would have been a general outbreak," he wrote. For one thing he argued for permission to allow the mountain Indians to return to the high country near Fort Apache, permission which was granted.[22] From San Carlos he ordered Captain

[19] *Ibid.*, 442.
[20] Cruse, *Apache Days*, 179–80.
[21] Crook to AAG, Division of the Pacific, September 27, 1882.—Hayes Collection.
[22] *Ibid.*, September 28, 1882.—Hayes Collection.

Emmet Crawford, Third Cavalry, to take over military control of the reservations, and to report to Crook directly. Lieutenant Gatewood, Sixth Cavalry, was assigned control of the White Mountain Apaches at Fort Apache. Lieutenant Britton Davis, fresh out of West Point, was to command the scouts at San Carlos. All were placed on "detached service as assistant chiefs of staff to the Commanding General of the Department."[23] Al Sieber was named chief of scouts, with Archie McIntosh and Sam Bowman as his assistants, and Mickey Free, enlisted as a scout with the pay of a first sergeant, was really interpreter.

Crook issued orders in his own picturesque and un-military language, to make clear to his officers and men what he demanded of them. He reissued his famous General Order No. 13 of April 8, 1873, in which he had urged the whites to treat the Apaches "as children in ignorance, not in innocence." To this he added General Order No. 43, dated October 5, 1882, which said in part:

> The commanding general, after making a thorough and exhaustive examination among the Indians . . . regrets to say that he finds among them a general feeling of distrust and want of confidence in the whites, especially the soldiery; and also that much dissatisfaction . . . exists among them. Officers and soldiers serving this department are reminded that one of the fundamental principles of the military character is justice to all—Indians as well as white men—and that a disregard of this principle is likely to bring about hostilities, and cause the death of the very persons they are sent here to protect. In all their dealings with the Indians, officers must be careful not only to observe the strictest fidelity, but to make no promises not in their power to carry out . . .
>
> Grievances, however petty, if permitted to accumulate, will be embers that smoulder and eventually break into flame. When officers are applied to for the employment of force against Indians, they should thoroughly satisfy themselves of the necessity for the application, and of the legality of compliance therewith, in order that they may not, through the inexperience of others, or through their own hastiness, allow the troops under them to become the instruments of

[23] Davis, *Geronimo*, 34–35.

oppression. . . . Each officer will be held to a strict accountability that his actions have been fully authorized by law and justice, and that Indians evincing a desire to enter upon a career of peace shall have no cause for complaint through hasty or injudicious acts of the military.

Crook continued his conferences with the Indians. On October 15 he held an important council with four hundred chiefs and head men at San Carlos, informing them that the old daily count would be reinstituted. "While every encouragement and assistance would be given Indians willing to be peaceful and to work, no mercy should be shown those who attempted to go on the warpath," it was reported. "If any Indians at the council felt disposed to break out, he thought it best for them to break out now and bring the question of supremacy to a test without more delay."[24] A *Star* correspondent remained at the reservation for three days in late October, filing a lengthy story on the councils which the indefatigable officer attended, somewhat reminiscent of those he had conducted a decade earlier. At one of them a White Mountain chief complained: "Our corn comes up finely, it looks well and grows fast for a time, but when it is knee high it turns yellow and dies, and that's the way with the Agents. They do first rate when they first come, but they soon change and instead of helping us they help themselves."[25]

Crook held his final conference on November 3 with every male Indian on the reservation not excused for illness, being present. He congratulated them on at last having a good agent,[26] and promised that the troops henceforth would not serve as a guard to protect those who would rob the Indians; the Apaches themselves must defend their own rights. To do this, Indian police would be enlisted again to maintain order, and the white soldiers would not be used unless the Indians were unable to govern themselves. Crook recognized that San Carlos was a poor place for so many, and promised that those who needed farming or grazing lands might select suitable portions of

24 *Star*, October 17, 1882.
25 *Ibid.*, November 5, 1882.
26 P. P. Wilcox, whom Crook strongly defended against the Indian ring.

the vast reservation, and go there to live under care of a chief, who would be held responsible for their discipline and behavior.[27]

To remind Southwesterners that the problems of Apacheria still were not all legalistic ones, such dispatches as this occasionally appeared in the newspapers:

ALBUQUERQUE, Dec. 7.—The news has been received of a terrible massacre of a party of Americans and Mexicans by the Apache chief Juh of Casa Grande in Chihuahua. The Indians have been very active of late in predatory excursions, and raiding and the settlers formed a party of about twenty men and started in pursuit. They were surprised near Casa Grande by Juh and his band numbering two hundred and completely surrounded. One of the party escaped through the lines and went to a settlement for aid, soon returning with a band of thirty men. The Indians however held the succoring party at bay and in the meanwhile massacred the entire party which had been surprised. They retreated toward the mountains . . .[28]

Jason Betzinez, who was an "apprentice" warrior in this fight, details the Indian side of it. He says it took place near Galeana, about fifteen miles from Casas Grandes, and that several Apaches rode as decoys to steal horses close to the settlement, in order to draw out the soldiers. The ruse worked, with a small body of Mexicans chasing the Indians some eight miles toward Casas Grandes, where the ambush had been laid. The Mexicans forted up on a small hillock, and the Apaches crept through the rocks toward them, firing as they moved up, each Apache rolling a stone in front of his head as a shield. An Indian named She-neah was creased by a rifle bullet, which enraged the Apaches, who then rushed in for the kill. All but one of the Mexicans were slain, and that one fled. "Geronimo shouted, 'Let him go! He will tell the rest of the soldiers in the town what has happened whereupon more Mexicans will come out to the rescue. In that way we can destroy other soldiers!'" Betzinez wrote. The Indians lost

[27] *Star*, November 4, 1882.
[28] *Ibid.*, December 8, 1882.

two men killed. The Mexicans lost twenty-one, including their commander, a major who "had been in immediate command of the enemy who killed Victorio and his band in 1881," Betzinez said. The fugitive raised the alarm, and soon another company of soldiers rode out of Galeana. The Indians mounted their ponies and rode toward the Mexicans, who dismounted and began to dig in. As it was near sunset, however, the Indians did not attack, but sat on the hillside, watching the Mexicans frantically digging. There was no further fighting.[29]

What had precipitated this action was evidence that sometimes the shoe was on the other foot. Typical of the bloodthirsty nature of relations between Mexican and Apache was the treachery at Casas Grandes itself, where Juh, Geronimo, and other leaders had led their bands seeking peace and liquor in the summer of 1882. They contacted some tame Apaches within the city, called "Janeros," since most of them had originally settled near Janos, and as a result the alcalde, a few soldiers, and other dignitaries met the Indians about three miles east of town.[30] "The smiling Mexicans told the Apaches that all past troubles were forgotten, there were no hard feelings, and that from now on they would be on friendly terms," wrote Betzinez. The whites cordially opened the town and its bottles to their guests, who proceeded to get drunk.

"Early the following morning, while most of the Apaches were lying in a stupor just outside the village walls, the Mexicans crept down among them and the butchery began." Bourke says that about a dozen of the warriors were killed and thirty women captured, among them a wife of Geronimo and the family of Chatto.[31] But the toll may well have been far higher. Betzinez said "not many got away" from among those sleeping closest to the village. He was the last to break away, explaining "I was fortunate in being a fast runner, always a good accomplishment when you tangle with your true, ever-

[29] Betzinez, *Geronimo*, 93–96.

[30] Most of this tale is based on Betzinez, *Geronimo*, 77–78, but Bourke, *Apache Campaign*, 23, Crook, *Autobiography*, and various writers refer to it. Betzinez has the most detailed account.

[31] Crook to AAG, Division of the Pacific, December 13, 1885.—Hayes Collection.

lasting friends, the Mexicans." Naturally, the Indians felt themselves abused in this incident, as indeed they were. But the Mexicans were exasperated, too, almost beyond measure by centuries of murder and pillage, and injury was not all on one side.[32]

Reports and rumors of hostilities below the border filled the Arizona air at this time. Nana was reported active in Chihuahua again, with the whole state in an uproar and under arms. Juh was said to be contemplating an extensive raid into Texas; no one knew where the next blow would strike.

Crook was concerned by the presence of large numbers of Chiricahuas from the United States in Sonora and Chihuahua, and likely to return to this country as raiders. With staff officers and scouts he rode to the extreme southeastern corner of Arizona and sent men deep into the mountains beyond, seeking to contact some party of hostiles from which he might secure a guide deep into Mexico. He hoped, he said, to spy out the location of the hostiles "and ascertain if they would be willing to come back and remain at peace upon the reservation," or so he wrote superiors. He actually had little faith in any such solution and already was thinking of leading an expedition to capture them. He thought perhaps he might send some scouts southward "and clean them out," and did send some as spies, but they found no one. Unfortunately, he confessed, "I found that the Mexicans were having a revolution that week," and his spies found so many troops milling around that they became afraid and returned. When,

[32] Crook, in a letter to the AAG, Division of the Pacific, March 28, 1883, gave his version of the affair: He was told that the Apaches "were anxious to accept terms, and open communication with the inhabitants of one of the small towns; they did not give the name of the town, but it could not have been far from Janos [Casas Grandes is about thirty-five miles from Janos], as the negotiations seem to have been maintained thro a party of Apaches, domesticated in that country and styled by the other Apaches, the 'Janeros.' The upshot of the whole affair, was that a small band of the hostile Apaches ventured in, were kindly received and plied with Aquacaliente; when they recovered consciousness those who had not previously escaped or been killed, found themselves to the no. of 35, tied hand and foot; the squaws say that they were carried off, but can't tell what became of them. I saw a floating paragraph in the newspapers last fall to the effect that the Mexicans had shot 35 Apaches to death on the plaza in one of the towns in Chihuahua; they may have been these very Apaches."—Hayes Collection.

on a later try, they found the hostiles, they were so savage that the scouts "did not dare go any further."[33]

The Mexican forces, when not fighting each other, had their hands full with the Apaches. A report from Hermosillo late in January, 1883, said that a detachment near Casa de Janos, twenty miles southwest of Janos on the Chihuahua frontier, was surrounded by thirteen hundred Apaches, more than twice the total of hostile men, women, and children at that time in Mexico. The report proved false, of course. So did one of a fight between Apaches and rancheros near Hermosillo. The Indians did kill three Mexicans forty-two miles north of Ures, and Garcia sent a company after them, though the Apaches escaped. So grave did the situation appear that Governor Luis Terrazas of Chihuahua authorized civilians to organize a militia to take on the enemy wherever found. Late in January one such company reported a success. The armed citizens of Temosachic, about one hundred miles south of Janos, surrounded an Apache camp in the foothills and attacked it without warning, killing a dozen Indians, capturing thirty-three, plus thirty-eight pack horses and fifty other animals. Then they hastened back toward town, but enroute were savagely attacked by the enraged Indians who had escaped the first assault, and six whites were killed as were four more Indians. But the posse clung to their prisoners and some of the booty and sped to Temosachic without further incident.[34] That is the white version.

Jason Betzinez's account indicates it was Juh's main band which was attacked "early one morning," and that only women and children were slain or captured, with Juh's wife among the dead and his only daughter seriously wounded. In the later skirmish two more warriors, considered among the Apaches' best, were killed, he wrote.[35] The incident led to much dissension in Juh's band, and may have contributed to Crook's success in Mexico later on. In something of a pout, Juh retired to a separate camp, and left Geronimo as the

---

[33] This series of operations is summarized in Crook to AAG, Division of the Pacific, March 28, 1883.—Hayes Collection.

[34] *Star*, February 10, 1883.

[35] Betzinez, *Geronimo*, 101–102.

dominant war leader in the main hostile encampment. Loco already was living apart, and if he led his people on any raids against the whites, no convincing account has been left. It is doubtful whether Loco ever caused serious depredations.[36]

[36] Crook wrote that Loco "was not at heart hostile to us, but was induced by Ju and Hieronimo to leave the reservation. . . . I am satisfied that if allowed to come back he will never return to the war path."—Crook to AAG, Division of the Pacific, March 28, 1883.—Hayes Collection.

XX

A New Raid

GENERAL CROOK was more convinced than ever that he would have to seek out and destroy the nest of hostile Apaches in the Sierra Madre, but to do this he would require two things: a reliable guide and an excuse, and permission, to cross the border. A reimplemented "hot pursuit" arrangement might make it possible to penetrate Mexico on such a mission, but even so he would have to await a raiding party from south of the line, and follow it back.[1] Meanwhile, however, he could make ready. He sent Crawford, Gatewood, Sieber, McIntosh, Mickey Free, and others to Willcox, a station on the Southern Pacific in southeastern Arizona, to prepare his expedition. "Forage, ammunition, and subsistence were brought in on every train," wrote Bourke,[2] even though Crook was not yet sure how his plans would work out. And then, abruptly, he got two of his needs in one package, a guide and a raid to use as an excuse.

On March 21, 1883, four men were idling about at a charcoal camp at Charleston, about ten miles southwest of Tombstone, when a rattle of gunfire announced the long-expected arrival of hostile Chiricahuas from south of the border. Three men were slain, while another escaped. The Indians then attacked a second camp, killing one man, and approached a tent where P. R. Childs, with the only gun among the whites, awaited them. The Indians stopped behind a corral thirty feet from the tent and called in Spanish and English for any occupants to come out. When no one emerged, the raiders fired into the tent. Seeing no movement there, two ran toward it. The

[1] See Crook to AAG, Military Division of the Pacific, March 7; Crook to AG, Army, Washington, April 18; Sherman to Crook, April 28; Crook to AG, Army, April 30, 1883, for his search for legal means to authorize the expedition he knew was necessary.—Hayes Collection.

[2] Bourke, *Apache Campaign*, 28.

foremost was shot dead by Childs.[3] The other took cover, and it is well for the whites of Arizona that he did so, for this Indian was to become a solution to the Apache problem, although at this time he made his way off with the other assailants. Within hours the Southwest knew that it had another Indian foray to contend with.

Even while the funeral of the four victims took place, Chihuahua, Chatto, and Bonito, leaders of the hostile party, struck again, killing three more unsuspecting miners at the Total Wreck plant. Once more the border country was in an uproar, and facts, rumors, and tales flourished everywhere. M. F. Joyce, who owned a Sulphur Springs Valley cow ranch, galloped out with a party of horsemen to alert his scattered cowboys. He arrived at a line camp to find they were already warned, a rider pulling in his spent horse and reporting he had been chased by five mounted Indians all the way from a water hole to camp. An unknown man was killed at Willow Ranch, a few miles farther down the valley. A report from Richmond, New Mexico, said that the Indians killed Jack Haynes and a stranger at the Palmer and Emerick camp, ten miles east of York's ranch. John Emerick was missing, believed killed. George Parks slipped wearily into Richmond with a report that the Indians killed five men at Swing Station, seven miles south of York's place. Everywhere it was the familiar old story, differing only in detail.

Buckskin Frank Leslie[4] and Captain Charles Young reached Tombstone from Swisshelm, about twenty-five miles east, with a hair-raising yarn of a fight. Leslie, jumped about half a mile from camp, barely beat the Indians in, he and Young standing off a siege at the ranch house all afternoon. The raiders fired the grass, hoping to burn them out, but without success. They attempted to shoot them out, and also failed. During the night they disappeared, just ahead of a Sixth Cavalry detachment. For miles around the countryside was

[3] This was Betzinez's cousin, Beneactiney, whom Chihuahua called "a very brave warrior."—Betzinez, *Geronimo*, 107. He was a former government scout.

[4] Leslie could "make a little truth cover a large area. As much fact as you could pick up on a pin point would last him a year," according to Charles F. Lummis, *General Crook and the Apache Wars*, 59–60.

burned out. More than fifty head of cattle and all the horses were run off.

Newspapers grew increasingly caustic. "The annual invasion of the Apaches is again upon us," muttered the *Star*. It urged that "these blood thirsty savages" either "be annihilated or removed." It added: "This is not the first bloody page in Arizona's history. This is not the first time our people have petitioned, prayed and appealed to the government for protection.... We have asked for bread; it has given us a stone. We have asked for meat; it has given us a serpent."

"The Apaches are pushing Arizonians to that length, where very soon forbearance must cease to be a virtue," warned the Phoenix *Gazette*. "If the military cannot suppress them . . . it is the proper thing for the citizens to take the matter in their own hands," said the Phoenix *Herald*. "If the government of the United States will remove all troops from Arizona," boasted the Tombstone *Republican*, it would "guarantee to find a competent man, who for one-half what it costs to maintain the troops . . . will take a contract to settle this Indian question at once and for all time." The Tombstone *Epitaph* was even sillier. It blamed the raid on General Crook, sarcastically hoping he was "stored away safely at Fort Whipple, while the soldiers at the different barracks are amply fortified against the attacks of the roving bands of Indians that are abroad for the purpose of plundering and murdering the citizens." It urged formation of a body of Tombstone rangers.[5]

Crook ignored the jibes and was even inclined to sympathize with the people of Tombstone and other exposed communities. In a telegram to Secretary of Interior Henry Teller, he said,

> So far as the threats by the people of Tombstone are concerned I am in full sympathy with them and should be glad to learn that the last of the Chiricahuas was under ground. They are an incorrigible lot. Ten years ago when the Apache bands were whipped on to the reservation, the Chiricahuas were specially exempted by the Government from this same subjugation. Since then it is believed they have killed not less than 1,000 persons in this country and in Mexico, they are constantly

[5] *Star*, March 27, 1883, which has a summary of press comment, and L.A. Pub. Lib.

trying to stir up mischief among the Agency Indians, and so long as they can run back and forth across the border, this Territory and New Mexico must look out for trouble. They are the worst band of Indians in America.[6]

San Carlos took on the appearance of an armed camp, because the raiders were expected there to seek recruits and ammunition. But the reservation Apaches were having none of it. "Guns and ammunition we had never suspected the Indians of having were produced, and a number of armed Tonto and San Carlos Apaches voluntarily took up the task of outposts in the neighboring hills."[7] Chihuahua did not raid San Carlos, after all. Instead the band pushed swiftly up the valley of the San Simon, thence to the Gila, and turned east to cross the New Mexico line near Ash Springs, north of Stein's Peak. This was probably March 27. They coursed the Burro Mountains, east of Silver City, and then, on the high road from Silver City to Lordsburg, they perpetrated a massacre that shocked the nation.

Federal Judge H. C. and Mrs. McComas and their six-year-old son, Charlie, were traveling by buckboard from Silver City to Leitendorf when, mute evidence revealed, they were attacked by Indians at the mouth of Thompson's Canyon, twenty miles north of Lordsburg. The attack, according to Betzinez, was by Bonito's group of the raiding band. Mrs. McComas, shot through the head, toppled from the buckboard. The body of the judge was found about two hundred yards south, shot in four places. Both were stripped naked. Little Charlie was made prisoner, and became the target for the most widespread and prolonged search in Apache war annals, but he was never found. The judge, fifty-two, was a well-known jurist and Mrs. McComas, thirty-three, was a sister of Eugene F. Ware, historian and later a U.S. pension commissioner. The bodies were discovered by Jim Baker, a stage driver, and recovered by four companies of the Fourth Cavalry commanded by Forsyth, and brought to Silver City for burial.[8]

[6] Crook to Teller, March 26, 1883.—Hayes Collection.

[7] Davis, *Geronimo*, 56.

[8] L.A. Pub. Lib.; Davis, *Geronimo* (Lakeside edition, footnote by Milo Quaife), 86n.

The raiders plunged south. Troops sought to cut them off short of the border, as did a party of Shakespeare, New Mexico, guards under Captain Jim Black,[9] but the raiders were not intercepted. They recrossed the border after a foray that would rival even the famous campaign of old Nana for daring and swift accomplishment. With twenty-six men, in six days, they had killed twenty-six whites and traveled not less than four hundred miles, riding sometimes seventy-five or one hundred miles a day, stealing fresh horses as they were needed. During the entire raid, it is said, Chatto did not sleep, except for the naps he could get in the saddle; when the party stopped to rest he stood guard until they were ready to ride again.[10]

On this whirlwind campaign but two Apaches were lost: Bene-actiney, killed at the charcoal camp, and a strikingly handsome young warrior named, variously, Tso-ay, Tzoe, Bariotish, Panayotishn, Coriotish, and perhaps others as well, who was Benactiney's companion in the attempt to slay Childs, and who could not forget the loss of his friend. When, later, the war party stopped on a high mountain, Tso-ay decided he had had enough of raiding, and determined to return to friends on the San Carlos reserve. His companions did not attempt to dissuade him, for in Apache society a man's individual decision must govern his actions, and Tso-ay left.[11]

Lieutenant Davis, in charge of the military at San Carlos while Crook organized his Mexico expedition to the southeast, was under considerable tension, he and the "tame" Apaches expecting momentarily an assault by the raiders. He wondered what would happen then, whether there would be another outbreak. He had confidence

[9] The first public guards organization in New Mexico was the Shakespeare Guards, created August 8, 1879, in Victorio's time. It took the field many times when Indians ventured close.—*Hidalgo County*, 108.

[10] Mrs. Eve Ball, of Hollywood, New Mexico, who has become an Apache authority by reason of her extensive interviews of descendants of the Chiricahua fighters, insists that Chihuahua was the real leader of this raid, and Chatto was distinctly an underling. As might be expected, newspapers were not consistent in the manner in which they described him and his activities. See the *Star*, June 20, 1883, for a sample. Britton Davis thought highly of him, as did Crook and Bourke. Chatto died in 1934 following an automobile accident.

[11] Betzinez, *Geronimo*, 117–18.

in the reservation Indians, but knew them well enough to predict nothing. "There still were many hundred disaffected Indians on the Reservation," he wrote. "If another outbreak should occur the massacre of all whites at the Agency was not at all improbable."[12]

Just at midnight on March 30, Davis had gone to bed but came wide awake as the door hinges creaked. In the dim light he saw the form of an Indian entering, gun in hand. The lieutenant reached for his own pistol, covered the intruder, and demanded his name. "Targar-de-chuse," the Indian whispered. He was one of the secret-service men Davis had enlisted. "Chiricahua come," he said. Davis leaped up, roused Bowman, and within half an hour took the trail with thirty scouts and half a dozen Tontos who volunteered, hoping there would be shooting. No one knew how many hostiles had reached the camp, twelve or fourteen miles up the river. Before dawn the place was surrounded, and at daylight the scouts moved in and captured Tso-ay, who smilingly surrendered. He was taken prisoner to San Carlos, where Davis hurried a wire to Crook. This was the break Crook had hoped for. He instructed Davis to enlist Tso-ay as guide and scout, if he were willing. The Apache was, and the lieutenant sent him on to Crook at Willcox, where the whites promptly nicknamed Tso-ay "Peaches," and by that name he is known to history.[13]

About this time a Chicago newspaper said that Davis had wired the following message, presumably to Crook, regarding the capture of this Indian, and the preliminary information Tso-ay had supplied about hostile activities:

> The Indian captured here this forenoon is Bariotish, of Eskiosh's band. He says: I left the Chiricahuas three days ago. There are two bands in Arizona [he meant two bands out raiding]—Chato's with twenty-five men, and Geommos [Geronimo's] with eighty men [then raiding for livestock in Sonora]. Juh was left in the Basuco

[12] Davis, *Geronimo*, 57.

[13] Although said to have been a full-blooded Indian, Tso-ay had a light, pink, and smooth complexion, and thus his nickname. He still was in irons when delivered to Crook who, after listening to him, ordered the fetters struck off. The Indian demurred, saying he wanted to wear his shackles "until his conduct should prove his sincerity." Crook had him freed anyway.—Bourke, *Apache Campaign*, 33.

Mountains, Mexico, with three men and five women. Loco is in a stronghold four days march southeast from Casa Grande with fourteen men, remnants of Victorio's band, and all the women of the bands now out of Natchel. Cochise's son [Naiche, or Nachez] is with Chato. Two bands left camp in Mexico twenty-two days ago. One came to the Whetstone Mountains, near Tombstone [Chato's band]; others came into Arizona farther east [this was the band raiding in Sonora under Geronimo; it did not enter Arizona]. He left the band near Pueblo Viejo [a Mexican hamlet two miles southeast of Safford on the Gila]. They intended to go north to the Mogollon Mountains. To-night they go south to a place where Col. Garcia had a fight last year. These Indians are all from San Carlos reservation except fourteen of Victorio's old band. They left the reservation a year ago. These are all the Indians in Mexico on the warpath controlled by Gerommas. Loco lives apart from them. The majority want to return to the reservation, and Loco is anxious to surrender, but the others will not let him. The Indian captured is ironed and in the guardhouse.[14]

As if Crook did not have enough to worry about, what with hostile raiders and all, he was now distracted by a hairbrained attempt of the people of Tombstone to solve the "San Carlos problem" in their own way. The goadings of the local press had at last borne fruit. On April 3 "the largest outpouring of people Tombstone has ever witnessed" gathered for a meeting presided over by Judge L. B. Peel. Speeches were made by H. C. Dibble, Benjamin Goodrich, Judge J. B. Southard, Colonel William Herring,[15] and others. The speakers declared that "the people must show the Government that they mean to protect themselves against the Apaches and thus force the Government to take sides, either with the Indians or whites. . . . The people here have no faith in the military and rely entirely on the rangers."[16]

All the Apache evil, the Tombstone residents appeared to believe, emanated not from Mexico, but from San Carlos. A Tombstone dis-

---

[14] L.A. Pub. Lib. The newspaper is unidentified.

[15] Herring later became attorney general of Arizona under Governor John N. Irwin.—Richard E. Sloan, *Memories of an Arizona Judge*, 95–98.

[16] L.A. Pub. Lib.

patch a week later, suggesting the sort of rumors on which they based their conclusions, reported that Texas Charlie, "a well-known scout," reported lots of Indian trails near Whitewater in the Sulphur Springs Valley, about twenty-two miles from Tombstone, although they must have been old or imaginary, since the raiders had long since re-entered Mexico. Anyway, Texas Charlie "left to join the Rangers," who were determined, despite Crook's orders to the military to arrest them on sight, to raid San Carlos and show those Indians that the people of Tombstone were on to their little game. Agent Wilcox wired Indian Commissioner Hiram Price a warning that the rangers were being organized, adding that "the result of such an invasion [of San Carlos] would be dangerous."[17] Another Camp Grant episode might drive hordes of tame Apaches off of the reservation and deluge the Southwest with blood as it had never been flooded even in the days of Mangas Coloradas. However, the authorities needn't have been so exercised.

The Tombstone Rangers, Davis wryly reported, proved to be "of the same general character as the Globe Rangers and under the same or a better brand of stimulant." They set out to massacre the San Carlos Indians, but at the southern edge of the reservation, "they met with an old Indian who was gathering mescal for a mescal bake. They fired at him, but fortunately missed. He fled north and they fled south. That ended the massacre."[18] Bourke added his deduction that the expedition had run out of whiskey and "expired of thirst."[19]

Crook's plans, meanwhile, developed rapidly. He had messaged various Mexican commanders, but receiving no reply, resolved to visit them in person. Leaving the organization of his expeditionary force to his competent officers, the general had gone into Mexico with Major C. S. Roberts, Bourke, and his engineer officer, Captain Gustav Joseph Fiebeger, after conferring with Ranald Mackenzie, commanding the District of New Mexico. He went by railroad to Guaymas, Hermosillo, and Chihuahua, meeting with General Luis E. Torres, governor of Sonora, General Jose Guillermo Carbo, Gen-

---

[17] *Star*, April 11, 1883.
[18] Davis, *Geronimo*, 55–56.   [19] Bourke, *Apache Campaign*, 30.

eral Bonifacio Topete, General Luis Terrazas, governor of Chihuahua, and others, seeking assurances that his command, if in "hot pursuit" south of the border, would be permitted to operate there for an extended period with no interference from Mexican troops.[20]

Bourke reported that the convention under which the expedition was to be carried out provided for crossing of the border when "in close pursuit of a band of savage Indians," in the "unpopulated or desert parts of said boundary line," at least two leagues from any encampment or settlement. The commander was to give notice, in advance, if possible, to the nearest military commander or civil authority, and the pursuing force was to retire as soon as it fought the band it was after, or lost the trail.[21] This ambiguous agreement obviously could be interpreted about as a commander chose, as Crook well knew. He was helped in his decision to invoke it by a message March 31 from General Sherman, to continue pursuit of the Chiricahuas "without regard to department or national boundaries,"[22] and it was in final preparation for that undertaking that he made this preliminary journey.

The Mexicans also had importuned their government for a liberal view of the border-crossing privilege, and Crook wired the Army adjutant general on his return: "We all recognize the fact that a literal construction of the terms of present convention . . . will bring about failure in the settlement of pending Indian hostilities. It is all important that we on the ground be permitted to vary these stipulations to the extent required by the best interests of the two Governments. . . . We are likely to have another such blood curdling raid as that of last month at any time, so long as any of these hostiles remain in the mountains, and all the troops on both sides cannot prevent it."[23]

[20] The best description of Crook's visits to Sonora and later to Chihuahua, are contained in Bourke's Diary, April 2, 1883, to April 17, 1883, vols. 64, p. 59, through 66, p. 17.

[21] The two-year agreement providing for "hot pursuit" crossing of the frontier was signed by the respective governments July 29, 1882.

[22] Schofield to Crook, March 31, 1883, Appendix D, Crook's *Annual Report*, 1883.—Hayes Collection.

[23] Crook to AG, Army, April 18, 1883.—Hayes Collection.

Within ten days Sherman freshly warned Crook of the necessity "to instruct you that *no* military movement must be made into, or within the Territory of Mexico, which is not authorized by the agreement . . . Negotiations for modifying now going on with Mexican Government, but it cannot be inferred that Gov't. will assent to any modification."[24] Crook tersely replied from the field that he was about to leave in pursuit of the savages "in accordance with the treaty." He had made clear that he would be outside normal communications for an extended period.[25] It also was clear that he was on his own.

If the expedition proceeded smoothly, succeeded, and there were no repercussions, Crook would be a hero and, more important to him, the Apache problem likely would be solved. If he failed, or if the diplomats decided to explode, his comb would be trimmed, to use his own expression, and he knew it. He had long since planned to go ahead. Willcox had futilely fought the Apaches defensively, the important civilian organizations had proven their incompetence to deal with them, the two governments had failed to treaty them into submission, the hostiles had more than held their own against Mexican regulars. Now Crook would have a go at them in his own way, on his own terms, carrying the fight to them wherever they could be found.

Crook started an expedition from Willcox on April 23, 1883, which was to establish a base camp at San Bernardino, in the extreme southeastern corner of Arizona.[26] There most of the troopers would be left to guard the border, while the general and his picked organization plunged southward. He would take only a token force of soldiers with him, depending upon Indians for the success of his war against Indians. Each man was allowed to carry the clothes he wore, a blanket, and 40 rounds of ammunition, and 160 rounds of extra ammunition and 60-days' rations for each man were on pack mules. The

[24] Sherman to Crook, April 28, 1883.—Hayes Collection. This message was delivered by courier to Crook April 30, on the eve of his entry into Mexico.

[25] Crook to AG, Army, April 30, 1883.—Hayes Collection.

[26] This famous old ranch often was virtually an Army headquarters during Apache war days. Of immense extent, it was bought by the famous John H. Slaughter in 1884.—Barnes, *Place Names*, 380; see also Allen A. Erwin, *The Southwest of John Horton Slaughter*, 139ff.

expedition would be officered by Crook, Bourke, Captain Fiebeger, Captain Adna Romanza Chaffee, Lieutenants Frank West and William Woods Forsyth, with Dr. George Andrews as surgeon. There would be 42 enlisted men of I Company of the Sixth Cavalry. Commanding the 193 Chiricahua, White Mountain, Yuma, Mohave, and Tonto scouts were Captain Crawford, Lieutenant James O. Mackay of the Third Cavalry, and Gatewood of the Sixth. Al Sieber was chief of scouts, with Archie McIntosh and Sam Bowman as assistants and Severiano and Mickey Free as interpreters. Five pack trains accompanied the column.

May 1 was departure day and "amid a chorus of goodbyes, and God-bless-yous from those left behind [we] pushed down the hot and sandy valley of the San Bernardino, past the mouth of Guadalupe Canyon, to near the confluence of Elias Creek," wrote Bourke.[27] So far as the nation was aware, Crook and his men at that point simply disappeared on this most daring of all Indian expeditions. Forty-two days would pass before their adventures would become known, and as time passed and concern mounted, rumors of all sorts circulated. Most were readily discountable, but one could not be too sure.

On May 10 General Sheridan's headquarters at Chicago revealed it did "not credit the rumors of disaster to Crook's column."[28] On May 28 Brigadier General Richard Coulter Drum, adjutant general at the War Department, while conceding that no word had been received from the expedition, was "disposed to credit the report that General Crook engaged the Apaches and defeated them. He thinks the stories to the effect that his Indian scouts turned upon and massacred Crook and command wholly sensational and improbable."[29] So did most rational men, even if the memory of Custer remained fresh; still, there was cause for worry. The little column was believed penetrating the almost impregnable heart of the Sierra Madre, where opportunities for ambush were everywhere. No one professed to know whether Crook's scouts would remain loyal. Scouts had

[27] Bourke, *Apache Campaign*, 57.
[28] *Star*, May 10, 1883.
[29] *Ibid.*, May 29, 1883.

mutinied at Cibicu. Might not these, in the heart of their historic sanctuary, be tempted to massacre the whites for their arms and plentiful ammunition, and revert to the wilderness? If not, mightn't they be tempted at least to warn their friends and relatives that the command was approaching, and thus give the hostiles opportunity to prepare a hot reception? These and other concerns arose. But there was no word.

Instead of printing the news hoped for, the territorial newspapers impatiently discussed the expedition editorially, with the *Star* almost alone expressing unshakable faith in Crook. "Considerable nonsense is being indulged in by the press regarding General Crook's expedition into Mexico," it scolded:

> The Phoenix *Gazette* of last Thursday [May 24] says: "It looks very much like General Crook had 'put his foot in it' by going over the line into Mexico," and intimates that his motives were probably prompted by jealousy inspired by the activity and valor of the expedition of the Tombstone rangers! Could anything be more absurd? . . . It is no picnic expedition . . . as some of the papers seem to imagine. . . . Crook has taken his life into his own hands and penetrated the stronghold of the Apache, a rough, rugged country, where the foot of white man has never trod, with his handful of men, for the purpose of putting an end to our trouble and settling the Indian question. He is in a dangerous position, but it is not the first time he has occupied such a one. . . . Crook conquered a large proportion of the Apache tribe long ere Tombstone and her chivalrous and truculent rangers came into existence. He has subjugated various tribes from the British Columbia line to Sonora, and now goes further in order to effect that peace which cannot otherwise be secured. [It is] certain that if he returns . . . without a victory, there is no use of any other officer undertaking a similar expedition . . .[30]

But the Arizona newspapers were not entirely without Indian news. There was always fighting somewhere in Mexico, or reports of fighting, even if there actually was none. Usually these stories concerned raids by Apaches, pursuit by the Mexicans, and orders by

[30] *Ibid.*, May 29, 1883.

General Carbo or someone else "not to take any prisoners, neither men, women or children." Occasionally there appeared a story out of the ordinary, and such was the singular account of perhaps the most intriguing figure of these perilous times, the asserted renegade, Zebina Nathaniel Streeter, often referred to in the press of that day as L. N., or I. N. Streeter, for no one knew him well.

This enigmatic figure, if reports of him are true, was almost unique in the Southwest, as being one of the very few white men to have fought with the Indians on their raids against other whites. In Apacheria there were no Simon Girtys. It is true that some say Victorio was a Mexican, which he was not, but even those who claim it admit he was raised as an Indian. There were whites, captured as children, who were raised as warriors and fought with their adopted people. And there were rumors of renegades, too. Back in 1870 a curious fellow dressed in "fancy buckskin coat, canvas pants, with fringing down the sides and moccasins" purchased corn at a ranch near Prescott and the *Miner* cautioned that "It is thought by some that the fellow . . . is . . . running with some band of Indians."[31] Conner reports a white man directing Indians in a fight. Again, he says, "It is certain that I saw a [white] man and became acquainted with him, who claimed to have lived with the Indians and I presume according to his own word that he actually wore the breech-cloth and ate horse flesh with them." He added that "there were men roaming these wilds who stripped and went naked with them awhile and then dressed themselves and deported themselves like civilized people awhile."[32] Byran P. D. Duppa in a Bradshaw fight in 1864 sent a bullet at an opponent who screamed, too late, "Don't shoot!" and afterward found that "it was a white woman, evidently about 30 years of age and dressed in all the paint and paraphernalia of the Apaches."[33] But there was no one save Streeter on record who, as an adult, became enamored of Apache ways and adopted them, even to fighting his own kind because his new friends did so.

[31] *Miner*, January 16, 1870.
[32] Conner, *Joseph Reddeford Walker*, 224–25.
[33] *Star*, February 24, 1894.

Streeter comes and goes like a wraith in scattered news reports from below the border. As early as 1879 the *Silver Belt* reported a rumor that "Streeter was recently killed by a Spanish officer in Janos in the State of Chihuahua. This is the same Streeter who was declared an outlaw by an act of our Legislature." But he wasn't killed, at least not then.[34] In the spring of 1883, it was reported he finally had been captured. The *Star* gave details of his extraordinary life, but many of them were fictitious. It said he first came into "notice in Arizona by his connection as clerk at the San Carlos agency during Governor Safford's administration. . . . While there he had some difficulty with officials, caused, it is said, by his giving aid and comfort to hostile Apaches. He left there suddenly and went straight for the camp of Juh and Geronimo. . . . Governor Safford offered a large reward for his apprehension, some stories placing the amount as high as $5,000. . . . He has never returned to Arizona." It continued alleging Streeter had generaled several Apache fights, spoke the language fluently, "and is said to have great influence with them."[35] Regardless of the validity of various aspects of the *Star*'s account, Streeter had led an extremely adventurous life. He was shot and killed in a small Sonoran town several years later, reportedly as the result of what used to be called "an affair of the heart."

Arizona newspapers knew that Mexican forces were to collaborate with Crook in this "final" subjugation of the Apaches. On May 11 the *Star* reported that the Mexican forces numbered almost four thousand, including one thousand cavalry. "Of course no such force is needed for a direct assault on the Apaches," it commented, "but it is determined on both sides to make a finale of these pests." The Mexicans, in fact, were first to draw blood, most of it their own.

Early in May, Torres returned to Hermosillo from the Sierra Madre with a tale of "the most savage fight ever made with the Apaches" at what he believed was their "long unknown stronghold [with] the trails of all the small bands depredating in Sonora and Arizona" leading to the place. He had pursued the Apaches for

[34] *Silver Belt*, August 29, 1879.
[35] *Star*, May 3, 1883.

twenty days on a trail which led him into the craggy, almost unknown wilds of the Moctezuma District. At Guamoso, Torres was joined by the veteran Garcia and near there struck a fresh trail, which they followed by forced marches for five days and as many nights. In the foothills of the Sierra Madre scouts espied the hostiles moving off, pursued rapidly, and twenty-five scouts struck a very strong body of Indians in a hidden stronghold of which they had known nothing, though it apparently had been used by the Indians for years, judging from the number of animal skeletons scattered about the generations of brush huts. The scouts bravely attacked, but were driven back to the main body of troops.

"The mountains being inaccessible for cavalry, the troops dismounted, made a march of twelve miles and found the Indians strongly entrenched on the crest of a large spur of high mountains," the *Star* reported. "The troops, 300 strong, made an attack at 1 o'clock. They had to climb the mountain on their hands and knees. The Indians, failing to do any damage by firing, rolled boulders down the mountainside without effect. The chief, supposed to be Juh . . . commanded the Indians [and] could be heard distinctly for a mile. It took two hours for the troops to gain the crest, and when reached two were shot dead. The fight on the summit lasted two hours. The troops, swinging behind the left of the Indians, made an attack by charging with bayonets and forcing them from their position. The Indians fled, leaving eleven bucks dead on the ground. Five soldiers were killed and eight seriously wounded. The Indians were driven for miles, and the trail showed much blood. A great many are supposed to be wounded."[36]

That is the Mexican side of the affair. The Apache version differs. Betzinez says that the fight took place near Oputo, and was brought about because of a furious grass fire that poured a towering column of smoke that served as a beacon. This brought the Mexicans, and Geronimo and Juh led their bands to safety, leaving a fighting detachment on the brink of the canyon to await the enemy. About noon of the next day, the Mexican soldiers arrived and started to cross the

[36] *Ibid.*, May 12, 1883.

canyon toward the Indians. The battle was a prolonged and bitter one, he said, with the Mexicans, although fighting bravely, taking a serious loss, and the Indians remaining in command of the site.[37]

Almost immediately the Apaches left on a major raid toward Chihuahua City, seeking prisoners to exchange with the Mexicans for Indians captured at Casas Grandes, and this expedition would probably not have been undertaken had they suffered serious losses in the canyon fight. The Mexicans promptly withdrew, and it would seem, therefore, that Betzinez's version is the more nearly correct.

Bourke, deep in Mexico, heard from the settlers, descriptions of the "most bloodthirsty fight ... in which, of course, the Apaches had been completely and ignominiously routed, each Mexican having performed prodigies of valor ... [but] they wouldn't go alone into their fields,—only a quarter of a mile off. . . . Peaches, our guide, smiled quietly, but said nothing, when told of this latest annihilation of the Chiricahuas."[38] Later, in the mountain profundities, a unit from Crook's command visited the site of the battle and judged it "conclusive that the Indians had enticed the Mexicans into an ambuscade, killed a number with bullets and rocks, and put the rest to ignominious flight."[39]

[37] Betzinez, *Geronimo*, 110–12.
[38] Bourke, *Apache Campaign*, 67.
[39] *Ibid.*, 86.

XXI

The Mexican Adventure

GERONIMO and his forty fighting men and five Mexican women captives were sweeping back toward their Sierra Madre retreat, when they camped one night and the chieftain gave an example of remarkable clairvoyance. Stuffing themselves on roasted beef around a campfire, the raiders were startled when Geronimo dropped his knife and blurted: "Our people whom we left at our base camp, are now in the hands of U.S. troops!" Betzinez, in writing of this, says, "I cannot explain it to this day. But I was there and saw it." Geronimo had received no word by messenger or smoke signal; he later predicted exactly how the returning party would be informed of the astonishing capture of their camp by Crook, and this prophecy, too, was fulfilled.[1]

Crook had marched hard and single mindedly to gain the heart of the Sierra Madre, for centuries the most secure of Apache retreats. On the second day the column had reached the Bavispe River, thirty miles northwest of the town of Bavispe, where a diarist noted that "The country is beginning to grow rough."[2] Bourke got "lost" in a canebrake and "nearly drowned in quicksand," crossing the stream to get back to the command.[3] The column continued southeastward,

[1] Like most primitive people, the Apaches were fascinated by individuals exercising any form of clairvoyance. Britton Davis tells, in *Geronimo*, 83, of a medicine man correctly predicting the time of arrival of Geronimo from Mexico. In a letter November 23, 1929, to Harry Carr of the Los Angeles *Times*, Davis discusses this.— Davis collection.

[2] One diary of the expedition, printed in the Tucson *Star*, June 17, 1883, is used extensively here, as "diarist," along with Bourke's more extensive diary and his *Apache Campaign*. Also employed is Crook's *Annual Report*, 1883, Appendix E, a complete account of the expedition. The diarist was not identified by the newspaper, but probably was Forsyth; see McClintock, *Arizona*, I, 246.

[3] Bourke, Diary, vol. 66, p. 84.

generally up the course of the river, camping within five miles of Bavispe on May 4. "Still nothing to indicate the presence of the hostiles," wrote the diarist, but Bourke, closer to the scouts, was shown pony tracks the Apaches said had been left by their quarry.[4] The next day Crook reached the towns of Bavispe and, farther on, Bacerac. Bourke and Fiebeger, inspecting the latter town, heard the thump of a drum. It was a Saturday night and a "baile," or dance, was about to begin. "We found that Zeiber [Al Sieber], Frank Monach [a packer] and others had bought out the whole stock of a 'tienda' which seemed to deal only in mescal," wrote Bourke:

> Everybody passing along the street was collared and "run in" and made to take a drink. An orchestra was recruited of a bass drum, a snare drum and 2 squeaky fiddles to play "for the drinks." None of them knew a note of music and whenever any special piece was called for, it was first necessary to whistle the air which the players readily caught and rendered with enthusiasm emphasized by the 2 drums. The orchestra was augmented after a while by the addition of a man with a sax-horn. He couldn't play and the horn had lost several keys, but he added to the noise and was welcomed with screams of applause. ... The new player was doing some good work with his horn when a couple of dancers whirled into him, knocking him clean off his pins and astraddle of the bass drum and drummer. Confusion reigned but only for a moment and good humor was restored by the liberal administration of mescal.[5]

On May 6 the command reached Huachinera, "a squalid hole with a squalid church," wrote Bourke. Peaches told him that the Chiricahuas, the bitter enemies of the residents, "came through this place when they started on their raid in March [and] ... sixteen of them entered the plaza of Huachinera in broad daylight and purchased tobacco."[6] In his book Bourke reported that "on each hand were the ruins of depopulated and abandoned hamlets, destroyed by the Apaches. ... The valley of the Bavispe had once been thickly popu-

---

[4] *Ibid.*, 87–88.
[5] *Ibid.*, vol. 67, pp. 7–8.
[6] *Ibid.*, 9–10.

lated; now all was wild and gloomy." The command reached the ranch of Tesorababi and, on the advice of Peaches, Crook decided to plunge into the heart of the Sierra Madre, traveling at first mostly at night. On May 7 the expedition remained in camp, then moving southeast, up the Bavispe tributary that heads out in the general direction of Cumbre, marching through foothills covered with rich grass and groves of oak, then cedar. Hills became steeper. Crook struck a trail made by Apaches driving cattle into the mountains. Advancing until midnight, the column camped in a deep canyon, ten miles into the mountains, so on May 8 they went on by daylight, hiking fifteen miles over so rough a trail that all, including the general, dismounted to scramble on afoot. "Climb! Climb! Climb!" wrote Bourke. "Up the summit of one crest only to learn that above it towered another; the country fearfully corrugated into a perplexing alternation of ridges and chasms."[7] The fresh trail was pulverized by hoofs of hundreds of stolen cattle and ponies, goaded along by the fierce hostiles. The expedition began to pass carcasses of butchered and mutilated livestock and even live animals escaped from the Indians. Six mules slipped off of the trail, but were rescued after rolling far down the slopes.

On a plateau seven thousand feet above the sea, in a country "grand and gloomy, the whole face of nature being cut by immense gorges and mountains apparently piled one on top of the other," as the diarist noted, the command bivouacked, near the farthest point of Mexican penetration. Dense pine coated the ridges; everywhere was rubbish left by the raiders: dress goods, saddles, letters, food, and other things. The scouts became "more vigilant, the 'medicine-men' more devotional," Bourke remembered. Next day there was more climbing. "Up! Up! Up!," Bourke jotted in his diary. "Perspiration running from every brow. . . . 'Look out!' comes the warning cry from those in the lead and then those in the rear dodge nervously from the trajectory of some piece of rock which, dislodged by the feet of horses or men, has shot downward, gathering momentum each second as if shot from a catapult. To look at this country is grand; to

[7] *Ibid.*, 15–16.

travel in it is Hell. And up and down these ridges, our Apache scouts, when the idea seizes them, ran like deer."[8] More mules tumbled over the precipices. "The country is almost impassable and looks as if the passage of men had been barred by the hand of the Almighty," wrote the diarist. "But nine miles were made during an entire day's march of about ten hours."

Crook now decided to send the scouts, with Crawford, Mackay, and Gatewood, and Sieber, McIntosh, Mickey Free, and others, on ahead. Crawford was ordered if he came on scattered parties, to attack, kill as many as he could, and capture any who might be willing to surrender. Should the Chiricahuas have the advantage of position, however, he should engage and hold them until reinforcements could arrive. He was not to kill women, children, or prisoners.[9] May 11 they left, the main command following along, a day or two behind. Four days later Crook got this terse note:

> Dear Gen'l:
>
> Scouts out yesterday report fresh trail of Indians going West, with horses & cattle. You had better camp at place packers designate until you hear from me again. I thought it best not to take mules with me,
>
> Resp'y,
> *E. Crawford*
>
> P.S. I don't think the Indians know we are in the country.

Later, that same day, May 15, came a sweating courier with a second message:

> Gen'l:
>
> The scouts ran across the Indians this A.M. in a cañon (2) two shots were fired at 2 Bucks and squaw by scouts which alarmed them and the whole camp is on the move. We will push after them as rapidly as possible. I think you had better come after us as rapidly as possible. Send whatever men can be spared. The scouts became very much excited. The bearer will bring you after us.
>
> Resp'y,
> *Crawford*

[8] *Ibid.*, 26–27.
[9] Bourke, *Apache Campaign*, 83.

The command hurried forward. "At 2 P.M. reports of distant musketry sounded in our ears," wrote Bourke in his diary. "Crawford and his scouts were fighting the Chiricahuas! There could be no mistake . . ."[10] Late in the afternoon Crawford returned with many of his scouts reporting they had attacked Bonito's village, killing seven (the figure later revised to nine) and capturing four children and a young woman, the daughter of Bonito. One child was the daughter of Nachez, and grand-daughter of Cochise. Bourke noted that the attack was solely by scouts with "no white troops being present; altho the result might have been better, yet it might also have been worse. Our scouts were too eager to engage, a serious fault it is true, but a virtue compared with a disinclination to do the same thing."[11] The woman said the rancheria belonged to Bonito and Chatto, and that "the Chiricahuas were anxious to make peace and talked of dispatching (2) two messengers to the San Carlos to ask for terms." Crook said he would camp four miles distant and "would there await for three (3) days any communication the enemy might wish to make." He gave the girl provisions and sent her with the oldest boy captured back to her people. With her went the general's most fervid hopes, but he would never reveal that he felt them.[12] His apparent reluctance, or disinterest, of course, was only a bluff or device to make more certain the surrender of the Apaches. It worked.

At noon May 17 two women came in; at three o'clock two others entered the white camp, and four additional women hovered on the bluffs outside. One who entered, the sister of Chihuahua, promised that he himself would come in the following morning, and he did, "a man upon whose lineaments great decision of character was imprinted. . . . Chihuahua had a very satisfactory talk with the commanding General, after which he was given permission to go out and hunt up the remnant of his band, promising to have them all back by to-morrow."[13] Before night forty-five Chiricahuas had come in; by

---

[10] Bourke, Diary, vol. 67, pp. 49–50.
[11] *Ibid.*, 53–54.
[12] *Ibid.*, 56–57.
[13] *Ibid.*, 65.

noon the next day the number was one hundred, and a woman reported that Loco had gone on to San Carlos with twenty families to give himself up. She was mistaken, however. Loco remained still. On May 20 at 8:45 A.M. a

> great commotion arose in camp. The scouts grasped their guns, took to the trees and set up a fearful yelling, the captive squaws and children were much more collected, but still added a fraction to the turmoil and yelled in response to cries directed at us from a pinnacle 1,000 ft. high commanding camp. It was a band of Chiricahuas wishing to come in but first anxious to learn how far they might commit themselves with safety. From our Apache scouts I obtained the information that this was a big raiding party which had been raising hell in Chihuahua. These Indians had with them a large herd of beef cattle and (5) five Mexican women & one child.

They perched above the camp like "vultures," as Bourke put it.

> They sent word that they wanted to talk with General Crook. His reply was to the effect that if they wished to see him they could come in without fear of molestation, that he did not intend to hurt them for the present and would refrain from active work for a day or two to allow such as were so inclined a chance to surrender. While we were eating supper, Hieronimo was ushered in to have a talk with General Crook. His men entered in the usual Apache style: (2) two by this trail and (2) by that, the fear of treachery ever present to their minds. . . . The aggregate imperceptibly swelled to 40 or more, a piratical gang surely, one that would have made the fortune of any manager who should place them on the stage as the "Pirates of Penzance." There wasn't a weak face in the line, not a soft feature. Each countenance was indicative of boldness, cunning and cruelty.
>
> General Crook received them coldly. The conference did not last many minutes and amounted to but little, but was followed by another and longer one as the night advanced.[14]

Geronimo sidled up to Crook again, and almost pleaded with him. His story was not all one-sided, he said. The Indians had been abused by crooked whites, as the general well knew. Geronimo said the

14 *Ibid.*, 73–77.

Mexicans had always proved treacherous. If the general would allow him to return to San Carlos, and guarantee him just treatment, he would gladly work for his own living and follow the path of peace. If he couldn't make peace, however, he and his men would die in these forbidding mountains, fighting to the end. He was surely not afraid of the Mexicans—Apaches killed Mexicans with rocks, he grinned, drawing attention to their most recent battle. But, Geronimo added frankly, he could not hope to fight forever against the Mexicans if the Americans and Apache allies entered the picture, too. Crook listened. He said little. Geronimo could make up his own mind what he wanted, peace or war. That the general said, and nothing else.[15]

This marked the tensest period of the most dangerous expedition ever undertaken by American forces during the frontier period. Geronimo was the key, though not by any means the most notorious of Apache chieftains of the day, even if he was the most intractable, and the most suspicious. If he came around, presumably the others would. If he bolted, the expedition would be a failure, no matter how much or little else would be accomplished. May 21 was the crucial day. Geronimo came at dawn to see Crook once more. It was said that Al Sieber sat in on this talk, clutching a revolver inside his shirt, and that he intended to blow out Geronimo's brains at the first suggestion of treachery. Although the report comes from Tom Horn, who wasn't there at all, it may well have been true, for it is in keeping with the characters of Crook, of Geronimo, and of Sieber.[16] But the Indian had determined upon peace. He begged to be taken back to San Carlos.[17] Meanwhile Chiricahuas of other bands kept coming in,

[15] Bourke, *Apache Campaign*, 103. Tom Horn, in his book, *Life*, 152, says he was interpreter and quotes Sieber as advising him, in a much-reprinted passage supposedly illustrative of the peril, to take a knife and "Stand while you are talking, forget that you may not live one more minute and think only of the talk." But Horn is betrayed by his own account, which shows he was not the interpreter and probably was not even there.

[16] McClintock, *Arizona*, I, 247. This passage is probably based on Horn's fictitious account, since Tom also described the meeting thus.

[17] Bourke, *Apache Campaign*, 104.

some sent by Chihuahua. Among them was the band of Ka-ya-ten-nae, a prominent warrior who had never been on a reservation. Some of the hostiles rode fine ponies which they had stolen, and drove pack animals and beef steers to be butchered to feed the ever-growing population of the camp.

Crook spoke plainly to Geronimo. "I am not taking your arms from you," he said, "because I am not afraid of you. You have been allowed to go about camp freely, merely to let you see that we have strength enough to exterminate you if we want to." He told the Indian that in asking to surrender and be protected at some reservation he was asking much, though if he and his people would pledge their word to keep good faith and remain on one, he would do what he could for them. "You must remember," he said, "that I have been fighting you for our people, and if I take you back and attempt to put you on the reservation the Americans and Mexicans will make a hard fight of it, for you have been murdering their people, stealing their stock and burning their houses. You have been acting in a most cruel manner, and the people will demand that you be punished. You see, you are asking me to fight my own people in order to defend your wrongs."[18] But he agreed to accept the surrender which, by this time, appeared as a great relief to the warrior.

Old Nana came in May 23 and had an interview with the general. Nana, wrote Bourke in his diary, "has a very strong face, one showing that he is powerful for good or evil. He has been reported killed no less than a dozen times in the past (3) three years, but seems to be able to get around at a lively gait yet. He is still prominent and influential among the Chiricahuas, altho the principal chief seems now to be Kow-tinne [Ka-ya-ten-nae], or "Looking Glass," a quite youthful man. . . . Fifteen (15) Indians all told form the band of Nane."[19] Three days later Loco and Crook had a talk, Loco saying what Crook already knew, that he was for peace.[20]

Geronimo asked that Crook remain while he and Nachez gathered

[18] *Star*, June 21, 1883.
[19] Bourke, Diary, vol. 68, pp. 6–7.
[20] *Ibid.*, 20.

their women and children and bands, now widely scattered, but the general could not do this, explaining that his rations were being eaten too swiftly and he was limited by treaty terms and admonitions from Sherman to remain in Mexico only so long as actual military operations required. That was accomplished. Plainly Crook was in a quandary. He could not insist too strongly that Geronimo return with him, if the Indian did not agree. Nor could he "arrest" him and bring him back in irons, for if he did, the wild Apaches would scatter like quail, all his work would be permanently undone, and the problem would not be solved perhaps for years. The best he could do was extract and accept a promise from this wily Indian that he would return to the reservation, even though neither Crook nor any other knowledgeable officer would have believed Geronimo under any normal circumstances. One could only hope. But it was the best, even the only, hope, and Crook accepted it. He gave Geronimo permission to round up his stragglers and come in as soon as he could.[21] But he refused the Indian's request for written passes, since he felt that with them the Indians might expose themselves, be killed as hostiles, and complicate matters when his passes were found on the bodies.

By May 29 many more Apaches had filtered in, by twos and threes, a grand tally on May 28 showing 123 warriors and 251 women and children, a total of 374. Of the Chiricahua great leaders, only Juh was missing. He had quarreled with others of the bands in March, and retired deeper into the mountains with his family and a brother. He never returned to raid in the United States.[22]

During all this time in the Sierra Madre, Crook and his forces

[21] *Star*, June 12, 1883.

[22] According to Cruse, in a letter to Davis October 8, 1927, Juh a short time later "went to Casas Grandes to get supplies—and got drunk on tequila and mounting his pony rode off to the mountains; on the rough trail he swayed too far, over-balanced the pony and both went over the precipice and Juh's neck was broken."—Davis Collection. Mrs. Eve Ball, however, confidante for many years of the late hostile Chiricahuas, heard from Asa, Juh's son, that Juh was probably not drunk at all, but died of a heart attack which led to his fall into a stream near Casas Grandes. Asa held his head out of the water for some time so he would not drown while some-one ran for a doctor, but Juh died before the physician arrived. Of course no inquest was held.—Interview, August 15, 1965.

had virtually no contact with the outside world. Once some scouts were fired on by Mexican soldiers who apparently took them for hostiles, emptied their firearms at them, and fled. A chase of fifteen miles after them was fruitless.

Crook broke camp May 30 and started north, arriving June 10 at Major James Biddle's headquarters on Silver Creek with 52 warriors, 273 women and children, and Nana, Loco, and Bonito. The movement to the border had resembled another exodus. Children, the old, and the ill were piled on mules, donkeys, or docile horses, but most walked, streaming along the trails, garlanded with cottonwood leaves against the sun, splashing gratefully in the cool mountain streams, dressing and curing game taken by the hunters, for the rations soon gave out. Apache scouts spent every available moment gambling with the Chiricahuas, fleecing them unmercifully, when they could. Bourke, always studying the Apaches, found "all the chiefs of the Chiricahuas . . . men of noticeable brain power, physically perfect and mentally acute—just the individuals to lead a forlorn hope in the face of every obstacle."[23]

The bands traveled the eastern slope of the high Sierra Madre, close to the summit, the days being hot, the nights frigid. Once down on the plains of Janos everyone helped fight a raging prairie fire. On Alisos Creek, near its junction with the Janos, they passed the ghastly field where Garcia had massacred scores of their people, a field white with scattered bones and hummocked with the graves of the Mexican dead. A few Indians preceded the main body to San Carlos. About twenty, including seven warriors, left the Sierra Madre independently of Crook, marched swiftly northward, crossed the border, and passed Stein's Peak to the Gila, went down its northern bank to the reservation, reaching there early in June. They cheerfully surrendered their firearms, only to discover that Agent Wilcox didn't want the responsibility of their care. He turned them over to the military, where they were held in close confinement, pending arrival of Crawford from Silver Creek with the bulk of the captives.

On June 23 there was great excitement at the San Carlos Agency.

[23] Bourke, *Apache Campaign*, 119.

In the foothills of a southerly mountainside arose a vast dust streamer. At its base were tiny figures that proved to be men on horseback, driven stock, and people trudging along on foot, nearing the end of their odyssey from deep in Mexico. Captain Crawford and four companies of cavalry, picked up at the border, and nearly two hundred Indian scouts formed the escort for the long line of Indians, headed by Loco and his family. Lieutenant Davis rode two miles from the agency to greet them and bring them in. The ex-hostiles were temporarily located in the bottomlands along the Gila and San Carlos rivers, close to the agency, where Crawford and Davis could keep eyes on them. The other Indians hated and feared them, but with the white officers the Chiricahuas soon became friendly. All but Ka-ya-ten-nae. He was apt to be found standing morosely in a corner somewhere, surly, suspicious, unbending. Spies told Davis that Ka-ya-ten-nae was sorry he had come in. He thought the hostiles should have fought it out in Mexico. He was followed by thirty-two young men, and Davis determined to keep a close watch on him.

Weeks followed with no sign of the other hostiles from Mexico. Crook was becoming uneasy. Finally he sent Davis to the border to await the hostiles and, if possible, speed them to the reservation. No one came. The old year was about worn out, but still there were no hostiles. Davis sent scouts as far into Mexico as they dared go, but they could not contact the wild Apaches. It looked as though General Crook had been betrayed. But he had not.

Suddenly on December 20 there appeared a party of thirteen Chiricahuas, eight warriors and five women and children. Then, on February 7, 1884, Chatto and nineteen others came in and were escorted at a rapid pace to San Carlos. Later that month Geronimo crossed the line, with his people and about three hundred fifty head of stolen livestock. Two civilian "officers," posing as a United States Marshal and Collector of Customs, intercepted them, ordering Davis to take Geronimo, his warriors, and the "smuggled" cattle to Tucson, where the hostiles would be "tried." The chance arrival of Bo Blake with a bottle of whisky at the camp saved the situation. The Army men got the civilians drunk, and Blake slipped Geronimo, his band

and his cattle, out of camp, making fast time for San Carlos, where they arrived safely.[24] Geronimo's cattle were taken from him at the agency and ultimately sold, bringing $1,762.50.[25] The proceeds were turned over to the Mexican government for distribution to their original owners.

[24] The account of the arrival of various bands of Chiricahuas at San Carlos is given in Davis, *Geronimo*, 69–101.

[25] Crook to AG, Army, August 16, 1884.—Hayes Collection.

XXII

Who Captured Whom—
or, Did Geronimo Take Crook

WHEN CROOK RETURNED from Mexico with prisoners and the promise that Geronimo and other ranking Apaches soon would come in, he became the lion of the hour. He was greeted at Tucson on June 19 by Mayor Charles M. Strauss and the citizens as the Southwest's greatest hero, and entertained the following evening at a resplendent banquet where his courage received its greatest test as Arizona Pioneer Charles Poston determinedly read a poem he had written for the memorable occasion. The first stanza is enough to suggest its merit:

> *Hail! to the Chief who comes from the mountains*
> *Of Mexico, laden with fame and with glory.*
> *To rest in the shade of our trees by our fountains.—*
> *His deeds will go down in song and in story.*[1]

With the dawn, Crook, followed by his willing staff, fled for the spartan comforts of Fort Whipple from where he issued General Order No. 10, summarizing the campaign and singling out for special commendation Captain Crawford, Lieutenants Gatewood and Mackay, Guides Al Sieber, Archie McIntosh, and Sam Bowman, and Interpreters Mickey Free and Severiano, but he made plain his conviction that the success was due primarily to the Apache scouts, and to the men who led them. But exactly how much of a success was the expedition?

Crook believed it a total vindication of his policy of using the scouts to conquer the wild Apaches, but even before it became apparent that the worst of the hostile warriors would not soon turn up

---

[1] *Star*, June 20, 21, 1883.

at the border as promised, Arizonans, or many of them, became skeptical. It is possible that many of them welcomed the growing doubts, for it was understood that "the continuance of the Apache wars means that more than $2 million annually is disbursed within Arizona's borders by the War Department,"[2] and that sum was not to be taken lightly. There were powerful and unscrupulous interests wanting no peace with the Apaches, for when peace came, the streams of funds spent by the military would dry up. It would not be too much for them to twist speculation about the measure of Crook's accomplishment into dark and evil suspicions that all was not as he had reported it to be. There began to be heard, perhaps as sly jokes at first, then as rumors, and finally as "fundamental facts," the suggestion that Crook had not really captured Geronimo in the Sierra Madre, but that the wily Apache had, in effect, captured Crook. Preposterous as this might seem, the theory persisted even after Geronimo finally did come in and, for that matter, exists yet in the reminiscences of some old timers.

Late in June or early in July, 1883, Crook went to Washington to confer about treatment of the surrendered Apaches with Secretary of War Robert Todd Lincoln, Interior Secretary Henry M. Teller, and Indian Commissioner Hiram Price. From this conference, at which no one else was present, came the report that Crook had virtually admitted that he had been captured by the Apaches, instead of accepting their submission. The report was stated publicly in some manner by State Senator Barnett Gibbs, of Texas, and was given very wide publicity across the nation, especially in the West. Crook had no comment at first, but John Bourke, at Philadelphia visiting his mother, was interviewed by a reporter for the Philadelphia *Press* which, on July 17, carried, in a lengthy story, his emphatic denial. "I do not know who State Senator Gibbs is," he said, "nor do I know where he got his information, which is without foundation, and, in fact, it is a lie. . . . General Crook achieved the main object of his expedition and" with what the reporter termed "an emphatic bang of his hand upon the table," Bourke added, Crook "was not defeated.

[2] Lummis, *General Crook*, 15.

296

I say this positively, without regard to the assertions of so-called state senators or of military dudes in Washington."

In a follow-up story the next day, the Philadelphia *Press* reported in a special dispatch from Washington that investigation showed there was no reason for "believing that Crook had even intimated such a thing. On the contrary, very little faith is placed in Senator Gibbs' charge." The dispatch suggested that the story may have originated with "a feeling of jealousy among certain frontier officers." The story continued: "To the direct question: 'Did Crook capture the Apaches, or did the Apaches capture Crook?' Secretary Teller replied: 'I do not know. I know nothing about the result of General Crook's campaign except what I heard from him at the conference and what I learn from his report to the War Department. He is an honorable man, and I suppose what he said was true.' " In an accompanying dispatch from Atlantic City, Secretary Lincoln stated that he had seen the "sensational dispatch" and denounced the report as "utterly without foundation, and said he could not understand how it could have originated." He listed those present at the conference and said it would have been impossible for anyone else to have overheard the conversation. "He further said that General Crook's campaign . . . had been in the highest degree satisfactory to the War Department." If both Lincoln and Teller were stating the truth, that left Price as the individual guilty of spreading the false report, if it was false. Yet Price, according to a sketch of his life, was not the sort of man to spread malicious gossip.[3]

Bancroft noted that the Chiricahuas "offered to surrender on the condition that past offences should be forgotten, and all be settled on the reservation. Because a successful prosecution of the campaign at this time and in this country [Mexico] was impossible, because to withdraw and await a more convenient opportunity of surprising the foe would involve renewed disaster to the scattered settlers, and because the Chiricahua outbreak had been caused to a considerable extent by unfair treatment, Crook accepted the terms."[4] He thus

[3] *Dictionary of American Biography.*
[4] Bancroft, *Arizona and New Mexico*, 571.

implies, what was probably true, that the Chiricahua submission was not entirely without terms which Crook felt obliged to accept, and in admitting something of this, the general may have given the impression at the conference that the surrender was something less than he desired. It was thus possible for others at the meeting to draw their own conclusions, and it may have been this fact that led to the distortion reported by Gibbs and its subsequent wide dissemination.

Once loosed upon the public, the story spread and was magnified beyond reason, as an article from the Chicago *Times*, "sometime in October, 1883," pasted in Bourke's Diary, attests. It reports an account purportedly given by a St. Louis rancher, Rochester Ford, who, on his return from Arizona, divulged himself of facts he had obtained "from personal knowledge and from interviews with officials in Arizona." A sample: "In the morning when Crook awoke, from behind every rock on both sides of the canyon he saw pointed down toward his camp the rifles of the Chiricahuas. Turning to Capt. Crawford . . . he said: 'We are surrounded and possibly shall all be massacred, and we might as well go to our fate bravely. Give me my shot-gun. I will go up on the side of the hill and pretend not to see them.' "[5] So widespread and persistent did the story become, that Bancroft himself said in a footnote: "There is extant in Arizona a theory that . . . General Crook, through placing too much confidence in his scouts, found himself really in the power of the Chiricahuas, and was obliged to accept Geronimo's terms. I have not attached much importance to this theory, though the events of 1885–6 tend somewhat to give it plausibility."[6]

Although Crook maintained his outward aloofness from these scurrilous attacks, inwardly he was boiling. On September 5, 1883, he wrote the Secretary of War:

I feel constrained to invite your attention to the gross misrepresentations which appear from time to time in the public press relative to my recent campaign in the Sierra Madre Mountains in Mexico. . . . It is believed, indeed it has become apparent that there has been a sys-

[5] Bourke, Diary, vol. 72, pp. 99, 102.
[6] Bancroft, *Arizona and New Mexico*, 572n.

tematic effort to grossly misrepresent the particulars of the capture and surrender of the Chiricahuas, and the real facts of the campaign. ... My letter to you of August 7, '83, is given to the associated press for publication throughout the country, not as written by me, but so garbled as to lead the public to believe by what purported to be my own words, a systematically prepared falsehood. ... I state in that letter that the Chiricahuas "surrendered with the understanding on their part, that their past misdeeds would not be punished," while the garbled publication is made to read: "they surrendered with the understanding that their past misdeeds would not be punished," thus making it appear that their understanding was my understanding and causing the public to believe the surrender of the Chiricahuas to me was the result of a bargain and that I agreed with them & promised they would not be punished for their previous atrocities, this too while, my original rep't of July 23, '83, states, "Hieronimo and others then said (after failing to get terms from me) we give ourselves up [to] do with us as you please." ... Ordinarily I would care little for this, but while I can overlook the design and intent to injure and misrepresent me, I cannot ignore the great damage likely to ensue from disingenuousness & misrepresentation to the end sought by me here in the solution of this intricate Indian problem. Moreover I am impelled to take notice of these matters, as it is the current belief that someone directly authorizes, countenances or favors publications calculated to mislead and to distort the facts and true situation. I have the honor to request that proper inquiry be made ...[7]

It is doubtful if such an inquiry were ever undertaken.

Meanwhile the rumor grew. Horn, in 1904, wrote nothing to indicate that he had heard of it, or gave it any credence, yet what he did write was used by some others as a chief support for the story. The capture hypothesis was summarized by McClintock in 1916, and enthusiastically promoted by Clum in 1928 as part of his perpetual attack upon the military.

In a section of his history labeled, "The Mysterious Treaty with Geronimo,"[8] McClintock gives a heavily inaccurate and slipshod re-

[7] Crook to Secretary of War.—Hayes Collection.
[8] McClintock, *Arizona*, I, 246–49.

view of Crook's meeting and discussions with the hostiles in the Sierra Madre, based to some extent on Horn's fictitious narrative and perhaps based otherwise on rumors current in Arizona at the time he wrote, but supported by nothing in the literature by participants of the campaign. Clum is even more inaccurate. "My personal convictions as to the actual facts relating to this particular campaign would lead me to state . . . that General Crook . . . met Geronimo and his band under conditions which practically placed the American troops at the mercy of the renegades and enabled their chief to dictate the terms of 'peace,' " he wrote. He quotes "Al Sieber, that brave and intrepid old scout and guide," as support for his thesis of the extreme danger to Crook at the mountain conferences, but does so on the sole authority of Tom Horn as quoted by McClintock. He cites the 1883 annual report of the Secretary of War to the effect that Crook returned with "53 male Indians," whom Clum asserted, without checking readily existing sources, were "53 boys," although the 52, the correct figure, were warriors in addition to 273 women and children. The former agent said the nine-month lag between Crook's return and Geronimo's arrival at the border left "in grave doubt" whether Crook had paroled Geronimo, or vice versa, "and a detailed study of the records [which Clum could not have made and written as he did] discloses a preponderance of evidence in favor of the renegades." Again, Clum turns to Horn as authority for the thesis that Geronimo had ordered Crook to come to his camp, instead of the other way around, remarks on Sieber's sitting there with a revolver under his shirt, "sure that the Americans all would be slain," adding that "neither the courage or the veracity of Al Sieber ever has been discredited." But the veracity of Tom Horn, from whom Clum extracted these details, most assuredly has been discredited, abundantly.

One more point taken by Clum should be refuted, indicating, as it does, his carelessness with the facts. "A very good photograph was made at the time of the asserted 'council,' when the general and his staff were 'arranging the terms of the surrender,' " in 1883, Clum asserts. "In this photograph are shown General Crook, Geronimo, Captain Bourke, Nana, Captain Roberts, Lieutenant Maus and others." Speaking of this photograph a few paragraphs earlier, Clum triumphantly reports that "The renegades insisted that General Crook should come to their camp for the conference, and . . . they further stipulated that the general and his party should come *unarmed*. The photograph of the 'council' does not reveal a single weapon."[9]

It is true that the famous photograph in question does not reveal any arms, in either white or Indian possession. But the important fact is that, as Clum should have known, this often-reproduced picture is not of some 1883 council in the Sierra Madre at all, but was taken three years later. It is of the March 25–27, 1886, conference between Crook and Geronimo at the Canyon de los Embudos, twenty-five miles south of San Bernardino, when Geronimo again agreed to surrender. Also it should be pointed out that Clum didn't even know who had accompanied Crook into the Sierra Madre, since he correctly lists as appearing in this picture Lieutenant Maus and Captain Roberts, neither on the 1883 expedition. No photograph was taken of the Sierra Madre conference because of a mishap. A Mr. Randall, "a citizen photographer," as Bourke described him,[10] went with the command into Mexico, but a mule carrying all his equipment on May 9 fell over a precipice and "Mr. Randall's photographic apparatus 'crushed to smithereens.' "[11] There went any hopes of recording the expedition pictorially for history. One can only conclude that Clum's theory was based on his wishful thinking, and has little support from existing data.

A close reading of Bourke's Diary, the diary presumably written by Forsyth, Crook's reports to his superiors and subsequent interviews, gives no credence whatever to the theory that he ever, at any time,

[9] Clum, "Geronimo," *NMHR*, Vol. III, No. 2 (April, 1928), 138–44.

[10] Bourke, Diary, vol. 66, p. 44.

[11] *Ibid.*, vol. 67, p. 24. It seems likely that Bourke's book, *An Apache Campaign*, which first appeared serially in *Outing Magazine* in 1885, and was published in book form the following year, may have been written at least in part to refute attacks on his good friend and commanding officer. Bourke must have had the criticisms in mind, since he takes pains to answer most of them which had by that time appeared in print.

was not in full command of the situation in the Sierra Madre. The records show, on the contrary, that the expedition, among the most daring and successful in American military annals, proceeded exactly as Crook reported on his return.

XXIII

Ka-ya-ten-nae

B Y THE MIDDLE OF 1884 Crook could affirm in his annual report that "for the first time in the history of that fierce people, every member of the Apache tribe is at peace," and he wrote Herbert Welsh of the Indian Rights Association his belief that "there is not in your own state of Pennsylvania a village of the same population more peaceable and law-abiding than the 5,000 Apaches on the San Carlos Reservation."[1] But, old soldier that he was, Crook knew that his charges remained among the most explosive of peoples.

He assigned with care the officers to control and live with the Indians, teaching them the ways of peace. Crawford was assigned to San Carlos, Britton Davis to stay with Geronimo, Chatto, and some of the wilder Chiricahuas, and Gatewood was sent to Fort Apache. Davis and Gatewood both were listed as in command of Apache scouts and had the most important and delicate of missions. Crook dreaded the necessity for assigning them to it. "These officers," he wrote, "constantly carried their lives in their hands; the service in which they were engaged was one of the greatest possible delicacy and danger, where the slightest indiscretion would have proved fatal to them. But it seemed, in my judgment, the only way in which the Indians could be reached and taught that subordination to authority, which is an essential requisite to any degree of advancement . . . toward a state of civilization. For this reason I allowed officers, the value of whose lives was inestimable, to engage in the most dangerous duty that ever falls to the lot of soldiers to perform."[2]

It would seem that, if there were any choice between them, Crook leaned toward Davis for the most arduous and exacting tasks. It was

[1] Crook to Welsh, July 16, 1884.—Hayes Collection.
[2] George Crook, *Resume of Operations Against Apache Indians, 1882–1886,* 5.

Davis who was sent to Turkey Creek to control the worst of the Chiricahuas. When the breakout occurred, it was Davis who had the difficult mission of taking his scouts deep into Mexico with Crawford, while Gatewood patrolled the soaring Mogollons and other New Mexico ranges for strays. Perhaps this was in part due to their contrasting physical qualities. Gatewood, tall and raw-boned, never was as robust as Davis, although he performed missions as arduous as any in the annals of Indian wars. One is forced to the conclusion, however, that had Davis remained in the service it might well have been he, instead of Gatewood, who entered the hostile camp alone and persuaded the mountain tigers to surrender. No man could have performed this duty more selflessly than Gatewood, but he happened to be the one called, although this in no way disparages his feat.

This conclusion about Davis does not originate directly from his own writings. His worthy chronicle of those years, *The Truth About Geronimo*, bears no hint that Davis realized he was something of a hero, nor does his personal correspondence. That he was popular with his fellow officers is plain, however, from their letters to him. Gatewood was admired, but he was more reserved.

Perhaps his extraordinarily long years with the scouts had something to do with that. Strangely, he seems never to have liked that work. Davis took it all as a great lark, a huge adventure, and his good-natured acceptance of the most astounding hardships shines through every page. He learned, while on the most delicate missions, to overcome his prejudice against the Apaches and developed a genuine respect and even affection for them. Gatewood, on the other hand, never liked Indians, never trusted them, was apparently delighted to be tucked away, later, on General Nelson A. Miles's staff. Although a hero to the end, he is not known to have ever more than tolerated the way of life forced upon him.

Any officer assigned to work with warlike Indians must find himself from time to time in ticklish situations. Davis often was in such. Time and again he was at the point of death; never did he falter. Sometimes the Indians themselves gave clear evidence that they liked and trusted him. When a crisis arose over distribution of rations, the major chiefs asked that Davis deal them out.[3] When Davis was in danger of assassination it was Chatto who saw to it he was not shot. When the great break was made, most of the important chiefs under his control remained loyal, even in the face of threats of death. While Davis was at Turkey Creek and Gatewood at Apache, the two must have seen a good deal of each other. There is nothing to indicate they were particularly close friends, but it was largely to rescue Gatewood's name from limbo that Davis wrote his book.

Stragglers continued to arrive at the reservation. One party of a score or so didn't reach San Carlos until May 15, 1884, two months after Geronimo had brought in the "last" of the hostiles. "This party should have come in with Geronimo," Crook conceded.[4]

The general was greatly concerned during these months with the Casas Grandes prisoners, the wives and families captured at that Mexican town after their husbands were murdered or chased away. They had been distributed as slaves, or what amounted to slaves, among various Mexican households, and Crook saw them as a constant threat to the peace of his charges. He sympathized with the Apaches' desire to be reunited. Repeatedly he urged Washington to negotiate with Mexican authorities for the captives' release, pointing out that so long as they were held, the warriors were bound to become increasingly restless, tempted to plunge back across the border and either forcibly free their people, gain hostages to trade for them, or at least avenge their loss.[5] In a letter to General Topete, commanding Mexican forces in Sonora, Crook charged that the Casas Grandes incident was responsible for the Chiricahua delay in coming in.[6] At last Mexico agreed to return minors whose relatives were at San Carlos, and adults who "elect to return," but this did not satisfy

[3] Crawford to Crook, April 6, 1884.—Hayes Collection.

[4] Crook to AAG, Division of the Pacific, May 17, 1884.—Hayes Collection.

[5] Crook to AAG, Division of the Pacific, July 11, 1884; Crook to AAG, Division of the Pacific, December 17, 1884; Crook to AAG, Division of the Pacific, April 24, 1885; etc.—Hayes Collection.

[6] Crook to Topete, November 22, 1883.—Hayes Collection.

Crook. "It is impossible," he reminded Washington, "to convince those [here] that the few of their relatives and friends captured in Mexico . . . are content to remain there . . . and just so long as any do so, there will exist an incentive to continue the forays which so long have vexed and endangered this border. It requires but a very slight pretext to induce these Indians to engage again in the hostilities which until two years ago has characterized their entire life."[7] At least some of the captives eventually were returned, but the relatives of Chatto and other leaders remained in Mexico for many long months.

There arose, too, the problem of Ka-ya-ten-nae. There is something almost noble about this Indian, a major figure among the more violent Apaches, but almost unknown to the whites. Ka-ya-ten-nae, Crook believed, ascended to the chieftainship of the Chiricahuas after the death of Victorio, although here he probably was in error.[8] The young warrior, however, was wild as a wolf and entirely unreconstructed. He stalked the reservation moodily. Crawford found him "very suspicious & . . . a bad man." McIntosh warned that Ka-ya-ten-nae was on the verge of a break, and more and more acted in "a surly and impudent manner."[9] Almost in desperation, Crawford enlisted the Indian as a scout, holding him "strictly responsible for the good behaviour of his band," and for a short time the warrior was content. Then Geronimo came in, and Ka-ya-ten-nae could live near him and Chatto on Turkey Creek, under the eyes of Davis and Sam Bowman.[10] The Indians scattered among the trees and established their rancherias up and down the stream, fifteen miles south of Fort Apache. The more suspicious and intractable, Mangus, Chihuahua, Geronimo and their bands, camped several miles from Davis, but Ka-ya-ten-nae stayed close by. Chatto became a first sergeant of scouts, and Davis soon regarded him as "one of the finest men, red or white,

[7] Crook to AGO, Army, April 7, 1885.—Hayes Collection.

[8] Crook made no distinction, except geographic, between the Warm Springs and Chiricahua Apaches, apparently believing them the same people as, historically, at least, they probably were.

[9] Crawford to Crook, November 20, 1883.—Hayes Collection.

[10] Crawford to Crook, March 24, 1884.—Hayes Collection.

I have ever met."[11] Chatto, Bonito, Zele, and Loco seemed satisfied with conditions on the reservation, glad they had come in, amiable and always ready for a chat or a joke. Nana, too, might have become friendly but was so old and, Davis thought, so crippled by rheumatism that he came to the officer's camp rarely.

On the other hand, Geronimo, Nachez, Chihuahua, and, above all, Ka-ya-ten-nae remained suspicious, untouchable, often restless. Crawford noted in a letter to Crook, however, that there was at least one compelling reason holding the late hostiles in, their women were tired of the war path "& being kicked and cuffed around," and liked the relative ease and luxury of their new camp. "I find that as long as I can keep them on my side I am all right," he wrote. "I find also they are like all the rest of womankind they cannot keep a secret but give everything away."[12]

Among Davis' scouts was a short, stocky Apache named Dutchy, who was to figure in the most extended correspondence, perhaps, of any Indian under Crook's control. Dutchy, so-named because of his German-like countenance, earlier had proved himself loyal, after his fashion. About ten years before, his father had killed a white man and taken to the hills. The agent, a religious man, had converted Dutchy and told him that only hell-fire would await both Dutchy and his father if the latter were not punished. Convinced, Dutchy went himself into the hills with a rifle, cartridges, a week's rations, and a sack in which to carry them. He returned with rations gone and in the bag the head of his father. "I do not vouch for the story," confessed Davis, "but it was accepted as true among those who should have known, Sieber and others."[13]

Now, when Ka-ya-ten-nae and his band became more unruly, Davis depended increasingly upon Dutchy, Chatto, and scouts he believed loyal. He heard spy reports that Ka-ya-ten-nae was stirring unrest, telling other Indians they had been fools to come in, brutally beating

---

[11] Davis note to National Archives in connection with photographs he gave to its collection.—Davis Collection.

[12] Crawford to Crook, March 24, 1884.—Hayes Collection.

[13] Davis, *Geronimo*, 116.

his wives against Army prohibition of that manly custom, and secretly making tizwin, also forbidden.[14] Davis called a meeting of the chiefs, but got nowhere. Shortly afterward Davis, by merest chance, avoided an ambush Ka-ya-ten-nae laid for him. He determined to arrest the Indian, but took the precaution of sending to Fort Apache for four troops of cavalry, which arrived just as the critical council was to get under way. Ka-ya-ten-nae had been sent for and angrily stalked in. In the resulting confrontation, only Dutchy and Chatto, Davis believed, protected him from being shot by Ka-ya-ten-nae and bravely assisted in his arrest.[15] The Indian was sent to San Carlos where Crawford had him tried by a jury of his tribe. He was sentenced to three years confinement and was delivered at Crook's orders to Alcatraz to serve his sentence. But the general intended to waste neither the opportunity nor Ka-ya-ten-nae. A man as influential as the spirited warrior could be of major assistance to him, if he could be brought around, and Crook laid plans to do that.

"His authority among his people for good or for harm is very considerable," Crook wrote his San Francisco headquarters:

> It was thought best that his relations with them should be severed for some time and he be so disciplined as to impress upon him the necessity of encouraging his people in good behaviour. . . . To this end I suggest that he be kept in irons at hard labor for one month and his confinement then relaxed, and he be permitted to go about the Island [of Alcatraz], and the city of San Francisco so that he may observe and become acquainted with the manner of living of the whites and thus learn something which may be of benefit to his people when he is re-

14 Betzinez, *Geronimo*, 126.

15 Britton Davis details this experience in *Geronimo*, 127–30. In explanatory notes accompanying the pictures he gave the Archives, Davis says, referring to the arrest: "Ka-e-ten-nae lost little time. The camp was hardly more than settled when he gave a tizwin party to a number of the most unruly young bucks, at which time he proposed that they kill me and return to their old haunts in Mexico. The motion was amended to wait until they finished the drunk. . . . The proposal was reported to me the same night by one of my secret service force (a woman). I arrested Ka-e-ten-nae the next morning . . ."

turned to the reservation, which I recommend be done at such time as the experience given him may be for their interests and his own.[16]

Ka-ya-ten-nae was to be of important assistance to Crook during troubles to come, although he remained to the end of his days a turbulent spirit, one not easily controlled and inclined to violence.[17]

And then there was Dutchy's case. Dutchy apparently had been identified in a killing that must have occurred near Camp Thomas in the 1882 Loco bust-out. In November, 1883, Crawford hastily wrote Crook that "I have just learned that the civil authorities at Solomonville . . . are getting up an indictment against 'Dutchey' . . . for murder. I suppose they will be coming along here some day with a warrant for his arrest & will call on me for the purpose of assisting them. In the event of a Sheriff coming here with a warrant do you wish me to turn 'Dutchey' over to him? They can never arrest him without the assistance of the military."[18] The general came immediately to Dutchy's rescue, not because he thought him innocent—whatever the crime Dutchy quite possibly had committed it, or something similar. But Crook reasoned that any attempt to press against this individual charges for depredations of which half the Chiricahuas were equally guilty could not fail to stampede the remainder off the reservation. They would think that their turn must surely come next. So he stalled the authorities while he wired Washington for instructions.

These Indians understand that their past offenses will be overlooked provided they behave themselves in the future, and I respectfully urge that the interests of the people of the U.S. and Mexico, should be considered before a step be taken which would very likely cause their return to the war-path. The arrest of "Dutchy" would be thought by every Chiricahua a breach of faith and even were he acquitted of the charge against him, the feeling of insecurity and want

[16] Crook to AAG, Division of the Pacific, August 2, 1884.—Hayes Collection.
[17] Betzinez, *Geronimo*, 180–81.
[18] Crawford to Crook, November 14, 1883.—Hayes Collection.

of trust in the intentions of the Government . . . would be so strengthened that the difficulties of their management would be much augmented even if an outbreak was prevented.[19]

Weighty as his arguments appear, they failed to influence the civil authorities, who tried by every means to arrest Dutchy. The tug and pull continued for many months. Despite a ruling by the Department of Justice that the case be held in abeyance, local civil officials in Arizona persisted in their attempts to extract the Indian from the military fold, even on one occasion sending an officer to arrest him while he was engaged as an Army scout, tracking Geronimo deep in Mexico. But all their efforts failed and Crook's policy, in the end, triumphed. Eventually Dutchy was sent east with the rest of the Chiricahuas after the final Geronimo surrender, and his case was at last forgotten.[20]

Some months later, Crawford was transferred at his request to his regiment in Texas and Captain Francis C. Pierce of the First Infantry brought in from duty with the Walapais to succeed him. Davis called this a "fatal" move.[21] Pierce unfortunately lacked Crawford's intimate knowledge of Apache character, and the stage was set for disaster.

[19] Crook to AGO, Army, May 25, 1884.—Hayes Collection.

[20] H. W. Daly, former chief packer for the Quartermaster Department, in "Scouts Good and Bad," *American Legion Monthly* (August, 1928), 70, wrote that he had heard Dutchy later went hostile, joined Geronimo, was captured with him, was sent east, and ultimately got into trouble in Oklahoma and was killed, or "if he wasn't he should have been." This can probably be discounted.

[21] Davis, *Geronimo*, 141.

XXIV

Geronimo—1

BRITTON DAVIS had no real inkling that the stage was being set for tragedy, a disaster that would cost the lives of ten American officers and men, nearly one hundred settlers and peaceful Indians, and no one could guess how many Mexicans, and that would be prolonged for nearly two years. It was from his camp that the Indians destined to become the Southwest's most notorious renegades would break out, yet the incident was in no way his fault. He had seen with some misgiving growing evidence of defiance of his authority. Chihuahua was a particular problem because he loved the forbidden tizwin and wanted the freedom to beat his women when he chose. He was "egged on" by Mangus who, in turn, was goaded into opposition to the young officer by Huera, Mangus' Mexican wife. She had "sufficient intelligence to be troublesome,"[1] was an expert tizwin maker, and hated the whites. Yet Mangus' personal following was small despite the fact he was a son of the redoubtable Mangas Coloradas, and neither Mangus nor Chihuahua really desired an outbreak.

Geronimo, third of the important "bad" Indians, was another case. "This Indian was a thoroughly vicious, intractable, and treacherous man," according to Davis' evaluation, based on months of close association. "His only redeeming traits were courage and determination. His word, no matter how earnestly pledged, was worthless."[2] Geronimo took advantage of the dissatisfaction of Chihuahua and Mangus, and the Southwest would suffer for it.

On May 18, 1885, telegraph keys in Apacheria began a cicadic chattering:

[1] Crook to AAG, Division of the Pacific, May 21, 1885.—Hayes Collection.
[2] Davis, *Geronimo*, 142–43.

About fifty Chiricahua Apaches under Geronimo left reservation near Fort Apache about dark last night and are thought to be making for Mexico. Troops are in pursuit and are sent out from all points to intercept them but I deem it prudent to advise you that you may warn the citizens.

GEORGE CROOK,
Brig. Gen'l.[3]

Such messages were sent to newspaper editors, to the governors of Sonora and Chihuahua, to appropriate Army commands. Again the terrible cry, "The Apaches are out!" echoed through the scattered communities. Once more the cavalry clattered out from Thomas, Grant, Bowie, Huachuca, Bayard, filing in trim blue lines behind hawk-eyed Apache scouts, making for the known waterholes, the mountain trails, the likely places for renegades to cross the border. Once more prospectors and lone travelers hastily threw their slender possessions on pack mules, grabbed lead ropes and jerked the infuriatingly slow beasts toward refuge. That is, those who heard the grim news fled; others did not hear, or were too slow. A few scoffed, the late arrivals, newcomers yet to learn of the terrors of Apache warfare. Some learned too late.

The uprising had been foreshadowed three days earlier, on Thursday, when Davis emerged from his tent at sunrise and found an ominous group of armed Indians, the chiefs and sub-chiefs and their followers, awaiting him. No women or children were present. Davis invited the leaders into his tent, where they squatted in a semicircle, some of them tizwin-drunk, demanding the right to brew the liquor, to beat their wives when the women needed it. They were tired of restrictions. Chihuahua told Davis that all of them had been drunk last night, and what was he going to do about it? The officer saw that an eruption was brewing and that he could no longer handle the situation. He promised to wire Crook for instructions.[4] He sent a telegram which read:

[3] Crook to Editor, Clifton *Clarion*, May 18, 1885.—Hayes Collection.
[4] Davis gives this story in detail in *Geronimo*, 144–51.

Capt. Pierce,
Comd'g San Carlos, A. T.

There was an extensive tiswin drunk here last night, and this morning the following chiefs came up and said that they, with their bands, were all concerned in it: Geronimo, Chihuahua, Mangus, Natchez, Zele and Loco. The wh[ole] business is a put up job to save those who were drunk. In regard to the others, I request instructions. The guard house here is not large enough to hold them all, and the arrest of so many prominent men will probably cause trouble. Have told the Indians that I would lay the matter before the General, requesting, at the same time, that their captives in Mexico be withheld. I think they are endeavoring to screen Natchez and Chihuahua.

(Sgd.) DAVIS, Lieut.[5]

Pierce, only two months at San Carlos, took the wire to Al Sieber for an opinion. Al had been gambling and drinking all night and was sleeping off a hangover when Pierce woke him up and handed him the telegram. "Oh, it's nothing but a tizwin drunk," he said, and handed it back to Pierce. "Davis will handle it." Pierce returned to his office, pigeonholed the message, and Crook never saw it for months. Disaster resulted. It is impossible not to place the fault squarely on Sieber's shoulders, although Pierce should still have forwarded the message.[6] Davis himself found it difficult to be too hard on the scout, preferring to remember the countless times Sieber had willingly jeopardized his life for others over the years.[7] Crook

[5] Appendix A, Report of Crook on Apache Operations, in the field, Fort Bowie, April 10, 1886.—Hayes Collection.

[6] A year later, in conversation with Davis, Crook said that had he received the message the outbreak might have been prevented, or the Indians taught a lesson they could never forget.—*Geronimo*, 149. Crook, in his *Resume of Operations*, 6, wrote: "I am firmly convinced that had I known of the occurrence reported in Lieutenant Davis's telegram . . . which I did not see until months afterwards, the outbreak . . . would not have occurred." He occasionally referred to the message in correspondence, but most of the officers serving under him did not know of it, and he bore much undeserved blame, as a result. Cruse wrote to Davis November 15, 1929, that he had "always held General Crook personally responsible for the outbreak," as he supposed he had ignored Davis' telegram of which Cruse had been aware.

[7] Davis, *Geronimo*, 36.

presumably accepted the incident as but another exigency on the harsh, bitter frontier. He never publicly blamed the scout.

The outbreak, Davis believed, was not premeditated. It stemmed, he thought, from "a certain class of Indians" more or less dissatisfied because "of their own worthlessness and a determination . . . not to be punished for offenses committed. . . . But this feeling was not general, by any means, nor in the ordinary course of events would it have led to such a culmination."[8]

As the days passed with no word from Crook the Indians' "fears . . . increased [and] Geronimo and Mangus determined to leave rather than remain and undergo the punishment which their fears pointed out to them." Sunday afternoon Davis umpired a baseball game between post teams at Fort Apache. Sam Bowman had learned that a breakout was imminent and sent word to the officer, but it reached him after the four o'clock eruption. Davis tried to wire Pierce, but the hostiles had cut the telegraph line, and the break could not be found immediately. The Apaches, wise by now in the way of repair crews, had cut the wire in a fork of a tree and tied the ends together with buckskin so that the break was all but invisible from the ground. Davis hurried to his tent, not noticing that three scouts slipped off through the brush, having failed in their Geronimo-inspired mission to assassinate the lieutenant and Chatto. They were foiled by guards Davis had assigned to the area as a precautionary measure.

Mangus and Geronimo already had gone to the other chiefs, "telling them that we had been killed, the scouts had deserted and that all of the Indians were going to leave the reservation. . . . Chihuahua and Natchez, frightened at the part they had previously

[8] This summary of the causes and chronology of the outbreak was written by Britton Davis as a report filed from Fort Bowie September 15, 1885, to the Adjutant General, Department of Arizona. It was reprinted textually in the *Army-Navy Journal*, October 24, 1885, under the heading: "The Difficulties of Indian Warfare." In some respects it is superior to his version in *Geronimo*, because it was written while the campaign was fresh in his mind, whereas the book developed from Davis' memory forty years later, checked against the recollections of surviving acquaintances. Hereafter cited as Davis, *Journal*.

taken, readily believed what was told them and gathering up the stock they had immediately around them, they followed Mangus and Geronimo."[9] Incorrigible old Nana also left, the total fleeing being thirty-four men, eight boys of fighting age, and ninety-two women and children. However, Loco, Zele, Bonito, and, of course, Chatto, refused to go out.[10]

Davis quickly rounded up his loyal Indians and, as soon as Gatewood arrived from Apache with a dozen White Mountain scouts, the officers took the trail, not hoping to overtake the enemy, but determined to discover their intentions. Trailing was slow during the night but a little after sunrise, Monday, "we came out on the crest of a ridge bordering a valley some fifteen or twenty miles wide. In the distance, on the opposite side of the valley, we could see the dust raised by the Indian ponies ascending another ridge."[11] Further pursuit was hopeless, so far as catching the hostiles was concerned, and Davis returned to Apache while Gatewood pressed on. At the fort Davis wired Crook that he, Captain Allen Smith, and Gatewood had followed the hostiles about sixty-five miles east to near Stevens' ranch on Eagle Creek, the Apaches "making for Black Range in New Mexico. Mangus is in command, they are traveling very rapidly. Chatto and ten other Chiricahua scouts returned with me, but are anxious to organize a sufficient number of scouts and start at once to hunt hostiles down. Chatto and Benito both very bitter."[12]

To this Crook replied by return telegrams, two on the same day. The first advised Davis to remind the Indians that "for more than a year I have been trying to get back to them their captives who were in Mexico and New Mexico and now just as they are beginning to return this trouble has occurred and unless it is satisfactorily settled up and peaceful times restored, all the business of returning the captives will have to stop."[13] In a second message Crook added that "as many of the Indians outside of the scouts as desire to go in pursuit

[9] Davis, "Difficulties of Indian Warfare," *Army-Navy Journal*, October 24, 1885.
[10] Crook to AAG, Division of the Pacific, May 21, 1885.—Hayes Collection.
[11] Davis, *Geronimo*, 151.
[12] Crook to AAG, Division of the Pacific, May 20, 1885.—Hayes Collection.
[13] Crook to Davis, May 21, 1885.—Hayes Collection.

should be encouraged and permitted to do so in order to get in among
the refugees [hostiles] and work upon the dissatisfied ones especially
Natchez . . . and thus . . . induce a return of those who are least guilty
and destruction of the ring-leaders if possible . . ."[14]

Much later Davis discovered that Chihuahua and Nachez had
learned, soon after the bolt, that "Mangus and Geronimo had lied to
them and frightened them into leaving."[15] The band was camped
briefly, with Geronimo, Mangus, and their people some distance
from Chihuahua's party. Chihuahua brooded over what he believed
the wrong, and then set out with his brother and a man named
Atelueitze, to kill Geronimo. But that Indian and Mangus, warned
in time, hastily gathered their band, mounted, and fled south. Nachez,
who had been camping with Mangus and Geronimo, decided that he,
too, had had enough and sent word to his wife and child, who were
with Chihuahua, to return to the reservation, that he would join
them soon. They did return as far as Eagle Creek, but there spotted
some scouts with Lieutenant Davis, who was again in the field pur-
suant to new instructions from Crook. Frightened, they returned and
rejoined Chihuahua.

Chihuahua's people, meanwhile, had intended to hide out north
of the Gila after Geronimo went south. They thought that when the
excitement died out, they could slip back onto the reservation. But
unfortunately Davis' scouts, reaching the place where Geronimo's
group went one way and Chihuahua's another, didn't know which
band to follow and decided to take the northern trail, figuring, no
doubt, that other troops and scouts farther south would cut the other.
The northern trail, however, was Chihuahua's. His band saw the
scouts coming after them like bloodhounds.[16] They abandoned all
hope of returning to the reservation, or most of them did, although a
few filtered back. The rest turned south for Mexico. Had it not been
for this incident, some eighty of the hostiles, including women and

[14] *Ibid.*

[15] Davis, "Difficulties of Indian Warfare," *Army-Navy Journal*, October 24,
1885.

[16] This was about ten days after the bust-out.—Davis, *Geronimo*, 152.

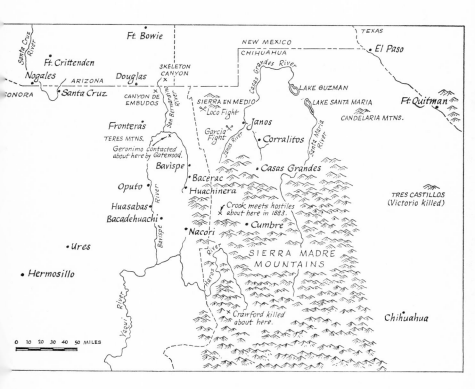

The Mexican Theater

children, would soon have surrendered and Geronimo's strength vastly reduced.[17] But Chihuahua was now committed. Henceforth he would prove himself unmellowed by time, again among the ablest of Chiricahua war leaders. While Geronimo fled to the sanctuary of the Sierra Madre, Chihuahua struck again and again, with telling effect.

As Davis and Gatewood scouted the wilderness, the route of the Indians, or of Chihuahua's party, at least, was being bloodily made clear. James H. Cook at that time was manager of a large cattle ranch three miles from a flyspeck mining town, Alma, about eighty miles northwest of Silver City.[18] About half-past nine one morning a horseman dashed up shouting that Indians had been chasing him after killing his companions ten miles west. Cook sent him on to warn the Alma miners and started his own men to filling gunny sacks with sand to barricade the windows and laying out ammunition and firearms. An Alma party clattered past, hunting Indian sign, but a few miles down the road they were ambushed and two were slain. A blood-covered horse galloped back to the ranch, giving a hint of what had happened. Cook and a cowboy rode out to bring in the ranch horses. From a hill Cook saw "a string of Indians, about twenty-five in number, part mounted, the rest on foot, moving toward the horses. . . . I immediately opened fire on the Indians with a 40-90 Sharps rifle at a range of about one thousand yards. This checked them, and they ran to cover in the rocks and brush. The horses in the pasture . . . stampeded . . . to their stable."

The next day Gatewood and his scouts, a pack train, and two troops of the Fourth Cavalry rode in, having "traveled about seventy miles over very rough mountain trails, hardly stopping for food or rest, and both men and horses were very tired. Many of their animals had lost their shoes, and traveling over the hard volcanic rocks had so worn their hoofs that they limped painfully." Captain Smith and Lieutenant James Parker were in command. The officers and their

[17] These incidents are all summarized in Davis, "Difficulties of Indian Warfare," *Army-Navy Journal*, October 24, 1885.

[18] James Cook, *Fifty Years on the Old Frontier*, 164–87. Although Cook believed, as did others, that it was Geronimo's band depredating in his vicinity, his account otherwise is accurate.

men pushed hard on the trail of the renegades, but it was a nearly impossible task. Captain Smith did make contact once, on Devil's Creek, although it was he who was attacked. Cook said he ran into the hostiles' rear guard, "cleverly concealed on the top of a bluff which could not be scaled by the troops."[19] The command had paused for a ten-minute break, to readjust saddles and rest their tired horses, when the shooting started. Captain Smith was rinsing his bandana in a stream. An Indian bullet punctured the handkerchief, but missed his hands. Three or four enlisted men were wounded and two cavalry horses killed; the troops believed they had wounded "some" of the enemy.[20]

The enemy trail now led southeast, in the general direction of Fort Bayard, and Cook volunteered to carry a message for Crook into the fort ahead of the troops, making the one hundred and ten miles in about twelve hours. A few hours later the Indians killed a number of whites within three miles of Silver City, on the trail Cook had just used.

Newspaper dispatches, sometimes accurate, often not, reflected the commotion in the Indian country, and the usual frustration because the hostiles could not immediately be caught. One dispatch claimed twenty-four persons had been killed in the Alma area, another reported others in the San Mateos, while a story datelined Silver City charged that "the Indian scouts are reported deserting to the hostiles," others charged additional killings here and there, and one bluntly said, "the military are doing nothing." Typical of them all was this one:

> SILVER CITY (N.M.), May 28.—Some particulars of the killing done by Geronimo's band near Silver City to-day are learned. . . .

[19] Cook, *Frontier*, 173.

[20] Crook to Colonel Bradley, Fort Bayard, May 24, 1885.—Hayes Collection. James Parker, *The Old Army: Memories, 1872–1918*, 156–65, tells the story of this fight in some detail, claiming that it was he who led the attack which broke up the "ambush," and that it was Captain Smith's folly which led the men into the trap in the first place. Parker in his book tends to credit himself with being an important figure in a campaign in which he was but a junior officer, and one not prominently mentioned by any other person who has published an account of it.

The family consisted of Phillips, wife and two children, aged 3 and 5 years. This morning Geronimo's band attacked him and his family, killing the entire family excepting the oldest child, a girl, whom they hanged on a meat-hook. The hook entered the back portion of her head, in which position she was found, still alive, by a rescuing posse of citizens and brought to Silver City, but only lived a few hours. The citizens think this is pretty rough, occurring within sight of a ten-company military post, and at present departmental headquarters.[21]

Perhaps it was the women who committed such atrocities; often it was. Whites who knew much about Indian warfare were apt to be more bitter against the women than the men. One dispatch, printed June 22, 1885, helped explain why. Commenting on the women of the hostiles, the unidentified writer says,

> I have been in these mountains and through these Indian raids for seven years, and to my personal knowledge the squaws are more cruel and blood-thirsty than the bucks. When Jim Cooney and Chick were killed in the Mogollons, in 1880, parties hidden saw squaws stick pieces of wood into their bowels while alive, then crush their heads to a jelly with rocks. I myself saw a bunch of twelve killed near Hillsboro whom the squaws literally hacked to pieces with knives. Any man who would not as quickly kill a squaw as a buck or rattle-snake knows nothing of them.[22]

Captain Allen Smith, in a message to Crook, reported, "The Indians are at least fifty miles ahead of me. They have fresh horses and have not made a camp yet. . . . Bayard may head them off. I will follow although my chances are small."[23] Crook sent Major Frederick Van Vliet and Captain Phillip L. Lee, both of the Tenth Cavalry, with seventeen officers and two hundred forty-five men to Bayard from San Simon and Clifton, respectively. They were too late to do more than rummage through the mountains for Indians that either had gone on or were too nimble to catch. As an aside, Crook had to pause to reassure the Mexicans that there was no possibility the

---

21 L.A. Pub. Lib. This collection includes a series of such dispatches.
22 *Ibid.* The name of the paper is not given.
23 Crook to Bradley at Bayard, May 22, 1885.—Hayes Collection.

hostile Apaches had broken out merely to help the troublesome Yaquis, who again were fighting the whites.

His main problem was, where were the hostiles? He knew that some were in the Mogollons, and thought all of them were; he had not yet learned of the split in the hostile camp and that Geronimo's band already was in Mexico, or close to the line. He carefully made his dispositions. On May 26 he wired San Francisco that "troops from Bowie are stationed at Stein's Pass and from Huachuca at mouth of Guadalupe Cañon to intercept hostiles if they should double back to go into Mexico by usual trails. Major Van Vliet... also Captain Smith with one hundred Fourth Cavalry, Captain Pierce and Indian scouts from San Carlos are at Fort Bayard and east of there . . . and Lieut. Davis with sixty Indian Scouts from Apache are still on their trail in pursuit into the mountains. What has made it so difficult to get any definite information in regard to the Indians is the rapidity of their march, having made about one hundred and thirty-five miles in two days over an exceedingly rough country."[24]

Crook planned to make his headquarters at Bayard (he soon was given command of the New Mexico units as well as those of Arizona), but before going he asked that Captain Crawford be sent back to his department from his Third Cavalry post in Texas.[25] He also requested some contract surgeons. The general was convinced that the campaign would be a long one, and he wanted to assure the health and treatment of his men. Drs. T. J. C. Maddox and Francis J. Ives were sent him. Crook dispatched a message to Davis via Bayard, hoping it could be forwarded to that hard-working officer in some way, urging him to "push on as rapidly as possible and use every exertion to carry out the instructions heretofore given you without reference to instructions or movements of any other troops."[26] He also warned commanders in key positions that the Indians were seeking to slip southward in small parties. Crook arrived at Bayard May

[24] Crook to AAG, Division of the Pacific, May 26, 1885.—Hayes Collection.

[25] Crook to Commanding General, Division of the Missouri, May 27, 1885.—Hayes Collection.

[26] Crook to Britton Davis, May 27, 1885.—Hayes Collection.

31, immediately wiring the presidio that the many outrages "indicates troubles similar to the Victoria outbreak, which will be very difficult to suppress."[27] He added in a separate telegram to Sheridan at Washington that "the condition of affairs is very bad. . . . The country is very much alarmed, and the most radical measures must be taken."[28]

After reviewing the situation with his customary thoroughness and making what troop dispositions seemed indicated, Crook reported to the presidio June 2 that the "Indians shortly after crossing New Mexican line evidently divided into small parties which raided in widely separated localities, while the women and children were hid away in the mountains. Troops have been following around the different raiding parties without result other than to break down their stock. It is impossible with troops to catch the raiding parties or afford citizens so scattered among the mountains protection from such parties." He said that Lieutenant Davis with sixty scouts was seeking to ferret out the enemy women and children among the mountains east of Duck Creek on the Upper Gila. Other troops, Crook revealed, were disposed in this fashion:

> Maj. Van Vliet with five troops of 10th. Cavalry and thirty Apache scouts, is moving north of Bayard towards Datil Range. Capt. Chaffee with one troop 6th. is in vicinity of Cuchillo Negro. Maj. [James Judson] Van Horn with Cavalry from Fort Stanton and Mescalero Scouts is scouting each bank of Rio Grande to prevent Indians crossing. Capt. Madden with two troops 6th. Cav'y is west of Burro Mtns. Capt. Lee with three troops 10th Cav'y is moving across Black Range between Smith and Van Vliet. Maj. Biddle followed trail of ten or fifteen Indians which crossed railroad near Florida Pass beyond Lake Paloma, Mexico.[29] . . . Troops are now moving into positions near all known water holes between railroad and Mexico to intercept Indians going south. Capt. [Henry] Lawton with three troops 4th. Cav'y and Lt. [George Henderson] Roach's scouts is in Guadalupe Canyon near boundary line. Maj. [Eugene

[27] Crook to AAG, Division of the Pacific, May 31, 1885.—Hayes Collection.
[28] Crook to Sheridan, May 31, 1885.—Hayes Collection.
[29] This was probably Geronimo's own band.

Beauharnais] Beaumont with two troops 4th. Cav'y is in Stein's Pass.[30]

At least twenty troops of cavalry and more than one hundred Indian scouts, perhaps twice that number, were now in the field, and yet the hostiles eluded them all, except when they chose to fight.

Britton Davis messaged Crook June 4 that the Indians had left the mountains, the scouts thinking they at last were headed for Old Mexico down the slot between the Animas and Chiricahua ranges, the route the hostiles had often used. Crook figured that by this time they had killed at least seventeen civilians, seven near Alma, five near Silver City, two near old Camp Vincent, and three near Grafton. They had done this, mostly, to get stock, arms, and ammunition, almost without loss to themselves. "But," said the general, "if after some of their number have been killed, the Indians are driven back into the United States, the number of people living in these mountains, and the property interests increased so enormously since the time of Victoria, there is no estimating the damage they will do. If the Indians get among these mountains again, such a wail will go up as was never heard before."[31] Such newspaper stories as this were not uncommon:

SAN FRANCISCO, June 5.—A San Simeon, New Mexico special says: Twenty-four cattlemen led by Parks and Fisher, who arrived here to-night, had an encounter with a band of about twenty-five Indians last night at the mouth of Doubtful Canyon. A hundred rounds were exchanged and two Indians are believed to be killed. The cattlemen brought with them a papoose, whose mother is supposed to have been killed in the encounter, also eighteen head of stock were captured.[32]

Crook had sent Crawford to Deming, New Mexico, thinking that the Indians might head south through the Floridas, as they some-

---

[30] Crook to AAG, Division of the Pacific, June 2, 1885.—Hayes Collection.

[31] *Ibid.*, June 8, 1885.—Hayes Collection.

[32] L.A. Pub. Lib. Eventually the captured child reached Safford, where it was raised by a white woman and became known as the "Doubtful Kid."—Letter, October 1, 1959, George Kerr, Lordsburg, to author.

times had before. Now he sent him west again, and wired him at Separ, east of Lordsburg:

> Davis reports this morning from Duncan [Arizona] that Indians passed that point night before last well mounted and traveling very fast. Davis will be in Bowie tonight for rations. I will instruct him to take thirty days rations and meet you at mouth of Guadalupe Cañon unless you desire some change. Davis has fifty-nine scouts. You had best take your own and Davis' scouts and follow Indians into the Sierra Madre. If you feel strong enough, leave Cavalry at Boundary. If you need more supplies, telegraph me. Pierce's pack train is available if you need it.
>
> GEORGE CROOK
> Brig. General.[33]

In pursuit of his policy to use the scouts to catch the hostiles, Crook wired the presidio for permission to hire two hundred more Apaches, stressed the necessity to hunt the Indians in Mexico "freed from the present vexatious treaty stipulations," and said he needed more pack mules.[34] A complete pack train was sent him from Cheyenne.

Crook believed that Geronimo led the band which went into Mexico past Palomas, the party Biddle had trailed, and that Mangus had six or seven warriors and a few women and children somewhere in the Black Range. That left the bulk of the hostiles, having now slipped past the troops at Stein's Pass, hastening for the border past Guadalupe Canyon. The only hope was that Captain Lawton could intercept this party, since Crawford and Davis would be far behind them. The General removed Al Sieber from Pierce's command and sent him in charge of a pack train from Bayard to Guadalupe Canyon, where he could join Crawford's column for the all-important drive into Mexico.

Captain Lawton was operating out of Huachuca, along with Captain Charles Allen Phelps Hatfield, in command of D Troop of the Fourth Cavalry, and Leonard Wood, at that time nominally an assistant surgeon, but who desired a combat command, and was given

---

[33] Crook to Crawford, June 5, 1885.—Hayes Collection.
[34] Crook to AAG, Division of the Pacific, June 5, 1885.—Hayes Collection.

one. On June 8 the three officers were on a scout, leaving in camp a noncommissioned officer and seven enlisted men. A telegram to Crook told what happened: "Courier just in from Lawton's camp reports while he, Wood and Hatfield were scouting in vicinity of Guadalupe Canyon, his camp was attacked by Indians about noon the eighth, five of his men killed, and two mules, five horses taken, and some camp equipments and stores burned. . . . Indian scouts say there were twenty-five or thirty Indians in the party."[35] No doubt it was Chihuahua's party that made the attack. A newspaper dispatch said that three wagonloads of government supplies, including several thousand rounds of ammunition, had been taken or destroyed when the Indians jumped the careless escort as the men were eating lunch.

Again newspapers of the area loosed their shrill cries. A Tombstone dispatch said "this city is wild to-night with rumors of all kinds. . . . A. J. Emanuel, who has a ranch at the south end of the Huachuca Mountains . . . reports that about 7 o'clock this morning he saw with a glass, apparently a large party of Indians between a body of soldiers and citizens, being pursued toward the Line."[36] Another: "A report [from Huachuca] says . . . that the united forces of soldiers and citizens had been fighting continuously all day in the north end of the San Jose Mountains, near the Mexican line. . . . The wildest rumors are current."[37] Still another: "Lewis Williams of Bisbee sends word by mail this morning: All is excitement and confusion now." From Benson: "Benson was thrown into excitement early this morning by the report that three Indians had been seen. . . . The Apaches are appearing on every hand [and] it keeps the people on constant anxiety."[38]

Not all of the reports were entirely imaginary. Chihuahua's band scoured the Chiricahua Mountains for stock and attacked ranches south of Bowie, and true tales of heroism filtered into the settlements. The Apaches' atrocious marksmanship saved the lives of some

[35] *Ibid.*, June 11, 1885.—Hayes Collection.

[36] Mr. Emanuel's instrument must have been a whisky glass; there were no hostiles at this time in the area at all. L.A. Pub. Lib.

[37] *Ibid.*

[38] *Ibid.*

individuals,[39] but others were not so fortunate. Typical was this account:

> Last night Daniels, accompanied by a man and a boy, followed a trail in the Dixie Canyon, Mule Mountains, ten miles from Bisbee. Daniels was in the advance, when he suddenly found himself in an ambuscade, and the Indians among the rocks shot and killed his horse. From appearances it seems that the animal must have fallen on him, pinning him to the ground. Helplessly entangled under the dead steed, Daniels, in spite of his skill with the rifle and great personal courage, was unable to defend himself, and the Indians shot him dead at their leisure, then cut his throat and mutilated his corpse. His companions escaped.[40]

Such tales abounded during the periods of Indian outbreaks. Similar outrages, of course, were perpetrated upon the red men by the whites, but these naturally were not reported.

Eventually the whirlwind flowed into Mexico. Crook sent his two expeditions, under Crawford and Captain Wirt Davis, plunging into the rocky wastelands after them. To guard against the hostiles' return into the United States, he cordoned off the border this way:

> The four troops 4th Cavalry from Fort Huachuca left on the fifth [of July] for their stations on the border and will be placed at Copper Canyon, Song Mountain, Solomon's Springs and Mud Springs. I expect on the ninth to send four more troops of the 4th. Cavalry from here, to be stationed at Willow Springs, San Bernardino, Skeleton Canyon and Guadalupe Canyon. Two companies of the 10th. Infantry are en-route to San Luis Pass. Three troops 6th. Cavalry left Separ to-day for the line in New Mexico. The stations have been selected with the greatest care so as to not only cover all known watering places, but also to give open country between these stations

[39] Whether the Indians often were good shots seems doubtful, although there must have been some exceptions. James Cook, himself an extraordinary marksman, wrote that "the Apaches . . . were, as a rule, very poor shots with firearms. Most of the white persons killed by them were fired upon at short range, from cover."— *Frontier*, 171. Opinions would differ, depending upon how narrow was one's escape, no doubt.

[40] L.A. Pub. Lib.

and the line. With each detachment of troops there will be stationed (five) Indian scouts who are to be used exclusively in watching and scouting in advance of line to prevent as nearly as possible the approach of any hostiles without the troops being notified. These dispositions will cover the line as thoroughly as possible from the Rio Grande as far west as it is thought probable the Indians will attempt to recross into the United States.

In rear of the advance line I shall place the troops of the 10th. Cavalry . . . to intercept parties should they succeed in sneaking through the first line. . . . These dispositions are the best that can be made, in my judgment . . . I have given orders for the search in the Sierra Madre to be most vigorous and to pursue any party which may attempt to return so closely as to endeavor to drive them towards the troops and force them to cross in daylight . . .[41]

Behind the mobile "second line" consisting of Tenth Cavalry troops, Crook stationed soldiers "on the railroad who might be sent to any desired point on the whole front, forming thus a third line."[42] In addition there were garrison troops of Forts Thomas, Grant, Bayard, and others at Ash Springs on the Gila, in the Mogollons and elsewhere, to form, "in reality a fourth line." Everything that could be done was done to prevent the Indians from slipping back across the border to raid, murder, depredate, loot, burn, and steal. But no one knew better than Crook that troops were virtually impotent when it came to sealing the line against the slippery Chiricahuas.

[41] Crook to AAG, Division of the Pacific, July 7, 1885.—Hayes Collection.
[42] Crook, *Resume of Operations*, 20.

XXV

Geronimo—2

IT WAS NOW EARLY SUMMER, and Crook had sent two columns into Mexico with orders to capture or destroy the hostiles, if they could. Captain Crawford, with Henry F. Kendall's Troop A of the Sixth Cavalry and ninety-two scouts under Britton Davis and Al Sieber, was ordered south on June 11. A month later, July 13, Captain Wirt Davis was also ordered into Mexico. He had a troop of the Fourth Cavalry, two pack trains, and a hundred Indian scouts under First Lieutenant Matthias W. Day.[1] Between them the columns were to work the Sierra Madre and associated uplifts, scouting them thoroughly. Their trails met and crossed from time to time as they searched the folds of the great range. Crawford's command paralleled Crook's 1883 route through Bacerac, Estancia, and Huachinera, then cut west, toward Oputo where, on June 21, a scout was shot by an American who took him for a hostile. Near Oputo the Apaches struck a fresh trail of hostiles.

Crawford sent a party of thirty Indians under Chatto on this trail,

---

[1] *Roster of Troops*, Department of Arizona. *Operating Against Hostile Chiricahuas July 14, 1885, In the Sierra Madre* (no office of publication or date) lists these parties: "Captain Emmet Crawford, Troop G, 3rd Cavalry, commanding. Captain H. M. Kendall, Troop A, 6th Cavalry, commanding troop. First Lieutenant Robert Hanna, Troop A, 6th Cavalry, with troop. First Lieutenant C. P. Egan, assistant surgeon, medical officer. Second Lieutenant Britton Davis, Troop L, 3rd Cavalry, commanding Indian scouts. Second Lieutenant C. P. Elliott, Troop H, 4th Cavalry, commanding Indian scouts. Troop A, 6th Cavalry. 92 Indian scouts. Two pack trains. Al. Sieber, Chief of Scouts. Mickey Free, interpreter." And: "Captain Wirt Davis, Troop F, 4th Cavalry, commanding. First Lieutenant H. P. Birmingham, assistant surgeon, medical officer. First Lieutenant M. W. Day, 9th Cavalry, commanding Indian scouts. Second Lieutenant R. D. Walsh, Troop B, 4th Cavalry, commanding Indian scouts. Troop F, 4th Cavalry. 100 Indian scouts. Two pack trains. G. B. Roberts, Chief of Scouts. Frank Leslie, Chief of Scouts." Copy in Southwest Museum Library, Los Angeles.

denying Davis and Sieber the opportunity to go along because, he said, they would prove only "an encumbrance." He later regretted it. On June 23 Chatto's party stumbled on a rancheria high on a mountainside, in a heavy rain. The hostiles and scouts saw each other at the same instant. Most of the former escaped, although Chatto captured fifteen, mostly women and children, and killed one. A scout was wounded and Chatto retook five Fourth Cavalry horses and a white mule, along with other items taken from soldiers killed at Guadalupe Canyon. The prisoners reached the line early in July.[2]

Crawford continued his scout to the south, following the mountains east of where the Bavispe joins the Haros to form the Yaqui. The country grew poorer and wilder. Somewhere near Nacori Chico the column swung north again, first along the Bavispe, then east into the ranges again. Wirt Davis and his command also continued working the main system, but behind them there was fresh activity.

Late in July a band of ten or twelve Indians, who had been hiding in the New Mexico mountains, swooped on the border from the north, driving forty or more head of stolen horses. Hatfield's and Wood's command took up the chase. A citizen named Tevis went with them some distance, leaving the column sixty miles deep in Old Mexico on July 28 and reporting, on his return, that the command was traveling swiftly on a fresh trail and had forced the enemy to drop the stolen horses, some broken down and ruined.[3] "Wood's scouts played out and came back," Forsyth reported to Crook from Fort Huachuca a short time later. "Fortunately Hatfield's were mounted and are with the command."[4]

Despite the vigorous activity of the troops, the territorial and national press demanded blood, and a fresh crescendo of abuse

[2] Crook to AAG, Division of the Pacific, June 28, 1885; Crook to General Pope, Presidio, July 3, 1885.—Hayes Collection. H. W. Daly, "The Geronimo Campaign," *Journal of the United States Cavalry Association*, Vol. XIX, No. 69 (July, 1908), 70, says that Davis, Elliott, and others were in the fight and that Nana was captured. He was mistaken. Nana also was falsely reported killed in August.

[3] Possibly this was James H. Tevis of Cochise days, who was in the country; see Chapter II.

[4] Crook to AAG, Division of the Pacific, July 30, 1885.—Hayes Collection.

mounted against Crook. Sometimes he felt that criticism went too far, and was intended to harm the whole campaign. On August 13 he wrote the AGO, Division of the Pacific, that: "So long as these newspapers confine their opposition to personal abuse of myself and our troops, I have no objection; but when their course is calculated to interfere with and prevent the settlement of this Indian question, I feel it my duty to bring the matter to the attention of proper authority."[5]

Crawford's command had topped out on the Sierra, spent a week there and, finding nothing, slipped back into Bavispe, sending pack trains north for more rations. While awaiting their return, Davis and Sieber with a dozen scouts went south of the river and up the Haros "as far . . . as they would go in fear of meeting Mexican troops, but no trail of the hostiles was found."[6] They did not go south quite far enough. Mangus and his small band were in that country, but east and south of where the scouting party turned around.

Freshly rationed, Crawford once more tackled the main range where, he felt convinced, the enemy must be, since he was no where else. Once atop it, a hostile trail was found, and Britton Davis and Sieber, working it out, came across another scouting party, from Wirt Davis' command, headed by Lieutenant Day and Charlie Roberts, one of his chiefs of scouts. Three days earlier they had struck a band they thought was led by Geronimo himself. They had killed a squaw and a youth on July 28, and now, August 7, they struck again, killing five and capturing fifteen, according to Britton Davis and the *Chronological List*. Crook, in an official report, tells it differently. Buckskin Frank Leslie, another of Wirt Davis' chiefs of scouts, brought him a message, Crook said, that reported:

Lieutenant Day and Mr. Roberts with seventy-eight scouts of his command, struck Geronimo's camp in the mountains a little north of east of Nakari [Nacori] on the seventh of August, and killed Chief Nana,[7] three other bucks and one squaw—one of the bucks the son of

[5] *Ibid.*, August 13, 1885.—Hayes Collection.
[6] Davis, *Geronimo*, 173.
[7] This was in error. Nana lived through the Apache peregrinations as far as

Geronimo. They captured fifteen women and children, among them three wives and five children of Geronimo's family, and Huera, the wife of Mangus. Geronimo was wounded and escaped, though trailed some distance by the blood.[8] Two other bucks and one squaw got away. On the twenty-ninth of July the scouts ambushed a party of four Chiricahuas in [Sierra de] Hoya Mountains and killed two of the bucks. In Geronimo's camp were captured thirteen horses and mules, besides saddles, blankets, dried meat, etc.[9]

The following day Crook called his headquarters' attention to the "excessive hardships and difficulties which both commands in the Sierra Madre have endured." He explained:

In the first place the whole country is of indescribable roughness. The Indians act differently than ever before, are split up in small bands and are constantly on the watch. Their trails are so scattered that it is almost impossible to follow them, particularly over rocks, which often delays the party following trails for several hours, even if the trail isn't entirely lost, while the party being pursued loses no time . . .

Owing to the rains which reports show to have been of more than usual severity, the troops have been almost continually drenched to the skin for the last month. . . . Mr. Leslie, who brought in Captain Davis's report, states that he swam the Bavispe River eleven times in one day, a stream that is usually easily forded. It should be understood that the Indians are so split up in small parties and are so constantly on the watch that our scouts are practically compelled to cover the entire region, and cannot even venture to follow trails where they pass over prominent points for fear of their pursuit being discovered. . . . In daylight they frequently have been obliged to conceal themselves in canyons where not only no rest was to be obtained, but where the extremely heavy mountain rains made their position one of great danger. At these times they have of course been separated from the pack trains for a period of from three to fifteen days . . .

Oklahoma where he died "at a great age—unreconstructed"; Lockwood, *Apache Indians,* 324.

[8] Geronimo was not wounded in this action, nor was Huera captured.

[9] Crook to AAG, Division of the Pacific, August 17, 1885.—Hayes Collection.

have been compelled to live for several days at a time on a half allowance of bacon, supplemented by acorns and roots.[10]

Crawford detached a party under Davis to follow Geronimo wherever he might go, picking up the trail from Day and Roberts. With Davis he sent Sieber, Mickey Free, Chatto, forty picked scouts, five pack mules, two packers, and a night herder. And a long, long chase it was. The wily Geronimo, if he it was, led them down off the eastern face of the Sierra into Chihuahua where he could steal plenty of fresh stock at will, then northward until he slipped across the line, having lost Davis and his weary party long before. Davis, after several adventures, made it to El Paso, from where he returned to Arizona by railroad. He soon resigned from the Army and entered private business in Mexico. Sieber, too, was done in and never served as chief of scouts in Mexico again.[11]

Crawford and Wirt Davis continued their scouts through the Sierra Madre until late September. On September 22, Davis' men had a brush with the enemy in the Teres Mountains,[12] losing a man killed and another wounded, for the killing of one and wounding of two hostiles. This same day Geronimo, at one o'clock in the morning, kidnapped his wife, child, and another woman from near Fort Apache, despite the greatest precautions against such an eventuality. Gatewood messaged Crook that "the only way to prevent [such incidents] is to put them in close confinement."[13]

Some of the hostiles again were interested in raiding north of the border, and on September 28 about twenty warriors crossed the line at Guadalupe Canyon. "Warn all the citizens to be on the watch constantly until Indians are run out of the country, as they are liable to come in on them when least expected," Crook cautioned prominent citizens at Clifton, Silver City, and Duncan. "Indians will be short of stock. Urge that all horses and mules be corralled and carefully watched in order that if the Indians attempt to re-mount themselves

[10] *Ibid.*, August 18, 1885.—Hayes Collection.
[11] For details of this scout, see Davis, *Geronimo*, 176–95.
[12] Crook to AAG, Division of the Pacific, September 28, 1885.—Hayes Collection.
[13] *Ibid.*, September 22, 1885.—Hayes Collection.

some of them may be killed."[14] Hot on the hostile trail came Crawford and Wirt Davis.

Crook's rapid deployment of troops frustrated the Indians for the moment. Unable to cross the San Simon Valley to the Stein's Peak Range, or unwilling to risk it, they took to the high Chiricahua Mountains, remaining there for several days despite the best efforts of Crawford's scouts to root them out. They killed two white men in the mountains before pressure from two companies of the Tenth Cavalry and Leonard Wood's troop of the Fourth became too heavy. By October 1 they had stolen fresh mounts and crossed into the Sulphur Springs Valley, where their trail was lost in darkness, and picked up at dawn again. Then, Crook was told, they galloped into the Dragoon Mountains, north of Tombstone. Troops, however, were so hot on their trail that they gave the enemy no pause, and the Indians fled southward again, by-passing Tombstone to the east. They touched base at the Mule Mountains, just north of Bisbee, then turned sharply east toward the Chiricahuas once more. Just when their new mounts were giving out, and it seemed that at last the troops might get their fight, Apache luck appeared again.

"By a circumstance maddening to the soldiers, they succeeded at this last gasp in capturing thirty of the best horses in Arizona. . . . It was no credit to the ranchmen of southeastern Arizona that the Indians got away with these mounts. At White Tail Canyon the cattlemen of the San Simon Valley had met for their fall roundup. Only the night before they had been warned that these dismounted Indians were in the vicinity; yet they went to sleep at a ranch house around which was lariated thirty crack cow ponies. The next morning the horses were gone; and, better mounted than ever, the Apaches were beyond pursuit."[15] During their hasty raid this war party had killed only three white men, but they had captured many horses and sent the countryside into turmoil.

[14] Crook to Colonel Eagan, Clifton, September 29, 1885.—Hayes Collection.

[15] Lockwood, *Apache Indians*, 283. Crook says that this incident occurred October 1, as the Indians left the Chiricahuas; Crook to AAG, Division of the Pacific, October 9, 1885.—Hayes Collection.

Crawford was sent to Fort Apache where his scouts were discharged, their six-month enlistments up, and fresh scouts enrolled. Colonel Bradley, at Fort Bayard, urged Crook to send Crawford on a scout through the Mogollons and Black Range as far as Hillsboro, since some hostiles of Geronimo's band were believed still hiding there, but Crook demurred. They were committing no depredations, he wired Bradley, and "I think it best to try and break up their main nest down in Old Mexico first."[16] Let the Mescaleros and Navahos deal with New Mexico renegades, he advised.

Early in November, 1885, came a slashing raid that rivaled the greatest such adventures in Apache history. A band of fewer than a dozen hostiles slipped across the border and entered the Florida Mountains in New Mexico, where they joined, briefly, a party of sixteen, also freshly across the line. On the way they had killed two Navaho scouts, another of the White Mountain people, and had left one of their own number with a broken leg to fend for himself as best he could in the Los Pinos Mountains of Old Mexico. Somewhere near the Florida Mountains the hostiles killed two civilians and a scout, and wounded a white soldier. Eleven of the Chiricahuas then faded into the stony mountains northwest of Hillsboro and the others dropped below the border and regained their highland sanctuary. So far as was known, they had suffered no loss. For three weeks the hostiles in New Mexico committed no depredations. Their leader, it was said, was a young brother of Chihuahua named Josanie,[17] a man relatively unknown to the whites until this time.

Then, on November 23, Lieutenant James Lockett, who had succeeded Gatewood in command at Fort Apache, notified Crook that a small band of hostiles had been seen within four miles of the fort and that his scouts were preparing to "go in pursuit." The telegraph line was cut at this point, and Crook could learn no more. When the wire was mended, he found that disaster had struck the White Mountain

16 Crook to Colonel Luther Prentice Bradley, November 14, 1885.—Hayes Collection.

17 Wellman, *Indian Wars*, 429, makes this name Ulzana, and says he was an Army scout during operations against Nana. Crook, *Resume of Operations*, 11, however, calls him Josanie, as does Ogle, *Western Apaches*, 233–34.

Apaches. The tiny band of hostiles had descended on the reservation and with grim fury had slain anyone they could catch save a few women, whom they stole. Early on the twenty-fourth they killed two herders in charge of the reservation beef herd and stole Bonito's bunch of horses. Just after daybreak they started up Eagle Creek trail, a fruitless pursuit hot after them. Lieutenant Charles Eben Nordstrom, Chatto, and ten soldiers, plus eighteen scouts, took up the trail. Troops all over the Southwest were alerted. Captain Crawford with one hundred scouts hurried to Bowie Station to intercept any hostiles coming that way. On November 27 Lockett telegraphed Crook that "it seems probable" the hostiles had slain eleven women, four children, and five men and boys, all with a view to punishing the Indians who had not taken to the warpath, and frightening others into joining them.[18] They suffered slight loss. Sanchez brought in the head of a Chiricahua named Azariquelch, but he was their only known casualty.

Fleeing southeastward, on fresh horses, the renegades wounded a man named Johnson near Black Rock, swept down through Aravaipa Canyon, doubled back and stole more horses in the Pueblo Viejo Valley, near Solomonville. A party of citizens, thinking the thieves were merely rustlers, whooped out on their trail, but were ambushed near Ash Peak and two killed. The trail then led through Ash Canyon toward Duncan on the Gila. Crook warned Bradley at Bayard to get out all of the troops and scouts he could and try to prevent the hostiles reaching either the Black or Stein's Peak ranges.[19]

The Southwest was again thoroughly alarmed, and Lieutenant General Philip Sheridan came out from Washington to confer with Crook at Bowie. They decided on a more aggressive policy in Old Mexico, seeking to break up the hostiles' base. In addition to Wirt Davis' command, below the border, Crawford was given a stronger force and crossed the line southbound on November 29.

However, the attention of the nation focused still on Josanie and his nine followers as they continued their spectacular raid. Scores of

[18] Crook to AAG, Division of the Pacific, November 25, 1885.—Hayes Collection.
[19] *Ibid.*, December 1, 1885.—Hayes Collection.

companies of troops and several hundred Indian scouts failed to bring this tight little band to bay. Fresh criticism of Crook arose, but some rose to his defense. A group of Arizona pioneers, headed by William S. Oury, Samuel Hughes, William Zeckendorf, and eighteen others, wrote a letter of encouragement to Crook, condemning the "continued and malignant attacks hurled against you by hungry penny-a-liners [from] sordid and malicious motives." They added, "We all know that though the chains of prejudice be thrown around you, true Justice will finally award you a heartfelt greeting and say, 'well done thou faithful servant.'" Crook replied with warm appreciation.[20] He knew, however, that into his experienced hands had been dropped an almost superhuman task. "The events of the past two weeks have clearly demonstrated that when Indians get through the line into rough country north of the railroad, it is practically impossible to do anything with them," he admitted in a letter to Bradley. "The country is so indescribably rough that any pursuit is almost a farce."[21]

Major S. S. Sumner wired Crook December 8 that Josanie and his band had killed two more white men near Alma and then fled into the Mogollons, although Lieutenant Samuel Warren Fountain with ten Navaho scouts and Troop C of the Eighth Cavalry was hard on their heels. Crook ordered Major Biddle to come down from Horse Springs with his forty scouts into the Mogollons from the northeast, to try and ambush the elusive nuisances. He warned Bradley "that the Indians have usually been two days at least in advance of our information," and to use "the utmost care in concealing" troop movements, with ambush parties traveling only at night, remaining concealed during the day.[22] Fountain struck the enemy on the cold evening of December 9 near the Papanosas, and thought he killed two, wounding others, but he had not. What he did, however, was unhorse the enemy, capturing fifteen mounts and all their blankets and supplies. Fountain thought there were sixteen in the party, which

[20] Group to Crook, December 5, 1885; Crook reply, December 8, 1885.—Hayes Collection.

[21] Crook to Bradley, December 6, 1885.—Hayes Collection.

[22] Crook to AAG, Division of the Pacific, December 9, 1885.—Hayes Collection.

would agree with the total of ten warriors plus six White Mountain squaws and a child. By way of retribution the next day Josanie raided Lillie's ranch at the head of the middle fork of the Gila, already scarred from previous battles, and killed both Lillie and a ranch hand named Prior. Then the renegades vanished, as though into the thin mountain air. Troops and scouts worked over the area—Horse Springs, Hillsboro, the Burro Mountains, the Alma region, and the country around Fairview—for days, but could find no hostile trace.

Sam Fountain and his troop, with some Navaho scouts, on December 19 were en route from the SW Ranch, near Alma, to Bayard for supplies. The Navahos, always loathe to work ahead when they sensed Apaches, were reluctant to break camp, so Fountain started off his column and wagon train, then returned to hustle up the scouts. Earlier he had sent a courier, a young Tennesseean, John T. Muir,[23] on toward Silver City with a dispatch for Colonel Bradley. Muir rode through a narrow gap and one-quarter mile beyond heard firing behind him, realizing that the column had ridden into ambush. He put spurs to his horse and arrived safely at Bayard with his dispatches. Lieutenant Fountain, meanwhile, had not regained his command when it fell into Josanie's trap. Dr. Maddox, the surgeon, was the first man hit.[24] The mortal wound did not knock him from his horse, but he dismounted and said to a trooper near him, "Babcock, save yourself. I shall be dead in a minute." A second bullet struck him in the head. Another man killed was Trooper Wishart, "One of the strongest men in the 8th Cavalry." His back was broken by a bullet, and he died in Lieutenant Fountain's arms. In all, five men were killed, Lieutenant De Rosey C. Cabell and an enlisted man wounded, and Josanie and his warriors slipped away without a scratch.[25]

Again the Alma area was ransacked. A freighter was killed, and the Indians stole what they wanted from his wagon and destroyed

[23] John Theodore Muir, born October 15, 1861, had come to New Mexico in 1880 and eventually became a noted rancher, legislator, and banker. His wife, Mrs. Emma Marble Muir, became a local historian. Both were friends of the author.— *Hidalgo County*, 85–86.

[24] Cook, *Frontier*, 182–83.

[25] Crook to AAG, Division of the Pacific, December 21, 1885.—Hayes Collection.

the rest. One brave sampled a cake of scented toilet soap he apparently mistook for candy. A row of teeth marks showed where he had attempted to bite it, and a deep dent where he had disgustedly hurled it against a sharp rock, so Jim Cook reported.[26] The toll grew. On Christmas Eve the harried Crook wired Sheridan:

> I am following the same steps which I indicated to you when here. . . . This party has been followed constantly. . . . That they have been energetically pursued is evidenced by the fact that up to yesterday they had not been able to remount themselves. Troops cannot catch them in that country except by accident, and the smallness of their numbers but adds to the difficulty. The whole force of the District of New Mexico is being used for this purpose either in pursuit or in anticipation of their future movements. Every effort which my experience suggests is being resorted to. . . . In pursuing Indians in this rough country troops must use precautions to prevent ambush. If they dont they run constant danger of attack.[27]

Christmas Day, however, Josanie remounted his band with good ranch horses stolen near Carlisle. Lieutenant David N. McDonald, who had led the Loco scout in the Stein's Peak Range four years earlier, took up the pursuit with M troop of the Fourth Cavalry, and was joined by Lieutenant George Lawson Scott with fifty all-but-worthless Navahos. They pushed the scouts energetically and trailed Josanie across the Gila, two miles below Duncan, while Crook warned all commanders south of the railroad to lay their ambushes well. "It is evident," he said, "that the Indians intend to lose no time in getting across the Border."[28]

McDonald and Scott were having troubles. They followed the hostile trail until about 1:30 P.M., December 26, when the Navahos balked. They "refused to go any further alleging a number of reasons, which were but excuses," Crook angrily reported. "Threats and persuasions failed to move them and they were marched back to

[26] Cook, *Frontier*, 178.
[27] Crook to Sheridan, December 24, 1885.—Hayes Collection.
[28] Crook to AAG, Division of the Missouri, December 26, 1885.—Hayes Collection.

the Gila below Duncan. Lieutenant McDonald endeavored to follow the trail but it led through an exceedingly rough rocky country and he found it impossible to keep it and in consequence was forced to abandon the pursuit. When he lost the trail it was in the Steins Peak range twenty-five miles north of Horse Shoe Cañon leading south."[29]

By the twenty-seventh the ten-man group was in the Chiricahuas, having killed a couple of whites near Galeyville on their way into those soaring peaks. Four troops of cavalry scoured the mountains, but found nothing but cold trails. A savage three-day blizzard covered the country with snow, obliterating all trails, and Josanie blithely fled into the warm sunlight of Old Mexico, secure from pursuit. In his two-month raid he had all but outdone Nana himself. He had traveled twelve hundred miles, killed thirty-eight people, stolen and worn out about two hundred and fifty horses and mules, and, although twice dismounted and several times near capture, had escaped into Mexico with the loss of but one man.[30]

Two columns, Wirt Davis' and Crawford's, continued their operations in Mexico, Davis with a troop of cavalry, but Crawford with only Indian scouts. He had information when he crossed the line that he might find a party of hostiles near Oputo; Davis had similar information about a group near Casas Grandes, on the other side of the Sierra. Sieber, having been recalled to San Carlos, had recommended to Crawford that Tom Horn be made chief of scouts, and this was done, Horn remaining with the command during its coming vicissitudes.[31] At, or near, Oputo, Crawford heard that the enemy was still farther south and so, pushing into a region "rugged almost

[29] *Ibid.*, December 27, 1885.—Hayes Collection.

[30] Ogle, *Western Apaches*, 233–34.

[31] Horn should be the best authority for this period, since he apparently was the only participant to publish a book about it. But his account is so hopelessly inaccurate and untrue as to be virtually worthless. For example, Horn, who has an excellent memory for some things, unaccountably confused Crook's and Miles's campaigns, lending weight to the theory that he did not write the "autobiography" bearing his name.

beyond description," south of the Haros River, he located the Chiricahuas on January 9, 1886.[32]

"Captain Crawford now decided to continue our march and attack the hostile camp at daylight the next morning. A hard day's march had already been made, but there was a chance we might be discovered and our present opportunity lost. The scouts requested the officers to take off their shoes and put on moccasins—this to avoid all noise if possible," reported First Lieutenant Marion P. Maus, commanding the scouts.

"All night the command toiled over the mountains and down into cañons so dark on this moonless night, that they seemed bottomless. However an hour before daylight, after an eighteen hour march, within a mile and a half of the hostile camp, tired and foot sore, many bruised from falling during the night's march, the four companies [of scouts] were disposed of as near by as possible, so as to attack the camp on all sides at the same time."[33]

The attack was made and, although most of the hostiles escaped, their herd and camp outfit were taken. The enemy realized that their sanctuary had been at last penetrated, and they sent in a woman to deal with Crawford. A meeting was arranged for the next day. The long, bitter, bloody, and infinitely tedious campaign seemed about over. But an ominous cloud had arisen on the horizon, unknown to Crawford. Governor Torres of Sonora had complained to Crook by letter that depredations were being committed against Mexican nationals by Apache scouts of Crawford's command. Crook had replied: "You cannot regret more than I do that any trouble, great or small, should arise between our military forces and the Mexican people. I have sent copies of your communication to Capt. Crawford by courier and directed him to make a thorough investigation and

[32] The following is based on Appendices I, K, and L and additions A through P to Appendix L to Crook's *Annual Report* for 1886, courtesy of the Hayes Collection. Appendices I, K, and L are each lengthy descriptions by Maus of the events that transpired, including the fatal wounding of Captain Crawford; additions A through P are documents, including statements by Horn and others, who were eyewitnesses to the shooting and subsequent events.

[33] Crook's *Annual Report*, Maus to Roberts, Appendix I, April 8, 1886.

report.... I further beg leave to assure you that if the outrages complained of are shown to have been committed by Apache scouts, the severest punishment shall be inflicted on the guilty parties."[34]

Crawford never received the dispatches. It seems possible that the tragedy which befell the brave captain may have been due to the alleged depredations and a resultant attitude by at least one Mexican command that the scouts were hostile and as much to be fought as Geronimo's party. That Mexican command also was stalking the Chiricahuas and included some Tarahumari scouts, bitter enemies of the Apaches. Among them was said to be Mauricio, proud bearer of the fancily nickel-plated rifle presented him by the state of Chihuahua for having slain Victorio more than five years earlier.

On this misty morning they approached the American camp, Crawford's Apaches mistaking them for Wirt Davis' scouts coming in from Chihuahua. Abruptly "the camp was alarmed ... by a shower of bullets." Maus, Crawford, and Tom Horn ran out to halt the shooting. "Although we tried in every way by waving handkerchiefs and calling out in Spanish who we were, they continued a sharp fire for about fifteen minutes, then it seemed we had made them understand that we were American soldiers and friends," wrote Maus:

> A party of them then approached and Captain Crawford and I went out about fifty yards from our position in the open and talked to them. ... I told them in Spanish we were American soldiers, called attention to our dress and said we would not fire.... Captain Crawford then ordered me to go back and ensure no more firing. I started back, when again a volley was fired.... When I turned again I saw the Captain lying on the rocks with a wound in his head, and some of his brains upon the rocks. This had all occurred in two minutes. He was said to be waving his handkerchief when shot. Mr. Horn was also wounded at the same time in the left arm.... *There can be no mistake; these men knew they were firing at American soldiers at this time.* I took command ...[35]

[34] Crook to Torres, January 11, 1886.—Hayes Collection.

[35] Crook's *Annual Report*, Appendix K, January 21, 1886. Daly, "Geronimo," *Journal U.S. Cavalry Association*, Vol. XIX, No. 69 (July, 1908), 89–90, suspects Dutchy fired the fatal bullet, but he has little eyewitness support.

The scouts fired back at the Mexicans. The Americans lost Captain Crawford, mortally wounded, and four men, including Horn, less seriously hit; the Mexicans lost about four killed and five wounded. Crawford died seven days and four hours later, remaining unconscious until he died.[36]

Negotiations opened with the Mexicans, who next day lured Maus to their camp and threatened him if he did not give them mules for their wounded, which he did. The next morning, to ease tension, Maus moved camp four miles where two women came in, said they wanted to talk, and a council was arranged. As a result, Maus took prisoner Nana and another warrior and some others, including the families of Geronimo and Nachez.[37] The others, including twenty-two warriors, agreed to come along shortly. Maus headed north. As he approached the border, Crook hastily sought assurances that no civil authorities would seek to arrest Nana, for to do so might stampede the lot back into the mountains and forestall the proposed meeting. The attorney general reassured him. On February 10 Crook received word from Maus that he was within five miles of San Bernardino and was confident that "all the hostiles intend to come in." Troops at one point fired on a small band of Indians heading north, but the latter evidenced their good faith by not shooting back.[38] Yet it was mid-March before all the Indians arrived at the rendezvous. They had insisted that Crook meet them without soldiers, and he advised the AAG, Division of the Pacific, that "I will have to play a heavy bluff game" with them, although he had five companies of infantry within call. The exasperating delay, Crook thought, was because "during the operations of last year the renegades had been

[36] The Mexican loss included Major Mauricio Corredor, First Lieutenant Juan de la Cruz, and two privates killed. For more on Crawford see Bernard C. Nalty and Truman R. Strobridge, "Captain Emmet Crawford, Commander of Apache Scouts: 1882–1886," *Arizona and the West*, Vol. VI, No. 1 (Spring, 1964), 30–40; see also *House Exec. Doc. 1*, 50th Cong., 1st Session, Serial 2532, *Papers Relating to the Foreign Relations of the United States* (June 26, 1888), p. 692; same series, *House Exec. Doc. 1*, 49th Cong., 2nd Session, Serial 2460, pp. 570–691; *Senate Report 756*, 53rd Cong., 3rd Session, Serial 3288, I, etc.

[37] Crook's *Annual Report* for 1886, Maus, Appendix I.

[38] Crook to AAG, Division of the Pacific, February 10, 1886.—Hayes Collection.

compelled to cache their plunder and broken down stock at different points widely separated, and they desire to collect this before they come in."[39]

Geronimo had named as the place of negotiations, the Canyon de los Embudos (Canyon of the Tricksters). Crook and his small party rode down that way from Fort Bowie, and crossed the line into Mexico. Tom Moore had taken a pack train out in advance; along with him had gone Alchise and Ka-ya-ten-nae, the latter released from Alcatraz at Crook's request to join the expedition. There also was a Tombstone photographer, C. S. Fly, who came with the general's permission. Contrabandista Springs were three miles across the line; the party watered there and then pushed on down the dry bed of the Rio de San Bernardino, a south-flowing tributary of the Bavispe, until opposite the Sierra de Embudos, then turned east into them by way of the canyon. A drove of wild pigs was flushed, and Ka-ya-ten-nae shot one through the head while his horse was going full speed, proving either that not all Apaches were atrocious shots, or that he was lucky that day. Horsemen guided the party to Lieutenant Maus's camp, on a low mesa overlooking a stream, plenty of good grass and wood close by. The rancheria of the hostiles was in a lava bed, atop a conical hill surrounded by steep ravines, some five hundred yards from Maus's camp and separated from it by a difficult arroyo. After Crook had lunch, Geronimo and some of the Chiricahuas warily approached.

Crook found the hostiles, "though tired of the constant hounding of the campaign, in superb physical condition, armed to the teeth, and with an abundance of ammunition." They were suspicious, independent, self-reliant, and

> . . . fierce as so many tigers—knowing what pitiless brutes they are themselves, they mistrust everyone else. We found them in camp . . . in such a position that a thousand men could not have surrounded them with any possibility of capturing them. They were able upon the approach of any enemy . . . to scatter and escape through dozens of ravines and cañons which would shelter them from pursuit until they

[39] Crook to Sheridan, March 12, 1886.—Hayes Collection.

reached the higher ranges. ... So suspicious were they that never more than from five to eight of the men came into our camp at one time, and to have attempted the arrest of those would have stampeded the others to the mountains.[40]

Bourke was assigned to record the negotiations verbatim and in due course this was published.[41] Both sides bluffed, to a degree. Crook knew he hadn't the force to annihilate the warriors and that if they fled it would take a campaign of months, perhaps years, to beat them once more into submission. Geronimo, Chihuahua, Josanie, and other Apache leaders, for their part, had the utmost respect for Crook's terse pledge that "they must decide at once upon unconditional surrender or fight it out. That in the latter event hostilities should be commenced at once and the last one of them killed if it took fifty years."[42] But Crook held more than one ace. The wisdom of his reform of Ka-ya-ten-nae now became apparent, for he sent this influential young warrior with Alchise, the son of Cochise and a staunch friend of Crook's, into the enemy camp. Before he did so he thoroughly impressed upon them their mission, made certain that they understood it perfectly and then, as was his custom, turned them loose to carry it out in their own way. They were charged with splitting the hostile camp.

Crook had no faith in swaying Geronimo toward surrender, but he thought Chihuahua and Nachez might be more amenable; he had heard rumors that the former wanted to come in. And so it proved. On the morning of the twenty-seventh Chihuahua sent word that he was sure the Chiricahuas would soon surrender, but whether they did or not, he would bring his own band into Crook's camp at noon.[43] With him came Geronimo and other influential leaders, including old Nana, whom Crook considered the brains of the hostile bands. The Apaches, other than Chihuahua, would agree only to surrender on condition they would be returned to the reservation after two

40 Crook, *Resume of Operations*, 9, 13–14.
41 This record has been printed almost textually in Davis, *Geronimo*, 200–12.
42 Crook, *Resume of Operations*, 10.
43 Bourke, *Border*, 478.

years' exile in the East. "As I had to act at once," Crook wired Sheridan, "I have to-day accepted their surrender upon [that] proposition."[44] Crook had entered into negotiations under the premise from Washington that he was authorized to secure the Indians unconditionally, with no promises made to them "unless it is necessary to secure their surrender." This, he would naturally infer, meant that if necessary, he might accept the surrender on the best terms he could get. Upon receipt of Crook's wire Sheridan hastened to the White House and conferred with President Cleveland, then dispatched a telegram to Crook advising him that "the President cannot assent to the surrender of the hostiles on the terms of their imprisonment East for two years with the understanding of their return to the reservation. He instructs you to enter again into negotiations on the terms of their unconditional surrender, only sparing their lives."[45] But it was too late.

A hard core of the Apaches had already fled once more to the mountains, leaving only Chihuahua, Nana, Josanie, and their women, to the number of seventy-five, under the white flag. Even with these it would be fatal to attempt renegotiation, besides a reflection on his honor, Crook knew. "To inform the Indians that the terms on which they surrendered are disapproved would in my judgment, not only make it impossible for me to negotiate with them but result in their scattering to the mountains, and I can't at present see any way to prevent it," he bluntly told Sheridan.[46]

The bolt of Geronimo, Nachez, and band—twenty men, thirteen women, three boys, and three girls in all—had been engineered by a white rascal named Bob Tribolett,[47] an American bootlegger and

[44] Crook, *Resume of Operations*, 10. Daly, "Geronimo," *Journal U.S. Cavalry Association*, Vol. XIX, No. 69 (July, 1908), has a version of this conference for which he is indebted to Fly's famous photograph, Bourke's transcript, and his own imagination. Most of it can be disregarded.

[45] Sheridan to Crook, March 30, 1886, *Resume of Operations*, 12.

[46] Crook, *Resume of Operations*, 14.

[47] He is called "Bob" by Thomas H. Rynning in *Gun Notches. The Life Story of a Cowboy-Soldier*, as told to Al Cohn and Joe Chisholm, 68. Daly, "Geronimo," *Journal U.S. Cavalry Association*, Vol. XIX, No. 69 (July, 1908), calls him "Charles." McClintock, *Arizona*, I, 255, says he was a Swiss who, years later, owned

rancher who, among other shadowy occupations, operated a mescal or whiskey dispensary about four hundred yards south of the line. Crook, after negotiating the surrender of the Chiricahuas, had left for Bowie, leaving Maus to escort the prisoners to the post. But en route they were met by Tribolett, or they encountered him, and soon he was doing the best business of his worthless life, selling liquor to Chiricahuas and scouts alike. Frank Leslie told Bourke he had seen "Tribolett sell thirty dollars' worth of mescall in less than one hour—all to Chiricahuas—and upon being remonstrated with, the wretch boasted that he could have sold one hundred dollars' worth that day at ten dollars a gallon in silver."[48] When they were drunk, Tribolett and his men sought to poison the Apaches' minds, telling them that certain death awaited them once they crossed the line. That night, the twenty-ninth of March, in a drizzling rain, Geronimo's reduced band stole away again.

Tribolett remains pretty much a man of mystery, but it seems probable that he was more than a mere dispenser of vile and expensive liquor to an occasional Indian. Nor is it likely to have been an accident that he pitched his camp so near the springs called Contrabandista. It would seem unlikely that such a man, with several followers, would at the risk of their lives bring only "three five-gallon demijohns of whiskey"[49] to within reach of the hostiles for the thirty dollars in sales that Bourke reports. It is more likely that he was well acquainted with the hostiles and that he was a man on a mission. If this is true, he was most likely motivated by the infamous "Tucson Ring" of contractors and others who counted on large profits from dealings with Army camps or in other ways benefited from a continuation of

a ranch two miles north of Fronteras, was arrested for planning a stage holdup; he and his three accomplices, two of whom had confessed, were started under guard for Arispe, to stand trial, but were shot "while trying to escape," as the phrase went. "There's no way of dealing with Tribolett," Crook told Lummis. "He has been tried before, but bought his way out. . . . Why, that man has a beef contract for our Army!"—Lummis, *General Crook*, 16. See Bancroft, *Arizona and New Mexico*, 459, for earlier Apache dealings with disreputable whites.

[48] Bourke, *Border*, 480–81.
[49] McClintock, *Arizona*, I, 254.

hostilities. It would seem not improbable that Tribolett was hired by some such elements to undertake the delicate and perilous mission of intercepting the hostiles and at any cost preventing them from reaching the United States, or arriving at a peace with the whites. Tribolett may well have been one of those mysterious figures of the border who dealt with the hostiles, kept them supplied with arms, ammunition, and bright-colored clothing, bought from them the stock they had stolen in Mexico and pointed them toward likely bunches of livestock in the United States which might bring a good price below the line. Crook called him a "designing man," as no doubt he was.[50]

McClintock records that Crook, in a Fort Bowie interview, confessed:

> This whole Apache business is full of complications that defy the best-directed efforts to surmount. I have had secret service men in Mexico who made special reports of the fact that the Mexicans traded with the Apaches at Casas Grandes and Nacori. . . . They steal stock from this side and sell it in Mexico; they do the same on this side, vice versa. This is the trade that built up Nacori. In two years that the Indians were on the reservation this town was nearly deserted, while now it is booming. When the Mexicans were remonstrated with, they said it was their own country and they would do as they pleased.[51]

It is on record that Crook received detailed reports on such matters from his spies in Mexican towns, and that he was well informed.[52]

General Crook wired the grim news to Sheridan, adding that Maus was in pursuit with eight scouts and about a week's rations, though two of the hostiles who had fled, on sobering up, surrendered and doubted that the lieutenant could catch the fleeing band. Maus abandoned the pursuit.

Sheridan was furious. He curtly wired Crook that the dispatch "has occasioned great disappointment. It seems strange that Geroni-

---

[50] Crook, *Resume of Operations*, 11.

[51] McClintock, *Arizona*, I, 255.

[52] Crook to Pope, November 19, 1885; Crook letters in the University of Oregon Library Collection.

mo and party could have escaped without knowledge of the scouts."[53] Usually taciturn, Crook resented the tone of the message and replied: "There can be no question that the scouts were thoroughly loyal and would have prevented the hostiles leaving had it been possible."[54] Later the same day he answered at greater length an earlier message from Sheridan in which Crook had been directed "to take every precaution against the escape of the hostiles, which must not be allowed under any circumstances. You must make at once such disposition of your troops as will insure against further hostilities by completing destruction of the hostiles" if necessary.[55] This impossible directive seared deeply and Crook replied:

> In reply to your dispatch of March thirtieth, to enable you to clearly understand situation, it should be remembered that the hostiles had an agreement with Lieut. Maus that they were to be met by me twenty-five miles below the line, that no regular troops were to be present. While I was very averse to such an agreement, I had to abide by it. . . . They were armed to the teeth, having the most improved guns and all the ammunition they could carry. The clothing and other supplies lost in the fight with Crawford had been replaced by new blankets and shirts obtained in Mexico. Lieutenant Maus with Apache scouts was camped at the nearest point the hostiles would agree to his approaching. Even had I been disposed to betray the confidence they placed in me, it would have been simply an impossibility to get white troops to that point either by day or by night without their knowledge, and had I attempted to do this the whole band would have been stampeded back to the mountains. . . . Even after the march to Bowie began we were compelled to allow them to scatter. They would not march in a body, and had any efforts been made to keep them together they would have broken for the mountains. My only hope was to get their confidence on the march through Ka-ya-ten-nae and other confidential Indians, and finally put them on the cars; and until this was done it was impossible even to disarm them.[56]

[53] Crook, *Resume of Operations*, 12.
[54] *Ibid.*, 13.
[55] *Ibid.*, 12.
[56] *Ibid.*, 13–14.

Sheridan, after receipt of this telegram, wired Crook: "I do not see what you can now do except to concentrate your troops at the best points and give protection to the people. . . . As the offensive campaign . . . with scouts has failed, would it not be best to take up defensive and give protection to the people and business interests of Arizona and New Mexico. . . . Please send me a statement of what you contemplate for the future."[57] Again Crook patiently explained the situation to Sheridan, with little hope of making him understand, and he reluctantly offered the only solution professionally possible:

> It has been my aim throughout present operations to afford the greatest amount of protection to life and property interests and troops have been stationed accordingly. Troops cannot protect property beyond a radius of one-half mile from their camp. If offensive movements against the Indians are not resumed they may remain quietly in the mountains for an indefinite time without crossing the line, and yet their very presence there will be a constant menace and require the troops in this Department to be at all times in position to repel sudden raids; and so long as any remain out they will form a nucleus for disaffected Indians from the different agencies in Arizona and New Mexico, to join. . . . I believe that the plan upon which I have conducted operations is the one most likely to prove successful in the end. It may be, however, that I am too much wedded to my own views in this matter, and as I have spent nearly eight years of the hardest work of my life in this Department, I respectfully request that I may now be relieved from its command.[58]

Sheridan, stubbornly convinced that the soldierly way was best in fighting Apaches, promptly transferred Crook to command of the Department of the Platte, effective April 28, and named Brigadier General Nelson A. Miles to succeed him in command of the Department of Arizona.[59]

[57] *Ibid.*, 15.

[58] *Ibid.*, 15–16.

[59] Months earlier there had been rumors that Miles was to succeed Crook; see the San Francisco *Bulletin*, January 5, 1886, which observed that "the two stars of General Pope are to be given away when General Pope retires in a couple of months and Miles wants a chance to earn them." Crook made major general before Miles, however.

XXVI

Geronimo—3

GENERAL MILES was an experienced Indian campaigner, but he lacked Crook's brilliance, thorough knowledge of the Apaches, originality, and perhaps even his integrity.[1] The officer came to Arizona imbued with Sheridan's notion that the proper way to fight the Apaches was with white troops, and he labored to put this into practice. At one time he had five thousand soldiers, one-fourth of the Regular Army of that day, under his command.[2] He ran his men literally ragged in the mountains of Mexico, and had little to show for it. Eventually he was forced to return to the methods of his predecessor to accomplish his mission. And it took a long time. Crook had believed that the original surrender had been made in good faith, and that the bolt of Geronimo could have been nullified, once he had gotten over his fright. But Miles's initial methods gave no room for that.[3]

The boom of a six-pounder at Fort Bowie on April 12, 1886, marked the arrival of Miles to assume command. He came in a six-mule ambulance, shook hands with General Crook, conferred with him at length, admonished the scouts to be good Indians when they got home, and settled into the command.[4] There remained out thirty-six hostiles, of whom twenty were men, seventeen in Geronimo's band and three with Mangus, somewhere in the Sierra.

Appreciating the value of rapid communications, Miles obtained a

[1] Miles "betrayed Crook and good Apaches both and lied to the nation," according to J. Frank Dobie, introduction to Bourke's *Apache Campaign*, 15. For an admiring view of him see Virginia W. Johnson, *The Unregimented General: A Biography of Nelson A. Miles.*

[2] Gatewood, "Surrender of Geronimo," *Proceedings*, 1929.

[3] Crook, *Resume of Operations*, 11.

[4] Lummis, *General Crook*, 54–55.

signal corps detachment to erect heliograph stations, the Army counterpart to Apache smoke signals, throughout the Indian country. Thirty stations were established on peaks in Arizona, New Mexico, and Old Mexico and, it was said, a message could be flashed by the sun's rays through the dozen stations from Nacori to Fort Bowie in a single hour. "In some instances the flashes of the mirror could be read fifty miles away. This system of signals kept all the forces constantly informed as to the movement of detachments and the whereabouts of the Indians. It is said that when the Indians discovered that messages were sent on the rays of the sun they lost all hope of escape."[5]

Initially Miles stationed his infantry in the passes, at the waterholes, and to guard supply bases, with cavalry for scouting and rapid concentration at threatened points. But he soon learned, as had his predecessor, that mounted cavalry was useless in chasing Apaches who, perceiving mounted men on their trail, scurried into the mountains where horsemen could not follow. Only dismounted soldiers, supplied by pack trains, could hope to prove effective.

Geronimo and Nachez led a raid across the border into the Santa Cruz Valley on April 27. Pursuit proved fruitless. The raiders split and operated almost at will over the country, even as far north as Fort Apache, where Gatewood was stationed, and San Carlos. One small group of raiders was struck by Captain T. C. Lebo, a veteran of the Victorio campaign, in the Pinito Mountains of Sonora on May 5. He lost a man killed and another wounded.[6] Captain Hatfield encountered another band in a small range between the Santa Cruz and San Pedro rivers south of the line, capturing the enemy's horses and camp equipment. But as he was making his way out of the mountains, the Apaches laid an ambush, killed his blacksmith and cook, wounded two sergeants, recovered the ponies and some arms and ammunition with no loss. Two days later this same band, or what was thought to be it, swung close to the White Mountain Reservation where one,

[5] Los Angeles *Times*, November 6, 1887.

[6] Lebo claimed he killed two and wounded one (see *Chronological List*), but Davis, *Geronimo*, 219, denied it.

Ki-e-ta, deserted and settled with his kinsmen who had not joined the renegades. Like Peaches, this Indian was to prove of value. Two minor skirmishes remained for white troops during the Geronimo campaign. On June 6 Troop B of the Fourth Cavalry had a brush with hostiles in the Patagonia Mountains of Arizona, but with no important results. July 13 Lieutenant Robert Alexander Brown, fresh out of West Point, commanding Indian scouts, captured the ponies and camp equipage of one party of hostiles. Captain Lawton, with his infantry and dismounted cavalry, didn't arrive until the enemy was long gone.

"Being deprived of their ponies and scant camp equipage meant little to the hostiles," noted Davis. "Seven times in fifteen months this happened to them, and seven times within a week or ten days they re-equipped themselves through raids on Mexican settlements or American ranches."[7]

To succeed Crook's Indian scout columns, Miles had organized a cavalry command under Lawton and Leonard Wood. Lawton was chosen, said Lockwood, in part "because of his extraordinary strength and toughness of physique and his confident belief that the Apaches could be outmaneuvered, worn down, and subjugated by white soldiers." Wood, too, was physically outstanding and shared Lawton's and Miles's belief in the superiority of the white soldier in such warfare. In fact, "Lawton and Wood alone of the white soldiers were able to endure to the end."[8] Their command was organized with one company of infantry, a troop of thirty-five picked calvary-men, twenty Indian scouts with Tom Horn as chief of scouts,[9] a hundred pack mules, and thirty packers. Five days in the Sonora mountains finished the cavalry, and the troopers joined the infantry afoot. From April through August these officers and men operated far down in Mexico, and had very little to show for it. By then Wood was garbed in nothing "but a pair of canton flannel drawers, and an

[7] *Ibid.*, 221.

[8] Lockwood, *Apache Indians*, 296.

[9] No writing I have seen gives Horn credit for the courageous, able work he did with the Lawton column; but he had the stuff of greatness if, lamentably, he had other less admirable qualities as well.

352

old blue blouse, a pair of moccasins and a hat without a crown."
Lawton, a giant of a man, wore "a pair of over-alls, an undershirt,
and the rim of a felt hat."[10]

Miles meanwhile had heard that the renegades were talking to the
Mexicans at Fronteras about possible surrender, so on July 13 he
sent Gatewood with Ki-e-ta, the former hostile, and Martine, another
Chiricahua, into Mexico from Fort Apache, thus seeking to close out
the campaign "by a return to the methods which constituted the dis-
tinctive feature of the policy adopted and followed" by Crook.[11]
Gatewood's first problem was to find the enemy.[12] He was given
written authority to call on any officer, except those operating in
Mexico, for whatever help he might need and was warned "not to go
near the hostiles with less than twenty-five soldiers as an escort."
This, the lieutenant suspected, was impossible; he could never get
close to the enemy with that size command. In rickety physical condition that could only be aggravated by field life, with scouts whose
loyalty might be suspect, wearied by a decade of work with Apaches
that was without parallel, in short, a man with every reason to reject
this summons, Beak Gatewood never gave refusal a thought.

The tall, rangy officer organized his expedition at Fort Bowie:
George Wratten, interpreter, Frank Huston, packer, and himself,
with, later, old Tex Whaley as courier. The Bowie commanding
officer could not part with enough soldiers to make up the escort
suggested by Miles, so Gatewood, no doubt heaving a sigh of relief,
left for Cloverdale. That border post also had no men to spare, so
Gatewood slipped across the border, shortly contacting a Fourth
Cavalry unit commanded by Lieutenant James Parker, also unable
to supply a twenty-five man escort. Gatewood journeyed then to
Carretas where he remained five days,[13] awaiting news "and to re-

[10] Herman Hagedorn, *Leonard Wood: A Biography*, I, 78.

[11] Crook, *Resume of Operations*, 24.

[12] The account that follows is based largely on Gatewood, "Surrender of
Geronimo," *Proceedings* (1929), 7–19. See also "Gatewood Reports to His Wife
from Geronimo's Camp," ed. by Charles Byars, *Journal of Arizona History*, Vol.
VII, No. 2 (summer, 1966), 76–81.

[13] On the Sonora-Chihuahua line, fifty miles south of the border.

cuperate from old injuries revived by the ride from Bowie." Persuading Parker to accompany him as a temporary escort, he then plunged south, determined to contact Lawton.[14] On August 3 Gatewood arrived at Lawton's camp on the Haros River, about two hundred and fifty miles by trail south of the line. "Lawton had no information of the hostiles' whereabouts, nor any news of them within two weeks. Having no escort—which I should of course have taken from Bowie—I put myself under Lawton's orders with the distinct understanding, however, that when circumstances permitted I should be allowed to execute my mission." Parker returned north. In a handwritten narrative of this campaign,[15] Leonard Wood said that Gatewood "had applied to be taken into Capt. Lawton's command," which might give the erroneous impression that he no longer desired to operate independently, whereas he was merely fulfilling Miles's injunction that he operate nowhere without a strong escort. Lawton and Wood, whose reduced command now counted about twenty-five men, had been aimlessly, and fruitlessly, searching southward from their Haros River camp, but had found nothing. Geronimo's hostiles were at this time far to the northeast, and Mangus and his band farther south than Lawton's men had looked, but doing no damage.

Hearing of Miles's information that the hostiles were near Fronteras, "we now marched north rapidly," wrote Wood, "passing through Nacori, where Capt. Crawford had been buried." The party hastened on, using the pack-mule trail which still exists, and meeting with no undue hardship. The trip was interrupted at Bacadehuachi, on the tributary of the same name just east of Bavispe. It was Sunday, August 15, when the party arrived, and nearly all of the scouts dashed eagerly into the village in search of mescal. "Gatewood's peace commission got awfully full," Wood wryly noted in his diary. In his narrative, written later, he explained that the trip was enlivened by

[14] Parker, *The Old Army*, 174–79, claims, far from merely providing an escort on request, that he took a reluctant Gatewood southward until they encountered Lawton, who was unhappy over assuming command of both Gatewood and Gatewood's mission. This must be taken with a large measure of salt.

[15] Manuscript in the Library of Congress, as is Wood's diary, difficult to read, but very valuable. Both are drawn on here.

354

"nearly all of our scouts getting gloriously drunk and shooting at each other or anything else they saw. They were brought to time however by their 1st Sergt and a few sober indians who would wait until an indian had fired off his gun and then run in and knock him down. For a time serious trouble was expected and it was feared that the troops would have to be used to bring them in, but it ended without serious trouble."[16]

The command continued north, moving so swiftly that it caught up with Lieutenant Parker's outfit. Rain had flushed torrents down the canyons and sometimes the command had to lay over a day or two waiting for the streams to subside. Then, on August 19, it was learned that two Chiricahua women, sent from the hostile camp to Fronteras,[17] had sought to treat with authorities about a surrender. At two o'clock on the morning of the twentieth Gatewood and his Indians, with six men detailed to him by Lawton, pushed ahead of the slower-moving column. Wood implies this was done by Lawton's order, saying his commander "sent Lt. Gatewood out that night with an escort with instructions to proceed to Fronteras or thereabouts and put his indians on the trail and let them go ahead on the trail, which they agreed to do." This narrative was written after the resulting controversy over whether Lawton or Gatewood should get credit for the surrender, a wordy battle in which, it should be noted, neither of the principals took part.[18] On its highest level, the dispute reflected the difference of opinion over whether Indian scouts or Army regulars had ended the war, but among Army officers it sometimes took on personal overtones. In his diary for the twentieth, Wood merely noted, "Gatewood with 22 scouts goes ahead."

Gatewood wrote that his party marched eighty miles before stop-

[16] Wood narrative, Library of Congress.

[17] About thirty miles south of present-day Douglas, Arizona.

[18] However, Captain R. G. Carter, "Lawton's Capture of Geronimo," *Collier's Weekly*, Vol. XXIV, No. 17 (January 27, 1900), 8, says: "Lawton . . . in a letter, dated Fort Huachuca, A. T., October 31, 1886, . . . says: 'I have been hard at work all summer, and you need not believe all the lies the newspapers tell you about the campaign. I got Geronimo myself, and feel very good over the complete success of my five months' work.' "

ping just outside of Fronteras, where he learned that the women had left with three ponies laden with food and mescal after Lieutenant Wilber Elliott Wilder had talked with them and persuaded the Mexicans to release them so they could carry back a summons to surrender.

"In the meantime," wrote Gatewood, "the Prefect . . . had secretly brought about two hundred Mexican soldiers into Fronteras and was planning to entice the Apaches there, get them drunk, and then kill all the men and enslave all the women and children," but Geronimo later told Gatewood that he had no intention of surrendering to the Mexicans, merely wishing to deceive them while his women bought supplies and his band rested. The prefect, however, not knowing that, warned the Americans not to follow the women lest they upset his plans. Gatewood nodded assent, took an escort of six or eight men Wilder offered him, along with Tom Horn and Jose Maria, and started as though for Lawton's camp, but about six miles south of town "darted up a convenient arroyo and circled around toward the north, so as to strike the trail of the squaws" which they found east of Fronteras. Members of the escort dropped off from time to time to keep Lawton informed, and his command followed, though at a discreet distance.

"Slowly and cautiously, with a piece of flour sacking on a stick to the fore as a white flag, we followed the squaws the next three days," wrote Gatewood, "over rough country full of likely places for ambush. By the third day the trail was very fresh." It joined that of the main body, and entered a narrow canyon leading down to the Bavispe River, about four miles away, "a canyon so forbidding that our two Indians, who were ahead, stopped to consider the situation. Hung up on a bush just before us was a pair of faded canvas trousers, which *might* be a signal for us to go forward without fear, and again might *not*." Finally the party bulled ahead, and found the canyon harmless. Gatewood crossed the Bavispe and made camp in a canebrake which probably was about opposite the present-day community of Morelos, twenty-five miles southeast of Fronteras. He placed a sentinel on a rounded hill behind the camp and sent the two Indians to scout the trail several miles in advance, leaving his white flag high on the withered stalk of a century plant, knowing "that it took more than any flag to make us bullet proof." All this time Geronimo had them clearly in his vision, and he examined the party closely through his field glasses and "wondered greatly what fool small party it was dogging his footsteps," as Gatewood later learned.

Sundown came, and with it Martine. The Chiricahua reported that the bronchos occupied a natural fortress in the Torres Mountains, four miles from Gatewood's camp. The scouts, risking their lives, had entered the stronghold and delivered General Miles's message. Geronimo had kept Ki-e-ta as hostage and sent Martine back to say he would talk only with Gatewood, and was offended because the lieutenant had not come directly to his camp himself! "Knowing Geronimo, I had my opinion of that," Gatewood observed. But Nachez, "the real chief if there was any," also sent word Gatewood's tiny group would be safe and invited the officer up right away. At this point Lawton's scouts, thirty in number, came into camp, and the captain with the rest of his command was supposed to be approaching. In the morning, on August 24, Gatewood moved ahead on the hostiles' trail, accompanied by Lawton's scouts.

Lawton, Wood, and Lieutenant Charles Clay had visited Fronteras, found the town "full of Mexican soldiers concealed in the different houses with a view of jumping the indians should they be fools enough to enter the town & talk," visited with Forsyth who had brought in a Fourth Cavalry command by a rapid march from Fort Huachuca, and worried briefly about Gatewood's Chiricahuas. This was because the two women had been overheard to remark that Geronimo's party "had no friends" among reservation Indians.[19] Wood's journal shows clearly that neither Lawton, Wood, their pack train, nor Indian scouts had the slightest idea where either the bronchos or Gatewood were. Not until a courier arrived from Gatewood did they learn of the existing situation, and its development was

[19] Wood narrative.

Gatewood's alone.[20] Before leaving for the hostile camp, Gatewood received this note hurried up by courier from Lawton:

> I have just arrived . . . and have rec'd your notes. My Pack Train got off the trail yesterday, and will not be in until in the night. I have sent Lt. [Abiel Leonard] Smith back on fresh horse to bring up your tobacco and some rations and will send them over to you as soon as they arrive. I have ordered them to come forward if it kills the mules. It will be too late for me to go over tonight, and besides I do not wish to interfere with you, but will come over if you wish me. Send a man back to conduct pack mules over, and write me what you want. I *hope* and *trust* your efforts will meet with success.[21]

About a mile from the hostile camp, some Chiricahuas appeared and urged that Lawton's scouts return to their own camp "and that any troops that might join [up] should remain there too," while Gatewood went on to meet Nachez. Holding his life in his hands, the lieutenant, accompanied the enemy to a selected council ground. Squads of hostiles came in, unsaddled, and turned their ponies out to graze. Geronimo was among the last to arrive.

"He laid his rifle down twenty feet away and came and shook hands, said he was glad to see me again, and . . . the tobacco having been passed around . . . he took a seat alongside as close as he could get, the revolver bulge under his coat touching my right thigh." The Indian said he was ready to hear what Miles had to say. The message was brief: "Surrender, and you will be sent with your families to Florida, there to await the decision of the President as to your final disposition. Accept these terms or fight it out to the bitter end." A silence fell, Gatewood remembered. "They sat there with never a movement, regarding me intently. I felt the strain. Finally, Geronimo passed a hand across his eyes, then held both hands before him making them tremble and asked me for a drink." Gatewood could

[20] Wood, Diary, for August 23, 24, 26, 27. These entries carry such remarks as, "No sign of Bronco trail." "Indian scouts said they did not know trail." "Capt. Clay & I started out early this morning [hoping] to cut Bronco trail."

[21] Davis, *Geronimo*, 228.

have shouted in relief! The Indian explained that his band had been on a three-day drunk with the mescal from Fronteras and he needed a drink to get straightened out. Fortunately Gatewood had brought no liquor, so Geronimo returned to the subject. He tried to bargain, but the officer said he had no power to enter into a discussion. During the long day Geronimo conferred first with his own people, then again with Gatewood, insisting that they be taken back to the reservation, or they would fight.

"I couldn't take him to the Reservation; I couldn't fight, neither could I run, nor yet feel comfortable," Gatewood confessed.

He explained that all their friends and relatives already had been sent to Florida,[22] and if they returned to the reservation they would have to live among their enemies. This shook them. After another private conference, Geronimo again approached Gatewood and said that while they had decided to continue the war, if they could find a beef they would have a barbecue and talk some more during the night. Fortunately a search disclosed no available steer. The Indians could not see holding a talk without meat, and Gatewood "was greatly relieved that I did not have to talk all night as well as all day."

Geronimo decided to continue the discussion. He asked searching questions about Miles, whom he had not met, "What is his age, his size, the color of his hair and eyes; is his voice harsh or agreeable; does he talk much or little, say less or more than he means? Does he look you in the eyes or not? Has he many friends? Do people believe what he says? Do officers and soldiers like him? Has he had experience with other Indians? Is he cruel or kind-hearted?" Geronimo listened intently to all Gatewood's answers, then grunted, "He must be a good man, since the Great Father sent him from Washington, and he has sent you to us." The Indians asked Gatewood to consider himself not a white man but one of them—what would he do? The lieutenant's reply: "Trust General Miles and surrender to him."

---

[22] This was almost true. The Chiricahuas under Chihuahua left April 7, 1886; on September 7 about 382 more left Fort Apache for Holbrook and Florida. The others went later.

Still they were not satisfied. Gatewood at length urged them to talk it over some more and went back to his own camp, reported to Lawton, and turned in for some much-needed sleep.

Early in the morning pickets set up a shout for "Bay-chen-day-sen," the Apache equivalent of "Beak," or "long nose," their pet name for Gatewood. He hurried beyond camp and, several hundred yards distant, met Geronimo and several of his band. They all sat down under an ancient mesquite, and again the officer was forced to go through his detailed description of Miles. Geronimo considered this. At length he said that the whole band, of twenty-four men, fourteen women and children, would go and meet the general and surrender to him. Geronimo asked that his party keep their arms until the surrender, that Lawton's men escort them to keep the Mexicans away, and that Gatewood personally travel with the hostiles, which he agreed to do. "We all entered the camp where, upon explanation of the whole matter to Lawton, he approved the agreement," Gatewood wrote.

From the foregoing it is clear that Geronimo's surrender, and the end of the Apache wars in the Southwest, were brought about primarily by Lieutenant Gatewood, and that Lawton and Miles merely implemented what he had done. This is not to disparage Lawton, nor reopen the old controversy, which had better been left dormant.

The remainder of the hostiles having come in, the party started for the United States, that day, August 25, for a meeting with Miles. But a big scare came on the twenty-eighth. About one hundred and eighty Mexican soldiers, thirsting for revenge, hurried up to the camp. They were commanded by the prefect of Arispe. "We caught sight of them at a distance of several miles," wrote Wood, adding that his scouts became excited, hurriedly swung on extra cartridge belts and "prepared for a fight. They have very little love for the Mexicans, and I suspect would not have objected to a fight. The packers also, some of them having been present in the killing of Capt. Crawford, had made preparations for a row. Geronimo kindly sent me word that he was on our side in case of a row."

Lawton ordered any officers whose horses were in to ride down and head off the Mexicans. Lieutenant Smith leaped on his mount and dashed off, and Wood flung his saddle on an animal and followed him. They found the Mexicans in a dense cane thicket. "All was confusion and they were discussing an advance," wrote Wood. "I remember telling them some big stories about the number of Scouts scattered about in the cane and the trouble likely to follow an advance." They were contemptuous of Wood's threats and very "cool" toward him, refusing to shake hands, "which may have been due to my rather peculiar appearance as at the time I was dressed in a pair of drawers, over these a gray shirt and over this a torn blouse, the whole surmounted by a wretched hat, and supported by moccasins much the worse for wear."

Most of the Mexicans camped in the canebrake, but ten or twelve went on to the American camp to see the Indians. About the time they arrived, Geronimo sauntered in with some of his men to see the Mexicans. "It was a meeting long to be remembered," wrote Wood. "The indians had decidedly the best of it, and looked upon the Mexicans with cool indifference" until Gatewood introduced Geronimo to the prefect. That individual hitched his revolver around to a handier spot, and Geronimo quickly "half-drew" his. "A most fiendish expression came over his face," wrote Gatewood, "the whites of his eyes at the same time turning red. But the Mexican put his hands behind him; Geronimo let his revolver slide back into its holster, and the danger of serious trouble was past."

A short conversation ensued between Indians and Mexicans, through various interpreters. "The deadly hatred and enmity of ages shone in the faces of both parties," Gatewood wrote. The prefect asked Geronimo why he had not surrendered at Fronteras. "Because I did not want to get murdered," retorted the Indian. Not all the Indians and Mexicans reflected mutual enmity, however. Some among the hostiles had been captives of the Mexicans in their boyhood, and one or two of the Mexicans captives of the Indians, and these gossiped freely.

From this point the mixed party moved uneventfully north along the valley of the San Bernardino toward Skeleton Canyon where the Indians were to meet General Miles. In one instance, however, trouble almost erupted. When the group arrived at Guadalupe Canyon they started to go into camp. "Suddenly four Indians, who had manifested uneasiness since their arrival, began to mount their ponies and leave camp, women and children going first," wrote Gatewood. "Then I learned that some of the [white] command had become inflamed with angry desires for vengeance for the killing of their comrades [in this canyon in 1885] and were proposing to attack the Indians." Lawton was absent, and Gatewood leaped on a mule and galloped after them. Geronimo pulled his pony to a walk, and the two men rode side by side, conversing in Gatewood's halting Apache. Geronimo asked Gatewood what he would do if the troops fired on the Indians. "I replied that I would try to stop it, but, failing that, would run away with him. Natchez, who had joined us, said, 'Better stay right with us lest some of our men believe you treacherous and kill you.' "

Old Geronimo, not trusting the white troopers, urged Gatewood to go with him direct to Bowie for a talk with Miles, but the lieutenant refused. He knew Miles wasn't there and feared that the hostiles would be fired on by some roving command. Yet the temptation to do as the Indian requested was considerable. White-trooper hatred for the Apaches was naturally extended to include a distaste for Gatewood as an "Indian lover," and this so bothered him that he asked Lawton to be transferred, now that he had completed his special mission. Lawton argued with him, finally telling him force would be used, if necessary, to keep him with the party.

The group at length reached Skeleton Canyon, but no Miles. Anxious days followed as the general delayed his arrival. Geronimo grew increasingly restless, "as uneasy as an old woman," as Wood put it, and the officers worried. Miles, it was reported, delayed his departure from Tucson so he could attend a banquet and did not arrive at Skeleton Canyon until September 3.[23]

[23] Parker, *The Old Army*, 183–86, writes that Miles at first refused to come to Skeleton Canyon, informing Lawton indirectly he was to assassinate Nachez and Geronimo. Parker says he protested, urged Lawton to demand Miles to come, which Lawton did. It would seem highly improbable for a junior officer to intercede in this manner between officers of much more rank, but Miles did appear reluctant.

One more hurdle remained. When Miles arrived, Nachez, the real chief of the hostiles, was gone. He was in the mountains, mourning a brother he feared killed in Mexico. Gatewood took interpreters and two scouts and went with Geronimo to Nachez's camp where he explained that the general had arrived and it would be disrespectful for Nachez to remain away, even to mourn. The chief came in, and the council was held, in several extended talks. The general repeated in substance the surrender terms announced by Gatewood. They were accepted, and Miles returned the following day by ambulance to Bowie, accompanied by Geronimo, Nachez, and a few others. They made it in one day while the rest of the party, coming by easy marches, took three. The night before Lawton reached Bowie, six hostiles, three men and as many women, fled back into Mexico, but the others surrendered as agreed.[24]

The problem of what the whites were to do with the Chiricahuas had long since been settled. All were to be sent east, to Fort Marion, Florida. There was some excuse for thus treating the war prisoners, for they had demonstrated their difficulty in settling down to reservation life. But it was not only the late hostiles who were to be sent east —the loyal Chiricahuas, the Army scouts, even non-Chiricahuas married to Chiricahuas, also were bundled up and shipped off. Included among them was Chatto and a party en route back from a formal tour of Washington whence they had been taken as an official delegation. Chatto wore with him into captivity a large silver medal the president had given him a few days before. Martine, Peaches, Ki-ye-ta, Dutchy, and countless others, the Indians who for thirteen dollars a month had risked their lives in loyal service to the Great Father, were sent along with the renegades, now that their services were no longer needed. Crook was outspoken in his comments on this treatment of the Apaches, particularly of the scouts, who had rendered such fine service. In his *Resume of Operations* he makes clear that termination of the Apache wars would have been impossible without their help:

24 Lockwood, *Apache Indians*, 313.

I assert that these Chiricahua scouts . . . did most excellent service, and were of more value in hunting down and compelling the surrender of the renegades, than all other troops engaged in operations against them, combined. . . . During the whole of the sixteen months [Geronimo's party was out] they did not receive an addition of a single Apache from the reservation. . . . During the entire course of the operations against them . . . the only hostiles killed or captured were in encounters with the scouts alone, except two men, one of whom was killed by a White Mountain Indian, near Fort Apache, and the other by an American near Fronteras, in Mexico, in March, 1886. During the entire campaign, from first to last, without any exception, every successful encounter with the hostiles was due exclusively to the exertions of Indian scouts, and it is the unanimous testimony of officers commanding scout companies, that the Chiricahuas were the most subordinate, energetic, untiring and, by odds, the most efficient of their command.[25]

It is true that Martine and Ki-e-ta received a bit of reward for their heroic services, but scarcely what they had expected. They told Herbert Welsh of the Indian Rights Association after they reached Fort Marion that they had been promised by Miles ten ponies apiece for their mission but, when it came time to be paid, received nothing like that. Instead they were then promised $100 apiece, but only $60 apiece was given them until "a military officer increased the amount to $100 out of his own pocket."[26]

Gatewood, in a letter to the editor of the *Army and Navy Register*, denied knowledge of such an offer, although it might have been made by Miles when he conferred with them at Fort Apache before sending them on the scout and before Gatewood had talked with them. At any rate, Gatewood said, "They were not promised ten ponies apiece, nor did they so understand it. In Mexico, days after having left General Miles, they told me that no definite pay was promised them, and they wanted to know what they would receive for their services, and if success of their mission would not increase

[25] Crook, *Resume of Operations*, 22–23.

[26] Herbert Welsh, "The Apache Prisoners in Fort Marion, St. Augustine, Florida," Indian Rights Association (1887), 9–10.

it. . . . Afterwards, at Fort Bowie, they were paid for their services and were satisfied with what was given them."[27] In 1927, after forty-one years with no recognition of their service, the two were placed on a small pension to which their enlistment entitled them.

Jason Betzinez recounts how the bulk of the Chiricahuas, having been gathered for a "routine count" at Fort Apache, were bluntly told they had become prisoners of war, were disarmed and shipped east.[28] On September 8 Geronimo and his party, including Martine and Ki-e-ta, were entrained at Bowie station while a Fourth Cavalry band played *Auld Lang Syne*, and shipped east, although their transit was not without incident. "A large force of cowboys gathered at the station of Deming [New Mexico] to welcome the train bearing the Apaches, but . . . when the train stopped, from it poured a large number of soldiers, whose determined attitude prevented a lynching party of the largest sort, one that had been carefully arranged."[29] The danger passed, the captives were moved on to San Antonio where they were held under close guard while a blizzard of telegrams between Sheridan, Miles, and other ranking officers sought to determine by whose orders the hostiles were being taken to Florida, and under what commitments, if any.[30]

Only one or two hostile parties remained in Mexico. Lieutenant

[27] In this letter is a curious passage where Gatewood assails the scouts in these words: "It is true that some of them [referring to Indians taken from Fort Apache to Fort Marion] have been in the service as scouts . . . there can be no doubt that much of the ammunition issued to them went into the belts of the hostiles. As far as my observation went in the earlier part of the campaign, Chatto and the other Chiricahua scouts could scarcely be considered faithful; they hindered rather than aided the operations of the troops. Before their removal was started from Fort Apache . . . they were plotting a more serious outbreak." This passage cannot be ignored, but, if written by Gatewood, is inexplicable, contrary to what was written by others almost equally qualified to judge. It is impossible to reconcile it with Gatewood's own narrative of the capture of Geronimo. Various explanations suggest themselves.

[28] Betzinez, *Geronimo*, 141.

[29] McClintock, *Arizona*, I, 264.

[30] For a summary of this correspondence, see Lockwood, *Apache Indians*, 306–13. Various official documents may also be consulted, among them *Senate Executive Document 117*, parts i and ii, 49th Congress, 2nd session.

C. B. Johnson was sent to hunt Mangus down, but failed to find a trace of him. Then, about the eighth or ninth of October, a rider galloped up to Britton Davis on the Corralitos Ranch he now was managing in Chihuahua, reporting he had been shot at by Indians who had driven off the ranch herd of fifty-three work mules and a bell mare. Davis, his foreman, and seven vaqueros tracked the Indians until he was sure they would cross the line, and then sent a telegram to Miles who dispatched Captain Charles L. Cooper of the Tenth Cavalry with twenty enlisted men and two scouts from Fort Apache to intercept them. Cooper cut off the enemy in an open flat near the Black Mountains. Mangus and his party surrendered without resistance and thus, as Davis points out, to Cooper goes credit for "the only actual *capture* of armed Indian *men* during the entire campaign."[31] Davis got fifty-one of his mules back. Mangus and his band of three men, three women, two half-grown boys, and four children, were sent to Fort Marion to join their fellow tribesmen.

And so, in a quiet surrender without a shot being fired, ended the most extensive (in numbers of white soldiers employed) campaign in the history of the border, and so ended the formal Indian wars in the Southwest. From 1866 until 1886 they had cost, according to the *Chronological List*, the lives of one hundred thirty-seven soldiers and twelve officers, but that list is far from complete. Many men, mortally shot, were carried as wounded alone, as, for example, Captain Crawford, who lived seven days after being shot in the brain, and two men of the Hembrillo Canyon fight, and numerous others. The tabulation itself is incomplete, many actions not appearing in it. Thus, it appears, the total casualties of the battles of Apacheria would top those of Custer's fight on the Little Big Horn, although admittedly they occurred over a much longer space of time. But when civilian casualties, including Mexican, are added, it will be seen that the fight for Apacheria was the most costly, in human lives, of any in the history of America.

There were many reasons for this, and here is not the place to go into them. Nor is it the purpose of this book to argue the morality of

[31] Davis, *Geronimo*, 232.

the conquest, and its rights and wrongs. That would take more specialized knowledge in a variety of fields than I have. But, morality aside, and it was, indeed, often cast aside, the conquest now was all but a fact. The day of the Indian fighter was about gone. Now had arrived the day of the company miner, the banker, the merchant, the teachers and housewives, and all of the others. A few bronchos would be left in the mountains of Mexico and Arizona. They would raid from time to time, and kill and steal and disappear. Troops would go after them, with the usual lack of success. But the Apache as a fighting force to be reckoned with militarily was but a memory in the ghostly peaks and endless deserts he had known so well and defended so bloodily.

Bibliography

SUCH A WEALTH of information has been published on the Indian wars in Apacheria as perhaps to be confusing to one unfamiliar with it, and who seeks basic works on the subject. Which of the many hundreds of titles are most fundamental, which less so? I do not pretend to omniscience, but have read most of the material, available and hard to come by, and therefore a word on the most important titles might be appropriate.

First, and most indispensable, of course, is Bourke's *On the Border with Crook*. Everyone should start with that. Fortunately it is again available in an economic edition. Along with it, one might read Crook's *Autobiography*, again in print. Bourke and Crook were active in Apacheria for about half of the period of its conquest, which roughly stretched from the Civil War to 1886. For the early period of the settlement of central Arizona, one should by all means read Conner's *Joseph Reddeford Walker and the Arizona Adventure*. This invaluable book should be read with some caution, not because Conner was dishonest, for he had not a false word in his vocabulary, but because he is often vague or does not adequately explain himself. The reader must do this for him. But for all of that, Conner is of fundamental importance. For the sympathetic treatment of the natives, see Lockwood's *The Apache Indians*, the only book mentioned here that is not readily available, except in public libraries. For the Apache side, as told by an Indian, see Betzinez's *I Fought With Geronimo*, superbly edited by Colonel W. S. Nye. And for a good-humored description of endlessly chasing the hostiles, read Britton Davis' *The Truth About Geronimo*, fortunately again in print; it may even be had in paperback.

None of these books covers the over-all story, except Lockwood's, almost, and for that I can only suggest my own, *Al Sieber, Chief of Scouts*, the first serious attempt to correlate the story of the conquest, and point up the relative significance of its various aspects.

There has been no really first-rate novel of this phase of the Indian wars, but one of the best is Paul I. Wellman's *Broncho Apache*, easily obtainable. It treats of incidents occurring after the conquest was completed, but is a good, picturesque tale, easily applicable to earlier years. The novels of Charles King, although too florid for modern taste, also reveal something of what soldiering was like on the Apacheria frontier. The books mentioned above should be, of course, but an introduction to a fascinating field.

Manuscript Materials, Unpublished Documents

Arizona Pioneers' Historical Society Archives, Tucson. Files of or pertaining to many Indian-war figures, including Albert F. Banta, Will C. Barnes, Mike Burns, Ed Clark, Corydon E. Cooley, William H. Corbusier, George Crook, Mickey Free, Frank C. Lockwood, Nelson A. Miles, Carlos Montezuma, Dan O'Leary, Al Sieber. George Crook, "The Apache Problem," typescript. Joseph F. Fish, "History of Arizona," unpublished manuscript.

Arizona State Department of Library and Archives, Phoenix. Newspapers, including a microfilm file of the *Arizona Silver Belt*, and some documents.

Bancroft Library, Berkeley, California. Vast newspaper file. Arizona manuscripts include brief biographical accounts of Samuel C. Miller, T. W. Boggs, Joseph R. Walker, Eben Stanley, George H. Stevens, General Oliver Otis Howard, and others figuring in Indian affairs. Loring, L. Y., "Report on Coyotero Apaches," unpublished manuscript.

Connor, Mrs. J. F., Englewood, New Jersey. Collection of Britton Davis' correspondence, including material from Thomas Cruse, George Morgan, George Converse, and other Indian fighters.

Corbusier, W. T., Long Beach, California. Many papers, including letters and other documents of Dr. William H. Corbusier, George O. Eaton, Charles King.

French, Albert Francis, Los Angeles. Documents and photographs relating to John Townsend.

Huntington Library, San Marino, California. Papers of Walter S. Schuyler, including letters from Crook. A. H. Nickerson, "Major General George Crook and the Indians," an unpublished manuscript.

Library of Congress, Washington, D.C. August V. Kautz Diary, 1875 to 1878. Leonard Wood Diary, 1886. Wood's handwritten narrative of 1886 Apache campaign into Mexico.

Los Angeles Public Library. Two books of clippings from newspapers of the 1860's through the 1880's relating to Indian affairs in Arizona.

Middleton, Leroy, Phoenix, Arizona. Recollections relating to Indian war in the Pleasant Valley area.

Phoenix Public Library. Some of James H. McClintock's papers relating to Arizona history.

New York City Public Library. Lamprey, Miss L., typewritten document, Acquisition 270128A, referring to Royal E. Whitman's late years.

Roberts, Brigadier General Charles D., Chevy Chase, Maryland. Diary for 1885, 1886.

Rutherford B. Hayes Memorial Library, Fremont, Ohio. Collection of hundreds of Crook documents, including *Annual Reports*, official correspondence, and other papers covering his Arizona service 1871–76 and 1882–86.

Sharlot Hall Historical Museum, Prescott, Arizona. Collections of documents and clippings, relating to Dan O'Leary, Al Sieber, Charley Spencer, and many other central Arizona pioneers.

Southwest Museum Library, Los Angeles. Munk Collection of Arizoniana, including more than one thousand articles, books, pamphlets, and other documents.

United States Government. National Archives and Records Service, Civil War Branch: *Apache Troubles*, 1879–1883, Document File 4327–1881, Record Group 94; Fort Mohave, A. T., Records of

U.S. Army commands, letters sent, vols. 4–6, 1859–67, Record Group 98; Selected Documents relating to activities of the Ninth and Tenth Cavalry in *Campaign Against Victorio, 1879–1880*, AGO, Letters Received 6058–1879, Record Group 94; Quartermaster Payrolls, Department of Arizona, 1872–86; Department of Arizona, Letterbooks, 1868–86; Department of Interior, Bureau of Indian Affairs, Arizona Superintendency, 1868–80, Record Group 75; *House Report 1084*, 1914, "Indian War History of the Army During the Years 1865–1886, compiled from War Department Records"; *House Exec. Doc. 1*, 49th Congress, "Report of the Secretary of War on Geronimo Campaign"; *House Exec. Doc. 1*, 49th Congress, 2nd Sess., Serial 2460, "Papers Relating to the Foreign Relations of the United States (Mexico)," pp. 570–691, concerning Crawford affair; *House Exec. Doc. 1*, 50th Congress, 1st Sess., serial 2532, "Papers Relating to Foreign Relations," p. 692; *Senate Report 756*, 53rd Congress, 3rd Sess., serial 3288, Crawford affair; *Senate Exec. Doc. 88*, "Letter from Secretary of War Transmitting Correspondence Regarding Apache Indians," 51st Congress, 1st Sess.; *Senate Exec. Doc. 117*, Parts I and II, 49th Congress, 2nd Sess.

University of New Mexico Library, Albuquerque, New Mexico. John G. Bourke, Diary, microfilmed from original at United States Military Academy Library, West Point, New York.

University of Oregon Library, Eugene. Collection of Crook letters and related documents, including Maus reports on shooting of Crawford.

Woody, Mrs. Clara T., Miami, Arizona. Documents on central Arizona history, particularly relating to King S. Woolsey and Pleasant Valley war.

Government Publications

American Decorations: A List of Awards of the Congressional Medal of Honor the Distinguished-Service Medal, Awarded under Authority of the Congress of the United States: 1862–1926. Washington, Government Printing Office, 1927.

Bourke, John G. "Medicine-Men of the Apache," Bureau of American Ethnology, *Ninth Annual Report*. Washington, 1892.

Centennial of the United States Military Academy at West Point, New York, 1802–1902. 2 vols. Washington, Government Printing Office, 1904.

Chronological List of Actions, &c., with Indians, from January 1, 1866, to January, 1891. Washington, Adjutant General's Office, 1891.

Crook, George. *Resume of Operations Against Apache Indians, 1882–1886*. Washington, Government Printing Office, 1887.

Federal Census—Territory of New Mexico and Territory of Arizona. Excerpts from the Decennial Federal Census, 1860, for Arizona County in the Territory of New Mexico, the Special Territorial Census of 1864 Taken in Arizona and Decennial Federal Census, 1870, for the Territory of Arizona. Washington, Government Printing Office, 1965.

Heitman, Francis Bernard. *Historical Register and Dictionary of the United States Army, from its Organization, September 29, 1789, to March 2, 1903*. 2 vols. Washington, Government Printing Office, 1903.

Hodge, Frederick Webb. *Handbook of American Indians North of Mexico*. 2 vols. Washington, Government Printing Office, 1907.

Medal of Honor Recipients: 1863–1963, Prepared for the Subcommittee on Veterans' Affairs of the Committee on Labor and Public Welfare, United States Senate. Washington, Government Printing Office, 1964.

Mooney, James. "The Ghost-Dance Religion," Bureau of American Ethnology, *Fourteenth Annual Report*. Washington, 1896.

Orton, Brigadier General Richard H. *Records of California Men in the War of the Rebellion 1861 to 1867*. Sacramento, State Office, 1890.

Palmer, William Jackson. *Report of Surveys Across the Continent in 1867–'68*. Washington, Government Printing Office, 1869.

Record of Engagements with Hostile Indians within the Military Division of the Missouri, from 1868 to 1882, compiled from official records. Washington, Government Printing Office, 1882.

Roster of Troops, Department of Arizona, Operating Against Hostile Chiricahuas, July 14, 1885, In the Sierra Madre. No publication place or date given.

Swanton, John R. *The Indian Tribes of North America.* Washington, Government Office, 1953.

U.S. Board of Indian Commissioners. *Peace with the Apaches of New Mexico and Arizona. Report of Vincent Colyer, Member of Board—1871.* Washington, Government Printing Office, 1872.

Van Zandt, Franklin K. *Boundaries of the United States and the Several States.* Geological Survey Bulletin 1212. Washington, Government Printing Office, 1966.

NEWSPAPERS

Florence-Tucson, Arizona, *Enterprise.*
Globe-Miami, Arizona, *Arizona Silver Belt.*
Los Angeles, California, *Los Angeles Times.*
Mesilla, New Mexico, *News.*
New York, New York, *Times.*
Philadelphia, Pennsylvania, *News.*
Phoenix, Arizona, *Arizona Gazette.*
Prescott, Arizona, *Arizona Miner.*
Prescott, Arizona, *Prescott Weekly Courier.*
San Francisco, California, *Daily Alta California.*
San Francisco, California, *Bulletin.*
San Francisco, California, *Call.*
Silver City, New Mexico, *Enterprise.*
Silver City, New Mexico, *Herald.*
Silver City, New Mexico, *Southwest.*
Tombstone, Arizona, *Tombstone Prospector.*
Tucson, Arizona, *Arizona Citizen.*
Tucson, Arizona, *Arizona Star.*

PRIMARY SOURCES

Banta, Albert Franklin. *Albert Franklin Banta: Arizona Pioneer.* Ed.

by Frank D. Reeve. Albuquerque, New Mexico, Historical Society of New Mexico, 1953.

Bartlett, John Russell. *Personal Narrative of Explorations and Incidents in Texas, New Mexico, California, Sonora, and Chihuahua, connected with the United States and Mexican Boundary Commission During the Years 1850, '51, '52, and '53.* 2 vols. New York, D. Appleton & Company, 1854.

Betzinez, Jason. *I Fought With Geronimo.* Harrisburg, Pennsylvania, Stackpole Company, 1959.

Bigelow, Lieutenant John, Jr. *On the Bloody Trail of Geronimo.* Ed. by Arthur Woodward. Los Angeles, Westernlore Press, 1958.

Bourke, John G. *An Apache Campaign in the Sierra Madre.* New York, Charles Scribner's Sons, 1886. New printing, 1953.

Bourke, John G. *On the Border With Crook.* New York, Charles Scribner's Sons, 1891.

Browne, J. Ross. *A Tour Through Arizona.* Tucson, Arizona Silhouettes, 1951.

Clum, Woodworth. *Apache Agent.* Boston, Houghton, Mifflin, 1936.

Conner, Daniel Ellis. *Joseph Reddeford Walker and the Arizona Adventure.* Norman, University of Oklahoma Press, 1956.

Cook, James H. *Fifty Years on the Old Frontier.* New Haven, Yale University Press, 1923.

Cremony, John C. *Life Among the Apaches.* San Francisco, A. Roman & Company, 1868, reprinted by Arizona Silhouettes, Tucson, 1954.

Crook, George. *General George Crook: His Autobiography.* Ed. by Martin F. Schmitt. Norman, University of Oklahoma Press, 1946. New ed., 1960.

Cruse, Thomas. *Apache Days and After.* Caldwell, Idaho, The Caxton Press, 1941.

Davis, Britton. *The Truth About Geronimo.* New Haven, Yale University Press, 1929.

Forsyth, George A. *Thrilling Days in Army Life.* New York, Harper & Brothers, 1900.

Gatewood, Charles B. "The Surrender of Geronimo," *Proceedings of the Annual Meeting and Dinner of the Order of Indian Wars of the United States.* Washington, 1929.

Gillett, James B. *Six Years with the Texas Rangers.* New Haven, Yale University Press, 1925. New ed., 1963.

Horn, Tom. *Life of Tom Horn: A Vindication.* Denver, The Louthan Company, 1904. Privately printed.

Lummis, Charles F. *General Crook and the Apache Wars.* Flagstaff, The Northland Press, 1966.

Marion, John H. *Notes of Travel Through the Territory of Arizona, Being an account of the trip made by General George Stoneman and others in the autumn of 1870.* Ed. by Donald M. Powell. Tucson, University of Arizona Press, 1965.

Miles, Nelson A. *Personal Recollections.* Chicago, The Werner Company, 1897.

Parker, James. *The Old Army: Memories 1872–1918.* Philadelphia, Dorrance & Company, 1929.

Pattie, James O. *Personal Narrative of James O. Pattie.* Ed. by William H. Goetzmann, Philadelphia and New York, J. B. Lippincott, 1962.

Pumpelly, Raphael. *Across America and Asia: Notes of a Five Years' Journey Around the World and of Residence in Arizona, Japan and China.* 4th ed. New York, Leypoldt & Holt, 1870.

Sloan, Richard E. *Memories of an Arizona Judge.* Stanford, Stanford University Press, 1932.

Sparks, William. *The Apache Kid, a Bear Fight and Other True Stories of the Old West.* Los Angeles, Skelton Publishing Company, 1926.

Summerhayes, Martha. *Vanished Arizona.* Chicago, The Lakeside Press, 1939.

Tevis, James H. *Arizona in the '50's.* Albuquerque, University of New Mexico Press, 1954.

SECONDARY SOURCES

Arizona: A Guide to the Grand Canyon State. Ed. Henry G. Alsberg and Harry Hansen, revised edition. New York, Hastings House, 1966.

Bancroft, Hubert Howe. *History of Arizona and New Mexico*. San Francisco, The History Company, 1889.

Bancroft, Hubert Howe. *History of the North Mexican States and Texas*. 2 vols. San Francisco, The History Company, 1884, 1889.

Barnes, Will Croft. *Arizona Place Names*. Tucson, University of Arizona, 1935. 2nd ed., revised and enlarged by Byrd H. Granger, University of Arizona Press, 1960.

Barney, James M. *Tales of Apache Warfare*. Privately printed, 1933.

Brandes, Ray. *Frontier Military Posts of Arizona*. Globe, Dale Stuart King, Publisher, 1960.

Carter, W. H. *From Yorktown to Santiago with the Sixth Cavalry*. Baltimore, The Lord Baltimore Press, 1900.

———. *The Life of Lieutenant General Chaffee*. Chicago, University of Chicago Press, 1917.

Clarke, Dwight L. *Stephen Watts Kearny: Soldier of the West*. Norman, University of Oklahoma Press, 1961.

Cleland, Robert Glass. *This Reckless Breed of Men*. New York, Alfred A. Knopf, 1950.

Comfort, Will Levington. *Apache*. New York, E. P. Dutton & Co., 1931.

Cozzens, Samuel W. *The Marvellous Country; or, Three Years in Arizona and New Mexico, the Apaches' Home*. Boston, Lee & Shepard, 1874.

Cullum, George W. *Biographical Register of the Officers and Graduates of the U.S. Military Academy at West Point, N.Y.* 8 vols. Boston, Houghton, Mifflin and Company, 1891–1910.

Deibert, Ralph Conrad. *A History of the Third United States Cavalry*. Harrisburg, Pennsylvania, Telegraph Press, 1933.

Diccionario Porrua: Historia, Biografia y Geografia de Mexico. 2nd ed. Mexico City, Libreria Porrua, 1965.

Dictionary of American Biography. 22 vols. New York, Charles Scribner's Sons, 1958.

Dunn, J. P., Jr. *Massacres of the Mountains*. New York, Archer House, Inc., n.d.

Erwin, Allen A. *The Southwest of John Horton Slaughter: Cattleman, Sheriff*. Glendale, Arthur H. Clark Company, 1965.

Farish, Thomas Edwin. *History of Arizona*. 8 vols. San Francisco, The Filmer Brothers Electrotype Company, 1915–18.

Fireman, Bert. *Historical Markers of Arizona*. 2 vols. Phoenix, Arizona Development Board, n.d.

Forbes, Jack D. *Apache, Navaho, and Spaniard*. Norman, University of Oklahoma Press, 1960.

Frazer, Robert. *The Apaches of White Mountain Reservation*. Philadelphia, Indian Rights Association, 1885.

Glass, Major E. L. N., compiler and ed. *The History of the Tenth Cavalry: 1866–1921*. Tucson, Acme Printing Company, 1921.

Goodman, David Michael. *A Western Panorama, 1849–1875: The Travels, Writings and Influence of J. Ross Browne on the Pacific Coast, and in Texas, Nevada, Arizona and Baja California, as the first Mining Commissioner, and Minister to China*. Glendale, The Arthur H. Clark Company, 1966.

Gregg, Josiah. *Commerce of the Prairies*. Norman, University of Oklahoma Press, 1954.

Hagedorn, Herman. *Leonard Wood: a Biography*. 2 vols. New York, Harper and Company, 1931.

Haight, Theron Wilber. *Three Wisconsin Cushings*. Madison, Wisconsin, Wisconsin History Commission, 1910.

Hamilton, Patrick. *The Resources of Arizona*. San Francisco, A. L. Bancroft & Company, 1884, 3rd ed.

Henson, Pauline. *Founding a Wilderness Capital: Prescott, A. T. 1864*. Flagstaff, Northland Press, 1965.

Hinton, Richard G. *The Handbook to Arizona*. San Francisco, Payot Upham & Company, 1878, rep. Tucson, Arizona Silhouettes, 1954.

History of Arizona Territory Showing Its Resources and Advantages; With Illustrations. No author cited. San Francisco, W. W. Elliott & Co., 1884, rep., Flagstaff, Northland Press, 1964.

Hunt, Aurora. *The Army of the Pacific*. Glendale, Arthur H. Clark Company, 1951.

———. *James H. Carleton, Frontier Dragoon*. Glendale, Arthur H. Clark Company, 1958.

Jackson, Orick. *The White Conquest of Arizona*. Los Angeles, The Grafton Company, 1908.

James, Henry. *The Curse of the San Andres*. New York, Pageant Press, 1953.

Johnson, Virginia W. *The Unregimented General: A Biography of Nelson A. Miles*. Boston, Houghton Mifflin Company, 1962.

King, James T. *War Eagle: A Life of General Eugene A. Carr*. Lincoln, University of Nebraska Press, 1963.

Lockwood, Frank C. *The Apache Indians*. New York, The Macmillan Company, 1938.

———. *Arizona Characters*. Los Angeles, The Times-Mirror Press, 1928.

———. *More Arizona Characters*. Tucson, University of Arizona, 1943.

Lutrell, Estelle. *Newspapers and Periodicals of Arizona 1859–1911*. Tucson, University of Arizona, 1950.

McClintock, James H. *Arizona: Prehistoric, Aboriginal, Pioneer, Modern*. 3 vols. Chicago, S. J. Clarke Publishing Company, 1916.

Miller, Joseph. *The Arizona Story*. New York, Hastings House, 1952.

National Cyclopaedia of American Biography. 20 vols. New York, James T. White & Company, 1898–1926.

Ogle, Ralph Hedrick. *Federal Control of the Western Apaches: 1848–1886*. Albuquerque, University of New Mexico Press, 1940.

Parsons, John E. *Smith & Wesson Revolvers*. New York, William Morrow & Company, 1957.

Peplow, Edward Hadduck. *History of Arizona*. 3 vols. New York, Lewis Historical Publishing Company, 1958.

Price, George F. *Across the Continent with the Fifth Cavalry*. New York, Antiquarian Press Ltd., 1959.

Prominent Men of Mexico. Mexico City, La Patria, 1888.

Raht, Carlysle Graham. *The Romance of Davis Mountains and Big Bend Country*. El Paso, The Rahtbooks Company, 1919.

Reid, Mayne. *The Scalp Hunters: A Romance of Northern Mexico*. London, Seeley and Co., Ltd., n.d.

Remington, Frederic. *Crooked Trails*. New York, Harper & Brothers, 1899.

Rice, William B. *The Los Angeles Star 1851–1864*. Berkeley, University of California Press, 1947.

Rister, Carl Coke. *The Southwestern Frontier: 1865–1881*. Cleveland, Arthur H. Clark Company, 1928.

Rynning, Thomas H. *Gun Notches: The Life Story of a Cowboy-Soldier*. New York, Stokes, 1931.

Santee, Ross. *Apache Land*. New York, Bantam Books, 1956.

Service Record World War I and II, Hidalgo County. Lordsburg, New Mexico, 1949.

Smith, Cornelius C., Jr. *William Sanders Oury: History Maker of the Southwest*. Tucson, University of Arizona Press, 1967.

Sonnichsen, C. L. *The Mescalero Apaches*. Norman, University of Oklahoma Press, 1958.

This Is Silver City: Stories and News Items from the Silver City Enterprise, 1882–1890. 3 vols. Silver City, Privately Printed, 1964, 1964, 1965.

Thrapp, Dan L. *Al Sieber, Chief of Scouts*. Norman, University of Oklahoma Press, 1964.

Van Tramp, John C. *Prairie and Rocky Mountain Adventures, or, Life in the West*. Columbus, Ohio, Segner & Condit, 1868.

Wallace, Andrew (ed.). *Pumpelly's Arizona*. Tucson, The Palo Verde Press, 1965.

Wallace, Ernest. *Ranald S. Mackenzie on the Texas Frontier*. Lubbock, Texas, West Texas Museum Association, 1964.

Weight, Harold and Lucile. *Wm. B. Rood: Death Valley 49er, Arizona Pioneer, Apache Fighter, River Ranchero*. Twentynine Palms, California, Calico Press, 1959.

Wellman, Paul I. *Broncho Apache*. New York, The Macmillan Company, 1936.

———. *The Indian Wars of the West*. New York, Doubleday and Company, 1947.

Wells, Edmund. *Argonaut Tales*. New York, Frederick H. Hitchcock, Grafton Press, 1927.

Wharfield, H. B. *Apache Indian Scouts*. El Cajon, California, privately printed, 1964.

———. *Cooley: Army Scout, Arizona Pioneer, Wayside Host, Apache Friend*. El Cajon, California, privately printed, 1966.

Who Was Who. Chicago, The A. N. Marquis Company, 1943.

Willson, Roscoe. *Pioneer and Well Known Cattlemen of Arizona*. 2 vols. Phoenix, Valley National Bank, 1951, 1956.

Wilson, Neill C., and Taylor, Frank J. *Southern Pacific: The Roaring Story of a Fighting Railroad*. New York, McGraw-Hill Book Company, 1952.

Wyllys, Rufus Kay. *Arizona, the History of a Frontier State*. Phoenix, Hobson & Herr, 1950.

Articles and Essays

Abarr, James W. "Fort Ojo Caliente," *Desert Magazine*, Vol. XXII, No. 4 (April, 1959), pp. 19–21.

Barnes, Will Croft. "The Apaches' Last Stand in Arizona," *Arizona Historical Review*, Vol. III, No. 4 (January, 1931), 36–59.

Barney, James M. "The Townsend Expedition," *Arizona Highways*, Vol. XIII, No. 3 (March, 1937), 12 *et seq.*

Blazer, A. N. "Beginnings of an Indian War," *New Mexico*, Vol. XVI, No. 2 (February, 1938), 22 *et seq.*

Bourke, John G. "General Crook in the Indian Country," *Century*, Vol. XLI, No. 5 (March, 1891), 643–60.

Brandes, Ray. "Don Santiago Kirker, King of the Scalp Hunters," *The Smoke Signal*, no volume, No. 6 (Fall, 1962), 2–8.

Byars, Charles, ed. "Gatewood Reports to His Wife from Geronimo's Camp," *Journal of Arizona History*, Vol. VII, No. 2 (Summer, 1966), 76–81.

Carter, R. G. "Lawton's Capture of Geronimo," *Collier's Weekly*, Vol. XXIV, No. 17 (January 27, 1900), 8 *et seq.*

Clum, John P. "Apache Misrule," *New Mexico Historical Review*, Vol. V, Nos. 2, 3 (April, July, 1930).

———. "Geronimo," *NMHR*, Vol. III, Nos. 1, 2, 3 (January, April, July, 1928).

———. "Victorio," *NMHR*, Vol. IV, No. 4 (October, 1929).

Corbusier, Dr. William F. "The Apache-Yumas and Apache-Mojaves," *American Antiquarian*, Vol. VIII, No. 5 (September, 1886), 276–84.

Daly, Henry W. "The Geronimo Campaign," *Journal of the United States Cavalry Association*, Vol. XIX, No. 69 (July, 1908), 68–103.

———. "Scouts Good and Bad," *American Legion Monthly*, Vol. V, No. 2 (August, 1928), 24–25, 66–70.

Davis, Britton. "The Difficulties of Indian Warfare," *Army-Navy Journal*, October 24, 1885.

Eaton, George O. "Stopping an Apache Battle," ed. by Don Russell, *Journal of the United States Cavalry Association*, Vol. XLII, No. 178 (July–August, 1933), 12–18.

Elliott, Charles P. "The Geronimo Campaign of 1885–6," *Journal of the United States Cavalry Association*, Vol. XXI (September, 1910), pp. 212 *et seq.*

Farmer, Malcolm F. "New Mexico Camps, Posts, Stations and Forts," Santa Fe, compiled and mimeographed under direction of the Library, Museum of New Mexico, n.d.

Frank Leslie's Illustrated Newspaper, no author; June 2, 1883, "General Crook's Apache Campaign," p. 233.

Gatewood, Charles B. "Campaigning Against Victorio in 1879," *The Great Divide*, no volume, no number (April, 1894), pp. 102–104.

Hall, Sharlot M. "First Citizen of Prescott: Pauline Weaver, Trapper and Mountain Man," Sharlot Hall Historical Museum, Prescott, Arizona, n.d.

Hanna, Robert. "With Crawford in Mexico," *Arizona Historical Review*, Vol. VI, No. 2 (April, 1935), pp. 56–65.

Hastings, James R. "The Tragedy of Camp Grant in 1871," *Arizona and the West*, Vol. I, No. 2 (Summer, 1959) 146–60.

Hill, Joseph J. "New Light on Pattie and the Southwestern Fur Trade," *Southwestern Historical Quarterly*, Vol. XXVI, No. 4 (April, 1923), 243–54.

Irwin, General B. J. D. "The Apache Pass Fight," *The Infantry Journal*, Vol. XXXII, No. 4 (April, 1928), 368–75.

Johnson, Carl P. "A War Chief of the Tontos," *Overland Monthly*, Vol. XXVIII (Second Series), No. 167 (November, 1896), 528–32.

Lyon, Juana Fraser. "An Apache Branch of Clan MacIntosh," *Clan Chattan*, Vol. IV, No. 2 (January, 1961), 15–18.

———. "Archie McIntosh, the Scottish Indian Scout," *Journal of Arizona History*, Vol. VII, No. 3 (Autumn, 1966), 103–22.

McClintock, James H. "Fighting Apaches—A Narrative of the Fifth Cavalry's Deadly Conflict in the Superstition Mountains of Arizona," *Sunset*, no volume, no number (February, 1907), 340–43.

Memorial and Affidavits Showing Outrages Perpetrated by Apache Indians in the Territory of Arizona for the Years 1869–1870. San Francisco, Francis & Valentine, Printers, 1871.

Merritt, General Wesley. "Three Indian Campaigns," *Harper's Magazine*, Vol. LXXX, No. 479 (April, 1890), 720–37.

Middleton, Hattie (Mrs. G. M. Allison). Account of Indian Fight in Pleasant Valley (no title). *Frontier Times*, June, 1928, reprinted: *True West*, Vol. XI, No. 4 (March–April, 1964), 28, 48, 50.

Murphy, Nellie. "Recollections of the Walapai," *The Native American*, Vol. VIII, No. 43, (December 21, 1907).

Nalty, Bernard C., and Strobridge, Truman R. "Captain Emmet Crawford, Commander of Apache Scouts: 1882–1886," *Arizona and the West*, Vol. VI, No. 1 (Spring, 1964), 30–40.

Nickerson, A. H. "An Apache Indian Raid, and a Long-Distance Ride," *Harper's Illustrated Weekly*, Vol. XLI, No. 2116 (July 10, 1897), 693–94.

Opler, Morris E. "A Chiricahua Apache's Account of the Geronimo Campaign of 1886," *New Mexico Historical Review*, Vol. XIII, No. 4 (October, 1938).

Poston, Charles. "Building a State in Apache Land," *Overland Monthly*, Vol. XXIV, No. 141 (September, 1894).

Rope, John, told to Grenville Goodwin. "Experiences of an Indian Scout," *Arizona Historical Review*, Vol. III, Nos. 1, 2 (January, April, 1936), 31–68; 31–73.

Sacks, Benjamin H. "New Evidence on the Bascom Affair," *Arizona and the West*, Vol. IV, No. 3 (Autumn, 1962), 261–78.

Shipp, Lieutenant W. E. "Captain Crawford's Last Expedition," *Journal of the United States Cavalry Association*, Vol. XIX (October, 1905), 280 *et seq.*

Smith, Cornelius C. "The Fight at Cibicu," *Arizona Highways*, Vol. XXXII, No. 5 (May, 1956), 2–5.

Smith, Ralph A. "John Joel Glanton, Lord of the Scalp Range," *The Smoke Signal*, No. 6 (Fall, 1962), Tucson, Arizona, Westerners, 9–16.

———. "Apache Plunder Trails Southward, 1831–1840," *New Mexico Historical Review*, Vol. XXXVII, No. 1 (January, 1962), 20–42.

———. "Apache 'Ranching' Below the Gila, 1841–1845," *Arizoniana*, Vol. III, No. 4 (Winter, 1962), 1–17.

———. "The Scalp Hunter in the Borderlands 1835–1850," *Arizona and the West*, Vol. VI, No. 1 (Spring, 1964), 5–22.

———. "The Scalp Hunt in Chihuahua—1849," *New Mexico Historical Review*, Vol. XL, No. 2 (April, 1965), 116–40.

Stevens, Robert C. "The Apache Menace in Sonora 1831–1849," *Arizona and the West*, Vol. VI, No. 3 (Autumn, 1964), 212–13, 218.

Thrapp, Dan L. "Dan O'Leary, Arizona Scout," *Arizona and the West*, Vol. 7, No. 4 (Winter, 1965), 287–98.

Tyler, Barbara Ann. "Cochise, Apache War Leader," *Journal of Arizona History*, Vol. VI, No. 1 (Spring, 1965), 1–10.

Utley, Robert M. "The Bascom Affair: A Reconstruction," *Arizona and the West*, Vol. III, No. 1 (Spring, 1961), 59–68.

Welsh, Herbert. "The Apache Prisoners in Fort Marion, St. Augustine, Florida," Indian Rights Association, Philadelphia, 1887.

———. "Report of a Visit to the Navajo, Pueblo, and Hualapais Indians of New Mexico and Arizona, 1885," Indian Rights Association, Philadelphia, 1885.

Wheat, Carl I. "Trailing the Forty-Niners Through Death Valley," *Sierra Club Bulletin*, Vol. XXIV, No. 3 (June, 1939), 74–108, and Plate XXXIII, following 62.

Williamson, Dan R. "Al Sieber, Famous Scout of the Southwest," *Arizona Historical Review*, Vol. III, No. 4 (January, 1931), 60–76.

Wilson, Benjamin David. "Benjamin David Wilson's Observations on Early Days in California and New Mexico," forward and notes by Arthur Woodward, *Historical Society of Southern California Quarterly*, no volume, no number, 1934, 74–150.

Woodward, Arthur. "Side Lights on Fifty Years of Apache Warfare 1836–1886," *Arizoniana*, Vol. II, No. 3 (Fall, 1961), 3–14.

Woody, Clara T. "The Woolsey Expeditions of 1864," *Arizona and the West*, Vol. IV, No. 2 (Summer, 1962), 157–76.

Index

Adam, Emil: 121, 122, 123

Agua Fria River: 27, 28, 36, 122, 132

Aguierre (Aggera), Trinidad: carried off by Indians, 85; breast pin "identified," 93

Alamo Canyon (Sacramento Mountains): 212

Alamosa River, New Mexico: xi

Alcatraz, Calif.: 230

Alchise (Apache leader): 256 & n., 343

Alder Creek (Mazatzal Mountains): 127

Aleman's Well, New Mexico: 192, 195–97

Alexander, Andrew Jonathan: 140–41

Alma, New Mexico: 318, 323, 336, 337

Almy, Jacob: 127, 135, 164; sent to San Carlos, 147; warned by Brown, 152; help of, asked, 153; killed, 153–54

Altar Wash, Arizona: xi

Amilyos, Chihuahua: 203

Animas Mountains, Valley: 178, 246, 323

Animas River: 183

Antelope Peak, Arizona: 25

Antonio (interpreter): 17

Antonio (Pima chief): 127

Apache, Fort: 99ff., 105, 121ff., 147, 157, 160, 182, 218ff., 259, 260, 303, 305, 306, 308, 314ff., 332, 334, 335, 351, 353, 364; army-agent bickering, 166–67; attacked after Cibicu, 226–27; Apaches shipped from, 365

Apache Indians: vii, viii, 62, 63, 111, 119, 126, 131, 163, 164, 201, 231,

254, 256; warfare, weapons, viii–x; Apache-Mexican plunder trade, 8 & n.; attack Israel-Kennedy train, 64–66; skirmish with Bourke, 69; slay Cushing, 74–76; depredations, massacre, 85–90; Crook confers with, 99; slay Stewart, 115–16; summary of depredations, 117–18; scouts at Salt River Cave fight, 127–30; surrender of, 137–40; Sonora depredations alleged, 169; Victorio killed, 208–209; depredate after Cibicu, 226–27; attack Fort Apache, 226–27; character of, 234; last Arizona action with military, 255; complain of mistreatment, 258–59; confer with Crook, 261–62; surrender in Sierra Madre, 283–93; all at peace, 303; Geronimo breakout, 312–15; women commit cruelties, 320; marksmanship of, 326 & n.; scouts accused of depredations, 340–41; surrender talks, 342–45; cavalry useless against, 351

Apache-Mohaves: see Yavapais

Apache Mountains: 70

Apache Pass: 15, 16ff., 24, 98, 170; California Column fight, 20; Victorio, Geronimo, presence, 23

Apache-Yuma Indians: vii, 155, 166

Aquarius Mountains, Arizona: 37

Aravaipa Apaches: viii, 82ff., 148

Aravaipa Canyon, River: xii, 64, 67, 82ff., 89ff., 99, 335

Aravaipa Mountains, Arizona: 70, 159

Arispe, Sonora: 360

Arizona: vii, x, xi, xii, 21, 53, 62, 108,

134, 146, 163, 166, 177, 198ff., 206, 229ff., 269ff., 298, 332, 333, 349; service in, dangerous, 56; population growth, 79; Crook arrives in, 94; growing up, 211–12; Crook returns to, 256; benefits from Indian wars, 296

Arizona Rangers (Indian fighters): 36–38

Arizona Volunteers (Indian fighters): 33–36

Army: organization in Apacheria, 53–56; rivalry with civilians, 53–54; geographical difficulties, 55; desertions from, 55–56; desertions encouraged, 86; Crook readies commands, 119

Arthur, Chester A.: 229

Ash Creek, Arizona: 177, 270, 327, 335

Ash Peak, Arizona: 335

Atelueitze: 316

Athapascan: vii

Azariquelch: 335

Babcock, John B.: 161, 164; reports Chan-deisi killed, 160

Babocomari River, Arizona: 76

Baby Canyon, Arizona: 132

Bacadehuachi, Sonora: 354

Bacerac, Sonora: 284, 328

Bache, Alfred B.: 158–59

Ba-coon (To-mas): 148ff., 149n.; saves Larrabee's life, 152–53

Bad Rock Mountain, Arizona: 124

Baege, Ludwig: 225

Baker, Jim: 270

Baker, Metcalf: 41

Bancroft, Hubert Howe: 297–98

Banghart, George: 61–62; loses favorite cow, 62

Banta, Albert: 97 & n.; in Davidson's Canyon fight, 115–16; castigates soldiers, 116

Barnes, Will C.: 239

Bascom, George Nicholas: 16ff.

Basuco Mountains, Sonora: 272–73

Bavispe, Sonora: 283, 284, 330, 354

Bavispe River, Sonora: xi, 283, 285, 329, 331, 343, 356

Bayard, Fort: 184, 192, 199, 312, 319ff., 335, 337

Baylor, George W.: 208

Beale's Pass, see Sitgreaves Pass

Beale's Springs: 40, 41, 48, 56, 105, 111

Bear Spring (Mogollon Plateau): 62

Bear Springs (Whetstone Mountains): 74

Beauford, Clay: 167 & n.; with Warm Springs operation, 172–75

Beaumont, Eugene Beauharnais: 322–23

Beaver Creek, Arizona: 138

Beneactiney: 267–68, 271

Benites, William O.: 225

Benjamin, Nathaniel: 40–41

Bennett, F. T.: 179

Benson, Arizona: 325

Berger, Charles: 207–208

Besias, Antonio (scout): 125; guided Salt River expedition, 124–25

Betzinez, Jason: 262ff., 270, 283, 365; Apache version of fight, 281–82

Beyer, Charles D.: 183–84

Biddle, James: 232, 292, 322, 324, 336

Big Bug, Arizona: 36

Big Dry Wash fight: 255–56; meaning of, 255–56

Big Prairie: xi

Big Rump (Wah-poo-eta): 59ff., 254; sites named for, 59; runs off herd, 60; killed, 61

Bill Williams Mountain, Arizona: 115

Bill Williams River, Arizona: vii

Bird, Henry C.: 225

Bisbee, Arizona: 325, 333

Biscuit Peak, Arizona: xi

Bitter Springs, Arizona: 48

Black Canyon, Arizona: 28, 132

Black Hills, see Mogollon Plateau

Black, Jim: 271

Black, Joseph P. G.: 115n.; tortured and killed, 115–16
Black Range (Arizona): 48
Black Range (New Mexico): x, 182, 184, 186, 192, 193, 197, 198, 214, 315, 322, 324, 335, 366
Black River, Arizona: 99, 258
Blake, John Y. F. (Bo): 235, 247, 293–94
Bliss, Fort: 178
Blocksom, Augustus P.: 183, 184, 186
Bloody Basin, Arizona: xi, 135
Bloody Tanks, Arizona: 31
Blue River, Arizona: 99
Board of Peace Commissioners: 102
Bomus, Peter S.: 124
Bonito (Apache leader): 232, 268, 287, 292, 307, 315; kills McComas family, 270; horses stolen, 335
Bourke, John Gregory: 34, 63ff., 101, 121ff., 131, 135, 256–57, 259, 267, 274, 283ff., 300, 301, 346; evaluation of Cushing, 63; describes fight, 65–66; Indian skirmish, 69; aide to Crook, 98 & n.; records cave fight, 125–30; records capture, 131–32; describes Apache surrender, 137–40; on mission to Cochise, 145–46; comments on Juh break, 233; on Mexico expedition, 274–75; analyzes fight story, 282; accompanies Crook, 283–93; defends Crook, 296–97; records surrender conference, 344
Bowie, Fort: 15, 55, 98, 183, 190, 312, 321, 324, 325, 335, 343, 348, 351ff.; Miles takes over, 350; Gatewood expedition organized, 353
Bowman, Sam (scout): 218–20, 218n., 260, 295, 306, 314; helps capture Peaches, 272
Bradley, Luther P.: 334, 335, 336, 337
Bradshaw Mountains, Arizona: 27, 61, 132, 135, 279
Brayton, George M.: 176n.
Breckenridge, Fort, Arizona: 18

Brent, Thomas Lee: 101
Briggs (stage driver): 19
Brown, James: 115–16
Brown, Robert Alexander: 352
Brown, Sam: 85
Brown, William H.: 121, 127ff., 131, 134–35, 153, 156; leads expedition, 124–25; leads Salt River Cave fight, 127–30; summary, 144; heads Cochise mission, 145–46; sent to Apache, 147; investigates San Carlos troubles, 151–52; warns Larrabee, Almy, 152
Buchanan, Fort, Arizona: 15, 16
Bully Bueno Mill: 36
Burgess (packer): 213
Burnett, George R.: 214
Burns, James: 125ff.; at Salt River Cave fight, 127–30
Burns, Mike: capture of, 126; Indian version of Cibicu, 227–28
Burro Mountains, New Mexico: 199, 240, 270, 322, 337
Butterfield Stage Line: 15, 19
Byrne, James J.: 207

Cabell, De Rosey C.: 337
Cabeza de Vaca, Alvar Nuñez: 6
Cameron, Camp, Arizona: 55
Camp Grant Massacre: 80ff., 111; approach to Grant, 89; massacre, 89–90; number killed, 90 & n.; perfunctory trial, 92–93; re-enactment threatened, 103–104
Camps, Army: see specific name
Cañada Alamosa, New Mexico: 100, 201
Candelaria Mountains, Chihuahua: 189, 207; Apaches massacre whites, 189 & n.
Canoa, Arizona: 3
Canyon Creek, Arizona: 142
Canyon de los Embudos: 301; site of surrender talks, 343–45
Capitan Chiquito: 82ff., 147; meets

Crook, 99; meets Colyer, 104; role at San Carlos, 148ff.

Carbo, Jose Guillermo: 274, 279

Carleton, James H.: 20, 31

Carlisle, New Mexico: 338

Carr, Andrew: 117

Carr, Camillo Casatti Cadmus: 59n., 122, 123; leads Big Rump fight, 59–60

Carr, Clark: 221

Carr, Eugene A.: 183, 190, 218, 220, 250; ordered take prophet, 221; arms scouts, 221; Cibicu expedition, 221–26; death rumored, 226; charged by Willcox, 229; admonished, 229

Carretas, Sonora: 353

Carrizal, Chihuahua: 209

Carrizo Creek, Arizona: 218, 221

Carrizo Mountains, Texas: 206

Carroll, Henry: in Victorio fight, 194–97

Carson, Kit: 7, 46

Carter, William H.: 223, 224

Casas Grandes, Chihuahua: 252, 262–63, 273, 282, 339, 347; prisoners concern Crook, 305–306

Casas Grandes River, Chihuahua: xi

Castle Creek, Arizona: 61

Cedar Springs, Arizona: 233–34

Cerbat Mountains, Arizona: 48

Cerro Colorado, Arizona: xi

Cervantes, Primitivo: 33, 35

Chaffee, Adna Romanza: 322

Cha-lipun: 140, 145; surrenders, 139–40

Chan-deisi (She-shet): 155, 158, 159; threatens Larrabee, 152–53; killed, 160

Chapman, Oliver: 162

Charleston, Arizona: 267

Chatto: 166, 236, 263, 268, 273, 287, 303, 305, 306, 308, 314, 315, 332, 335, 363; raid summary, 271; comes in, 293; attacks hostiles, 328–29

Chemehuevi Indians: vii, 39

Cherry Creek, Arizona: 69

Cherum Peak, Arizona: 49

Chevlon Fork, Arizona: 255

Cheyenne, Wyoming: 324

Childs, P. R.: 267–68, 271

Chihuahua (Apache leader): 166, 236, 268, 270, 306, 307, 311, 313, 316, 317, 334, 345; surrenders, 287–88; challenges Davis, 312; bolts with Geronimo, 314–15; tries to kill Geronimo, 316; almost comes in, 316–17; attacks Guadalupe Canyon party, 325; surrenders, 344

Chihuahua (city and state): 7, 8, 9, 13, 31, 203, 208, 264, 274, 280, 282, 288, 332, 341, 366

Chile (Apache leader): 256

Chino Valley: 57, 62, 121

Chiricahua Apaches: vii, viii, 16, 168ff., 177, 181, 199, 208, 231ff., 255, 256, 259, 264, 267ff., 284ff., 297, 298, 299, 303, 304, 305, 309, 318, 341; raiding into Mexico, 144; Crawford locates, 340; attacked by, 340; appearance of, 343–44; women talk surrender, 355; order Lawton's scouts back, 358; surrender, 363; sent to Florida, 363, 365, 366

Chiricahua Mountains, Arizona: xii, 98, 245, 323, 325, 333, 339

Chivaria, Juan: 28; party kills Big Rump, 61–62

Chunz: 125 & n., 155, 156ff., 159, 164; hostility at San Carlos, 148–54; escapes attack, 158; tracked, killed, 160–61

Cibeque Creek, (Cibicu) Arizona: xi, 220ff., 229, 230, 232, 254, 278; engagement on, 221–26; Mike Burns version, 227–28; mutineers hanged, 230

Cienega, Arizona: xi, 73

Clark, Ed (scout): 114 & n., 119, 121

Clay, Charles: 357

Clendenin, D. R.: 46, 48

Cleveland, Grover: 345
Clifton, Arizona: 238, 320
Cloverdale, New Mexico: 246, 332, 353
Clower, Edward: 40
Clum, John Philip: 162n., 169, 231–32, 233, 299; arrives at San Carlos, 162; description, personality, 163; meets Eskiminzin, 163; disputes started, 164; first moves for Indians, 164–65; accepts removal policy, 165ff.; tackles Camp Apache dispute, 166–67; transfers Indians, 167; dispute with Desalin, 167–68; ordered to remove Chiricahuas, 170–71; ordered to remove Warm Springs, 172; does so, 172–75; resigns, 177; accepts "Crook-capture" theory, 300–301
Cochinay: 148ff., 156ff., 158, 159; killed, 160
Cochise: 13ff., 34, 63, 72, 98, 100, 112, 144–45, 168–69, 232, 273, 287, 344; birth and description, 14; difficulties with Bascom, 17–18; Apache Pass fight, 20; whether killed Cushing, 77; Crook's mission to, 145–46; Bourke's description of, 146; dies, 169
Cochise head: xii
Colorado River: vii, x, xi, 6, 39
Colvig, John L. (Cibicu Charley): killed by Indians, 254 & n.
Colyer, Vincent: 102, 102–103n., 107, 114, 118, 129, 141; establishes reservation, 103; tours Arizona, 103–105; meets Crook, 14; assailed, 104; approves reservations, 105; "decapitation" of, 105
Comanche Indians: 181, 199
Concepcion (interpreter): 148ff.
Concho, Fort, Texas: 197
Connell, Charles T.: 254
Connell, Francis J.: 9–10
Conner, Daniel E.: 21–22, 24–25, 279; description of Woolsey fight, 29–31; defense of, 31; describes Indian-

killing expeditions, 32–33; on white barbarity, 35
Conover, James L.: 41
Contrabandista Springs, Sonora: 343
Cook, James H.: 318–19, 338
Cook's Canyon, New Mexico: 202
Cooley, Corydon E.: 103 & n., 124
Cooney, Jim: 198, 320
Cooper, Charles L.: captures Mangus, 366
Copper Canyon, Arizona: 326
Coronado, Francisco Vásquez de: 6
Corral de Piedras, Chihuahua: 208
Corralitos Ranch, Chihuahua: 366
Costello (soldier): 69
Cox, William: 148
Coyotero Apaches: viii, 167; Crook talks with, 99
Craig, Fort: 59, 201
Crawford, Emmet: 209, 260, 267, 292, 293, 295, 298, 304, 306, 307, 308, 309, 310, 323–24, 326, 328ff., 335, 339, 348, 360, 366; on Mexican expedition, 283–93; goes ahead, 286; reports scouts action, 286; attacks camp, 287; assigned to San Carlos, 303; returned to Arizona, 321; returns from Mexico, 335; locates, attacks, hostiles, 340; mortally wounded, 341–42
Cremony, John C.: 11
Crittenden, Fort: 73, 76, 109, 115–17
Crook, George: 94, 113, 114, 118, 123, 126, 130, 131, 132, 134, 135, 137, 141, 147, 162, 164, 168, 255, 258ff., 265, 269, 271, 272, 274, 282, 301, 302, 305, 307, 314ff., 328ff., 334, 335, 338, 346, 350; Bourke's characterization of, 96; considers Apache and Mexican scouts, 97, 99, 100; brush with Apaches, 101; defends Tucsonians belligerence, 104; meets Colyer, 104; readies offensive, 106; delay forced, 107; assails Whitman court action, 108–109; angered by

Howard-Whitman association, 109; prepares offensive, 119–20; Indian Bureau disputes, 124; describes Turret Mountain fight, 136; describes offensive success, 138–39; praised by Schofield, 143; plans Cochise whipping, 144–45; mission to Cochise, 145–46; reports agent rascalities, 146–47; comments on San Carlos troubles, 151; organizes campaign against renegades, 156ff.; pays Delshay bounty twice, 161; on Cibicu, 225–26; estimates Loco losses, 248–49; reassigned to Arizona, 250; returns, 256; meets 400 Apaches, 261–62; studies Mexico operation, 267; estimates casualties, 269–70; visits Mexico, 274–75; newspapers comment on, 278; Mexican expedition, 283–93; recovers Mexican captives, 288; hailed and assailed, 295–300; attitude toward Davis-Gatewood, 303–305; seeks Casas Grandes prisoners, 305–306; sends Ka-ya-ten-nae to prison, 308–309; efforts for Dutchy, 309–10; comments on Davis message, 313n.; plans for long campaign, 321–23; makes border dispositions, 326–27; criticism against mounts, 330; describes Indian war difficulties, 331–32; confers with Sheridan, 335; defended in Tucson, 336; replies to Torres complaint, 340–41; surrender talks, 342–45; describes "ring" activities, 347; explains to Sheridan, 347–49; relieved, 349; his methods used by Miles, 353; pays tribute to scouts, 363–64

Cruse, Thomas: 202, 209–10, 217ff., 259; in San Andres fight, 196–97; in Cibicu fight, 221–26

Cuchillo Negro River, New Mexico: xi, 194, 214, 322

Cumbre, Sonora: 285

Cummings, Fort: 203 & n., 207

Curtis, John A.: 68

Cushing, Alonzo: 63

Cushing, Howard Bass: 31, 63ff., 98; bravery of, 63; description of, 66; first Arizona scout, 66–67; attacks raiders, 67; almost drowned, 68; many scouts, 69–70; roving command, 70; last scout, 72–77; killing of, 75; praised by Mowry, 77; memory of, monuments to, 78; remains moved, 78n.

Cushing, William Barker: 63

Cut-Mouth Moses: 256

Daly, George: 215

Dandy Jim (scout): 224; hanged, 230

Daniels: 326

Date Creek: 59, 61, 105, 111, 113, 121ff.

Datil Range, New Mexico: 322

Davidson's Canyon, Arizona: 115–16

Davis, Britton: 260, 274, 293, 303, 306, 307, 308n., 310, 311, 316, 318, 321, 322, 323, 324, 328–29, 330, 332; captures Peaches, 271–72; comparison with Gatewood, 303–305; escapes ambush, 308; his Apaches break-out, 312–15; wires Crook, 313; pursues hostiles, 315; comments on Indian losses, 352; Mangus steals mules of, 366

Davis, Fort: 204

Davis Mountains, Texas: 13, 181

Davis, Wirt: 244, 326, 328, 329, 330, 331, 332, 333, 335, 341; continues Mexican operation, 339

Dawson, Byron: 183–84

Day, Matthias W.: 184 & n., 328, 330, 332

Day, William L.: 132–33

Defiance, Fort: 97, 103

Dead Shot (scout): 224; hanged, 230

Deine, James: writes of Spencer fight, 44–45

Delafield, Wisconsin: 78

Delaware Indians: 10
DeLong, S. R.: 87
Delshay: 124, 125, 127, 140, 159, 160, 161 n., 254; description of, 140; history of, 140–41; misses Colyer, 141; surrenders, 142–43; fears Pimas, Maricopas, 141; causes difficulties, 155; killed twice, 161
Deming, New Mexico: 323: Geronimo lynching planned, 365
Desalin: tracks down Chunz, 160–61; kills Delshay, 161; slain, 168
Devil's Creek, New Mexico: 319
Diamond Rim: xi
Dibble, H. C.: 273
Dick (scout sergeant): 185
Disappointment Creek, Arizona: 67
Dos Cabezas Mountains, Arizona: xi, 98, 175
Doubtful Pass: 19–20, 24, 239, 248, 323 & n.; McDonald-Forsyth fights in, 242–44
Dragoon Mountains: xi, 146, 169, 170, 235, 333
Dripping Springs Mountain, Arizona: 67
Drum Barracks, California: 82, 84
Drummond, George W.: 58
Duck Creek, New Mexico: 322
Dudley, L. Edwin: 166
Duncan, Arizona: 324, 332, 335, 338–39
Dunn, J. P., Jr.: 11
Duppa, Byran P. D.: 279
Duran, Manuel (scout): 66ff.
Durango: 12–13
Dutchy (scout): 308, 310 n., 363; description of, 307; his troubles, 309–10
Dye, Joe: 29, 30

Eagle Creek, Arizona: 315, 316, 335
Eagle Mountains, Texas: 204
Eagle Springs, Texas: 204
Eames: 11

East Clear Creek, Arizona: 255
East Verde River, Arizona: 123, 132
Eighth Cavalry: desertions from, 56
Elder, Anthony, 19
El Dorado Canyon, Camp, Arizona: 55
Elias: 36
Elias, Jesús Maria: 80 ff.
Elliott, William: 154
Ellit, Lew (scout): 119, 132
El Paso, Texas: 207, 209, 332
Emanuel, A. J.: 325
Emerick, John: 268
Epizootic: 132
Eskiminzin: 80 ff., 110, 147, 156, 167; comes in, 82; refuses move to White Mountains, 82; meets Colyer, 104; pays Whitman tribute, 111; role in San Carlos troubles, 148 ff.; surrenders, 159; meets Clum, 163
Espejo, Antonio de: 6
Essick, Charles L.: 153–54
Estancia, Sonora: 328
Ewing, Thomas: 34
Extermination thesis: 32–33

Fairview, New Mexico: 337
Felmer, Joe (scout): 66 ff., 66 n., 97, 119; kills Kargé, 70; guides Salt River expedition, 124–25; at cave fight, 128–30
Fichter, Hermann: 75–76
Fiebeger, Gustav Joseph: 274, 284
Finley, Leighton: 204
Fish Creek, Arizona: 31
Fish, Joseph F.: 86 & n.
Flood (soldier): 44
Florence, Arizona: 68
Florida: 358–59, 363, 365, 366
Florida Mountains, New Mexico: 186, 323, 334
Fly, C. S. (photographer): 343
Foran, Thomas F.: 225
Ford, Rochester: spreads anti-Crook story, 298
Forsyth, George Alexander: 235, 270;

operations against Loco, 240–45; reaches Tupper camp, 247; continues into Mexico, 248–49; meets Garcia, 249

Forsyth, William Woods: 301, 329, 357

Fort Apache (White Mountain) Reservation: 111, 142–43, 169, 189, 351

Fort Rock, Arizona: 43, 56

Forts, Army: *see* specific name

Fossil Creek, Arizona: xi, 123

Fountain, Samuel Warren: chases Josanie, 336–37; ambushed, 337

Four Peaks, Mazatzal Mountains, Arizona: 126, 127

Fowler, O. B.: 22

Francisco, Warm Springs leader: 189

Fredonia, New York: 78

Free, Mickey: 15 ff., 260, 267, 286, 295, 332

French, Camp, New Mexico: 201

French, J. Hansell: 192

Fresco River, New Mexico: 200

Frink, Captain: 238

Fronteras, Sonora: 34, 353 ff.; Mexicans plan trap at, 356

Gadsden Treaty: 7

Galeana, Chihuahua: 262–63

Galerita, Francisco (Papago chief): 88 & n.

Galeyville, Arizona: 245, 339

Galiuro Mountains, Arizona: 70, 82

Gallegos, Chihuahua: 203

Gallegos, Manuel: 33 ff.

Gallup, New Mexico: 178

Garcia, Lorenzo: 251, 252–53, 265, 273, 281, 292; fights Loco, meets Forsyth, 249–50

Garvey, Thomas: 115; fights Delshay, 124

Gatchell-Curtis: train attacked, 68

Gatewood, Charles Baehr: 182 & n., 190, 247–48, 260, 267, 286, 295, 318, 332, 334, 351; chases Victorio, 184–85; describes Morrow's Mexican pursuit, 186–89; in San Andres fight, 196–97; precipitates Mescalero action, 197–98; assigned to Fort Apache, 303; comparison with Davis, 303–305; pursues hostiles, 315–18; assigned by Miles, 353; contacts Lawton, 354–55; pushes ahead, meets Geronimo, 355–59; Geronimo surrenders, 360; Gatewood achieves surrender, 360; averts new bolt, 362; talks Nachez in, 363; comments on scouts, 364–65, 365n.

General Springs: 101, 255

George (Apache leader): 232

Geronimo: 23, 166, 170, 172, 189, 199, 217, 236, 272, 273, 280, 281, 295, 299, 301, 303, 305, 306, 307, 310, 313, 314, 316, 317, 321, 324, 330, 331, 341, 342, 350, 354, 365; captured, 173–74; perhaps fled with Juh, 232–33n.; at ambush, 262–63; becomes leader, 265–66; clairvoyance of, 283; meets Crook, 288; kills Mexicans "with rocks," 289; surrenders, 289–90; comes in, 293; possibility "captured" Crook, 296–300; Davis' evaluation of, 311; bolts reservation, 314–15; kidnaps his family, 332; surrender talks, 342–45; bolts again, 345; leads new raid, 352; last skirmishes, 352; talks with Gatewood, surrenders, 358–60; faces down Mexicans, 360–61; almost bolts again, 362; sent to Florida, 365

Gibbs, Barnett: 296–97, 298

Giddings, John James, 19

Gila River: vii, viii, x, xi, 11, 12, 33, 67, 68, 82, 85, 99, 111, 123, 130, 151, 156, 199, 237 ff., 270, 292, 293, 316, 322, 335, 337, 338

Gileno Apaches: viii

Gilmore, J. C.: 205–206

Gilson (freighter): 236

Gleason (scalp hunter): 11 ff.

Globe, Arizona: 68, 230, 234, 254, 258

Globe Rangers: 255, 274
Gold: in Arizona, 24–25; effect on Indians, 24
Golden, Patrick: 57–58
Goodhue, George: 26
Goodrich, Benjamin: 273
Goodsight Mountains, Chihuahua: 187
Goodwin, Fort: 55
Goodwin, John N.: 34
Gordon, Charles G.: 247; wounded at Fort Apache, 227
Grafton, New Mexico: 323
Grand Army of the Colorado: 45ff.; dissolved, 48
Grand Canyon: x
Grand Jury of Arizona: blast against Tiffany, 257, 257–58n.
Granite Wash, Arizona: 135
Grant, Fort: 55, 64ff., 80ff., 99, 103, 105, 111, 121ff., 131ff., 144, 145, 147, 148, 151, 157ff., 163, 183, 233, 239, 274, 312, 327; Bourke's description of, 64; Indians come in, 81
Grant, Ulysses S.: 92, 102, 107
Green (soldier): 74; killed in Cushing fight, 74–76
Green, John: 103 & n.
Gregg, John Irvin: 54; Gregg-McDowell dispute, 54–55; desertions from command, 55; with Williams in ambush, 58
Greiner, John: 13
Grierson, Benjamin Henry: 204, 206; in San Andres operation, 195–97; Mescalero operation, 197–98
Grijalba Merejildo (scout): 119, 153ff.
Gross (sergeant): 192
Guadalupe Hidalgo, Treaty of: 7
Guadalupe Canyon, Arizona: 321, 322, 324, 325, 326, 329, 332, 362
Guadalupe Mountains, Texas: 64
Guamoso, Sonora: 281
Guaymas, Sonora: 274
Guilfoyle, John F.: attacked by Nana, 212–13; follows, repeatedly attacks

Nana, 213; attacks Nana in San Mateos, 214; forced to quit, 214
Guzman Mountains, Chihuahua: 187

Hagan, Jack: 184
Hall, Sharlot: 237
Hall, William Preble: 117
Halleck, Henry Wager: 53, 55
Hardscrabble Mesa, Arizona: xi
Hardy, William H.: 39, 54–55
Hardyville, Arizona: 39, 40, 43, 48; Hardyville-Prescott toll road, 54–55
Haros River, Sonora: 329, 330, 340, 354
Harrington, R.: 69
Hart, H. L.: 177
Haskell, A. S.: 189, 190
Hassayampa River, Arizona: 28, 33
Hasson, Patrick: inept fight, 41–43; successful fight, 43
Hatch, Edward: 172, 175, 178, 180, 190, 193, 199, 200, 203, 214; describes fighting Victorio, 193; Hembrillo Canyon fight, 194–97; Mescalero operation, 197–98; reluctant to help Parker, 201–202; president Carr court of inquiry, 229
Hatfield, Charles Allen Phelps: 324, 325, 329, 351
Havasupai Indians: vii
Hayes, Rutherford B.: 207
Haynes, Jack: 268
Heliograph network: 351
Hell Canyon, Arizona: xi, 57, 133
Hembrillo Canyon, New Mexico: 194–96, 366
Henely, Austin: 172
Henry, Guy V.: 100, 102
Hentig, Edmund C.: 223, 227, 230; killed at Cibicu, 224
Hermosillo, Sonora: 250, 265, 274, 280
Herring, William: 273
Hillsboro, New Mexico: 183, 320, 334, 337
Hoag, Ezra: 232, 233

Hodges, Tom: 36ff., 57–58
Hooker, Ambrose: 182, 186
Hooker, George: 133
Hooker, Henry: 234
Hooper & Co., Tucson: 251
Hopkins, J. W.: 87
Horn, Tom: 289 & n., 299, 300, 339n., 342, 352, 356; made chief of scouts, 339; wounded with Crawford, 341
Horse Shoe Canyon, New Mexico: 244–45, 339
Horse Springs, New Mexico: 336, 337
Hostiles: differences among, 316
Howard, Guy: 183
Howard, Oliver Otis: 112, 113, 118, 144–46, 147, 168; assigned to Arizona, 107 & n.; sides with Whitman, 107ff.; meets Whitman, relationship to, 109; meets Whitman's Apaches, 110–11; accomplishments, 111–12
Huachinera, Sonora: 284, 328
Huachuca, Fort: 183, 312, 321, 324, 326, 329, 357
Huachucua Mountains, Arizona: xii, 73, 325
Hualapais Mountains, Arizona: 46
Hualpai, Camp: 114, 121
Huera (Mangus' wife): 311, 331
Hughes, Samuel: 336
Hugh's Ranch, Arizona: 117
Hurle (Hurrle), George: 221, 222, 223
Huston, Frank (packer): 353
Hutton, Oscar (scout): 34

Indian Ring: possible implication in massacre, 86; part in removal policy, 165–66; implication suspected in Geronimo outbreak, 346–47
Irwin, Bernard J. D.: 18
Israel, Newton: 64ff.; wagon train destroyed, 64–66
Ives, Francis J.: 321

Jackson, David: 7

Jacobs, Ed C.: 147
James, Bill: 26n.
Janeros Apaches: 263
Janos, Chihuahua: 19, 187, 190, 252, 264, 264n., 265, 280, 292
Jay, Leroy: 36n.
Jaycox, Walapais Charley: 122
Jeffords, Thomas: 145–46, 145n., 168–70, 189, 190; nature of Chiricahua agency, 168; criticisms against, 168–69
Jim, Sergeant (scout): 200–201
"Johnny-behind-the-deuce": escapes jail, 211–12
Johnson, C. B.: 366
Johnson, James: 10ff.
Jones, Thaddeus Winfield: 205
Jones, W. T.: 186
Jornada de Muerte: 192
Josanie (Ulzana): 344, 345; great raid of, 334–39; summary, 339
Jose Maria (interpreter): 356
Joyce, M. F.: 268
Juan José Compa: 10ff.
Judson, Andrew: 41
Juh: 170, 186, 189, 190, 199, 231, 239, 254, 264, 272, 280, 281; may have killed Cushing, 77; strikes wagon train, struck by Rucker, 178–79; bolts reservation, 232; skirmishes with Willcox, 234; sends up for Loco, 235–36; successful ambush, 262–63; reasons, 263–64; band attacked, 265–66; remains in Sierra Madre, 291; death of, 291n.
Jumpoff Gulch, Arizona: xi
Junior, Elijah Stout: 148; role in San Carlos troubles, 148–50

Kargé: 70
Ka-ya-ten-nae: 290, 293, 307, 348; description of, 306; arrested, shipped to Alcatraz, 307–309; helps Crook at surrender talks, 343–45
Kearny, Stephen Watts: 13

Kemp, Charles: 7, 12
Kendall, Henry F.: 328
Kennedy, Hugh: 64ff; wagon train destroyed, 64–66
Kennon, Dr.: 184
Kershaw (bugler): 117
Ki-e-ta: 364–65; deserts raiders, 352; sent with Gatewood after Geronimo, 353; goes ahead, 357; shipped to Florida, 363
Kilmartin, John: 75–76
Kingman, Arizona: 40
Kirker, Santiago: 9n.
Kitchen, Pete: 73
Knodles, Sam: 41
Knox, Felix (gambler): 237
Kurtz (soldier): 245

Lacey, D. B.: 255
La Paz, Arizona: 25
Larrabee, Charles F.: appointed agent, 147, 148; feuds with Wilbur, 148ff.; difficulties, 149–54; meets hostiles, 150; asks military assistance, 151; asks Almy for help, 153; quits, 154
Las Palomas, New Mexico: 172
Lawton, Henry: 322, 324, 325, 352, 357, 362, 363; description of, 352–53; contacted by Gatewood, 354; follows Gatewood, 356; scouts join Gatewood, 357; in dark about Gatewood's movements, 357–58; approves Geronimo's surrender, 360
Le Beau, Alexander: 207
Lebo, Thomas Coverly: 206, 351
Lee, James: 92
Lee, J. G. C.: 92
Lee, Phillip L.: 320, 322
Lemon, J.: 56–57
Lennan, Cyrus: 28–30; death and burial of, 30
Leon, Jose de (scout): 114 & n.
Leslie, Buckskin Frank: 268 & n., 330, 331, 346
Lillie's Ranch, New Mexico: 337

Lincoln, Camp: *see* Fort Verde
Lincoln, Robert Todd: 296–97
Linton, L. M.: 36n.
Lipan Apaches: viii, 207
Little Colorado River, Arizona: x, 102
Livingstone, Edward D.: 224
Lockett, James: 334–35
Lockwood, Frank C.: 86, 233, 352
Loco: 100n., 166, 250, 254, 266 & n., 273, 288, 292, 293, 307, 309, 313, 315, 338; bolts with Victorio, 177–78; target of hostiles, 234; description of, 234–35; persuaded to flee, 235; campaign southwards, 236–50; wounded, 247; losses, 248–49; fights Garcia, 249; surrenders to Crook, 290
Long, Jack: 185; in decisive Victorio battle, 200–201
Lordsburg, New Mexico: 235, 238, 239, 240, 270, 324
Loring, Frederick W.: 105
Los Angeles, California: 11
Los Angeles County: 62
Los Huerigos, Sonora: 246
Los Pinos Mountains, Sonora: 334
Lowell, Fort: 53, 55, 70, 98, 157, 182–83
Lynx Creek, Arizona: 24, 33

McCleave, William: confirms Big Rump killing, 61
McClintock, James H.: 67, 299, 300, 347
McCloud, William (scout): 115, 119, 121
McComas, Charlie, Judge H. C., and Mrs.: 270
McCormick, Richard C.: 31
McCoy, Mason (scout): 119, 121
McDonald, David N.: 241n., 245; ambushed by Loco, 240–44; pursues Josanie, 338–39
McDonald, John: 133
MacDonald, John F.: 222, 223; kills prophet, 225

McDowell, Fort: 55, 56, 69, 100, 104, 105, 111, 122ff., 131, 135, 141, 142, 143

McDowell, Irvin: 53; Gregg dispute, 54–55

McEver's Ranch, New Mexico: 215

McGregor, Thomas: 133

McIntosh, Archie (scout): 95 & n., 97, 100, 115, 119, 121, 125, 157, 189, 190, 260, 267, 286, 295, 306; chases sheep thieves at night, 114–15; guides Salt River expedition, 124–25; on mission to Cochise, 146; warns of San Carlos trouble, 152; guides Bache expedition, 158–59

Mackenzie, Ranald S.: 245, 249, 274

McLane, Fort: 21

McLellan, Curwen B.: 190; leads Victorio fight, 194–97

McMillenville, Arizona: 254

McNary, Arizona: 100

McPherson, Camp: 55, 59

Mackay, James O.: 286, 295

Madden, Dan: 207, 322

Madden, Emery S.: 207

Maddox, T. J. C.: 321; killed, 337

Magdalena, Sonora: 15

Magruder, Sam Eckles: 238

Malpais Spring, New Mexico: 195

Maney, James: 208

Mangas Coloradas: 12ff., 18, 19, 215, 274, 311; birth and description, 12–13; activities, 13–14; Conner's description of, 21; capture and death of, 21–23

Mangus (Apache leader): 306, 311, 313, 315, 316, 324, 330, 331, 350, 354; bolts with Geronimo, 314–15; finally captured, shipped east, 366

Manning, W. C.: 124

Maricopa Indians: vii, x, 6, 24, 28ff., 31, 34, 35, 60ff., 126, 141

Marinette, Arizona: 28

Marion, John (editor): assails Colyer, 104–105

Martin, J. W.: 245

Martine (scout): 364–65; sent by Miles with Gatewood, 353; goes ahead to Geronimo, 357; shipped to Florida, 363

Martinez, Jesusa: 15–16, 16n.

Mason, Julius Wilmot: 121; avenges Wickenburg massacre, 113

Massai Point, Arizona: xii

Mauricio (Tarahumari scout): kills Victorio, 208–209; may have killed Crawford, 341

Maus, Marion P.: 300–301, 347, 348; reports Crawford incident, 340–42; fails to hold hostiles, 346

Maxey, Arizona: 258

Mazatzal Mountains, Arizona: vii, xi, 56, 125ff., 135, 140, 142

Meinhold, Charles: 105

Merrill (soldier): 56–57

Merritt, Charles W.: 180

Merritt, Wesley: 157; describes Pinal fight, 157–58

Mescal Mountains, Arizona: 125

Mescalero Apaches: viii, 181, 199, 334; fought by Cushing, 64; warriors join Nana, 212; as scouts, 322

Mescalero Reservation: 180, 181, 194, 196; disarming of Indians, 197–98

Mesilla, New Mexico: 19, 186

Mestas, Stanislaus: survives Indian attack, 237–38

Mexicans: as scouts, 97; slay drunken Apaches, 263–64; Crook's version thereof, 264n.

Mexican soldiers: 203, 208–209, 262–63; permission urged for "hot pursuit," 275; fight Apaches in Sierra Madre, 280–81; irregulars kill Crawford, 341–42; lay ambush at Fronteras, 357; threaten Geronimo surrender, 360–61

Mexico: x, xi, xii, 98, 168, 179, 181, 189, 193, 194, 195, 197, 202, 206ff., 215, 231, 234ff., 259, 265, 269, 273,

276, 283ff., 293, 304, 305–306, 310, 321, 322, 324, 326, 332, 350, 353ff., 365; Chiricahuas raid into, 144; Tucson Rangers penetrate, 251–53; Crook visits, 274–75; Crook expedition into, 283–93; Josanie regains, 339; surrender talks within, 343–45

Miami, Arizona: 31

Michler, Frank: 133, 135

Middleton children, Cliff, Della Lee: 230

Middleton, Hattie: 230

Middleton, Henry: wounded in attack, 230

Middleton, William, Ranch, Arizona: attacked by Indians, 229–30, 229–30n.

Miguel (Apache leader): 103; Crook talks with, 99

Miles, Nelson A.: 304, 352ff., 360, 362, 365, 366; named to succeed Crook, 349; summary of, 350; organizes column, 352; turns to Gatewood and scouts, 353; Gatewood relays message to Geronimo, 358; Geronimo asks about, 359–60; accepts surrender, 363; "promises" to scouts, 364

Miller, Camp: 56

Miller, Daniel H.: saves Cushing, 68; in Cushing's last fight, 76

Miller, Samuel C.: 24; biography, 24n.; murders Wauba-Yuba, 40

Miller, William: 224

Mills, Anson: 190

Mimbreno Apaches: viii, 10, 177, 199

Mimbres Mountains, New Mexico: 184

Mineral Creek, New Mexico: 198

Ming, Dan: 180 & n., 255; chases Loco, 236

Moctezuma, Sonora: 281

Mogollon Apaches: viii

Mogollon Mountains, New Mexico: x, 198, 273, 304, 321, 327, 336

Mogollon Rim (Tonto Rim), Plateau,

Arizona: x, xi, 100, 121, 123, 137, 142, 159

Mohave, Fort: 39, 46, 48, 51, 55, 62

Mohave Indians: 39

Monach, Frank (packer): 284

Monica Springs, San Mateo Mountains, New Mexico: 214

Montgomery, Robert H.: 121, 122, 123

Moody, Henry: 230

Moore, Alexander: 72; shies from fight, 98

Moore, Isaiah N.: 18

Moore, Thomas (packmaster): 101, 343

Moquis villages: 6

Morby (Sergeant): 245

Morrow, A. P.: 182, 184, 185, 190, 192, 193, 200, 202; recaptures horses, 186; follows Victorio into Mexico, 186–89, 188n.

Mose (scout): 221, 223

Mott, John: 65; account of Cushing's last fight, 72–77

Mt. Geronimo, Arizona: xii

Mowlds, Mrs.: 233

Mowry, Sylvester: praises Cushing, 77

Mud Springs, Arizona: 326

Muir, John T.: 337 & n.

Mule Mountains, Arizona: xi, 326, 333

Murphy (two soldiers): killed, 56–57

Music Mountain, Arizona: 58

Nachez: 232, 235, 236, 254, 273, 287, 290, 307, 313, 316, 342, 344, 358, 362, 363; bolts with Geronimo, 345; raids with Geronimo, 351; reassures Gatewood, 357

Nachi: 15

Nacori Chico, Sonora: 329, 347, 351, 354

Nana: 166, 209, 264, 271, 292, 300, 307, 329n., 330, 330–31n., 339, 345; with Victorio at San Andres, 196; escapes massacre, 209; great raid of, 212–16; surrenders to Crook, 290;

described by Bourke, 290; flees with Geronimo, 315; Maus captures, 342; "brains" of hostile band, 344

Nanni-Chaddi: leader of Salt River hostiles, 127–30

Nantje (scout): 127

Natanes Plateau, Arizona: xi, 69, 177

Nation, William: 117

Na-ti-o-tish: 254

Navaho Indians: vii, viii, 31, 62, 97, 126, 183, 184, 236, 334, 336, 337, 338–39

Nealy, Sam: 19

Neiss, Michael: 19

Nelson, William: 103–104

Netterville, W. McC.: 141

New Bedford, Massachusetts: 147

New Mexico: viii, x, 10, 12, 21, 53, 62, 166, 169, 170, 172ff., 177ff., 189ff., 202, 212, 231 ff., 256, 270, 304, 322, 329, 334, 349; tormented by Victorio, 186

Ne-zhar-titte (prophet): 150 & n.

Nickerson, Azor H.: 95 & n., 123; chases sheep thieves, 114–15; sends columns out, 122; describes Taylor's death, 134

Niza, Marcos de: 6

Nobles, Nat (packer): 220, 221

Noch-ay-del-klinne (prophet): 221, 228; Crook enlists as scout, 99; description of, 217; leads Apache revivals, 218; nature of them, 220; captured by Carr, 222; killed at Cibicu, 225

Nolan, Nicholas: 206

Nolgee: 170, 190; attacks train, attacked by Rucker, 178–79

Nordstrom, Charles Eben: 335

Notzin: 226

Oak Creek, Arizona: 138

Oaks and Willows, Camp: 42

Ogilby, Frederick D.: dispute with agent, 166–67

Ogle, Ralph Hedrick: 86–87, 147

Ojo Caliente: see Warm Springs

Ojo Caliente Apaches: see Warm Springs Apaches

Ojo del Pino, Chihuahua: 204

O. K. Smythe & Babcock: 238

O'Leary, Dan (scout): 42–43, 46, 114, 119, 121, 135; guides troops against Scherum, 48–51

Oñate, Juan de: 6

Oposura, Sonora: 11

Oputo, Sonora: 281, 328, 339

Oury, William S.: 19–20, 80ff., 108; biography, 87n.; describes organization and raid, 87–89; defends Crook, 336

Outlaw Mountain, Arizona: xi

Overton, G. E.: 176n.

Owens, William McK.: 57

Pack trains: Crook's concern for, 106

Paiute Indians: 39, 48, 119, 121, 126

Palomas Lake, Chihuahua: 187, 322

Palomas River, New Mexico: xi, 200

Papagoes Indians: x, 111; role in Camp Grant Massacre, 88–92

Papanosas, New Mexico: 336

Par-a-muck-a: 29

Parker, Charles: 214

Parker, H. K.: 208; guide in decisive Victorio fight, 199–201; extent of victory: 202

Parker, James: 318, 319n., 353, 355, 362n.; accompanies Gatewood, 354

Parks, George: 268

Patagonia, Patagonia Mountains, Arizona: 15, 352

Pattie, James Ohio: 6

Peaches (Tzoe): 282, 284, 285, 352; abandons raiders, 271; captured, 272; his story, 272–73; shipped to Florida, 363

Peacock Springs, Arizona: 41, 48, 51

Pedro (Apache chief): 103, 160, 226;

Crook meets at Apache, 99; rejects removal, 167
Peel, L. B.: 273
Peeples, Abraham H.: 25, 28
Peloncillo Mountains, New Mexico: 246
Pennington, James: 85
Pesqueira, I. (Sonora governor): 169
Phillips family: massacred, 320
Pierce (soldier): 74
Pierce, Francis C.: 314, 321, 324; assigned to San Carlos, 310; pigeonholes Davis message, 313
Pierson, Ed: 236
Pima County, Arizona: 251–52
Pima Indians: 6, 24, 28, 31, 35, 104, 111, 126ff., 141; fight with Big Rump, 59–60; help kill Big Rump, 61
Pinal Apaches: viii, 15, 16, 31; attack train, 64–66; punished by Cushing, 67
Pinal Creek, Arizona: 31, 68
Pinal Mountains, Arizona: vii, 67, 68, 70, 85, 98–99, 125, 157ff., 233
Pinito Mountains, Sonora: 351
Pinos Altos, New Mexico: 20
Pinto Creek, Arizona: 68, 158
Pionsenay: kills Rogers, Spence, 169–70; wounded, 170; sparks San Carlos emeute, 177
Piper, O. F.: 100
Pleasant Valley, Arizona: 229–30
Point of Mountain, Arizona: 108
Ponce (Warm Springs leader): 175, 189
Pope, John: 53, 199
Postle, Robert: 33
Poston, Charles: 295
Potrero, Arizona: 73
Prescott, Arizona: 24ff., 36, 37, 40, 41, 43, 53, 61, 62
Price, George F.: 122, 123, 132
Price, Hiram (Indian Commissioner): 274, 296–97
Price, William Redwood: 46; negotiates peace, 51–52

Pueblo Indians: 207
Pueblo Viejo, Arizona: 273, 335
Puerco River, New Mexico: 192
Puerto del Dado, Arizona: 15, 16

Quitman, Fort, Texas: 203 & n., 204ff., 207

Raccoon Creek, Arizona: 125
Rafferty, William Augustus: chases, fights, Loco, 245–47
Ramirez, Captain: 252
Randall (photographer): 301
Randall, George M.: 124, 135, 156, 157; commands fight at Turret Mountain, 135–37; captures Delshay, 140–43; leads Chunz expedition, 157–58
Rattlesnake Springs, Texas: 204–206
Red Canyon, San Mateos Mountains, New Mexico: Nana attacks whites, 213–14
Red Rock country, Arizona: 121, 122
Reed, Walter: 180
Reese, Aquila Asbury Jr.: 48
Reidt, Charles: 34
Reilly, Ben: 158–59
Removal policy: 165; possible promoters, 165–66; Indian removal from Verde, 166; from Apache, 167; some Chiricahuas removed, 170–71; folly of removal, 171; Warm Springs removed, 172–75; removals criticized, 176n.; concentration policy reaffirmed, 179; women, children, removed, 179–81
Renegades: 279–80
Reno, Camp, Arizona: 56, 57, 59, 124, 140
Reno Pass, Arizona: 56
Reservation: *see* specific name
Reventon, Arizona: 3, 4
Reyes, Bernardo: captures Ross, 252–53
Rhodes, William B.: *see* Rood
Rice, Willard (scout): 119 & n., 122

Rice, William F.: 121, 122, 135, 154; fights hostiles, 123
Rich Hill, Arizona: 25, 28
Richmond, New Mexico: 240 & n., 268
Rillito Creek, Arizona: 89
Rincon Peak, Arizona: xi
Rio Grande River: vii, x, xi, 62, 177, 192, 201, 203ff., 212, 213, 322, 327
Rip: 173–74
Rising Sun: 140
Risque, John P.: 238
Roach, George Henderson: 322
Roberts, Charlie (scout): 330, 332
Roberts, Cyrus Swan: 274, 300, 301
Roberts, Isaac: 207
Roberts, James E. (agent): dispute with military, 166–67
Robideau, Michel: 6
Robinson, William W.: 81, 83, 90; defends Whitman, 93–94
Rockwell, C. H.: 145–46
Rogers (storekeeper): 169
Rood (Rhodes), William B.: 3ff.
Roosevelt Dam, Arizona: 69
Ross, William J.: 101, 121; aide to Crook, 98 & n.; leads civilians to fight Apaches, 251–53
Royall, William B.: 129
Rucker, John Anthony (Tony): 176n.; attacks Juh, 178–79
Rucker, L. H.: defeated by Victorio, 192–93
Russell, Fort D. A.: 255
Russell, S. A. (agent): 197–98

Sacaton, Arizona: 82
Sacramento Mountains, New Mexico: 196, 212
Sacramento Valley, Arizona: 46
Safford, Arizona: 273
Safford, Anson P. K.: 92, 95, 97, 280; as Indian fighter, 70–72; comments on Cochise, 168–69
Sagotal: 236

Salt River: 28, 31, 33, 59, 69, 99, 124ff., 131, 142, 254
Salt River Cave fight: 127–30, 130n., 131; hostile casualties, 130; one hostile escapes, 130
San Andres Mountains, New Mexico: x, 192, 213; Victorio fight in, 194–97
San Angelo, Texas: 197
San Antonio, Texas: 365
San Bernardino, Arizona: 276, 301, 326, 342
San Bernardino River, Sonora: 343, 361
San Carlos Apache Reservation: 111, 147ff., 159, 160, 162ff., 169ff., 178ff., 182, 189, 198ff., 230, 231ff., 254ff., 270ff 303ff., 321ff., 351; difficulties, 147–54; hostility among Indians, whites, 176–77; conditions deplored, 257 & n.; captives arrive from Mexico, 293; law abiding, 303; stragglers arrive, 305
San Carlos Apaches: viii, 220, 270
San Carlos, Chihuahua: 203
San Carlos River, Arizona: 67, 69, 99, 151, 293
Sanchez (chief): 222, 224, 335
San Diego, California: 107
San Franciscan Mountains, New Mexico: x
San Francisco Mountains, Arizona: 62, 121
San Francisco River, Arizona: 239
San Jose, New Mexico: 213
San Lorenzo, Chihuahua: 203
San Luis Mountains, Sonora: 246, 326
San Mateo Mountains, New Mexico: 192, 213, 319
San Nicholas Springs, New Mexico: 195
San Pedro River, Arizona: 64, 67, 82, 87, 89, 152, 351
San Simon Valley, Arizona: 240, 245, 270, 320, 333
Santa Catalina Mountains, Arizona: 160
Santa Cruz, Sonora: 15, 73

Santa Cruz River, Arizona: xi, 72ff., 85, 89, 116, 351
Santa Fe, New Mexico: 8, 12, 193, 217
Santa Fe Trail: 62
Santa Maria, Chihuahua: 206
Santa Maria River, Arizona: vii
Santa Maria River, Chihuahua: xi
Santa Rita mines, New Mexico: 10
Santa Rita Mountains, Arizona: 13, 116
Santa Rosalia, Chihuahua: 209–10
Santa Teresa Mountains, Arizona: 99
Santo: 82
San Xavier, Arizona: 87, 93
Sawed-off Butte, Arizona: xi
Scalp hunting: 8ff.
Scherum: 39, 46, 48; fight with Young-Stevenson party, 48–51; negotiates peace, 51–52
Scherum's Canyon, Arizona: 49 & n.
Schofield, George W.: 237 & n.
Schofield, John M.: 107, 109, 143
Schurz, Carl: 259
Schuyler, Walter Scribner: 143, 147, 159, 160, 161; troubles with Delshay, 154–55; on handling Indians, 155
Scott, George Lawson: 338–39
Scouts: impetuousness of, 125; evaluation of, 126; effectiveness, 139; Crook credits success to, 295; more needed, 324; paid tribute by Crook, 363–64; curious comments by Gatewood, 364–65, 365n.; Paiutes, 48, 121; Navahos, 97, 126, 336–39; Lipans, 207; Pueblos, 207; Mescaleros: 334; *see also* Mexicans as scouts
Separ, New Mexico: 235, 240, 324, 326
Severiano: 226, 295
Shakespeare, New Mexico: 239 & n., 271
Sheridan, Philip: 179, 322, 338, 345, 347, 350, 365; confers with Crook, 335; objects to surrender terms, 345; furious over escape, 347–49; relieves Crook, 349

Sherman, William Tecumseh: xii, 53, 179, 275, 291; escapes Indians, 239; warns Crook, 276
Shirland, Edmond D.: 21
Sieber, Al: 97, 113n., 119, 121, 159, 166, 167, 223, 235, 248, 260, 267, 284, 295, 300, 307, 324, 328–29, 330, 332, 339; leads Walapais scouts, 113; with Schuyler against Delshay, 154–55; assails Forsyth, 245; with Rafferty-Tupper, 245–47; chief of scouts with Crook, 283–93; part in Geronimo-Crook talk, 289–90; misjudges Davis message, 313
Sierra Ancha Mountains, Arizona: 125
Sierra Aniba, Arizona: 70
Sierra Blanca Mountains, Texas: x
Sierra de Hoya, Sonora: 331
Sierra Diablo, Texas: x, xi
Sierra Enmedio, Sonora: 246–48
Sierra Madre: xi, 7, 171, 190, 235, 280–81, 283ff., 296ff., 318, 324, 328ff.
Signal Peak, Arizona: 67
Silver City, New Mexico: 10, 181, 207, 270, 318–19, 323, 332, 337; burial team out, 239
Silver Creek, Arizona: 292
Simms: killed by Indians, 85
Simpson, W. H.: civilian killed with Cushing, 74–75
Sitgreaves Pass, Arizona: 46
Skeleton Canyon, Arizona: 326; Miles meets hostiles, 362–63
Skippy (scout): 230
Skinya: 169–70
Skirmish Canyon, Arizona: 70
Slawson, John: 238
Smith, Abiel Leonard: 358, 360–61
Smith, Allen: 315, 318–19, 320, 321
Smith, G. W.: 215
Socorro, New Mexico: 207
Solomon's Springs, Arizona: 326
Solomonville, Arizona: 258, 309, **335**
Sonderegger, John: 224

Song Mountain, Arizona: 326
Sonoita River, Arizona: 15, 72ff., 116
Sonora: 7, 9, 11, 13, 31, 67, 73ff., 84,
    170, 264, 280, 352
Southard, J. B.: 273
Southern Pacific Company: 202, 235,
    239, 267
Spanish-Apache conflict: 7–8
Spear, Augustus A. (Gus): 46, 119 &
    n., 121
Spence (storekeeper): 169
Spencer, Charlie (scout): 44–45, 62
Squaretop Hill, Arizona: xi
Standwood, Frank: 85, 90
Stanton, Fort: 62, 177–78, 194 & n.,
    322
Stanton, William: 223, 224, 225
Stauffer, Rudolph: 114 & n., 133
Steins, New Mexico: 240
Steins Peak Range, New Mexico: x, 19,
    178, 235, 239ff., 270, 292, 321, 323,
    324, 333, 335, 338–39; Forsyth bat-
    tle in, 244–45
Sterling, Albert D.: 254; killed by In-
    dians, 236 & n.
Stevens, George H.: 145–46, 145n.,
    147, 167, 315; ranch attacked by
    Loco, 237–38
Stevenson, Jonathan D.: 48ff.; expedi-
    tion against Scherum, 48–51
Stewart, George: 117
Stewart, Reid T.: 115–16
Stoneman, George: 82ff., 87, 89, 102;
    rebuffs Whitman, 84; appears to free
    Tucsonians, 87; relieved, 94 & n.
Strauss, Charles M.: 295
Streeter, Zebina Nathaniel (renegade):
    279–80
Sturgeon, D. B.: 22
Sugarfoot Jack: 26, 26n., 32–33
Sugar Loaf Mountain, Arizona: 56
Sullivan, John: 224
Sulphur Springs: 98, 170, 268, 274, 333
Sulphur Springs, Texas: 206
Summary, Apacheria conquest: 366

Sumner, E. V.: 13
Sumner, S. S.: 336
Sunflower Valley, Arizona: 57, 141
Superstition Mountains, Arizona: 125ff.,
    131ff., 157; mountains cleaned, 131–
    32
SW Ranch, New Mexico: 337
Swain, Gus: 133 & n.
Sweeney, Martin: 164–65, 165n.
Swilling, Jack W.: 21; confirms Big
    Rump killing, 61
Swing Station, New Mexico: 268
Swisshelm, Arizona: 268
Sycamore Creek (Mazatzals), Arizona:
    57, 130

Tarahumari Indians: 341
Tar-gar-de-chuse: 272
Tauelclyee: 170; kills Desalin, 168
Taylor, F. B.: 215
Taylor, George W.: 133–34
Taylor, Sergeant: 70
Taylor, Alfred B.: 127, 135
Taza, son of Cochise: 15; succeeds
    father, 169; fights with Skinya, 170
Teller, Henry M.: 296–97
Temosachic, Chihuahua: 265
Tempe, Arizona: 157
Temporal Canyon, New Mexico: 182
Teres Mountains, Sonora: 332
Terran, Sergeant: 57–58
Terrazas, Joaquin: 210, 252; traps
    Victorio, 208–209
Terrazas, Luis (Chihuahua governor):
    265, 274
Tesorababi, Sonora: 285
Tevis, James H.: 329 & n.
Texas: 195, 198, 208, 264, 321;
    Rangers, 203
"Texas Charlie": 274
Texas Pacific Railroad: 207
Theely: 56–57
Thomas, Camp: 232, 233, 235, 237,
    309, 312, 327
Thompson, Free: 19–20

Thompson's Canyon, New Mexico: 270
Three Rivers, New Mexico: 195
Tiffany, J. C.: 218, 220, 231, 235; Grand Jury blast against, 257–58
To-mas: *see* Ba-coon
Tombstone, Arizona: 267, 268, 273ff., 278, 333; Rangers, 273–74
Tonto-Apache Indians: vii, 114, 126, 133, 155, 161, 166, 270, 272; attack Crook, 101; kill trio, bringing down vengeance, 133–34
Tonto Basin, Arizona: 56, 120, 121ff., 137, 140, 254
Tonto Creek, Arizona: xi, 59, 69, 130, 133, 142, 254
Tonto Jack: 29
Topete, Bonifacio: 274, 305
Torres, Luis E. (Sonora governor): 274, 280; complains to Crook, 340–41
Torres Mountains, Sonora: 357
Touey, Timothy A.: 176n., 196
Townsend, John (scout): 119 & n., 132
Townsend's ranch, Arizona: 122, 123
Trahen, William: 36n.
Traverse, Lieutenant: 46
Tres Alamos River, Arizona: xi, 85
Tres Castillos Mountains, Chihuahua: 208
Trescott, H. L.: 238
Trevino, Geronimo: 190
Tribolett, Bob: 345–46n.; uses whiskey to incite Geronimo, 345–46
Troy, Corporal: 44
Tubac, Arizona: 3, 6, 15, 85
Tubac, Camp, Arizona: 55
Tucson, Arizona: 3, 6, 13, 19, 20, 24, 33, 53, 62, 64, 70, 78ff., 108, 115–16, 160, 183, 233, 238, 293, 362; Crook arrives at, 95; armed rowdies threaten Apaches, 103–104; moral tone of, 211; sends civilians against Indians, 251–53; hails Crook, 295
Tucson Ring: *see* Indian Ring
Tulerosa, New Mexico: 180, 194, 197

Tupper, Tullius C.: 183; chases, fights Loco, 245–47
Turkey Creek, Arizona: 36, 304, 305, 306
Turnbull Mountains, Arizona: 70
Turner, George: 230
Turret Mountain, Arizona: xi, 130, 161; battle of, 136–37, 137n.
Twaddle, Harvey: 36; killed by Indians, 36–37

Ulzana: *see* Josanie
Union, Fort: 178, 236
Union Pass, Arizona: 46, 48
Ures, Sonora: 265

Valle, Adolph I.: 204, 206
Valois, Gustavus: 214–15
Van Horn, James Judson: 322
Van Horn's Wells, Texas: 204
Van Vliet, Frederick: 320, 321, 322
Verde, Fort: 34, 102, 104, 105, 114, 121ff., 133ff., 137ff., 143; history of, 102n.
Verde (San Francisco) River, Arizona: 25, 28, 33, 57, 59, 102, 121, 123, 131, 135ff.
Victorio: 23, 166, 171 & n., 190, 192, 202, 203, 211, 215, 231, 234, 252, 256, 263, 273, 279, 306, 322, 323, 341, 351; agrees to removal, 175; unhappy at San Carlos, 175–76; leads outbreak, 177–78; "good Indian" at Warm Springs, 178; whites in quandary over, 179; refuses fresh removal, 179; bolts, 179–80; surrenders again at Warm Springs, 180; bolts for good, 181; depredations begin, 182; ambushes Dawson, 183–84; fights Gatewood, 185; pursued into Mexico, 186–89; fight in Hembrillo Canyon, 194–97; Victorio weakening, 198; decisive battle with Parker's scouts, 200–201; stalemated in Texas, 204–206; grand scheme to eliminate him,

207–208; Victorio killed, 208–209; Cruse's version, 209–10
Viele, Charles Delavan: ambushes Victorio, 205–206
Vincent, Camp, New Mexico: 323
Vock Canyon: see Scherum's Canyon

Waite, Elizabeth Ann: 109
Walapai Indians: vii, 39ff., 58, 119, 123, 310; fight Young-Stevenson, 48–51; negotiate peace, 51–52; scouts avenge Wickenburg massacre, 113
Walapais Charley: 39; negotiates peace, 51–52
Walapais Valley, Arizona: 48
Walapais War: begins, 40–41; peace comes, 51–52
Walker, John D.: 34, 35; biography of, 34n.
Walker, Joseph Reddeford: 20–21, 24ff.; founding of Prescott, 24–25
Wallace (stage driver): 17–18
Wallen, Camp: 55, 74–76
Walnut Grove, Arizona: 133
Walsh, John: 117
Ward, Felix: see Mickey Free
Ward, John: 15–16, 16n.
Ward, Santiago: 16, 16n.
Ware, Eugene F.: 270
Warfield, Sergeant: 65; saves Cushing, 68
Warm Springs Agency: 178ff., 183, 186, 193, 200–201
Warm Springs (Ojo Caliente) Apaches: vii, viii, 169, 171–80, 231, 234ff.; difficulties at Ojo Caliente, 172
Washburn, Hiram H.: 33, 34
Washington (son of Victorio): raids toward San Carlos, 199; killed, 203
Watts, Charles H.: 154
Wauba Yuba: 39; murder of, 40
Weaver, Pauline: 7, 25
Wells, A. B.: 46, 48
Wells, Edmund: 42
Welsh, Herbert: 303, 364

West Clear Creek, Arizona: 138
West, Frank: 176n.
West, Joseph R.: 21–23
Whaley, Tex: 353
Wheeler, George M.: 105
Whetstone Mountains, Arizona: 74, 273
Whipple, Fort: 26, 40, 42, 53, 55, 102, 104, 114, 122ff., 133ff., 157ff., 239, 269, 295
White Mountains (Sierra Blanca), Arizona: x, 82, 152
White Mountain (Sierra Blanca) Apaches: viii, 167, 177, 232, 238, 260, 334–35, 337; Crook talks with Indians at, 99
White River, Arizona: 99, 100
White Sands, New Mexico: 213
White Tail Canyon, Arizona: 333
Whitewater, Arizona: 274
Whitman, Royal Emerson: 80ff., 95 & n., 103–104; arrives in Arizona, 80; record and history, 80–81, 81n.; receives Indians, 81; agrees to feed them, 82; surrenders reach 500, 83; arrangements for Indians, 83–84; rebuffed by Stoneman, 84; hostility mounts against, 85; hears of attack, 90; Indians continue to have faith in, 92; attack on, 93–94; Howard sides with, 107; Court-martial and charges, 107–109; Crook angered anew, 109; describes Howard's meeting with Indians, 110–11; subsequent history, 111n.
Wickenburg, Arizona: 33, 123, 134
Wickenburg (Loring) Massacre: 105; massacre avenged, 113
Wilbur, R. A.: 147; effect on San Carlos, 147; sinister record, 147–48; incites Indians, 148–54; responsibility in Almy murder, 149–54
Wilcox, P. P. (agent): 274, 292
Wilder, Wilber Elliott: 356
Willcox, Arizona: 267, 272, 276
Willcox, Orlando: 189, 190, 220, 230,

231, 232, 235, 276; prefers charges against Carr, 229; in Indian skirmish, 234; relieved, 250
Williams, James Monroe: 57ff., 57n.; wounded at Music Mountain, 58–59; resigns, 59
Williams, Josephus: 162
Williams, Lewis: 325
Williamson Valley, Arizona: 114
Willow Grove, Camp: 43
Willow Springs, Arizona: 326
Willows, The, Arizona: 37, 40, 45, 48
Wilson, Benjamin D.: escapes from Apaches, 11–12
Wilson, Robert P.: 114
Winchester Mountains, Arizona: xi
Wishart (soldier): 337
Wolf (soldier): 69
Wood, Leonard: 324–25, 329, 333, 352, 354, 357–58; description of, 352–53; explains Gatewood mission, 355; on Mexican threat, 360–61
Wood, Rube: 254
Woodson, Albert E.: 122, 123, 133, 135
Woodworth, Ira: 40
Woolsey, King S.: 27ff., 36; poisons Indians, 27; leads campaign against Indians, 27ff.; fights with them, 28–31
Wooster, L. B.: 85

Wratten, George (interpreter): accompanies Gatewood, 353
Wright, John T.: 22

Yampai Valley (Truxton Wash), Arizona: 58
Yaqui Indians: vii, 321
Yaqui River, Sonora: xi, 329
Yavapais Indians: vii, 57–58, 104, 119, 126, 155, 166; heavily defeated, 113; menace ended, 113
Yavapai Rangers: *see* Arizona Rangers
Yeaton, Franklin: 64 & n.
Yesques, Jose M.: 93
Young, Charles: 268
Young, Ewing: 7
Young, Samuel Baldwin Marks: 48ff., 56; leads expedition against Scherum, 48–51; negotiates peace, 51–52
Yount, John P.: 75–76
Yuma Bill (scout): in Loco ambush, 240–44; killed, 243–44
Yuma, Fort: 55

Zabriskie, J. W.: 258
Zeckendorf, William: 336
Zele (Apache leader): 307, 313, 315
Zuñi: vii
Zuñiga, Ignacio: 7

The Conquest of Apacheria has been cast on the Linotype in Caslon Old Face. The matrices were cut from original Caslon letters resulting in exact and faithful reproduction of William Caslon's eighteenth-century typographic design. Handset Caslon was selected as display type to complement the text.